Jane Eyre

THE GRAPHIC NOVEL
Charlotte Brontë

QUICK TEXT VERSION

Script Adaptation: Amy Corzine
Artwork: John M. Burns
Lettering: Terry Wiley
Design & Layout: Jo Wheeler & Carl Andrews
Publishing Assistant: Joanna Watts
Additional Information: Karen Wenborn

Editor in Chief: Clive Bryant

Jane Eyre: The Graphic Novel
Quick Text Version

Charlotte Brontë

First UK Edition

Published by: Classical Comics Ltd
Copyright ©2008 Classical Comics Ltd.

Acknowledgments: Every effort has been made to trace copyright holders of
material reproduced in this book. Any rights not acknowledged here will be
acknowledged in subsequent editions if notice is given to Classical Comics Ltd.

All enquiries should be addressed to:
Classical Comics Ltd.
PO Box 7280
Litchborough
Towcester
NN12 9AR
United Kingdom
Tel: 0845 812 3000

info@classicalcomics.com
www.classicalcomics.com

ISBN: 978-1-906332-08-2

Printed in the UK

This book is printed by Hampton Printing (Bristol) Ltd using biodegradable vegetable inks, on
environmentally friendly paper which is FSC (Forest Stewardship Council) certified (TT-COC-002370) and
manufactured to the accredited Environmental Management Standard ISO 14001. This material can be
disposed of by recycling, incineration for energy recovery, composting and biodegradation.

The publishers would like to acknowledge the
design assistance of Greg Powell in the completion of this book.

The rights of John M. Burns and Terry Wiley to be identified as the Artists of this work have been
asserted in accordance with the Copyright, Designs and Patents Act 1988 sections 77 and 78.

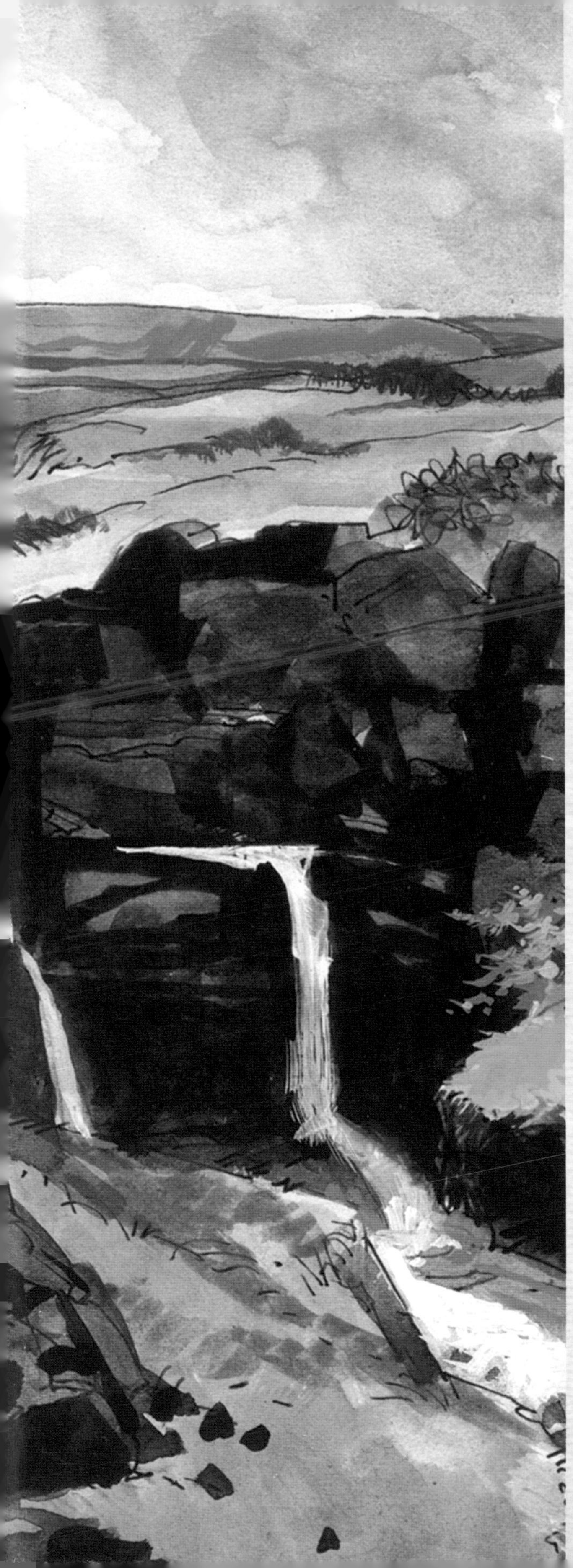

Contents

Dramatis Personae

Jane Eyre

Mr. Edward Fairfax Rochester
Owner of Thornfield Hall

Young Jane Eyre

Mr. Reed
Jane's uncle

Mrs. Sarah Reed
Jane's aunt

John Reed
Jane's cousin

Eliza Reed
Jane's cousin

Georgiana Reed
Jane's cousin

Miss Bessie Lee
Maid at Gateshead Hall

Miss Abbott
Maid at Gateshead Hall

Mr. Lloyd
Apothecary

Mr. Brocklehurst
Manager of Lowood School

Miss Maria Temple
*Superintendent at
Lowood School*

Helen Burns
*Jane's friend at
Lowood School*

Miss Alice Fairfax
*Housekeeper at
Thornfield Hall*

Adèle Varens
Jane's pupil

Céline Varens
Adele's mother

Grace Poole
Maid at Gateshead Hall

Lord Ingram

Lady Ingram

Miss Blanche Ingram
*Daughter of Lord and
Lady Ingram*

Miss Mary Ingram
*Daughter of Lord and
Lady Ingram*

**Bertha Mason
Rochester**

Richard Mason
Bertha's brother

Mr. Briggs
A solicitor from London

Pilot
Mr. Rochester's dog

St. John Rivers

Mary Rivers
Sister to St. John

Diana Rivers
Sister to St. John

Rosamond Oliver
Friend of St. John Rivers

The Birth of Jane Eyre

Charlotte Brontë's *Jane Eyre* was a huge success when it first appeared in 1847. It was a year of great achievement for the Brontë sisters of Haworth: the publication of Anne Brontë's *Agnes Grey*, and Emily Brontë's *Wuthering Heights* also taking place that same year.

That success, however, was set against a family history full of loss and sadness.

Despite the many advances made in medical science during the nineteenth century, potentially fatal diseases were still extremely common. Charlotte had to cope with her mother's death when she was only five years old; and then, four years later, two of her sisters were lost to tuberculosis.

Young Charlotte was fortunate enough to have a caring father and aunt to look after her – but what about an infant who had lost both parents?

It was usual for orphaned children to be looked after by relatives; and while the kindness of that act cannot be denied, the emotional impact of the loss of parents on the child, coupled with the stresses felt by the family looking after an extra person in the household, could provide the background to an unhappy childhood – especially for a poor, plain little girl, thrust into the home of her spiteful cousins and an uncaring aunt.

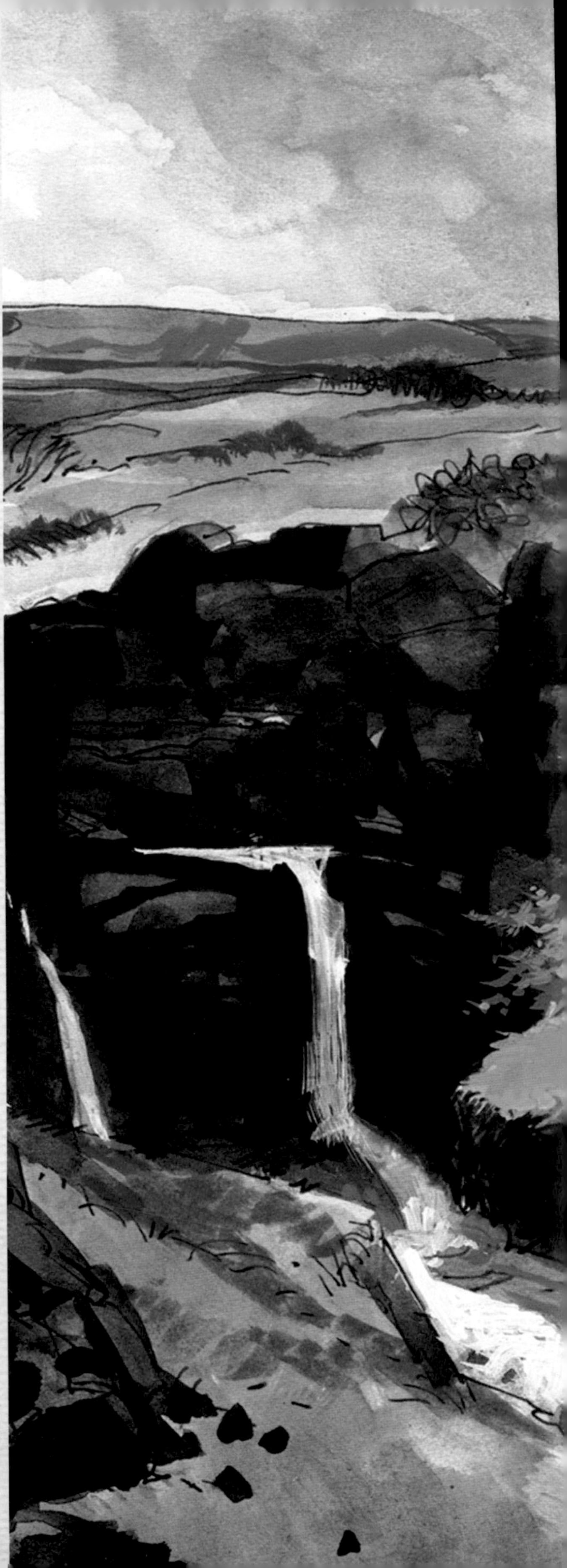

Jane Eyre

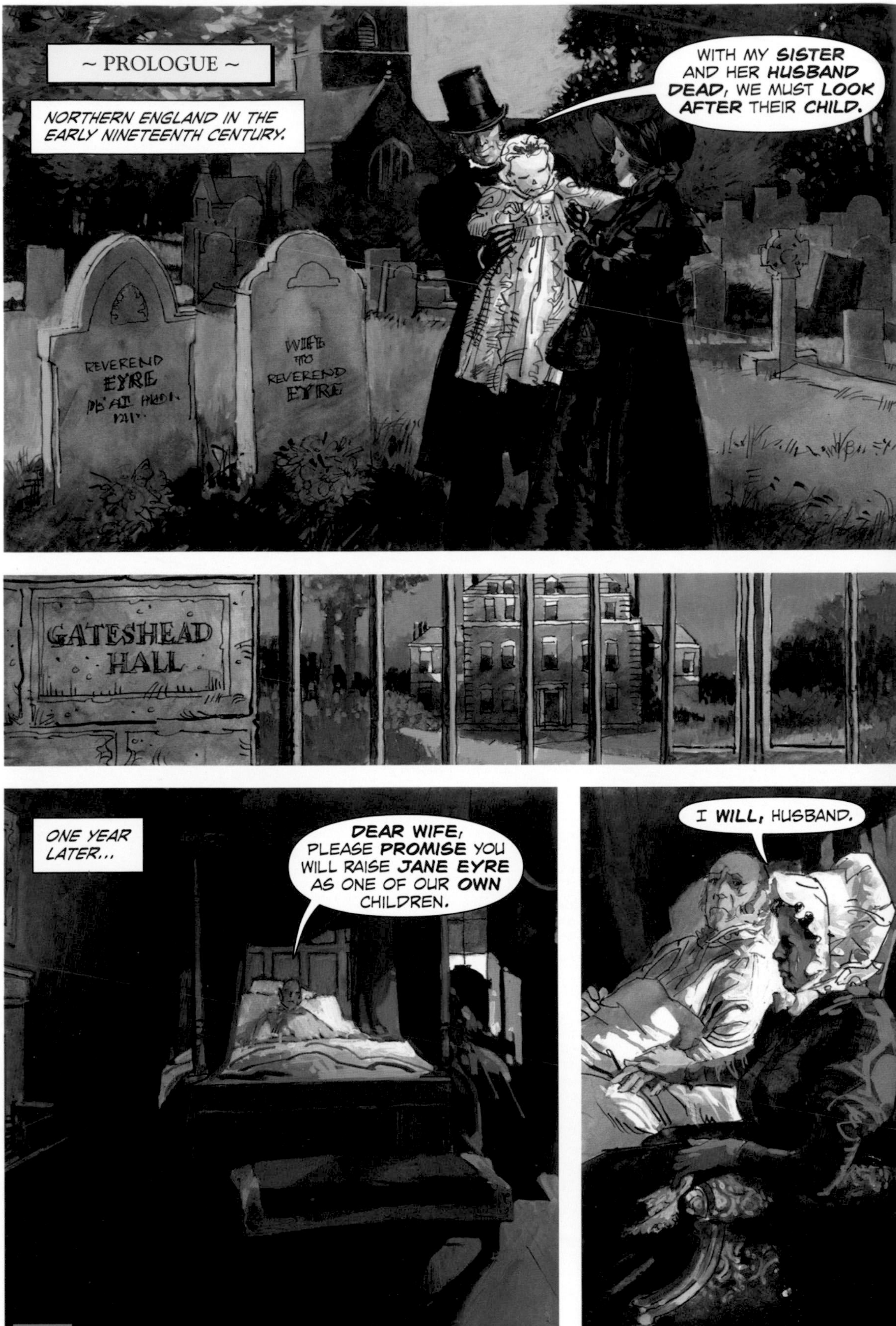
~ PROLOGUE ~
NORTHERN ENGLAND IN THE EARLY NINETEENTH CENTURY.
WITH MY SISTER AND HER HUSBAND DEAD, WE MUST LOOK AFTER THEIR CHILD.
REVEREND EYRE
WIFE
REVEREND EYRE
GATESHEAD HALL
ONE YEAR LATER...
DEAR WIFE, PLEASE PROMISE YOU WILL RAISE JANE EYRE AS ONE OF OUR OWN CHILDREN.
I WILL, HUSBAND.

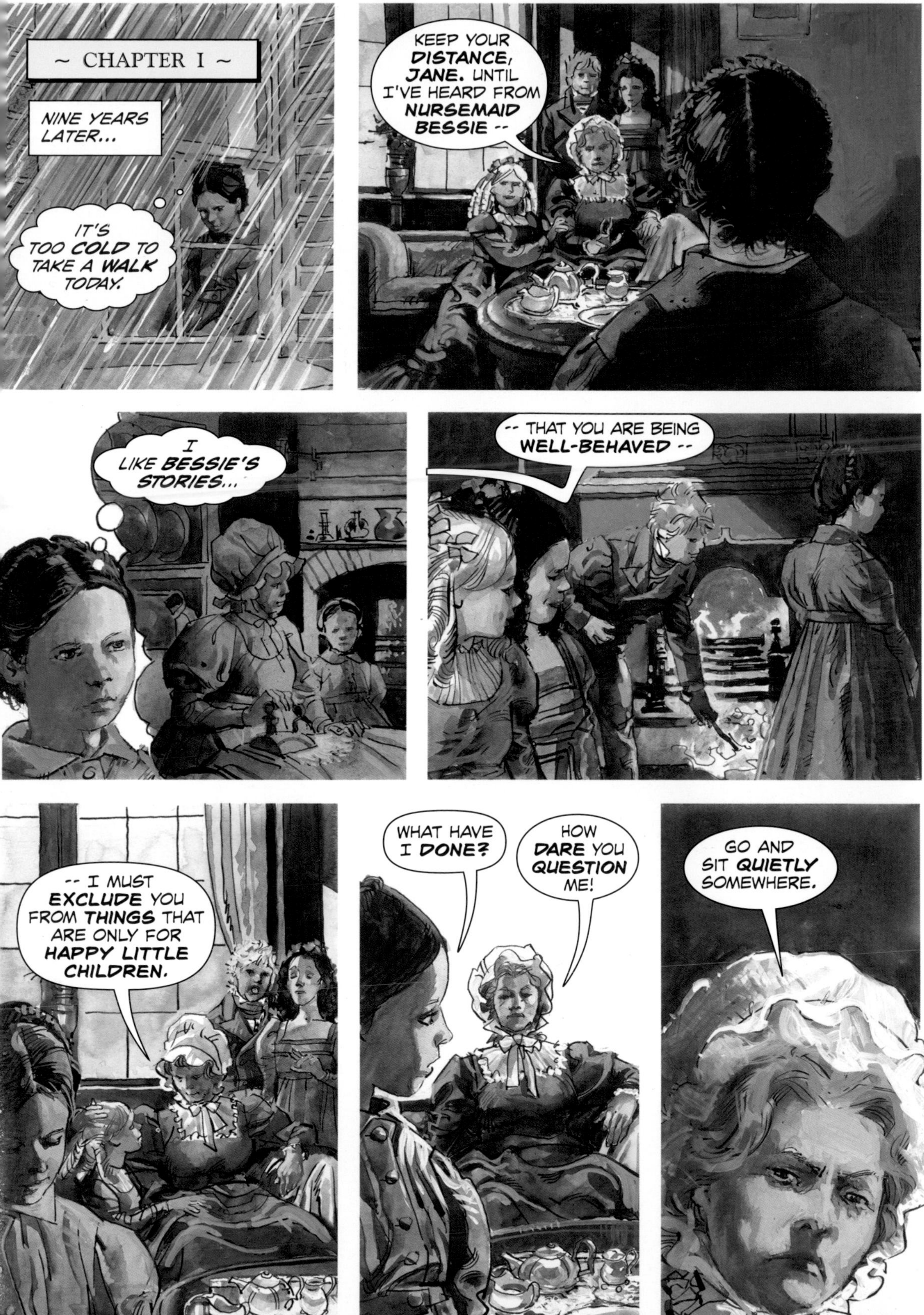
~ CHAPTER I ~
NINE YEARS LATER...
IT'S TOO COLD TO TAKE A WALK TODAY.
KEEP YOUR DISTANCE, JANE. UNTIL I'VE HEARD FROM NURSEMAID BESSIE --
I LIKE BESSIE'S STORIES...
-- THAT YOU ARE BEING WELL-BEHAVED --
-- I MUST EXCLUDE YOU FROM THINGS THAT ARE ONLY FOR HAPPY LITTLE CHILDREN.
WHAT HAVE I DONE?
HOW DARE YOU QUESTION ME!
GO AND SIT QUIETLY SOMEWHERE.

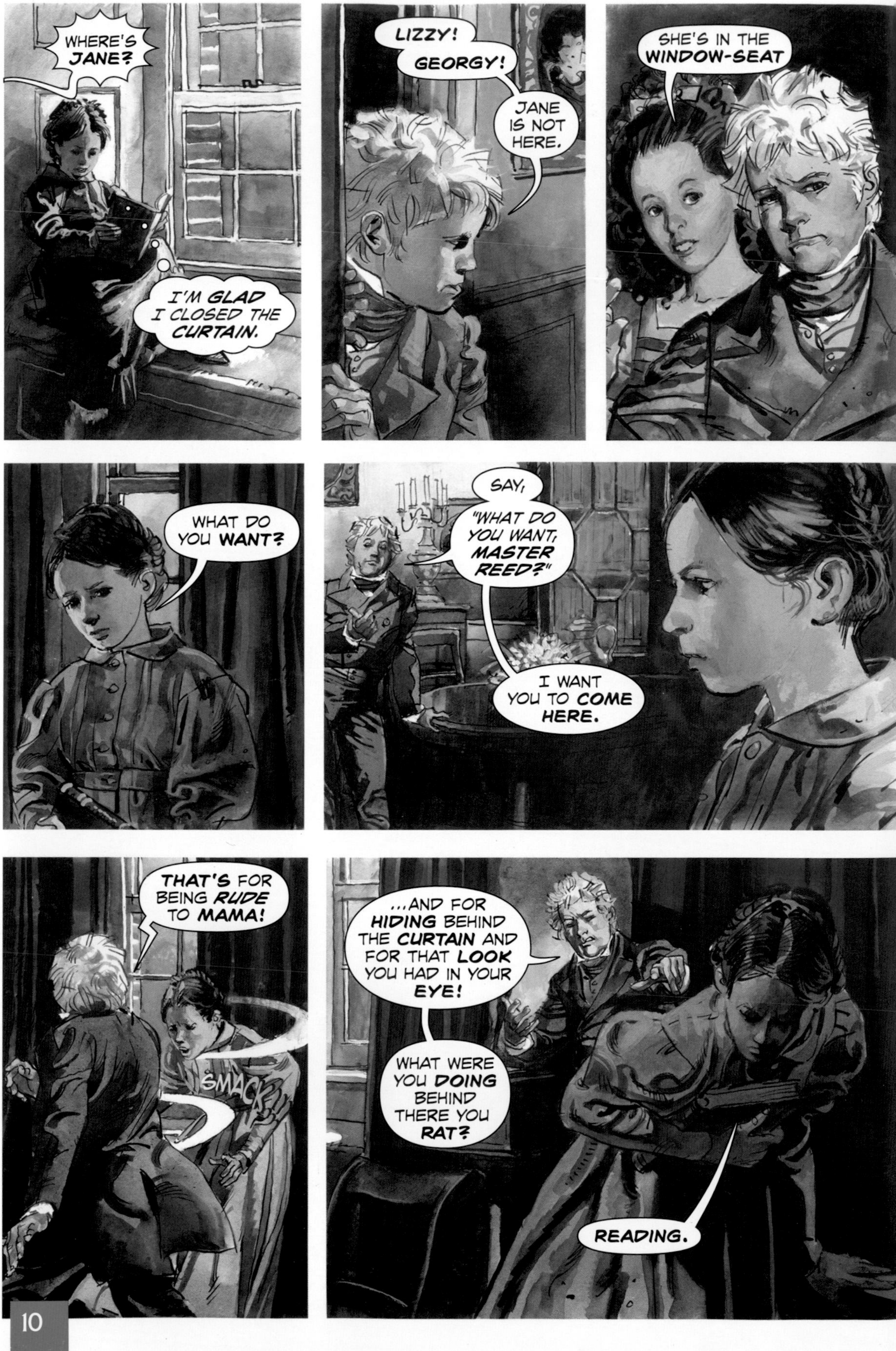
WHERE'S JANE?
I'M GLAD I CLOSED THE CURTAIN.
LIZZY!
GEORGY!
JANE IS NOT HERE.
SHE'S IN THE WINDOW-SEAT
WHAT DO YOU WANT?
SAY, "WHAT DO YOU WANT, MASTER REED?"
I WANT YOU TO COME HERE.
THAT'S FOR BEING RUDE TO MAMA!
SMACK
...AND FOR HIDING BEHIND THE CURTAIN AND FOR THAT LOOK YOU HAD IN YOUR EYE!
WHAT WERE YOU DOING BEHIND THERE YOU RAT?
READING.

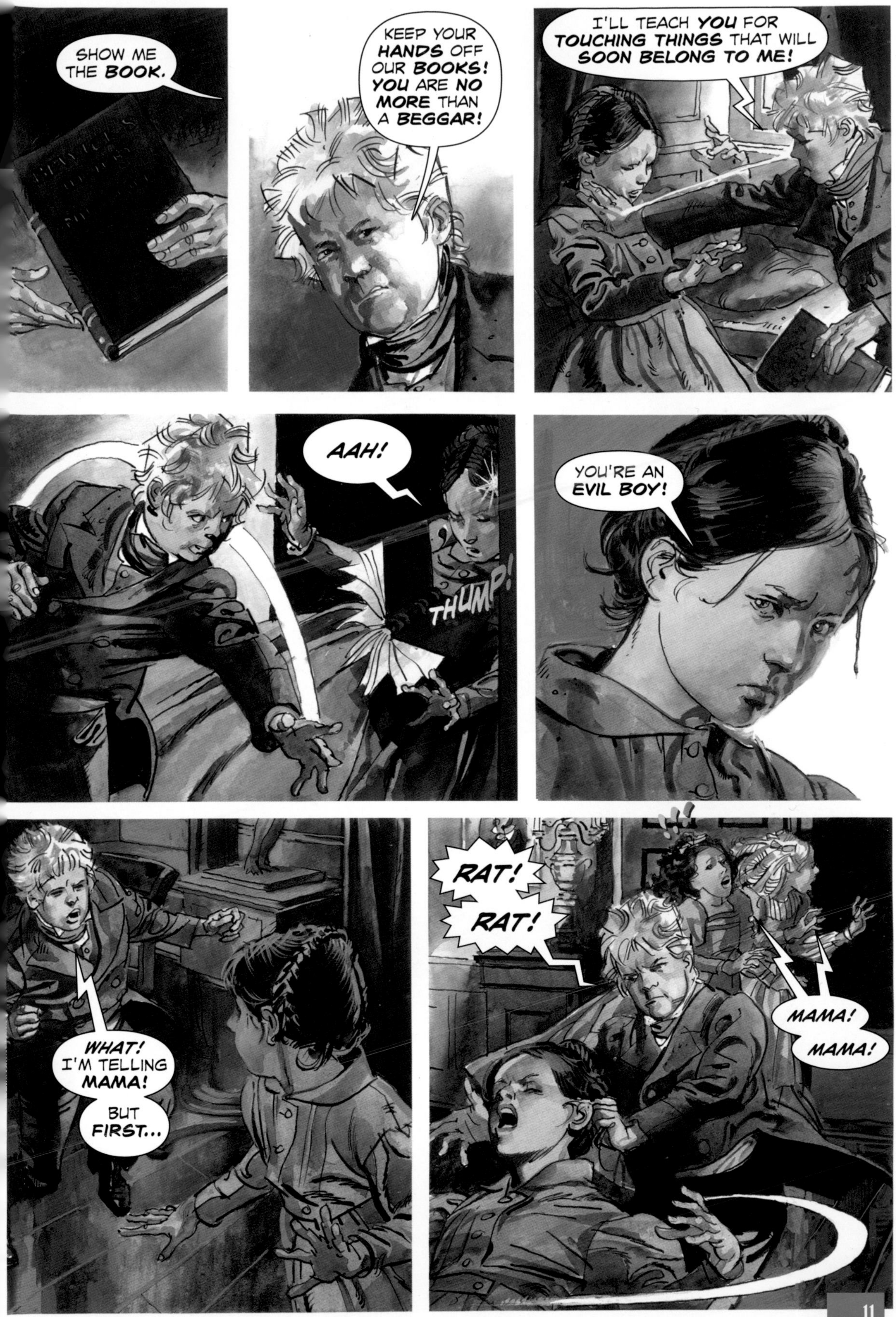
SHOW ME THE BOOK.
KEEP YOUR HANDS OFF OUR BOOKS! YOU ARE NO MORE THAN A BEGGAR!
I'LL TEACH YOU FOR TOUCHING THINGS THAT WILL SOON BELONG TO ME!
AAH!
THUMP!
YOU'RE AN EVIL BOY!
WHAT! I'M TELLING MAMA!
BUT FIRST...
RAT!
RAT!
MAMA!
MAMA!

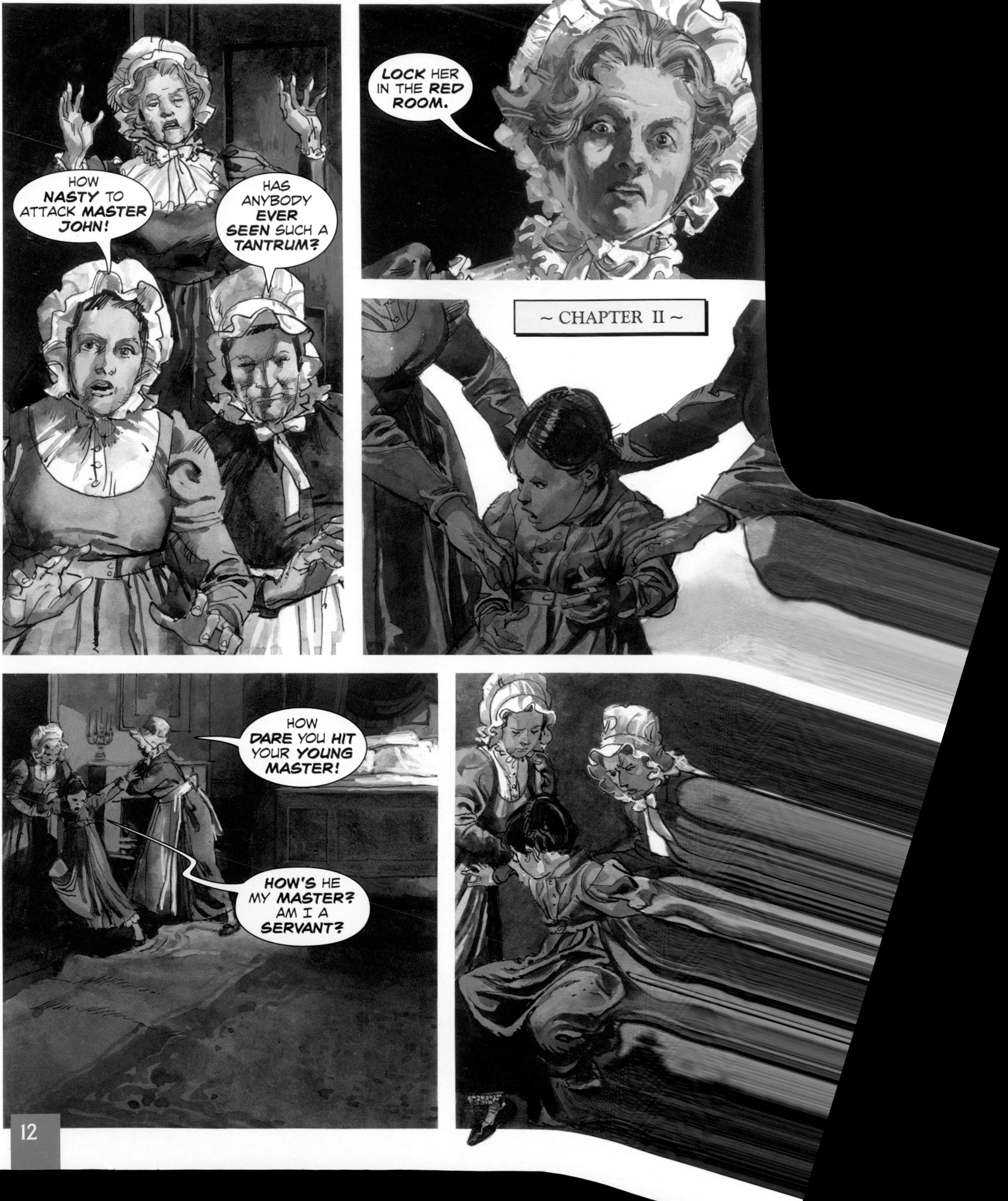
HOW NASTY TO ATTACK MASTER JOHN!
HAS ANYBODY EVER SEEN SUCH A TANTRUM?
LOCK HER IN THE RED ROOM.
~ CHAPTER II ~
HOW DARE YOU HIT YOUR YOUNG MASTER!
HOW'S HE MY MASTER? AM I A SERVANT?

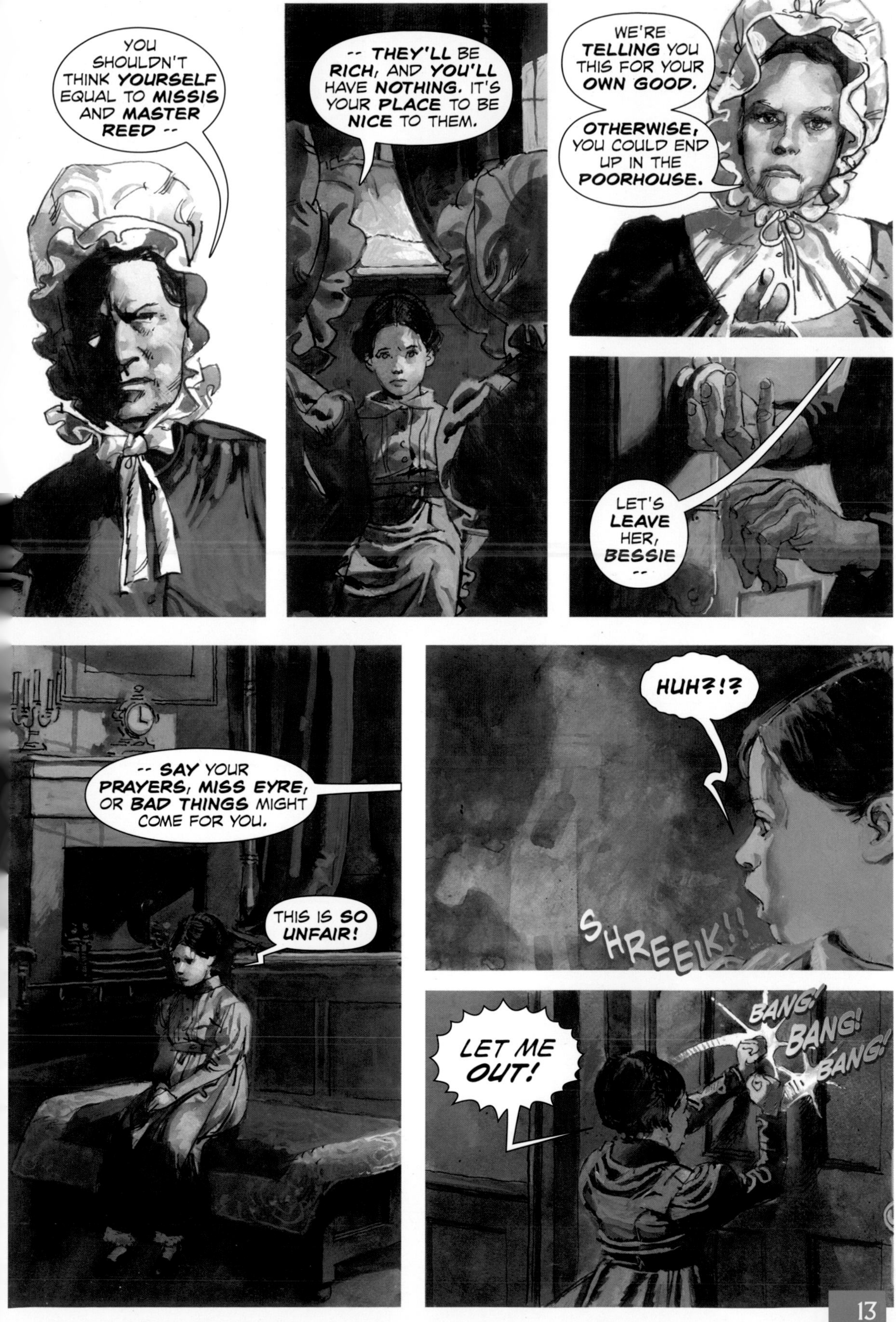
YOU SHOULDN'T THINK YOURSELF EQUAL TO MISSIS AND MASTER REED --
-- THEY'LL BE RICH, AND YOU'LL HAVE NOTHING. IT'S YOUR PLACE TO BE NICE TO THEM.
WE'RE TELLING YOU THIS FOR YOUR OWN GOOD.
OTHERWISE, YOU COULD END UP IN THE POORHOUSE.
LET'S LEAVE HER, BESSIE --
-- SAY YOUR PRAYERS, MISS EYRE, OR BAD THINGS MIGHT COME FOR YOU.
THIS IS SO UNFAIR!
HUH?!?
SHREEIK!!
LET ME OUT!
BANG!
BANG!
BANG!

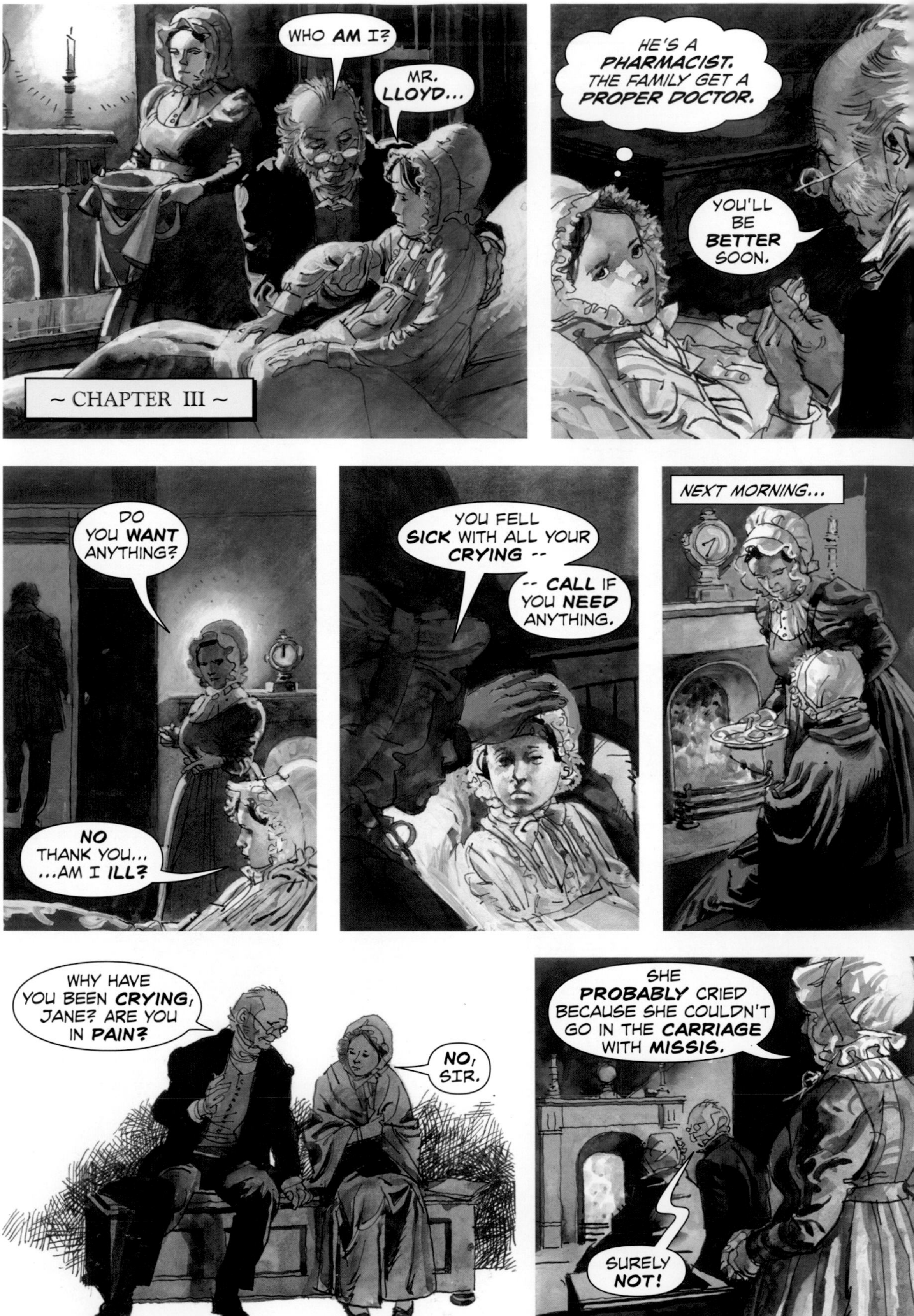

~ CHAPTER III ~
WHO AM I?
MR. LLOYD...
HE'S A PHARMACIST. THE FAMILY GET A PROPER DOCTOR.
YOU'LL BE BETTER SOON.
DO YOU WANT ANYTHING?
NO THANK YOU... ...AM I ILL?
YOU FELL SICK WITH ALL YOUR CRYING --
-- CALL IF YOU NEED ANYTHING.
NEXT MORNING...
WHY HAVE YOU BEEN CRYING, JANE? ARE YOU IN PAIN?
NO, SIR.
SHE PROBABLY CRIED BECAUSE SHE COULDN'T GO IN THE CARRIAGE WITH MISSIS.
SURELY NOT!

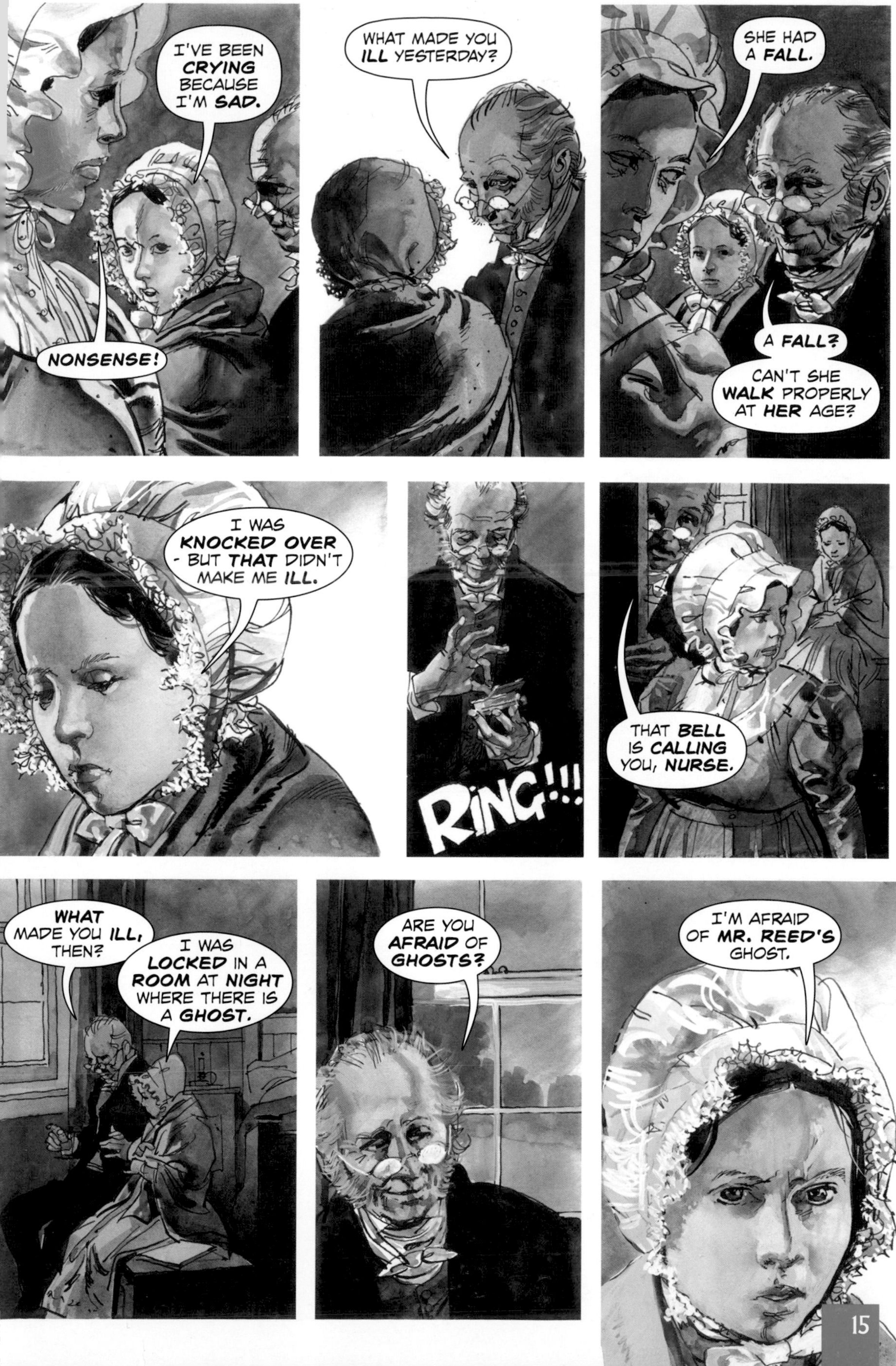
I'VE BEEN CRYING BECAUSE I'M SAD.
NONSENSE!
WHAT MADE YOU ILL YESTERDAY?
SHE HAD A FALL.
A FALL?
CAN'T SHE WALK PROPERLY AT HER AGE?
I WAS KNOCKED OVER - BUT THAT DIDN'T MAKE ME ILL.
RING!!!
THAT BELL IS CALLING YOU, NURSE.
WHAT MADE YOU ILL, THEN?
I WAS LOCKED IN A ROOM AT NIGHT WHERE THERE IS A GHOST.
ARE YOU AFRAID OF GHOSTS?
I'M AFRAID OF MR. REED'S GHOST.

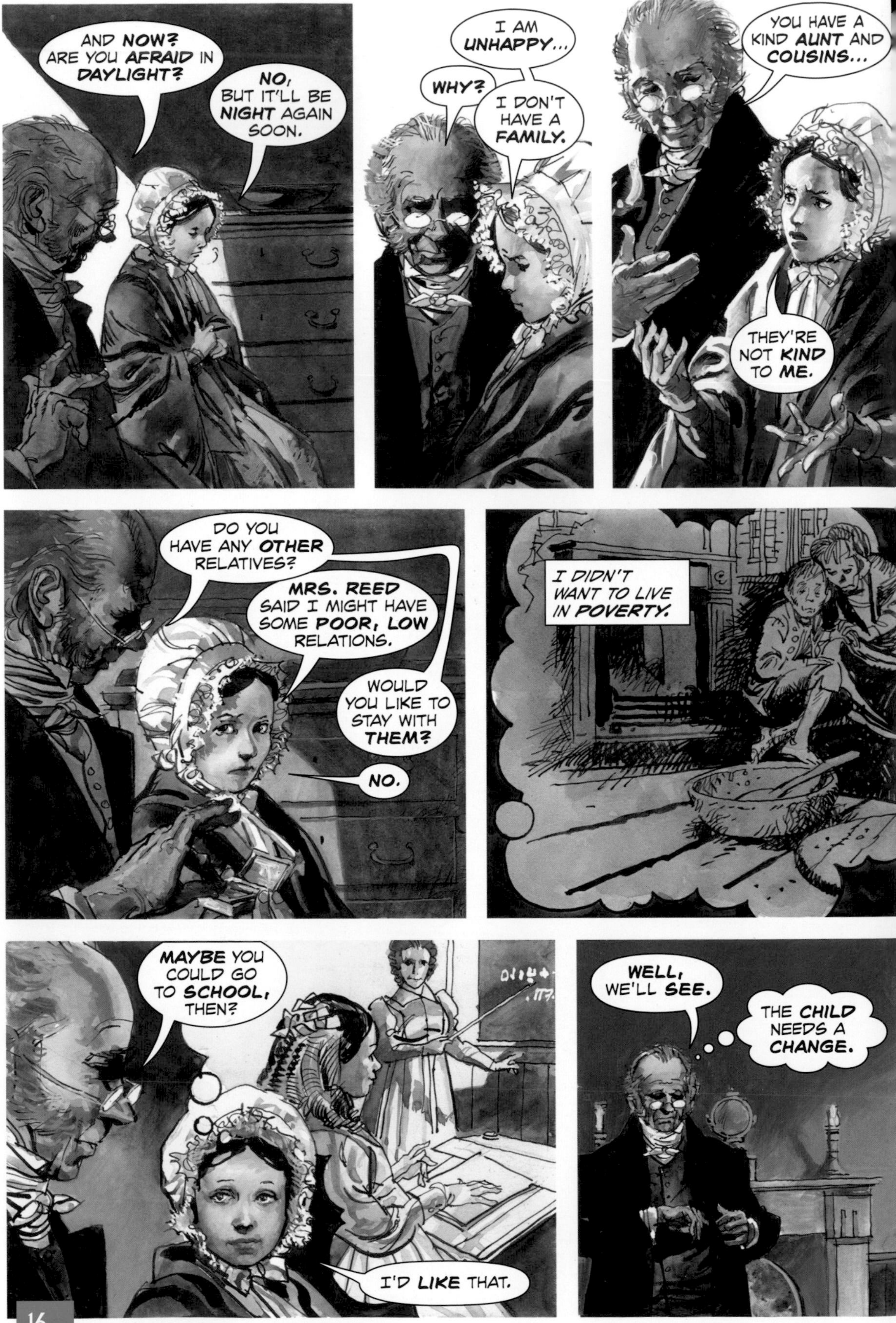
AND NOW? ARE YOU AFRAID IN DAYLIGHT?
NO, BUT IT'LL BE NIGHT AGAIN SOON.
I AM UNHAPPY...
WHY?
I DON'T HAVE A FAMILY.
YOU HAVE A KIND AUNT AND COUSINS...
THEY'RE NOT KIND TO ME.
DO YOU HAVE ANY OTHER RELATIVES?
MRS. REED SAID I MIGHT HAVE SOME POOR, LOW RELATIONS.
WOULD YOU LIKE TO STAY WITH THEM?
NO.
I DIDN'T WANT TO LIVE IN POVERTY.
MAYBE YOU COULD GO TO SCHOOL, THEN?
I'D LIKE THAT.
WELL, WE'LL SEE.
THE CHILD NEEDS A CHANGE.

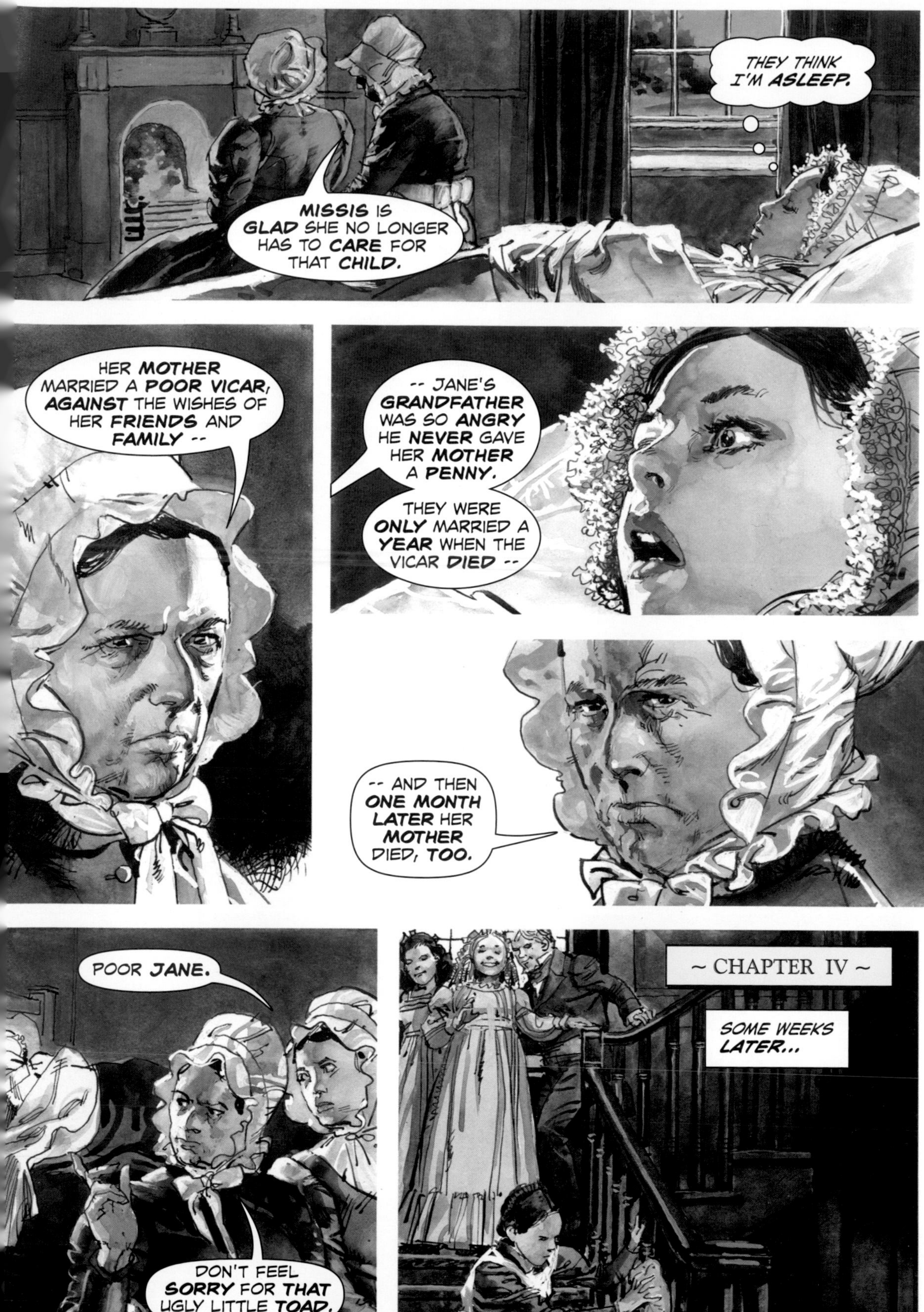

THEY THINK I'M ASLEEP.
MISSIS IS GLAD SHE NO LONGER HAS TO CARE FOR THAT CHILD.
HER MOTHER MARRIED A POOR VICAR, AGAINST THE WISHES OF HER FRIENDS AND FAMILY --
-- JANE'S GRANDFATHER WAS SO ANGRY HE NEVER GAVE HER MOTHER A PENNY.
THEY WERE ONLY MARRIED A YEAR WHEN THE VICAR DIED --
-- AND THEN ONE MONTH LATER HER MOTHER DIED, TOO.
POOR JANE.
DON'T FEEL SORRY FOR THAT UGLY LITTLE TOAD.
~ CHAPTER IV ~
SOME WEEKS LATER...

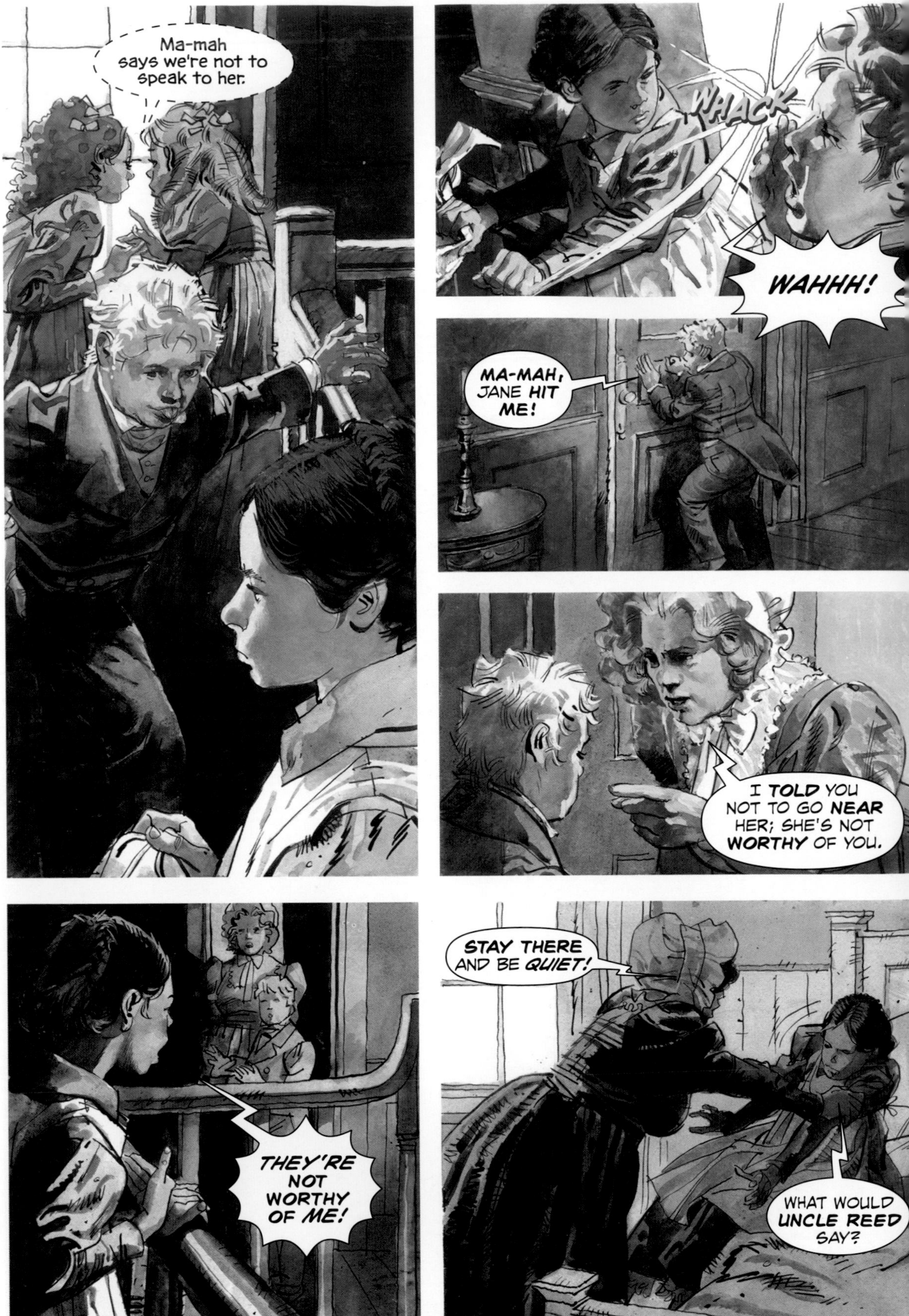

Ma-mah says we're not to speak to her.
WHACK
WAHHH!
MA-MAH, JANE HIT ME!
I TOLD YOU NOT TO GO NEAR HER; SHE'S NOT WORTHY OF YOU.
THEY'RE NOT WORTHY OF ME!
STAY THERE AND BE QUIET!
WHAT WOULD UNCLE REED SAY?

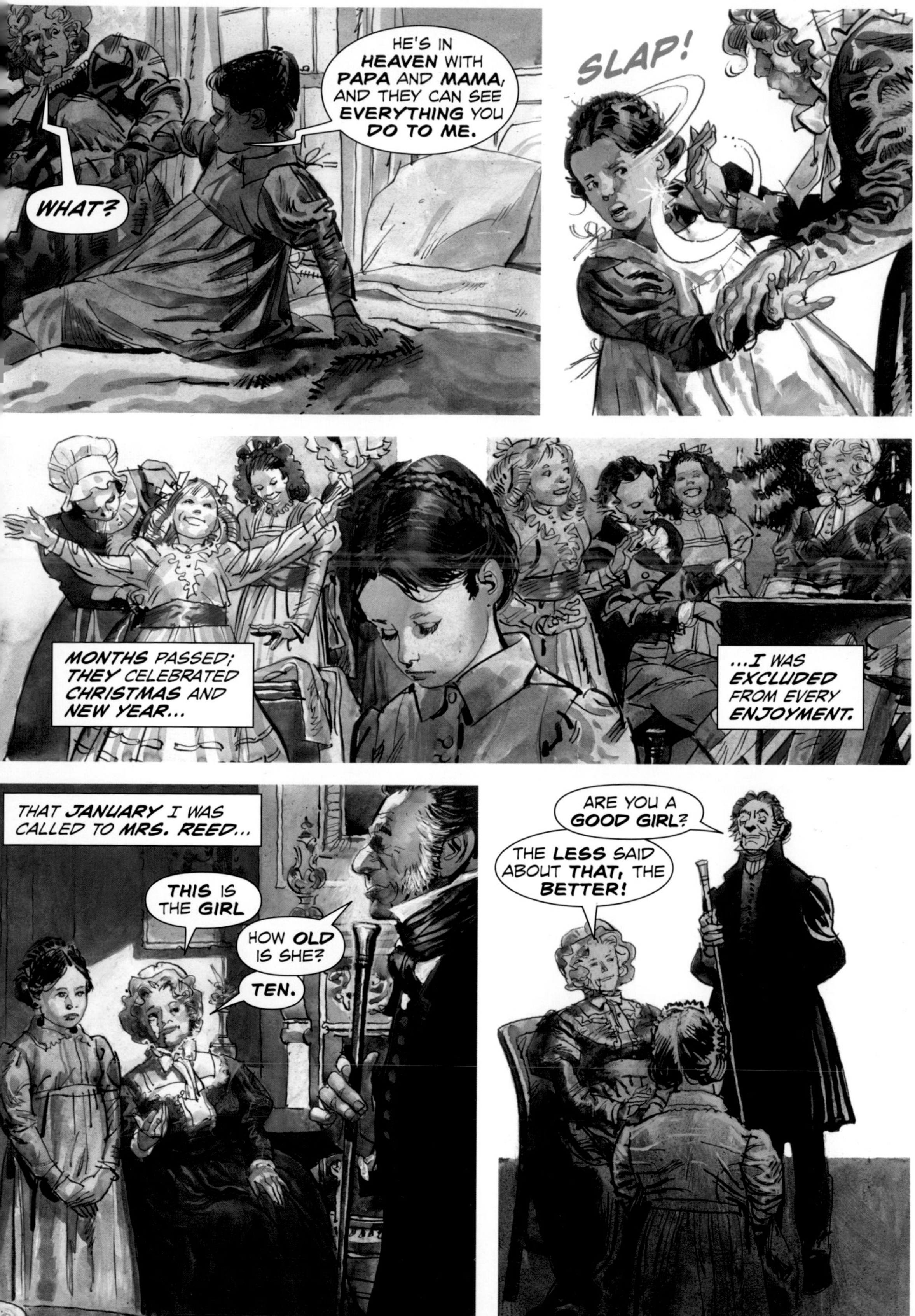
HE'S IN HEAVEN WITH PAPA AND MAMA, AND THEY CAN SEE EVERYTHING YOU DO TO ME.
WHAT?
SLAP!
MONTHS PASSED; THEY CELEBRATED CHRISTMAS AND NEW YEAR...
...I WAS EXCLUDED FROM EVERY ENJOYMENT.
THAT JANUARY I WAS CALLED TO MRS. REED...
THIS IS THE GIRL
HOW OLD IS SHE?
TEN.
ARE YOU A GOOD GIRL?
THE LESS SAID ABOUT THAT, THE BETTER!

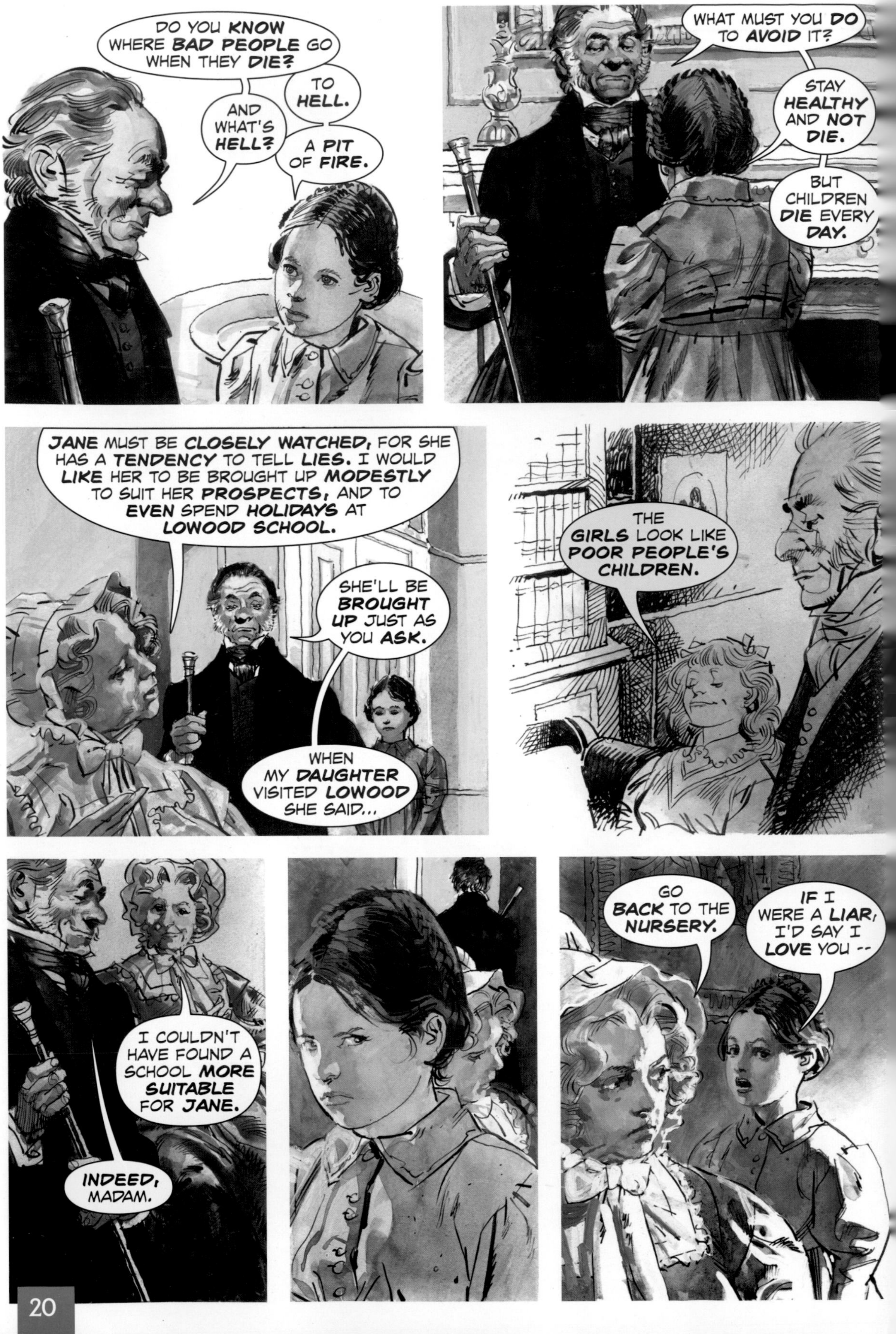
DO YOU KNOW WHERE BAD PEOPLE GO WHEN THEY DIE?
TO HELL.
AND WHAT'S HELL?
A PIT OF FIRE.
WHAT MUST YOU DO TO AVOID IT?
STAY HEALTHY AND NOT DIE.
BUT CHILDREN DIE EVERY DAY.
JANE MUST BE CLOSELY WATCHED, FOR SHE HAS A TENDENCY TO TELL LIES. I WOULD LIKE HER TO BE BROUGHT UP MODESTLY TO SUIT HER PROSPECTS, AND TO EVEN SPEND HOLIDAYS AT LOWOOD SCHOOL.
SHE'LL BE BROUGHT UP JUST AS YOU ASK.
WHEN MY DAUGHTER VISITED LOWOOD SHE SAID...
THE GIRLS LOOK LIKE POOR PEOPLE'S CHILDREN.
I COULDN'T HAVE FOUND A SCHOOL MORE SUITABLE FOR JANE.
INDEED, MADAM.
GO BACK TO THE NURSERY.
IF I WERE A LIAR, I'D SAY I LOVE YOU --

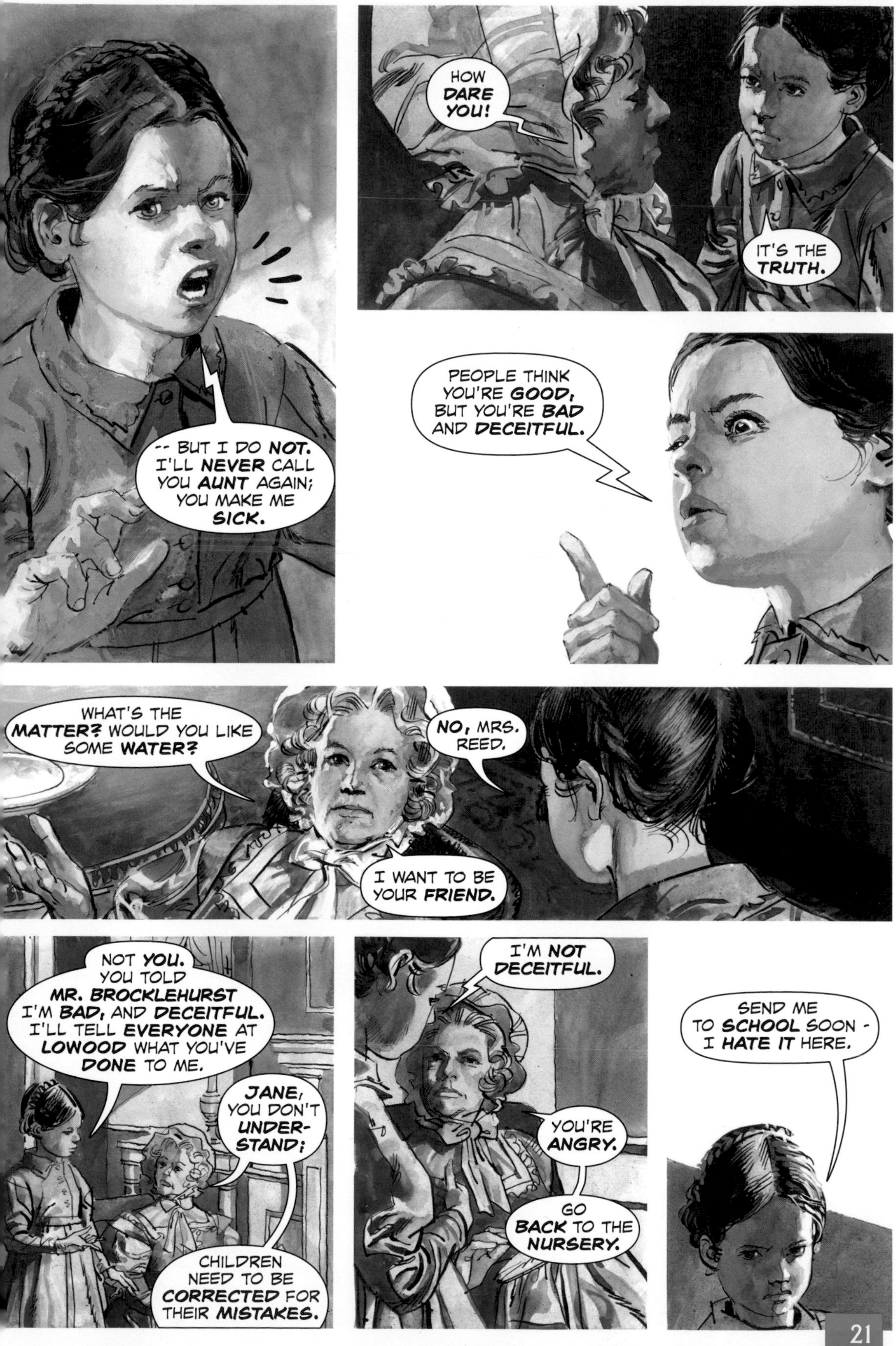
-- BUT I DO NOT. I'LL NEVER CALL YOU AUNT AGAIN; YOU MAKE ME SICK.
HOW DARE YOU!
IT'S THE TRUTH.
PEOPLE THINK YOU'RE GOOD, BUT YOU'RE BAD AND DECEITFUL.
WHAT'S THE MATTER? WOULD YOU LIKE SOME WATER?
NO, MRS. REED.
I WANT TO BE YOUR FRIEND.
NOT YOU. YOU TOLD MR. BROCKLEHURST I'M BAD, AND DECEITFUL. I'LL TELL EVERYONE AT LOWOOD WHAT YOU'VE DONE TO ME.
JANE, YOU DON'T UNDER-STAND;
CHILDREN NEED TO BE CORRECTED FOR THEIR MISTAKES.
I'M NOT DECEITFUL.
YOU'RE ANGRY.
GO BACK TO THE NURSERY.
SEND ME TO SCHOOL SOON - I HATE IT HERE.

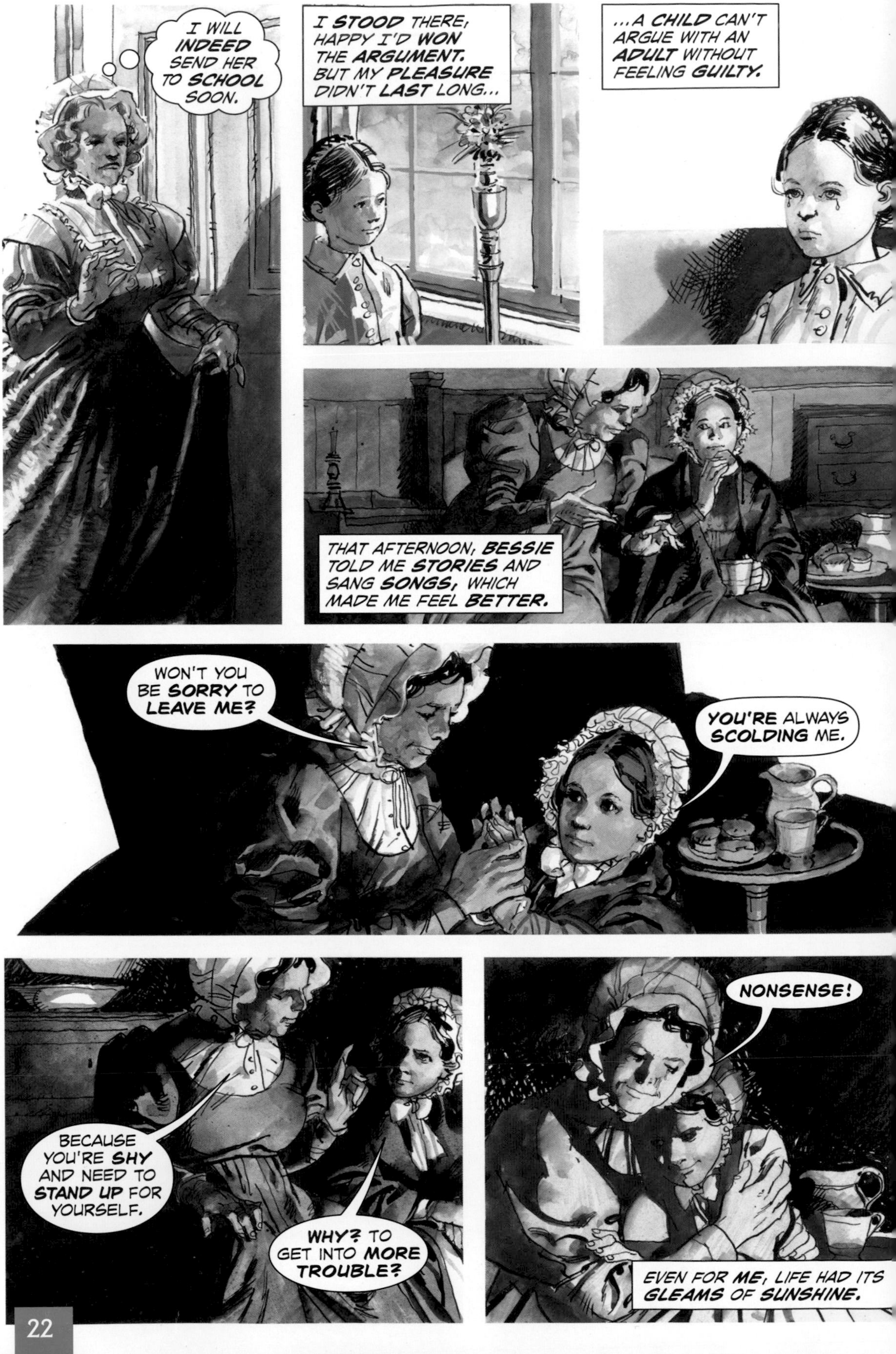

I WILL INDEED SEND HER TO SCHOOL SOON.
I STOOD THERE, HAPPY I'D WON THE ARGUMENT. BUT MY PLEASURE DIDN'T LAST LONG...
...A CHILD CAN'T ARGUE WITH AN ADULT WITHOUT FEELING GUILTY.
THAT AFTERNOON, BESSIE TOLD ME STORIES AND SANG SONGS, WHICH MADE ME FEEL BETTER.
WON'T YOU BE SORRY TO LEAVE ME?
YOU'RE ALWAYS SCOLDING ME.
BECAUSE YOU'RE SHY AND NEED TO STAND UP FOR YOURSELF.
WHY? TO GET INTO MORE TROUBLE?
NONSENSE!
EVEN FOR ME, LIFE HAD ITS GLEAMS OF SUNSHINE.

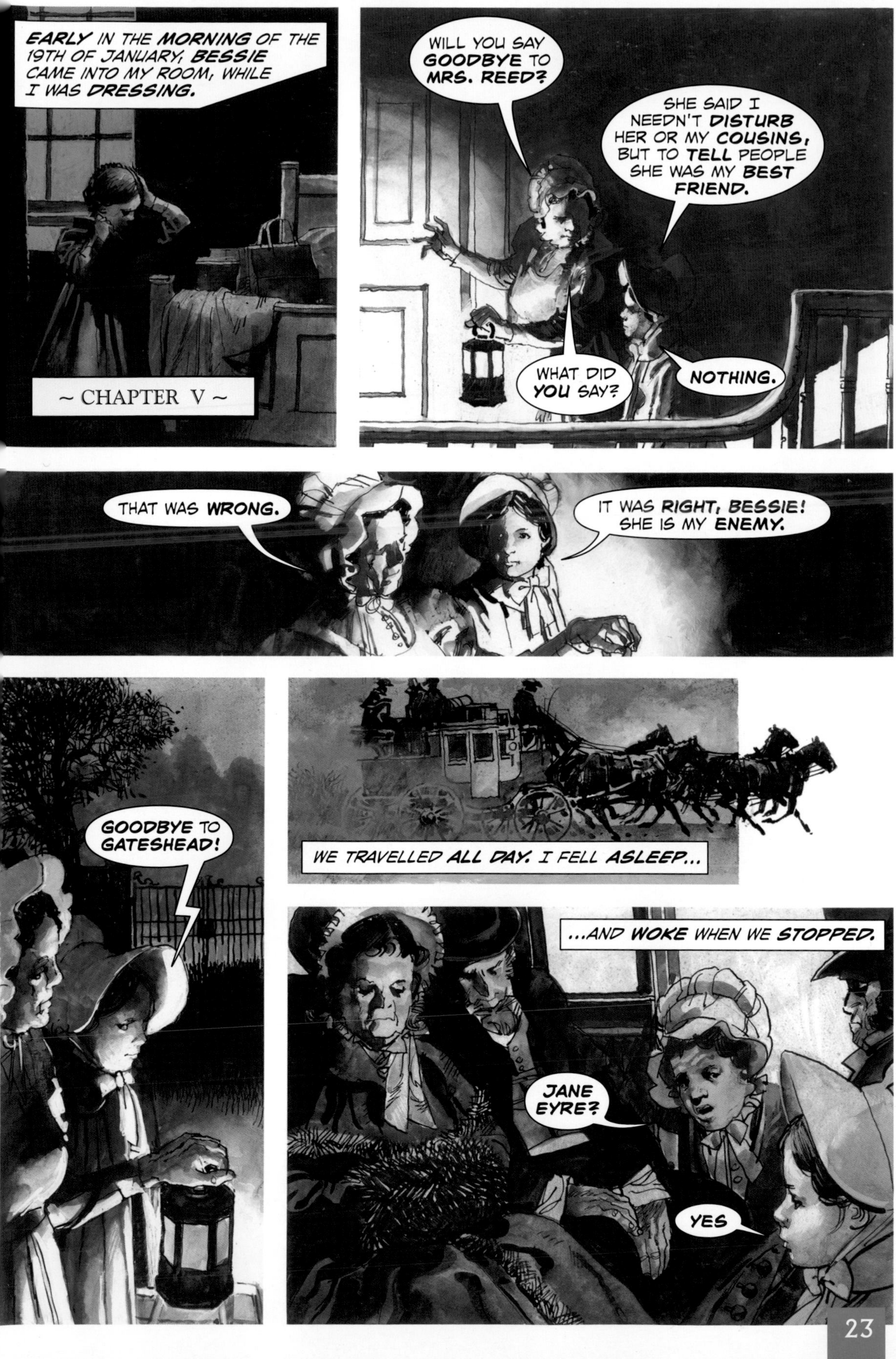
EARLY IN THE MORNING OF THE 19TH OF JANUARY, BESSIE CAME INTO MY ROOM, WHILE I WAS DRESSING.
~ CHAPTER V ~
WILL YOU SAY GOODBYE TO MRS. REED?
SHE SAID I NEEDN'T DISTURB HER OR MY COUSINS, BUT TO TELL PEOPLE SHE WAS MY BEST FRIEND.
WHAT DID YOU SAY?
NOTHING.
THAT WAS WRONG.
IT WAS RIGHT, BESSIE! SHE IS MY ENEMY.
GOODBYE TO GATESHEAD!
WE TRAVELLED ALL DAY. I FELL ASLEEP...
...AND WOKE WHEN WE STOPPED.
JANE EYRE?
YES

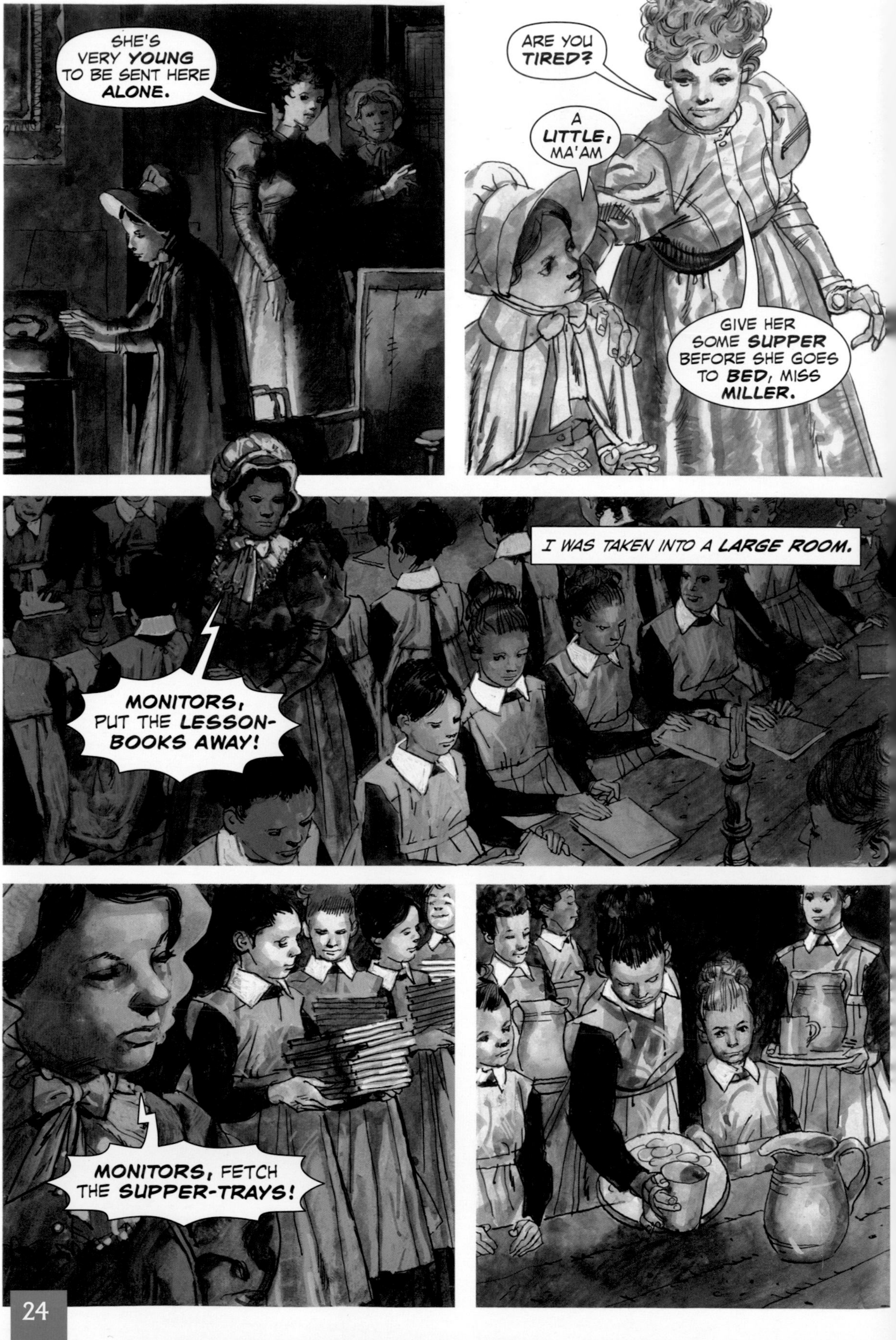

SHE'S VERY YOUNG TO BE SENT HERE ALONE.
ARE YOU TIRED?
A LITTLE, MA'AM
GIVE HER SOME SUPPER BEFORE SHE GOES TO BED, MISS MILLER.
I WAS TAKEN INTO A LARGE ROOM.
MONITORS, PUT THE LESSON-BOOKS AWAY!
MONITORS, FETCH THE SUPPER-TRAYS!

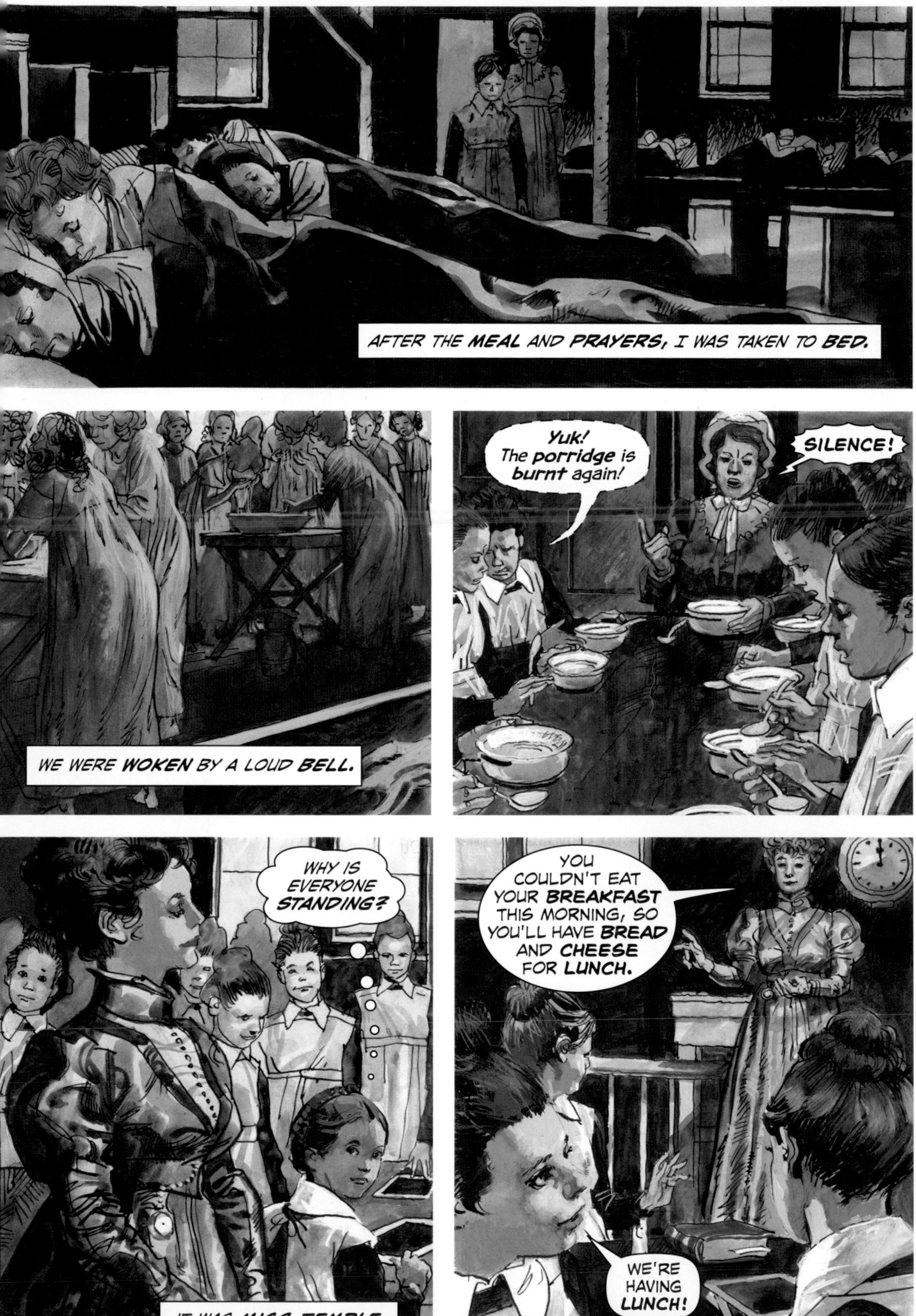
AFTER THE MEAL AND PRAYERS, I WAS TAKEN TO BED.
WE WERE WOKEN BY A LOUD BELL.
Yuk! The porridge is burnt again!
SILENCE!
WHY IS EVERYONE STANDING?
IT WAS MISS TEMPLE.
YOU COULDN'T EAT YOUR BREAKFAST THIS MORNING, SO YOU'LL HAVE BREAD AND CHEESE FOR LUNCH.
WE'RE HAVING LUNCH!

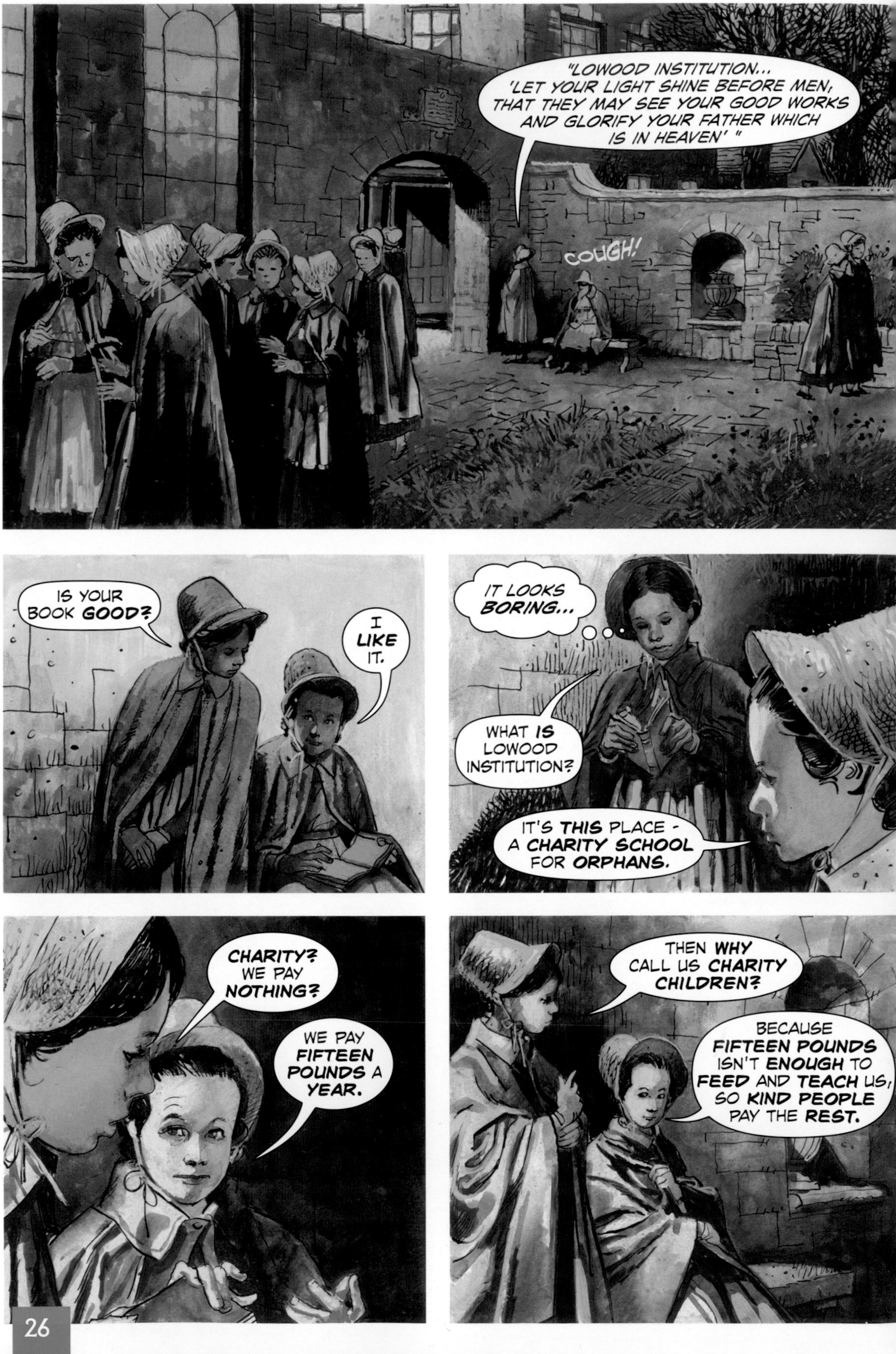
"LOWOOD INSTITUTION... 'LET YOUR LIGHT SHINE BEFORE MEN, THAT THEY MAY SEE YOUR GOOD WORKS AND GLORIFY YOUR FATHER WHICH IS IN HEAVEN' "
COUGH!
IS YOUR BOOK GOOD?
I LIKE IT.
IT LOOKS BORING...
WHAT IS LOWOOD INSTITUTION?
IT'S THIS PLACE - A CHARITY SCHOOL FOR ORPHANS.
CHARITY? WE PAY NOTHING?
WE PAY FIFTEEN POUNDS A YEAR.
THEN WHY CALL US CHARITY CHILDREN?
BECAUSE FIFTEEN POUNDS ISN'T ENOUGH TO FEED AND TEACH US, SO KIND PEOPLE PAY THE REST.

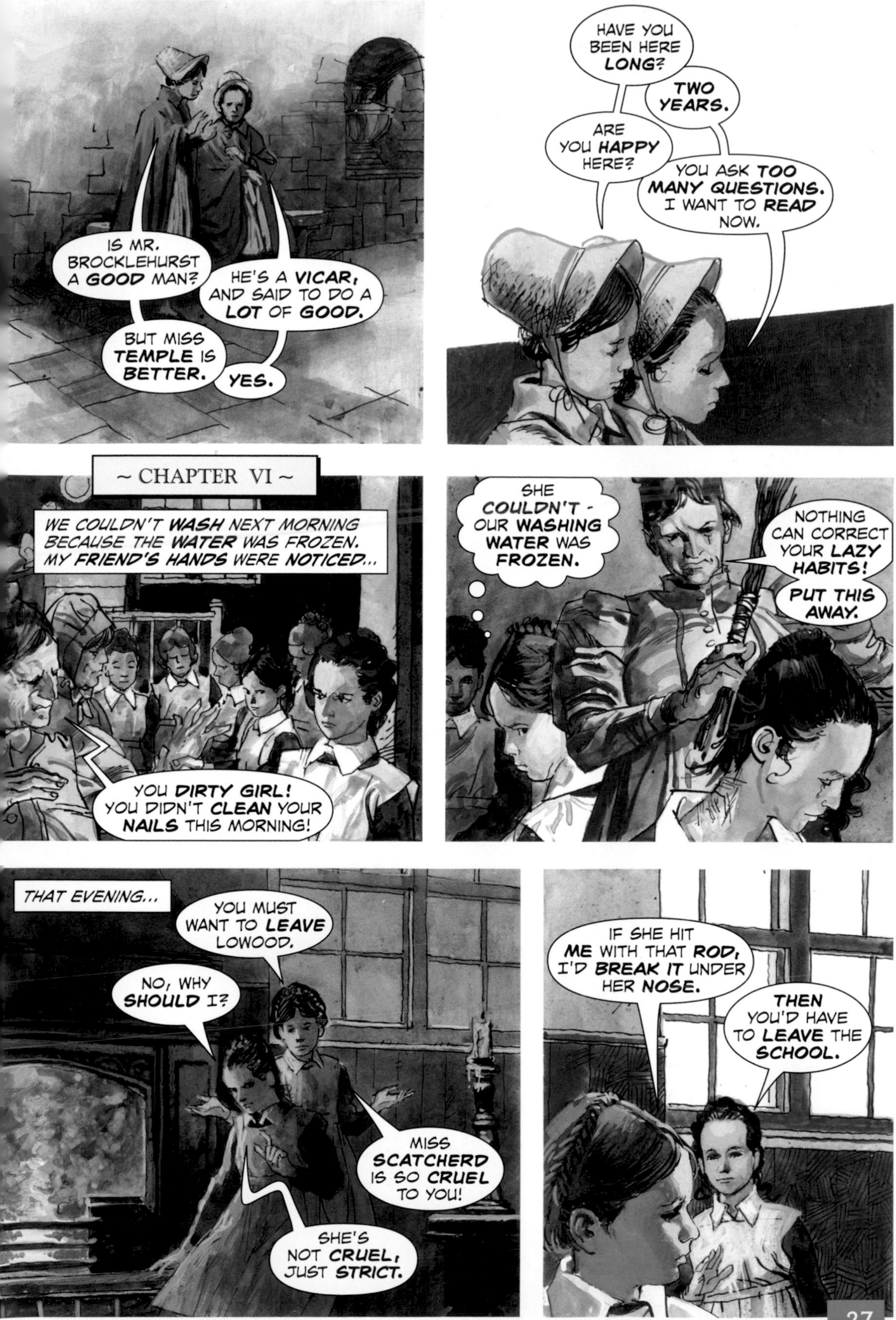
IS MR. BROCKLEHURST A GOOD MAN?
HE'S A VICAR, AND SAID TO DO A LOT OF GOOD.
BUT MISS TEMPLE IS BETTER.
YES.
HAVE YOU BEEN HERE LONG?
TWO YEARS.
ARE YOU HAPPY HERE?
YOU ASK TOO MANY QUESTIONS. I WANT TO READ NOW.
~ CHAPTER VI ~
WE COULDN'T WASH NEXT MORNING BECAUSE THE WATER WAS FROZEN. MY FRIEND'S HANDS WERE NOTICED...
YOU DIRTY GIRL! YOU DIDN'T CLEAN YOUR NAILS THIS MORNING!
SHE COULDN'T - OUR WASHING WATER WAS FROZEN.
NOTHING CAN CORRECT YOUR LAZY HABITS!
PUT THIS AWAY.
THAT EVENING...
YOU MUST WANT TO LEAVE LOWOOD.
NO, WHY SHOULD I?
MISS SCATCHERD IS SO CRUEL TO YOU!
SHE'S NOT CRUEL, JUST STRICT.
IF SHE HIT ME WITH THAT ROD, I'D BREAK IT UNDER HER NOSE.
THEN YOU'D HAVE TO LEAVE THE SCHOOL.

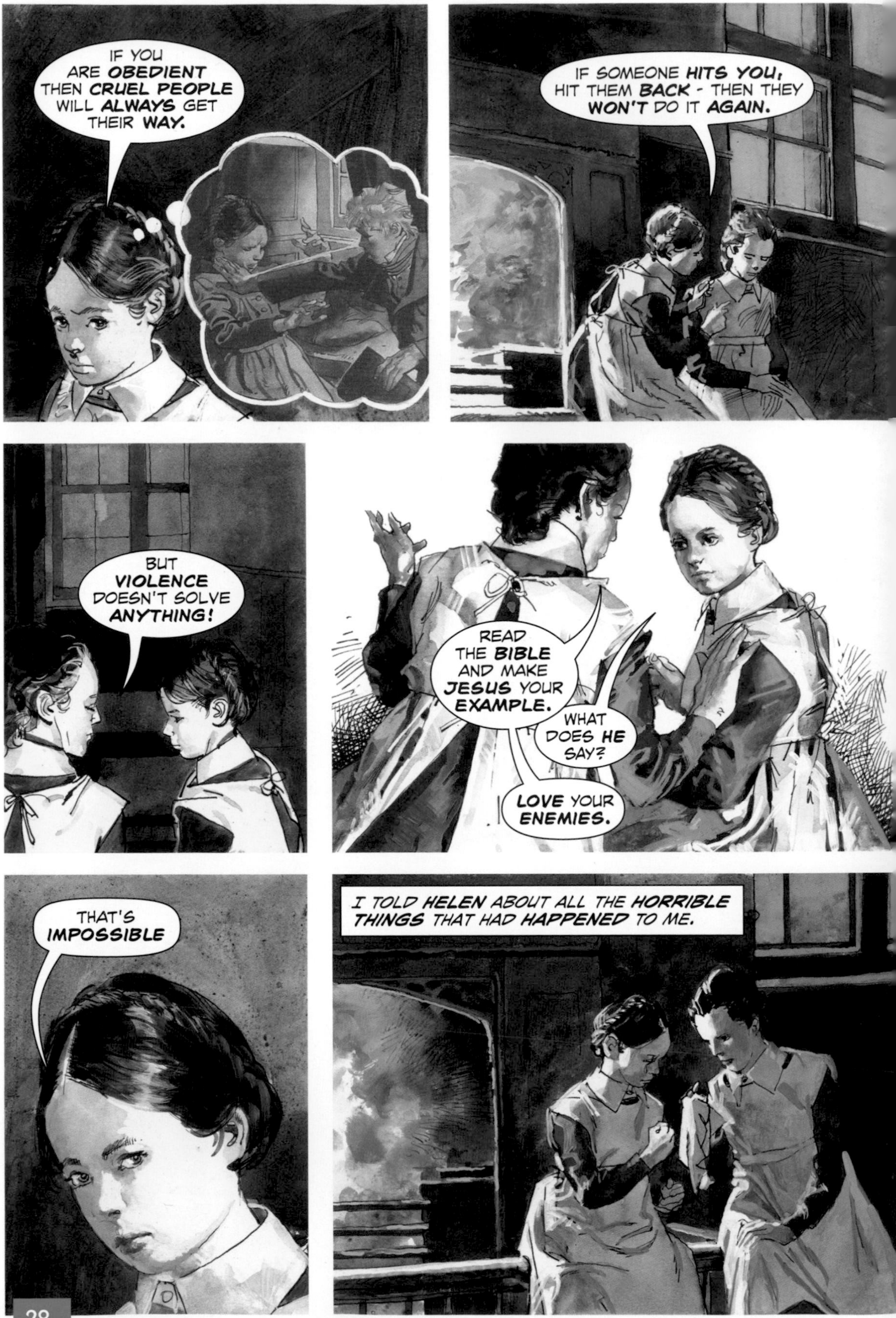
IF YOU ARE OBEDIENT THEN CRUEL PEOPLE WILL ALWAYS GET THEIR WAY.
IF SOMEONE HITS YOU, HIT THEM BACK - THEN THEY WON'T DO IT AGAIN.
BUT VIOLENCE DOESN'T SOLVE ANYTHING!
READ THE BIBLE AND MAKE JESUS YOUR EXAMPLE.
WHAT DOES HE SAY?
LOVE YOUR ENEMIES.
THAT'S IMPOSSIBLE
I TOLD HELEN ABOUT ALL THE HORRIBLE THINGS THAT HAD HAPPENED TO ME.

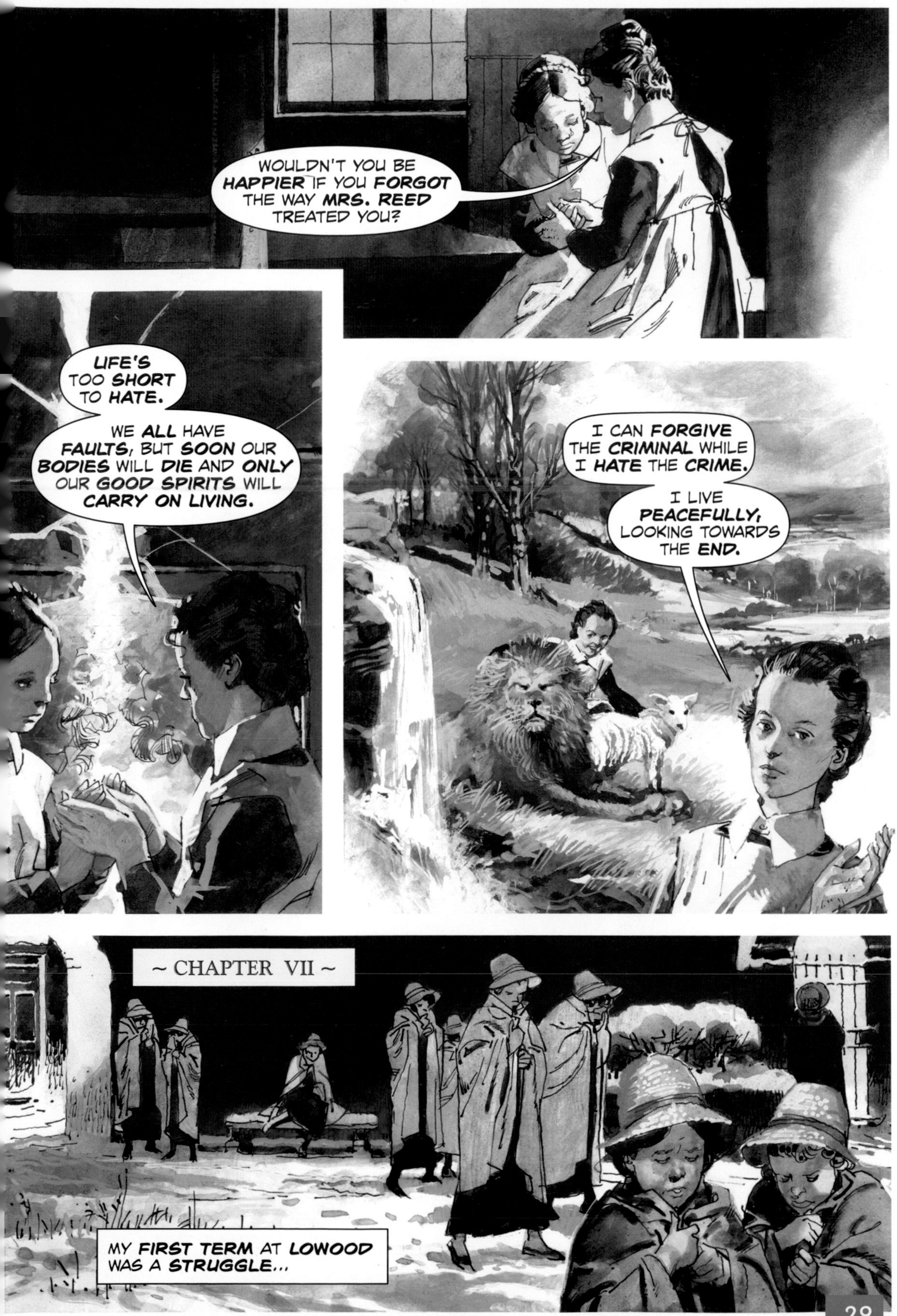
WOULDN'T YOU BE HAPPIER IF YOU FORGOT THE WAY MRS. REED TREATED YOU?
LIFE'S TOO SHORT TO HATE.
WE ALL HAVE FAULTS, BUT SOON OUR BODIES WILL DIE AND ONLY OUR GOOD SPIRITS WILL CARRY ON LIVING.
I CAN FORGIVE THE CRIMINAL WHILE I HATE THE CRIME.
I LIVE PEACEFULLY, LOOKING TOWARDS THE END.
~ CHAPTER VII ~
MY FIRST TERM AT LOWOOD WAS A STRUGGLE...

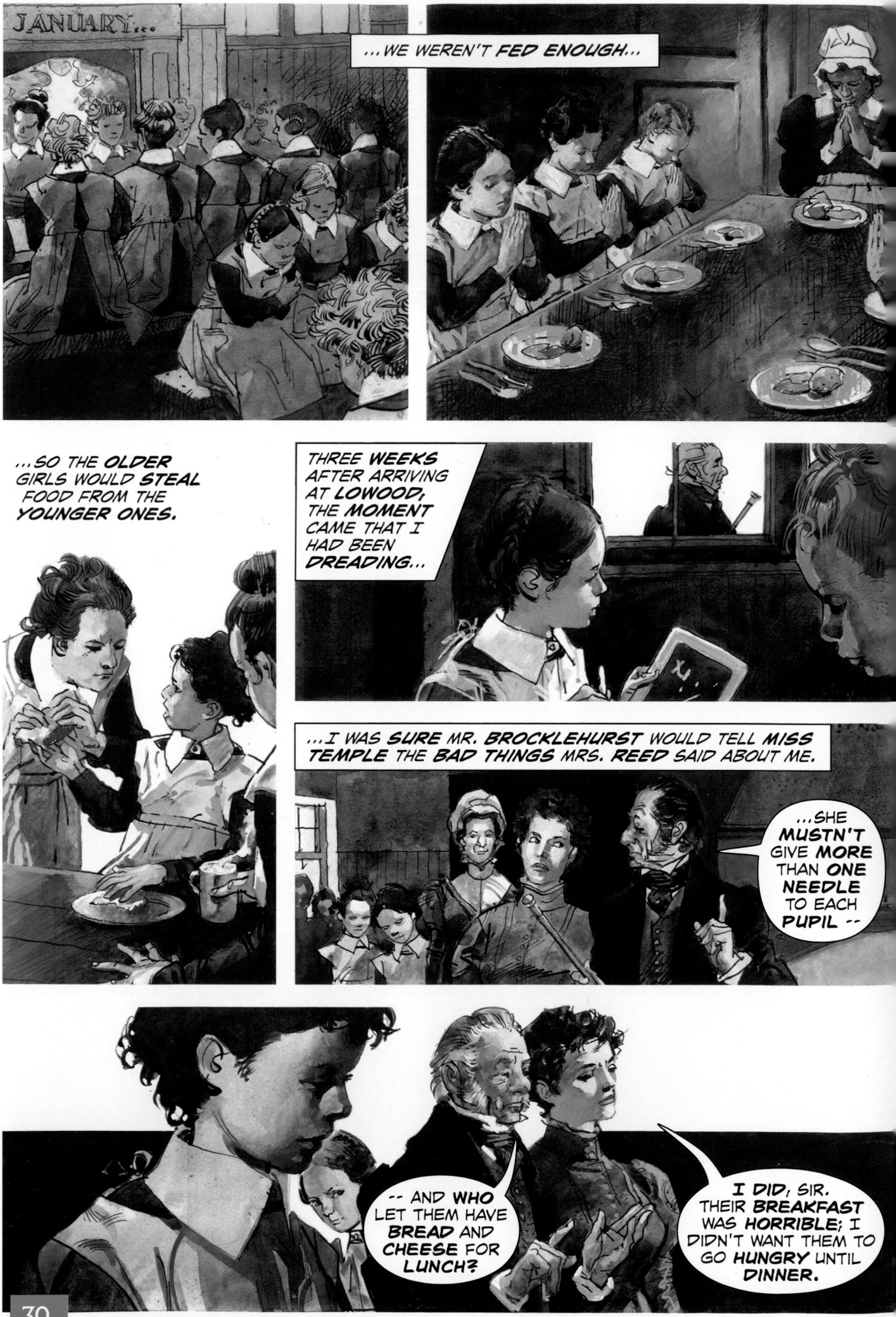
JANUARY...
...WE WEREN'T FED ENOUGH...
...SO THE OLDER GIRLS WOULD STEAL FOOD FROM THE YOUNGER ONES.
THREE WEEKS AFTER ARRIVING AT LOWOOD, THE MOMENT CAME THAT I HAD BEEN DREADING...
...I WAS SURE MR. BROCKLEHURST WOULD TELL MISS TEMPLE THE BAD THINGS MRS. REED SAID ABOUT ME.
...SHE MUSTN'T GIVE MORE THAN ONE NEEDLE TO EACH PUPIL --
-- AND WHO LET THEM HAVE BREAD AND CHEESE FOR LUNCH?
I DID, SIR. THEIR BREAKFAST WAS HORRIBLE; I DIDN'T WANT THEM TO GO HUNGRY UNTIL DINNER.

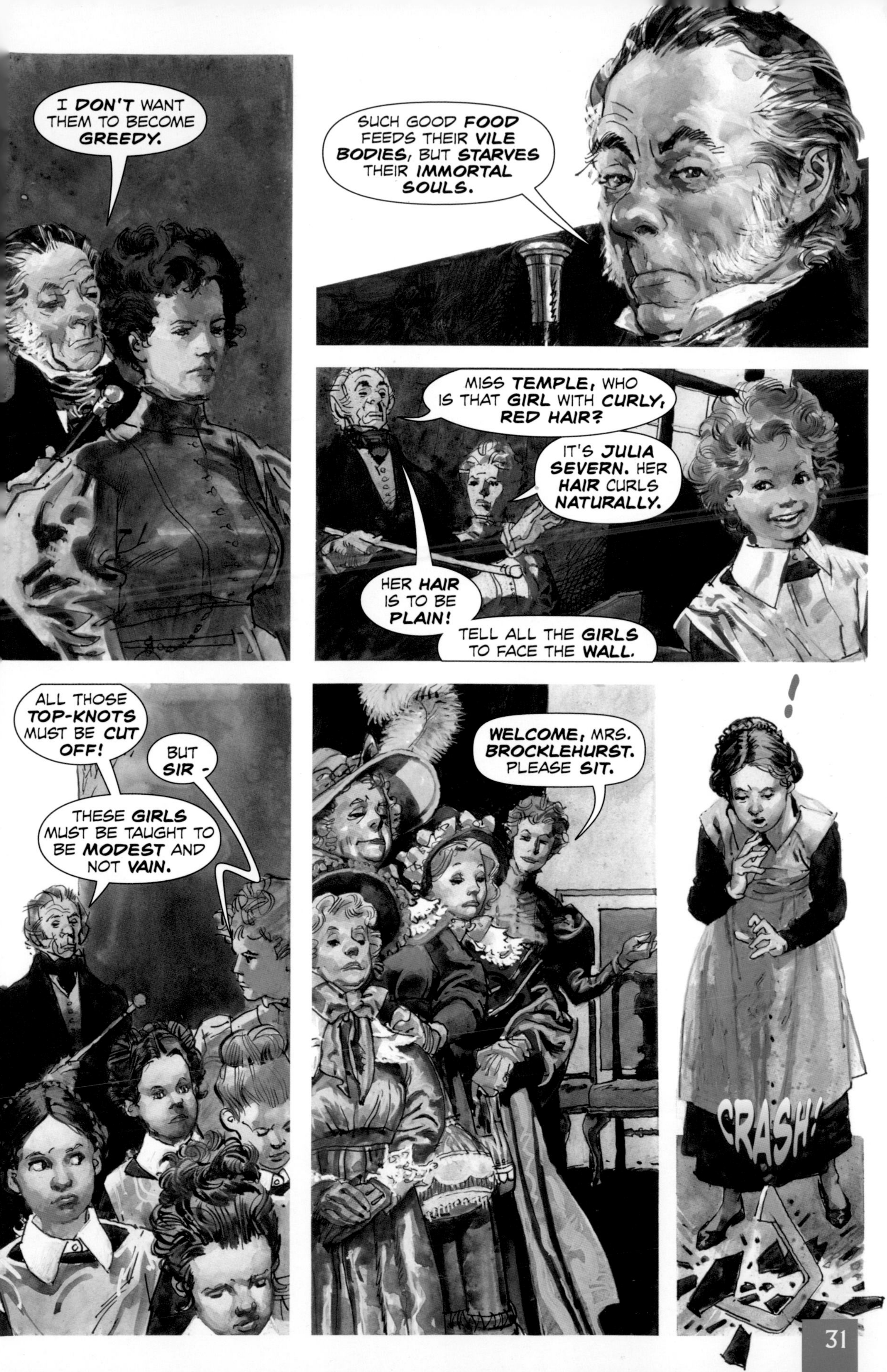
I DON'T WANT THEM TO BECOME GREEDY.
SUCH GOOD FOOD FEEDS THEIR VILE BODIES, BUT STARVES THEIR IMMORTAL SOULS.
MISS TEMPLE, WHO IS THAT GIRL WITH CURLY, RED HAIR?
IT'S JULIA SEVERN. HER HAIR CURLS NATURALLY.
HER HAIR IS TO BE PLAIN!
TELL ALL THE GIRLS TO FACE THE WALL.
ALL THOSE TOP-KNOTS MUST BE CUT OFF!
BUT SIR -
THESE GIRLS MUST BE TAUGHT TO BE MODEST AND NOT VAIN.
WELCOME, MRS. BROCKLEHURST. PLEASE SIT.
!
CRASH!

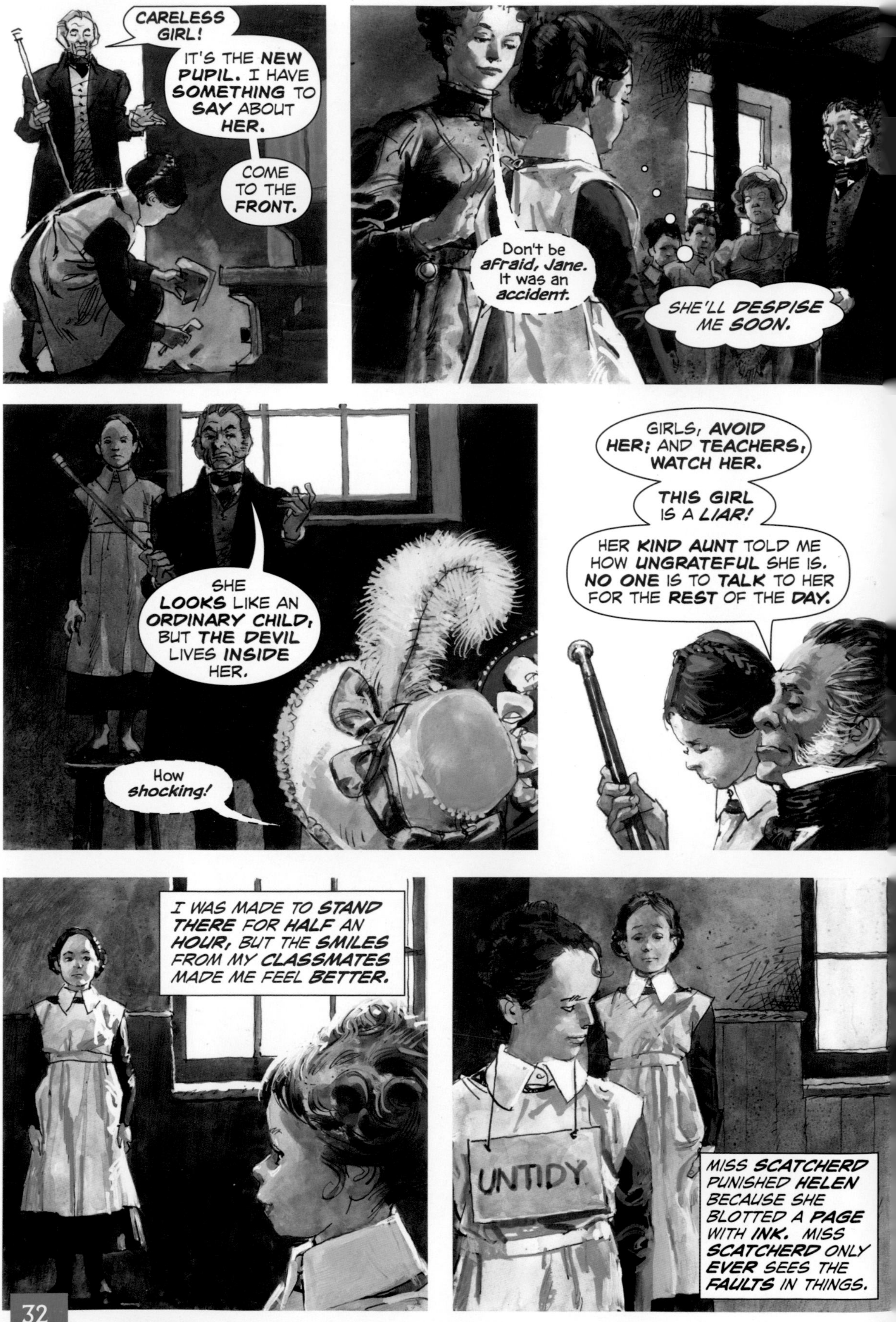

CARELESS GIRL!
IT'S THE NEW PUPIL. I HAVE SOMETHING TO SAY ABOUT HER.
COME TO THE FRONT.
Don't be afraid, Jane. It was an accident.
SHE'LL DESPISE ME SOON.
SHE LOOKS LIKE AN ORDINARY CHILD, BUT THE DEVIL LIVES INSIDE HER.
How shocking!
GIRLS, AVOID HER; AND TEACHERS, WATCH HER.
THIS GIRL IS A LIAR!
HER KIND AUNT TOLD ME HOW UNGRATEFUL SHE IS. NO ONE IS TO TALK TO HER FOR THE REST OF THE DAY.
I WAS MADE TO STAND THERE FOR HALF AN HOUR, BUT THE SMILES FROM MY CLASSMATES MADE ME FEEL BETTER.
UNTIDY
MISS SCATCHERD PUNISHED HELEN BECAUSE SHE BLOTTED A PAGE WITH INK. MISS SCATCHERD ONLY EVER SEES THE FAULTS IN THINGS.

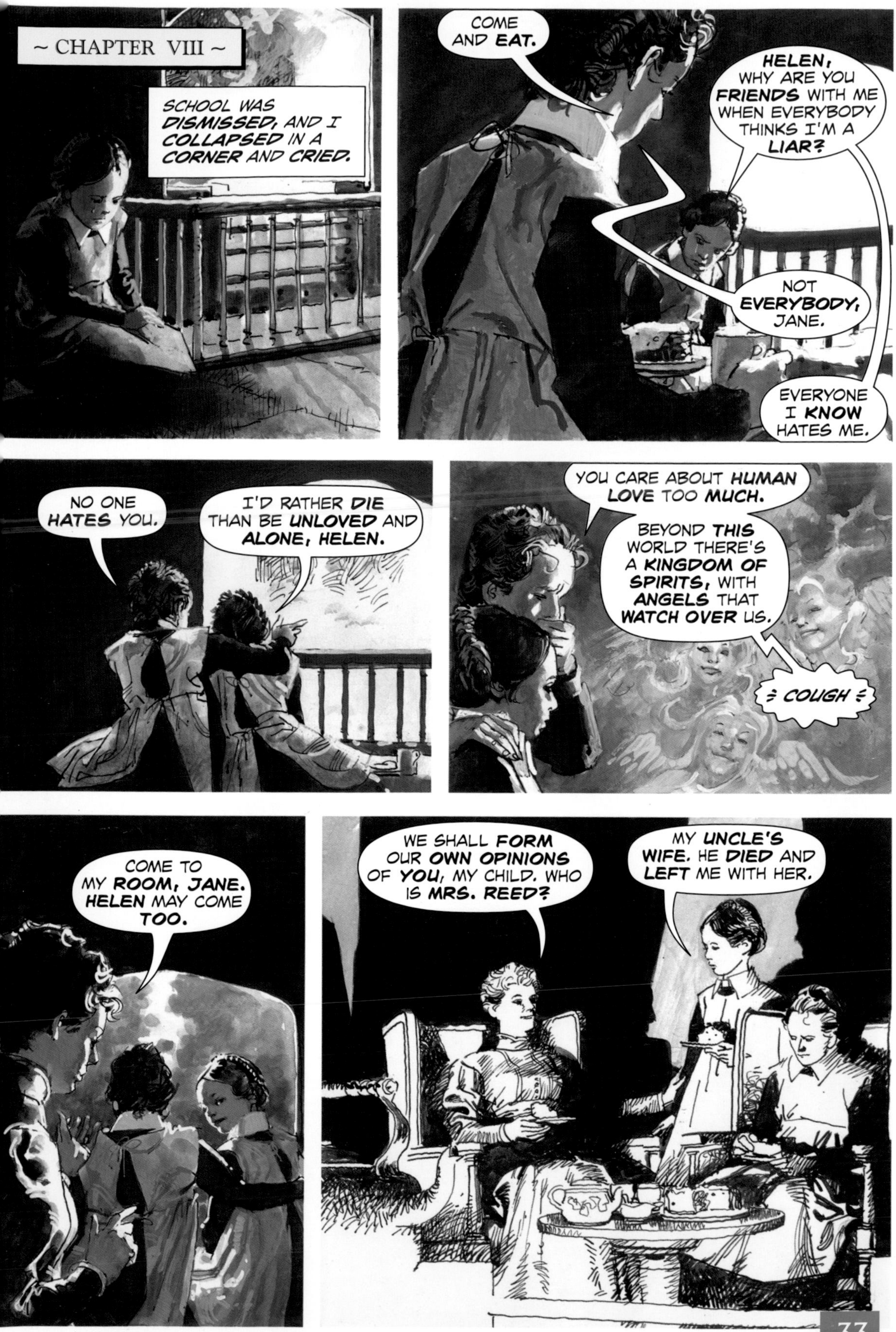
~ CHAPTER VIII ~
SCHOOL WAS DISMISSED, AND I COLLAPSED IN A CORNER AND CRIED.
COME AND EAT.
HELEN, WHY ARE YOU FRIENDS WITH ME WHEN EVERYBODY THINKS I'M A LIAR?
NOT EVERYBODY, JANE.
EVERYONE I KNOW HATES ME.
NO ONE HATES YOU.
I'D RATHER DIE THAN BE UNLOVED AND ALONE, HELEN.
YOU CARE ABOUT HUMAN LOVE TOO MUCH.
BEYOND THIS WORLD THERE'S A KINGDOM OF SPIRITS, WITH ANGELS THAT WATCH OVER US.
COUGH
COME TO MY ROOM, JANE. HELEN MAY COME TOO.
WE SHALL FORM OUR OWN OPINIONS OF YOU, MY CHILD. WHO IS MRS. REED?
MY UNCLE'S WIFE. HE DIED AND LEFT ME WITH HER.

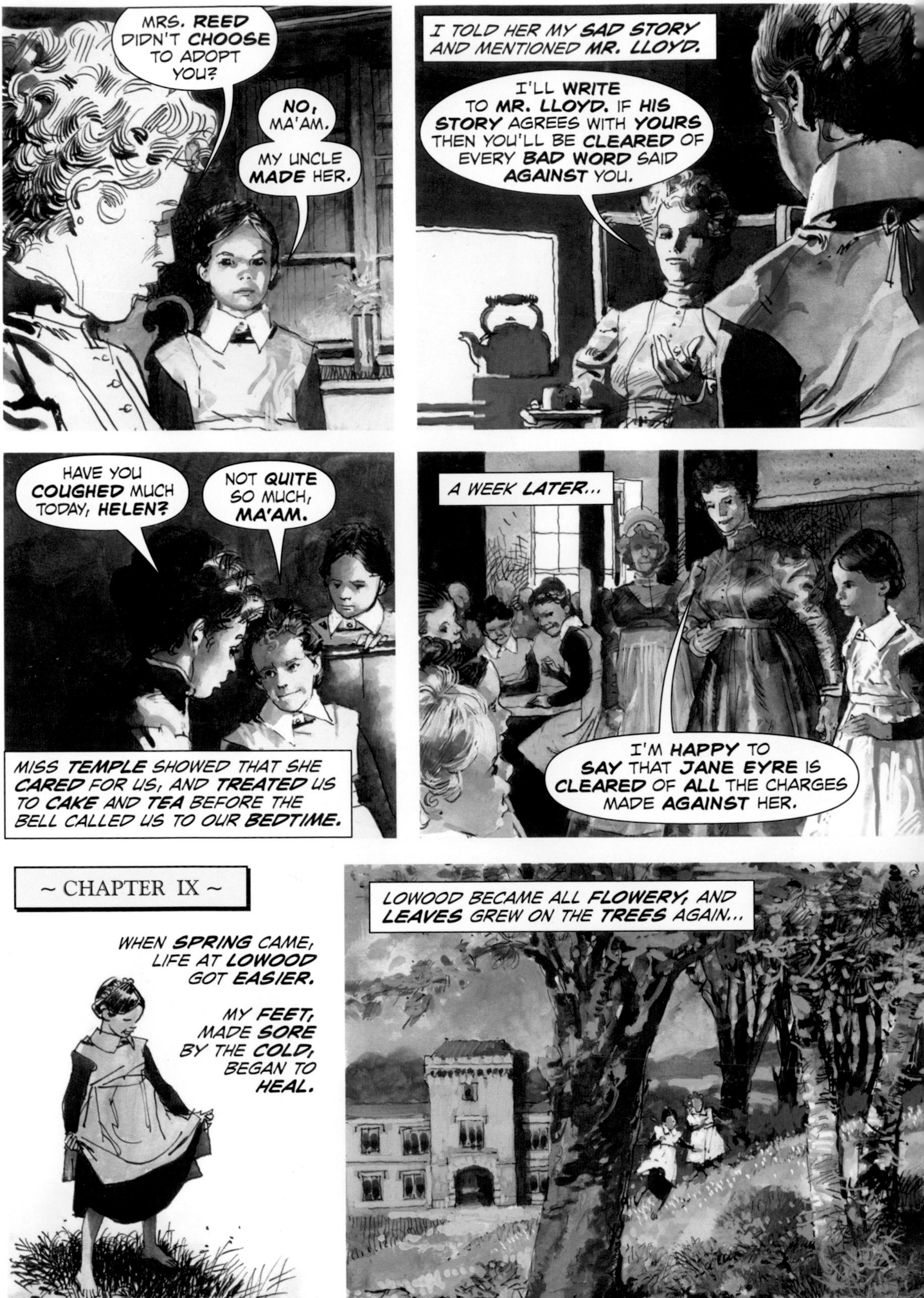
MRS. REED DIDN'T CHOOSE TO ADOPT YOU?
NO, MA'AM.
MY UNCLE MADE HER.
I TOLD HER MY SAD STORY AND MENTIONED MR. LLOYD.
I'LL WRITE TO MR. LLOYD. IF HIS STORY AGREES WITH YOURS THEN YOU'LL BE CLEARED OF EVERY BAD WORD SAID AGAINST YOU.
HAVE YOU COUGHED MUCH TODAY, HELEN?
NOT QUITE SO MUCH, MA'AM.
MISS TEMPLE SHOWED THAT SHE CARED FOR US, AND TREATED US TO CAKE AND TEA BEFORE THE BELL CALLED US TO OUR BEDTIME.
A WEEK LATER...
I'M HAPPY TO SAY THAT JANE EYRE IS CLEARED OF ALL THE CHARGES MADE AGAINST HER.
~ CHAPTER IX ~
WHEN SPRING CAME, LIFE AT LOWOOD GOT EASIER.
MY FEET, MADE SORE BY THE COLD, BEGAN TO HEAL.
LOWOOD BECAME ALL FLOWERY, AND LEAVES GREW ON THE TREES AGAIN...

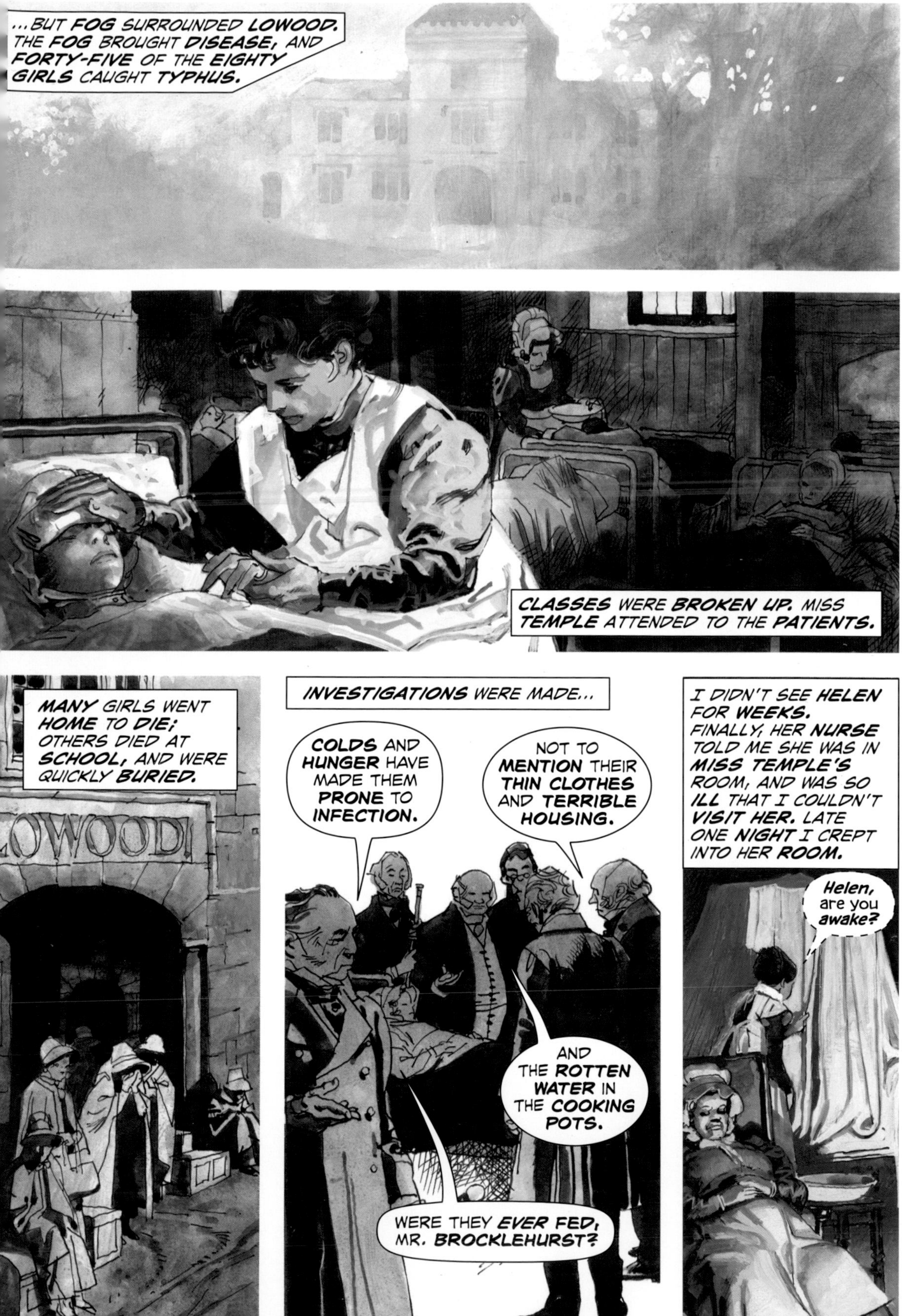
...BUT FOG SURROUNDED LOWOOD. THE FOG BROUGHT DISEASE, AND FORTY-FIVE OF THE EIGHTY GIRLS CAUGHT TYPHUS.
CLASSES WERE BROKEN UP. MISS TEMPLE ATTENDED TO THE PATIENTS.
MANY GIRLS WENT HOME TO DIE; OTHERS DIED AT SCHOOL, AND WERE QUICKLY BURIED.
OWOOD
INVESTIGATIONS WERE MADE...
COLDS AND HUNGER HAVE MADE THEM PRONE TO INFECTION.
NOT TO MENTION THEIR THIN CLOTHES AND TERRIBLE HOUSING.
AND THE ROTTEN WATER IN THE COOKING POTS.
WERE THEY EVER FED, MR. BROCKLEHURST?
I DIDN'T SEE HELEN FOR WEEKS. FINALLY, HER NURSE TOLD ME SHE WAS IN MISS TEMPLE'S ROOM, AND WAS SO ILL THAT I COULDN'T VISIT HER. LATE ONE NIGHT I CREPT INTO HER ROOM.
Helen, are you awake?

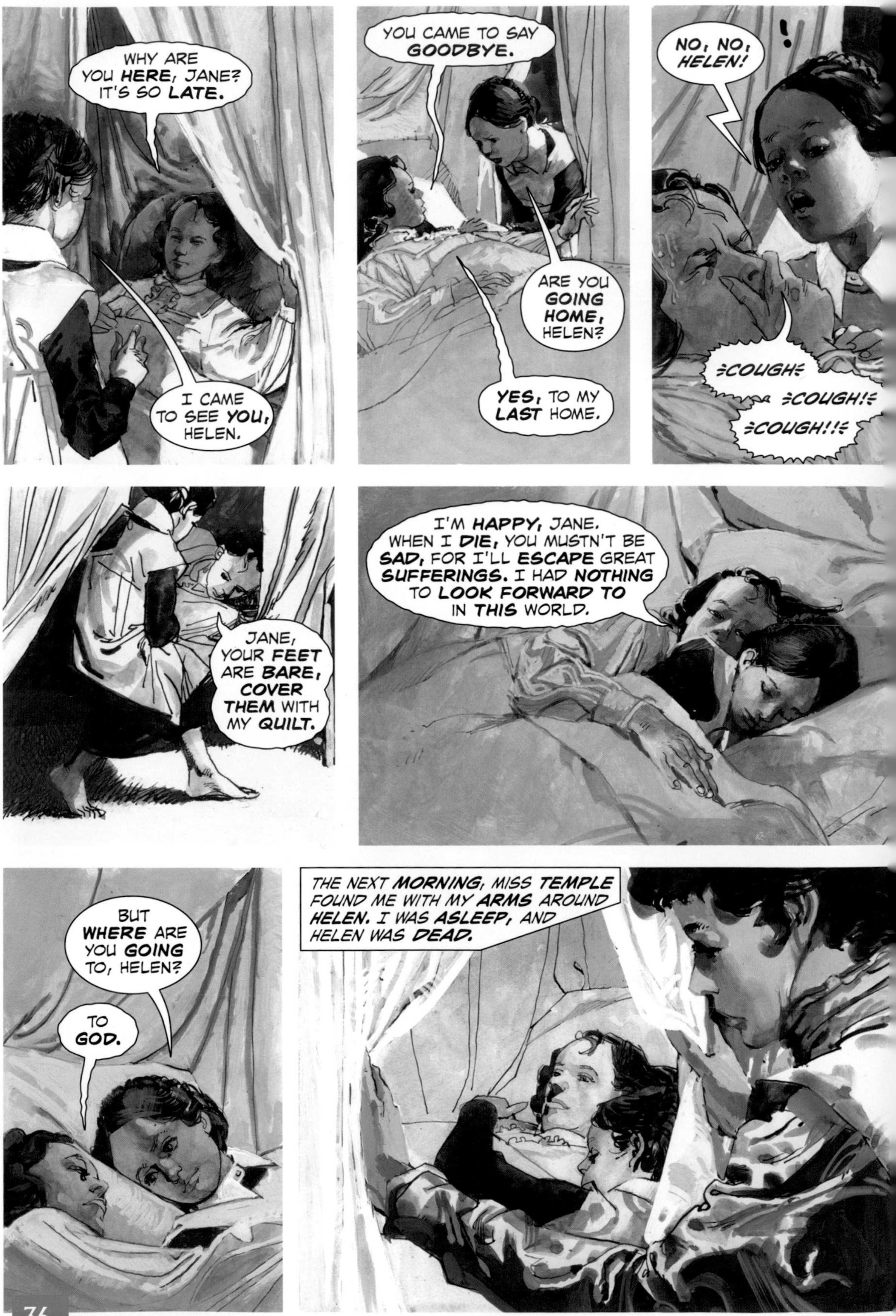
WHY ARE YOU HERE, JANE? IT'S SO LATE.
I CAME TO SEE YOU, HELEN.
YOU CAME TO SAY GOODBYE.
ARE YOU GOING HOME, HELEN?
YES, TO MY LAST HOME.
NO, NO, HELEN!
!
COUGH
COUGH!
COUGH!!
JANE, YOUR FEET ARE BARE, COVER THEM WITH MY QUILT.
I'M HAPPY, JANE. WHEN I DIE, YOU MUSTN'T BE SAD, FOR I'LL ESCAPE GREAT SUFFERINGS. I HAD NOTHING TO LOOK FORWARD TO IN THIS WORLD.
BUT WHERE ARE YOU GOING TO, HELEN?
TO GOD.
THE NEXT MORNING, MISS TEMPLE FOUND ME WITH MY ARMS AROUND HELEN. I WAS ASLEEP, AND HELEN WAS DEAD.

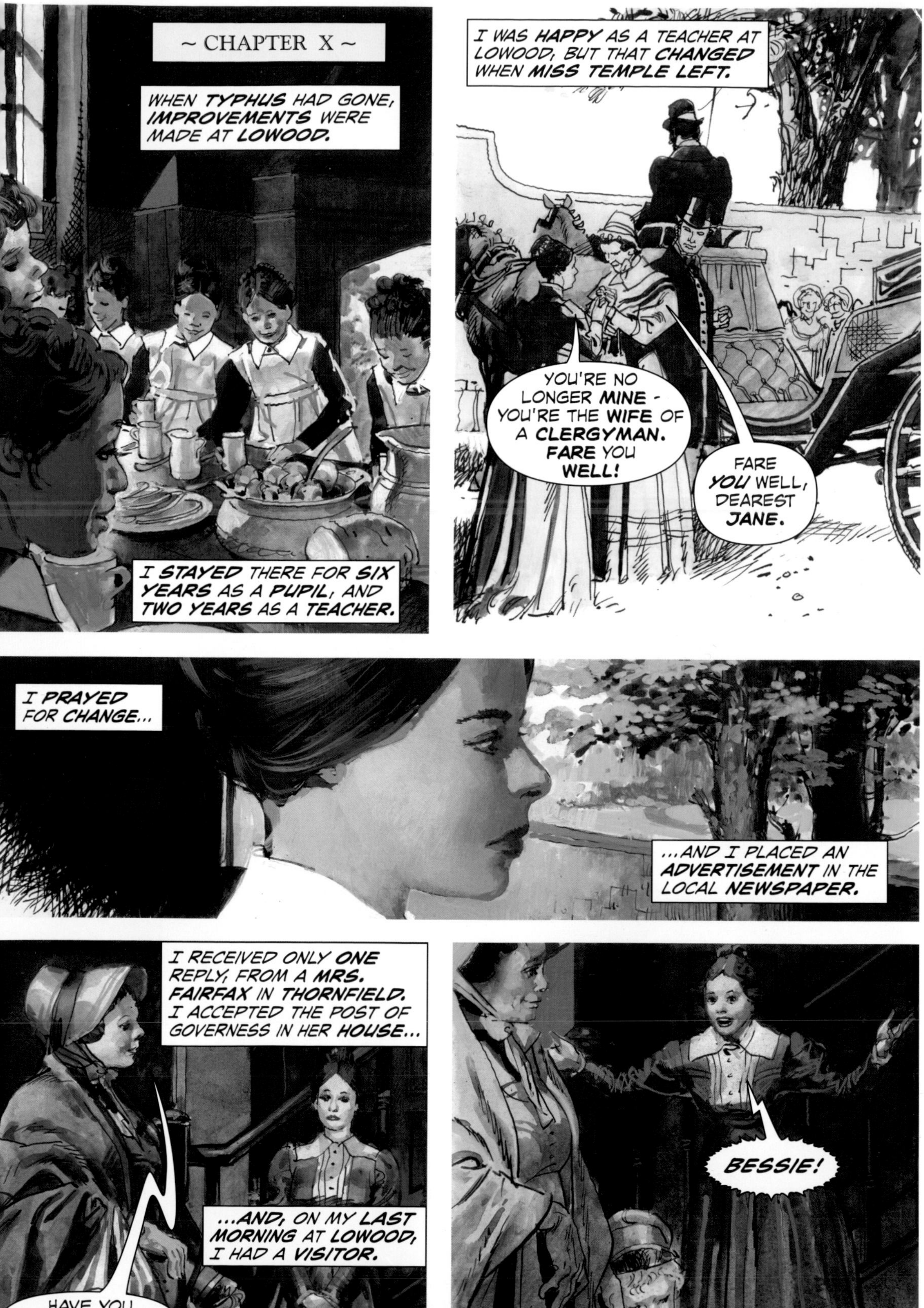
~ CHAPTER X ~
WHEN TYPHUS HAD GONE, IMPROVEMENTS WERE MADE AT LOWOOD.
I STAYED THERE FOR SIX YEARS AS A PUPIL, AND TWO YEARS AS A TEACHER.
I WAS HAPPY AS A TEACHER AT LOWOOD, BUT THAT CHANGED WHEN MISS TEMPLE LEFT.
YOU'RE NO LONGER MINE - YOU'RE THE WIFE OF A CLERGYMAN. FARE YOU WELL!
FARE YOU WELL, DEAREST JANE.
I PRAYED FOR CHANGE...
...AND I PLACED AN ADVERTISEMENT IN THE LOCAL NEWSPAPER.
I RECEIVED ONLY ONE REPLY, FROM A MRS. FAIRFAX IN THORNFIELD. I ACCEPTED THE POST OF GOVERNESS IN HER HOUSE...
...AND, ON MY LAST MORNING AT LOWOOD, I HAD A VISITOR.
HAVE YOU FORGOTTEN ME, MISS JANE?
BESSIE!

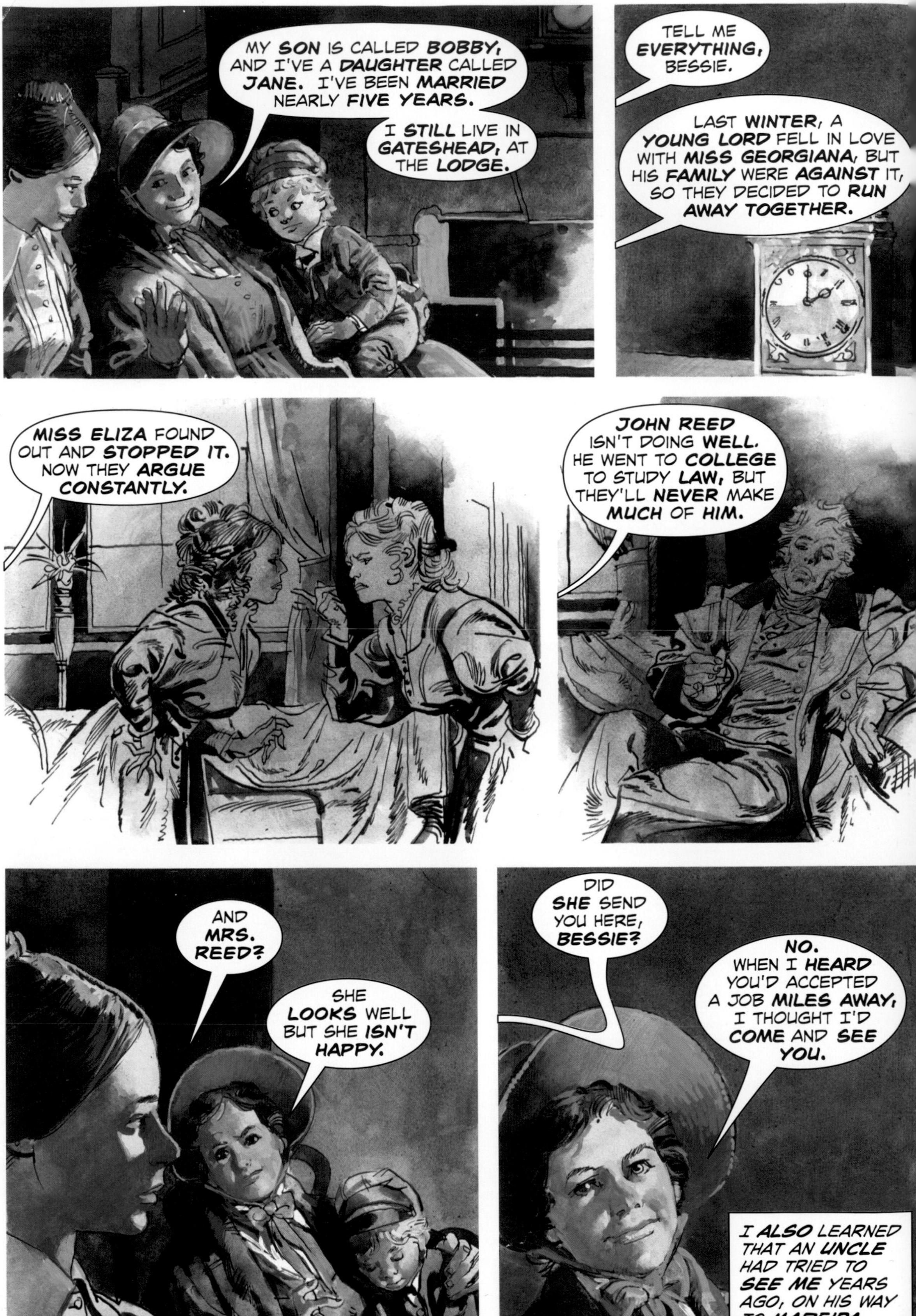
MY SON IS CALLED BOBBY, AND I'VE A DAUGHTER CALLED JANE. I'VE BEEN MARRIED NEARLY FIVE YEARS.
I STILL LIVE IN GATESHEAD, AT THE LODGE.
TELL ME EVERYTHING, BESSIE.
LAST WINTER, A YOUNG LORD FELL IN LOVE WITH MISS GEORGIANA, BUT HIS FAMILY WERE AGAINST IT, SO THEY DECIDED TO RUN AWAY TOGETHER.
MISS ELIZA FOUND OUT AND STOPPED IT. NOW THEY ARGUE CONSTANTLY.
JOHN REED ISN'T DOING WELL. HE WENT TO COLLEGE TO STUDY LAW, BUT THEY'LL NEVER MAKE MUCH OF HIM.
AND MRS. REED?
SHE LOOKS WELL BUT SHE ISN'T HAPPY.
DID SHE SEND YOU HERE, BESSIE?
NO. WHEN I HEARD YOU'D ACCEPTED A JOB MILES AWAY, I THOUGHT I'D COME AND SEE YOU.
I ALSO LEARNED THAT AN UNCLE HAD TRIED TO SEE ME YEARS AGO, ON HIS WAY TO MADEIRA.

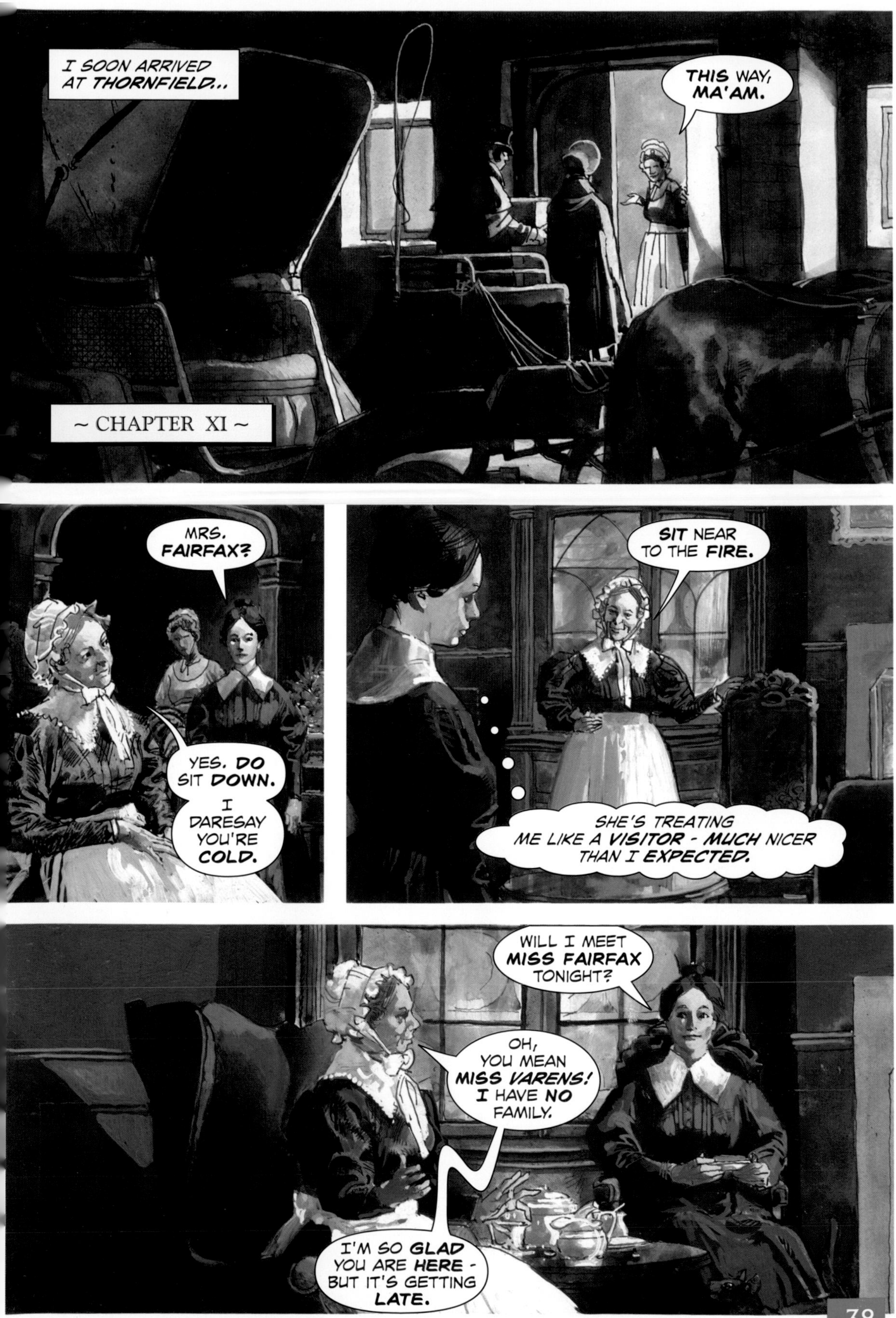
I SOON ARRIVED AT THORNFIELD...
~ CHAPTER XI ~
THIS WAY, MA'AM.
MRS. FAIRFAX?
YES. DO SIT DOWN.
I DARESAY YOU'RE COLD.
SIT NEAR TO THE FIRE.
SHE'S TREATING ME LIKE A VISITOR - MUCH NICER THAN I EXPECTED.
WILL I MEET MISS FAIRFAX TONIGHT?
OH, YOU MEAN MISS VARENS! I HAVE NO FAMILY.
I'M SO GLAD YOU ARE HERE - BUT IT'S GETTING LATE.

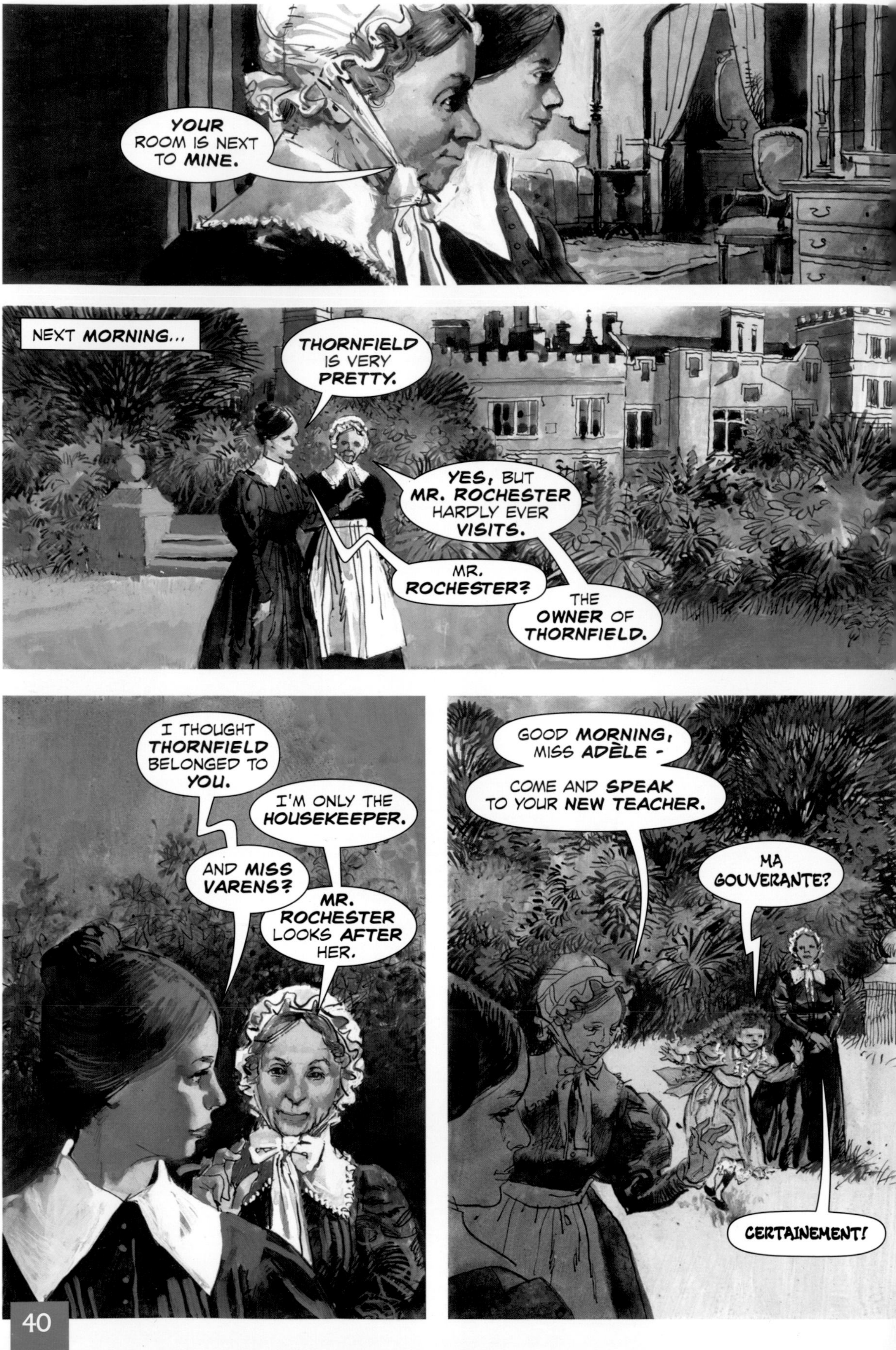
YOUR ROOM IS NEXT TO MINE.
NEXT MORNING...
THORNFIELD IS VERY PRETTY.
YES, BUT MR. ROCHESTER HARDLY EVER VISITS.
MR. ROCHESTER?
THE OWNER OF THORNFIELD.
I THOUGHT THORNFIELD BELONGED TO YOU.
I'M ONLY THE HOUSEKEEPER.
AND MISS VARENS?
MR. ROCHESTER LOOKS AFTER HER.
GOOD MORNING, MISS ADÈLE -
COME AND SPEAK TO YOUR NEW TEACHER.
MA GOUVERANTE?
CERTAINEMENT!

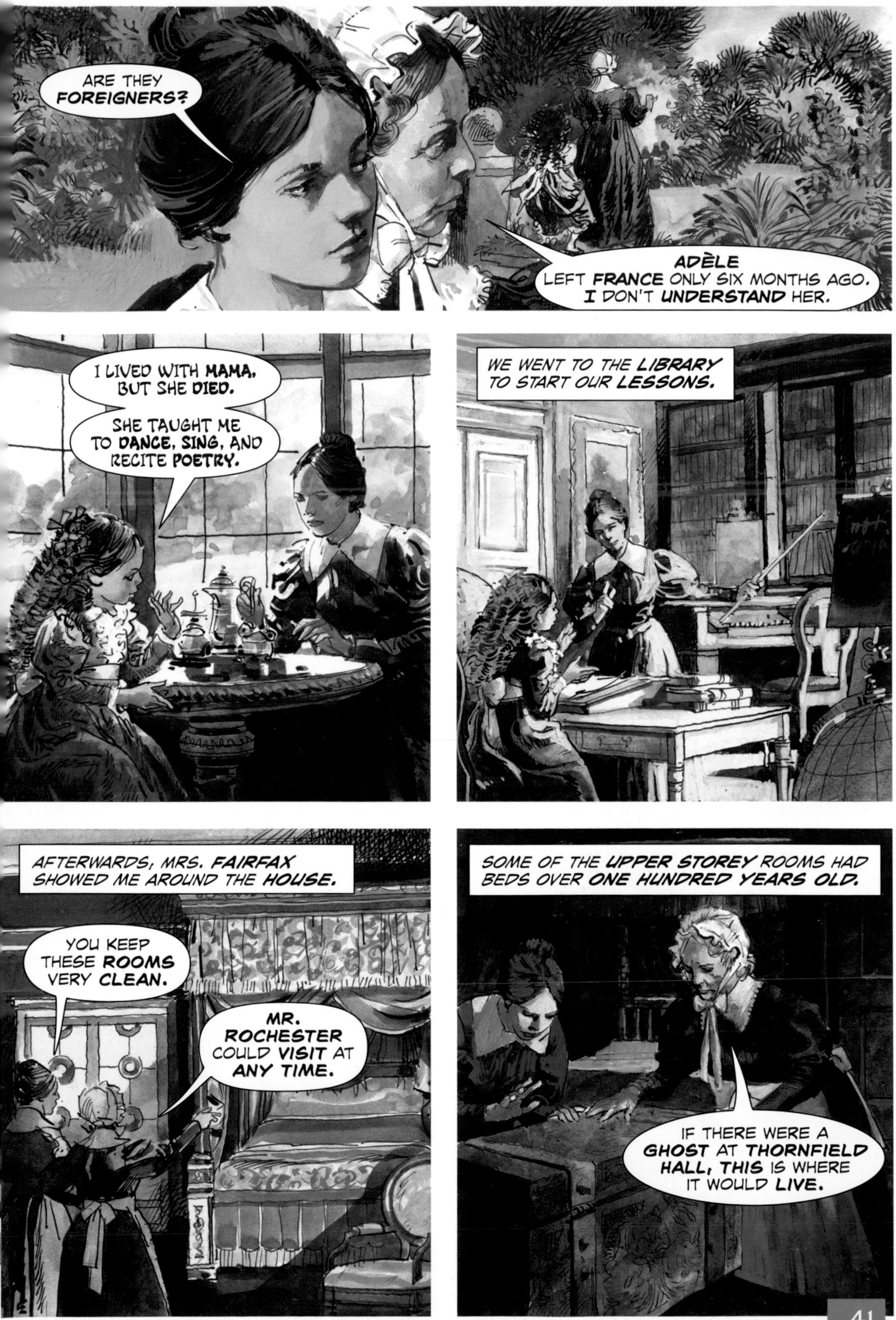
ARE THEY FOREIGNERS?
ADÈLE LEFT FRANCE ONLY SIX MONTHS AGO. I DON'T UNDERSTAND HER.
I LIVED WITH MAMA, BUT SHE DIED.
SHE TAUGHT ME TO DANCE, SING, AND RECITE POETRY.
WE WENT TO THE LIBRARY TO START OUR LESSONS.
AFTERWARDS, MRS. FAIRFAX SHOWED ME AROUND THE HOUSE.
YOU KEEP THESE ROOMS VERY CLEAN.
MR. ROCHESTER COULD VISIT AT ANY TIME.
SOME OF THE UPPER STOREY ROOMS HAD BEDS OVER ONE HUNDRED YEARS OLD.
IF THERE WERE A GHOST AT THORNFIELD HALL, THIS IS WHERE IT WOULD LIVE.

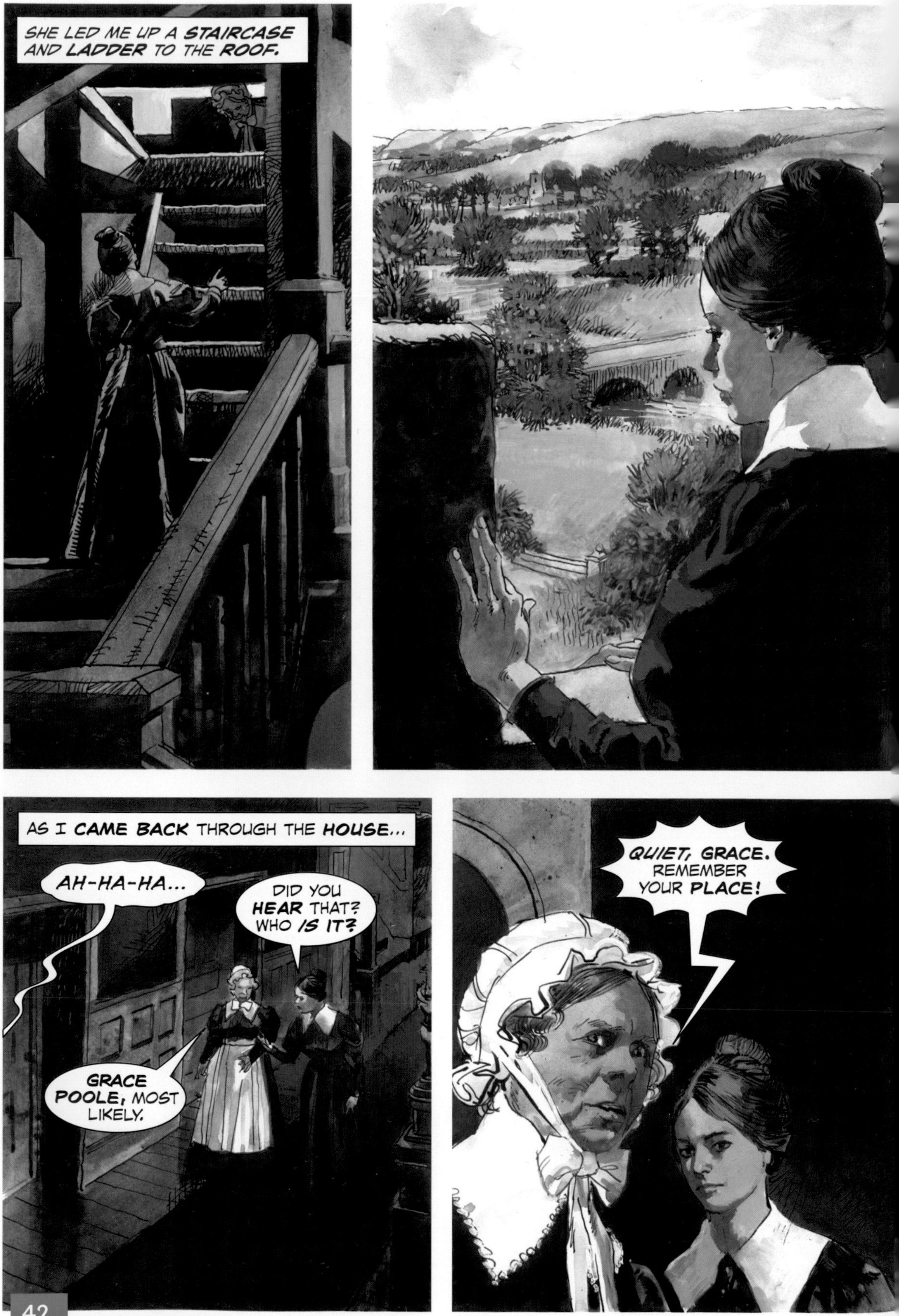
SHE LED ME UP A STAIRCASE AND LADDER TO THE ROOF.
AS I CAME BACK THROUGH THE HOUSE...
AH-HA-HA...
DID YOU HEAR THAT? WHO IS IT?
GRACE POOLE, MOST LIKELY.
QUIET, GRACE. REMEMBER YOUR PLACE!

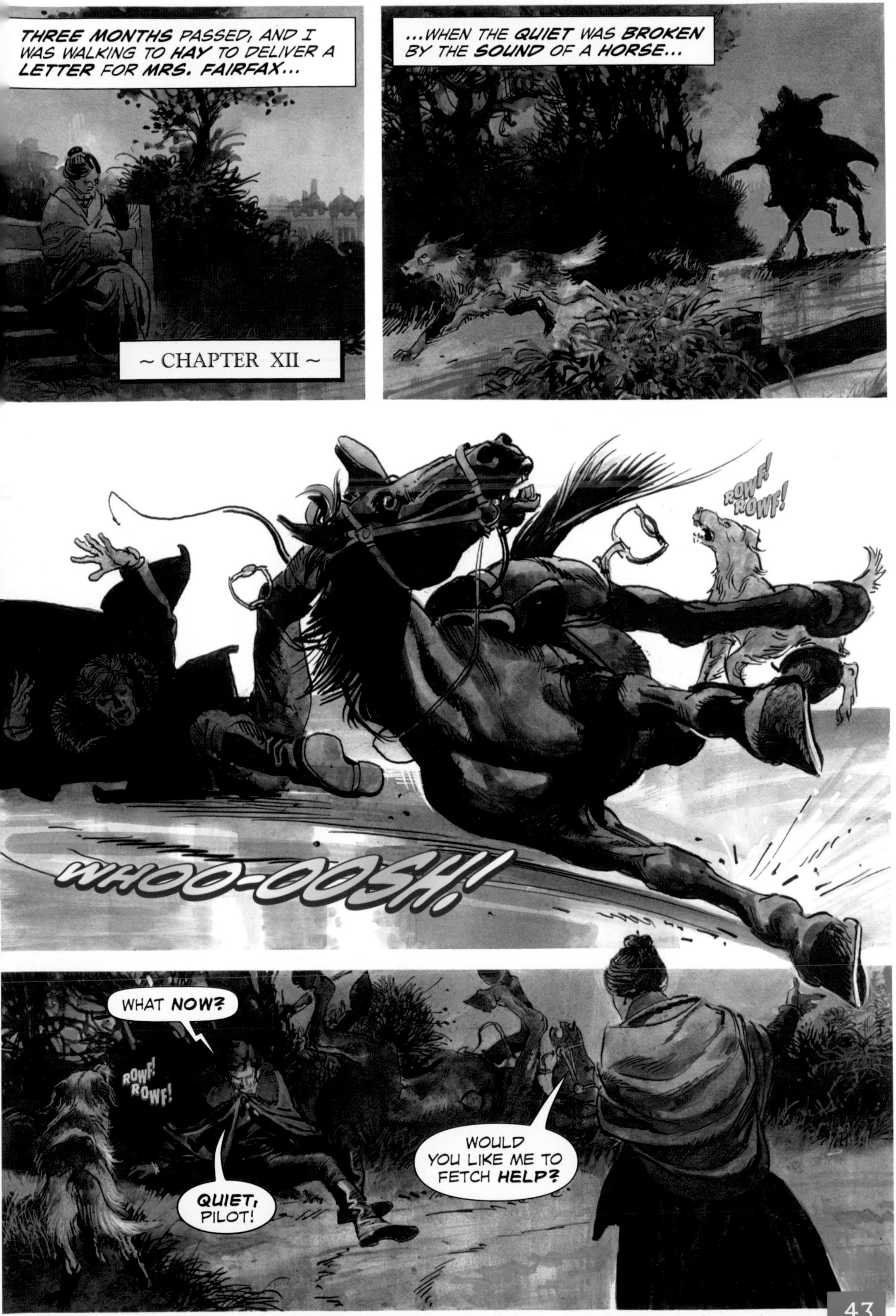
THREE MONTHS PASSED, AND I WAS WALKING TO HAY TO DELIVER A LETTER FOR MRS. FAIRFAX...
~ CHAPTER XII ~
...WHEN THE QUIET WAS BROKEN BY THE SOUND OF A HORSE...
ROWF! ROWF!
WHOO-OOSH!
WHAT NOW?
ROWF! ROWF!
QUIET, PILOT!
WOULD YOU LIKE ME TO FETCH HELP?

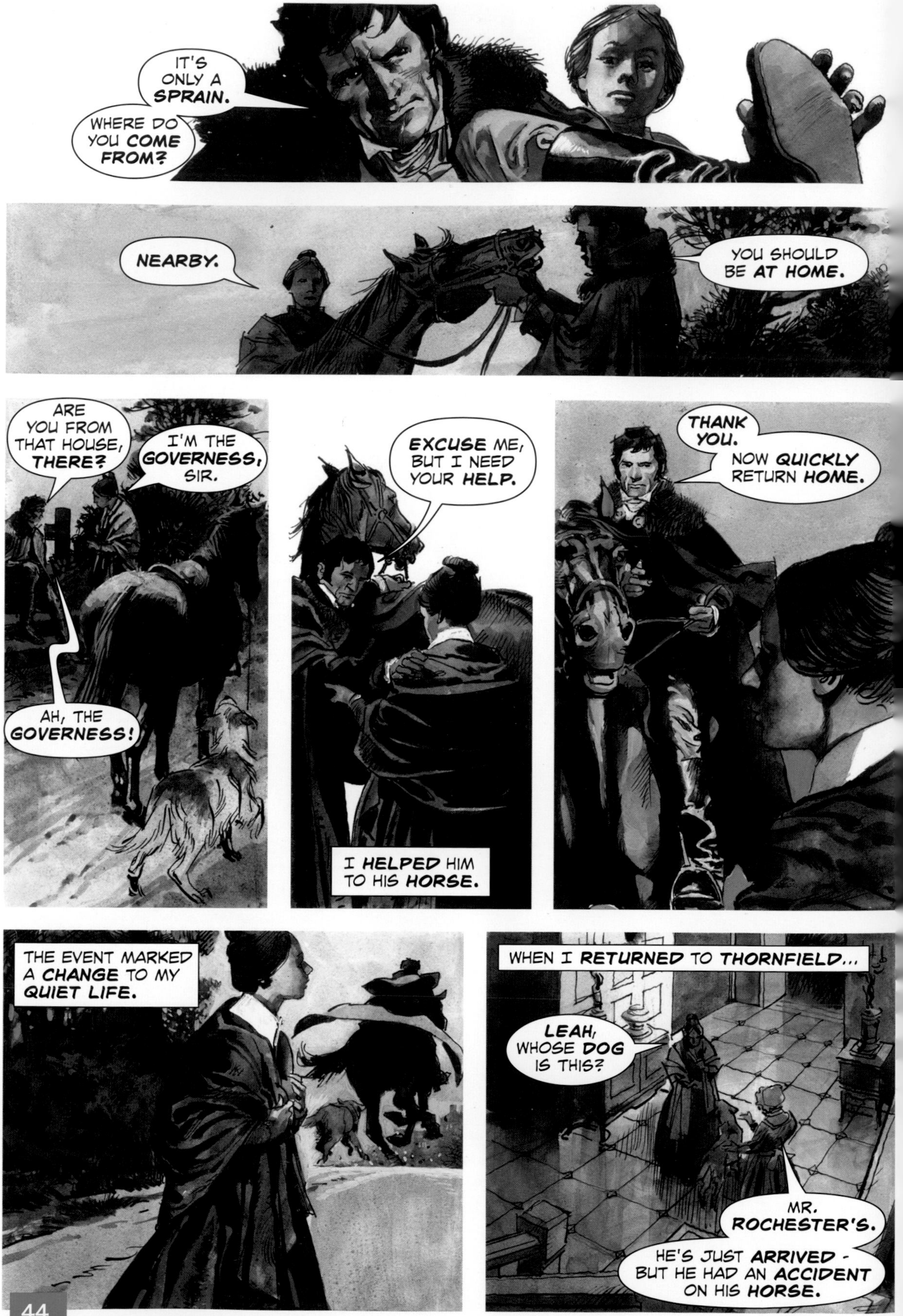
IT'S ONLY A SPRAIN.
WHERE DO YOU COME FROM?
NEARBY.
YOU SHOULD BE AT HOME.
ARE YOU FROM THAT HOUSE, THERE?
I'M THE GOVERNESS, SIR.
AH, THE GOVERNESS!
EXCUSE ME, BUT I NEED YOUR HELP.
I HELPED HIM TO HIS HORSE.
THANK YOU.
NOW QUICKLY RETURN HOME.
THE EVENT MARKED A CHANGE TO MY QUIET LIFE.
WHEN I RETURNED TO THORNFIELD...
LEAH, WHOSE DOG IS THIS?
MR. ROCHESTER'S.
HE'S JUST ARRIVED - BUT HE HAD AN ACCIDENT ON HIS HORSE.

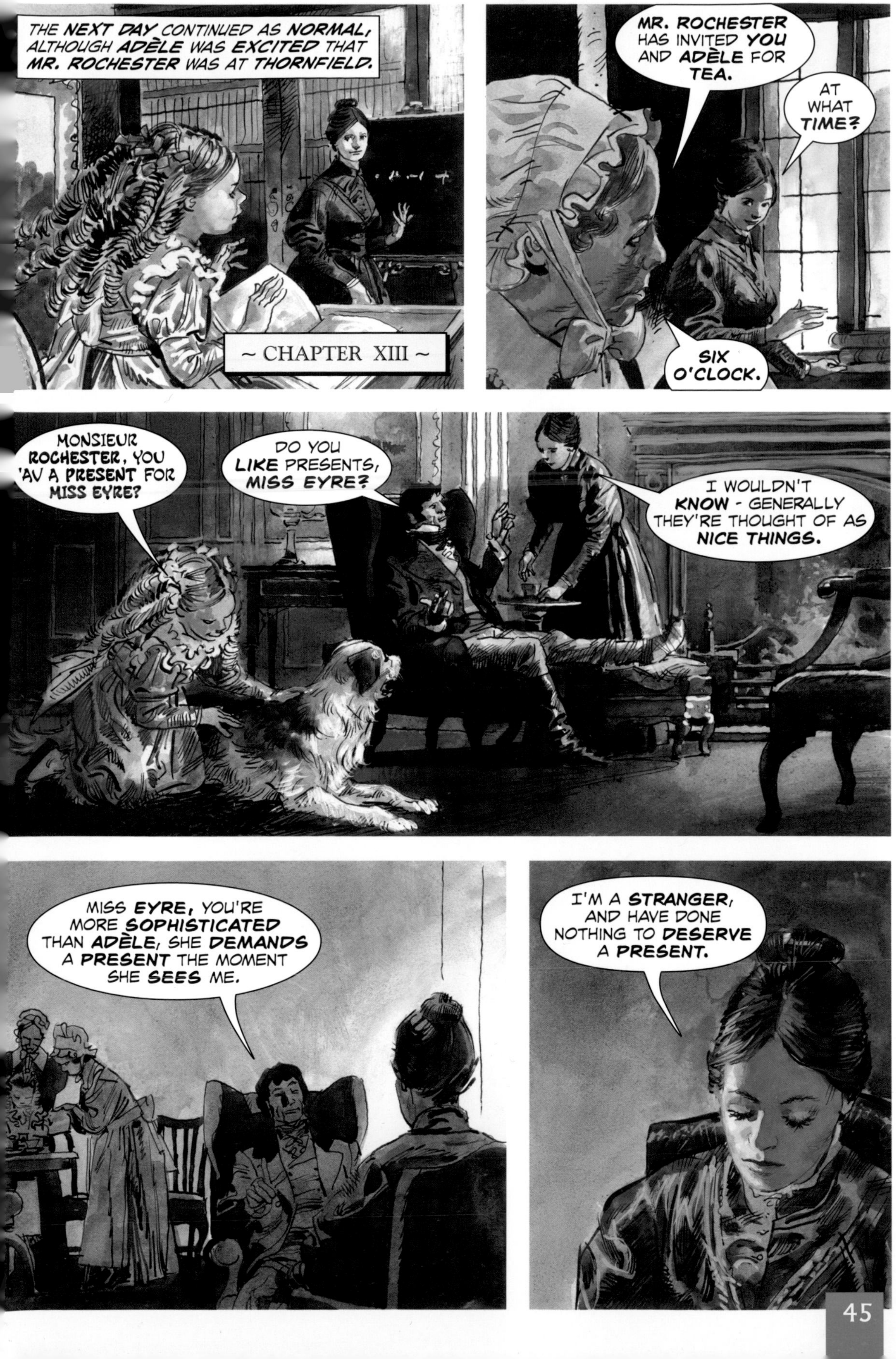
THE NEXT DAY CONTINUED AS NORMAL, ALTHOUGH ADÈLE WAS EXCITED THAT MR. ROCHESTER WAS AT THORNFIELD.
~ CHAPTER XIII ~
MR. ROCHESTER HAS INVITED YOU AND ADÈLE FOR TEA.
AT WHAT TIME?
SIX O'CLOCK.
MONSIEUR ROCHESTER, YOU 'AV A PRESENT FOR MISS EYRE?
DO YOU LIKE PRESENTS, MISS EYRE?
I WOULDN'T KNOW - GENERALLY THEY'RE THOUGHT OF AS NICE THINGS.
MISS EYRE, YOU'RE MORE SOPHISTICATED THAN ADÈLE, SHE DEMANDS A PRESENT THE MOMENT SHE SEES ME.
I'M A STRANGER, AND HAVE DONE NOTHING TO DESERVE A PRESENT.

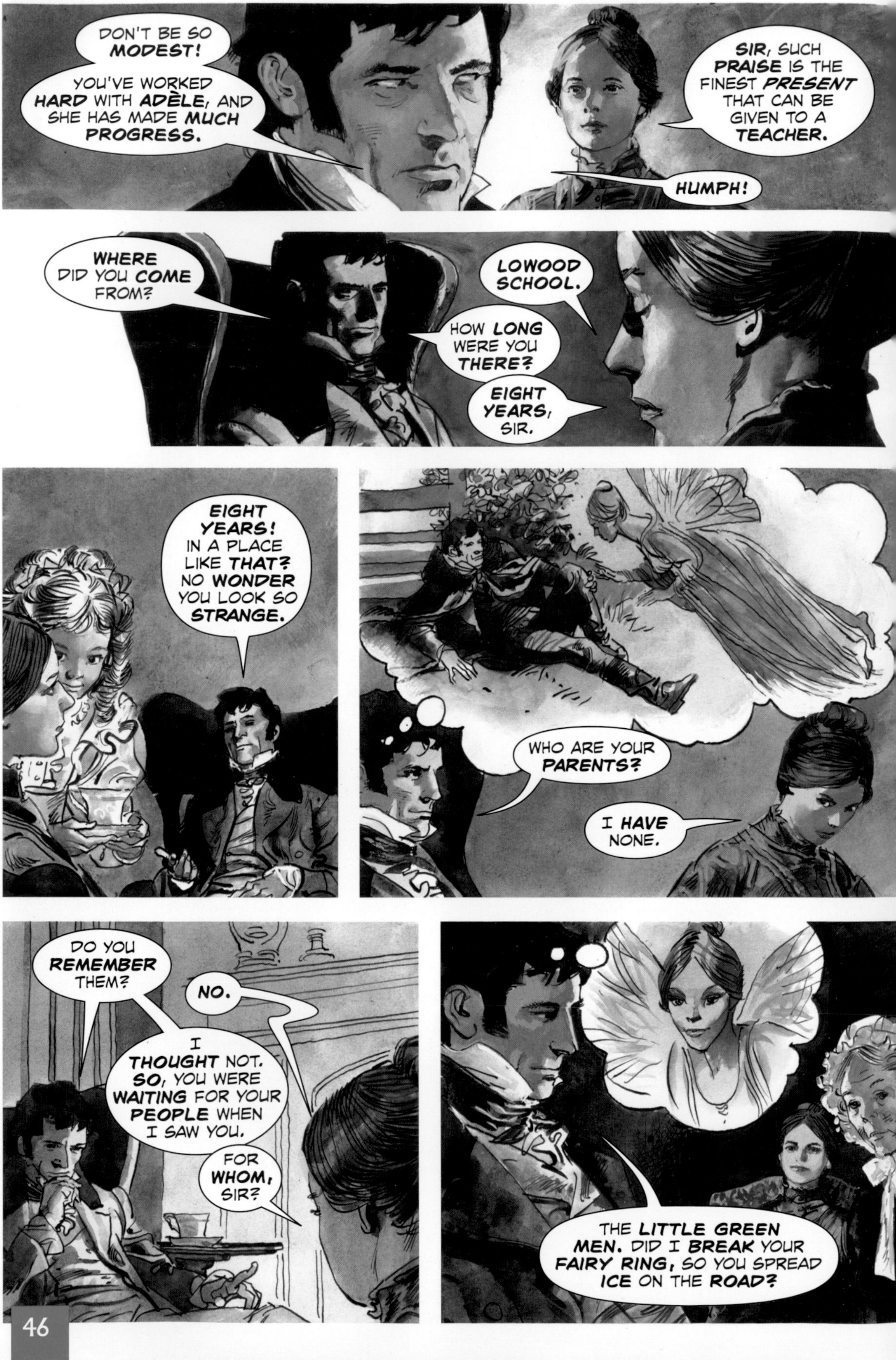
DON'T BE SO MODEST!
YOU'VE WORKED HARD WITH ADÈLE, AND SHE HAS MADE MUCH PROGRESS.
SIR, SUCH PRAISE IS THE FINEST PRESENT THAT CAN BE GIVEN TO A TEACHER.
HUMPH!
WHERE DID YOU COME FROM?
LOWOOD SCHOOL.
HOW LONG WERE YOU THERE?
EIGHT YEARS, SIR.
EIGHT YEARS! IN A PLACE LIKE THAT? NO WONDER YOU LOOK SO STRANGE.
WHO ARE YOUR PARENTS?
I HAVE NONE.
DO YOU REMEMBER THEM?
NO.
I THOUGHT NOT. SO, YOU WERE WAITING FOR YOUR PEOPLE WHEN I SAW YOU.
FOR WHOM, SIR?
THE LITTLE GREEN MEN. DID I BREAK YOUR FAIRY RING, SO YOU SPREAD ICE ON THE ROAD?

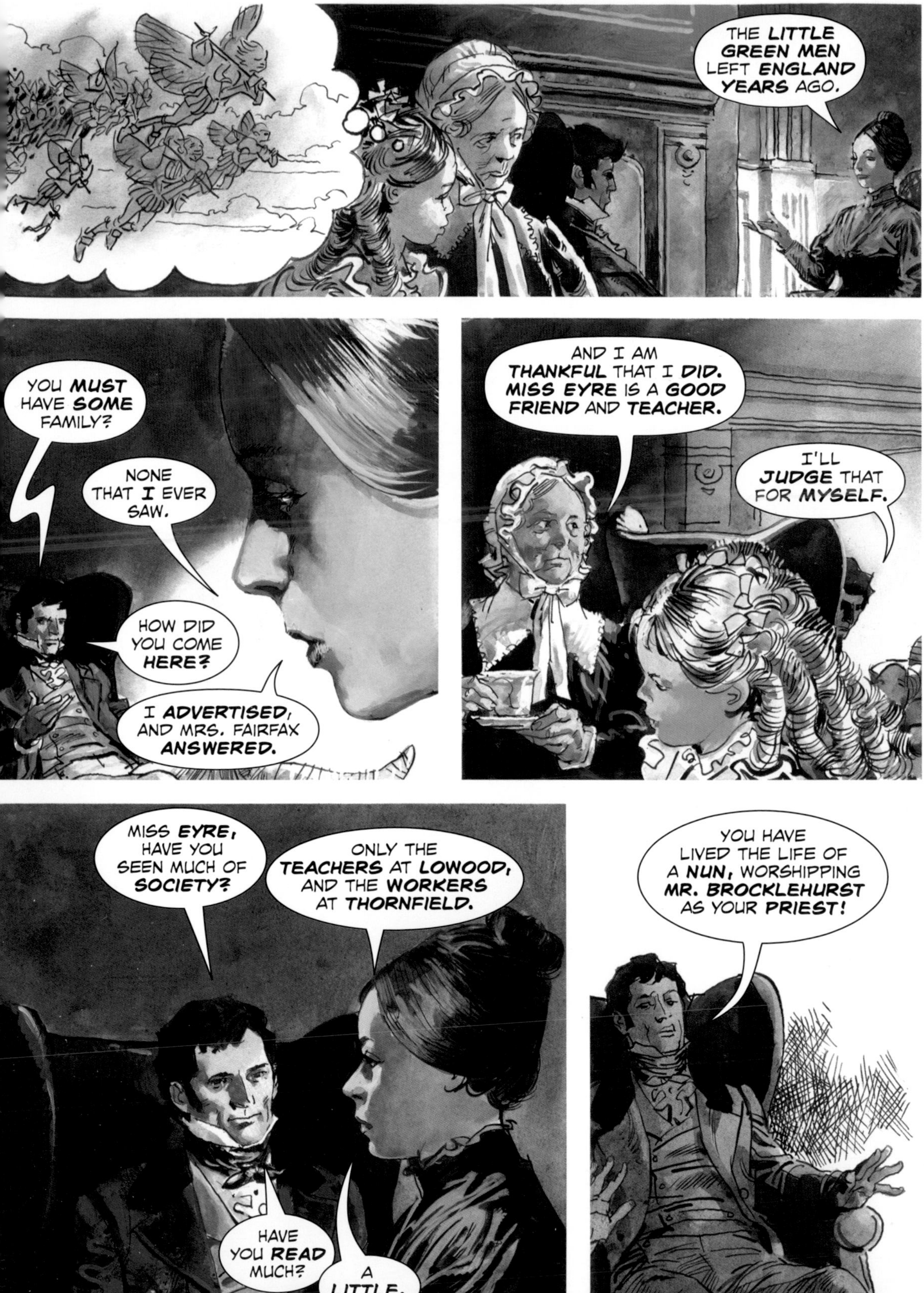
THE LITTLE GREEN MEN LEFT ENGLAND YEARS AGO.
YOU MUST HAVE SOME FAMILY?
NONE THAT I EVER SAW.
HOW DID YOU COME HERE?
I ADVERTISED, AND MRS. FAIRFAX ANSWERED.
AND I AM THANKFUL THAT I DID. MISS EYRE IS A GOOD FRIEND AND TEACHER.
I'LL JUDGE THAT FOR MYSELF.
MISS EYRE, HAVE YOU SEEN MUCH OF SOCIETY?
ONLY THE TEACHERS AT LOWOOD, AND THE WORKERS AT THORNFIELD.
HAVE YOU READ MUCH?
A LITTLE.
YOU HAVE LIVED THE LIFE OF A NUN, WORSHIPPING MR. BROCKLEHURST AS YOUR PRIEST!

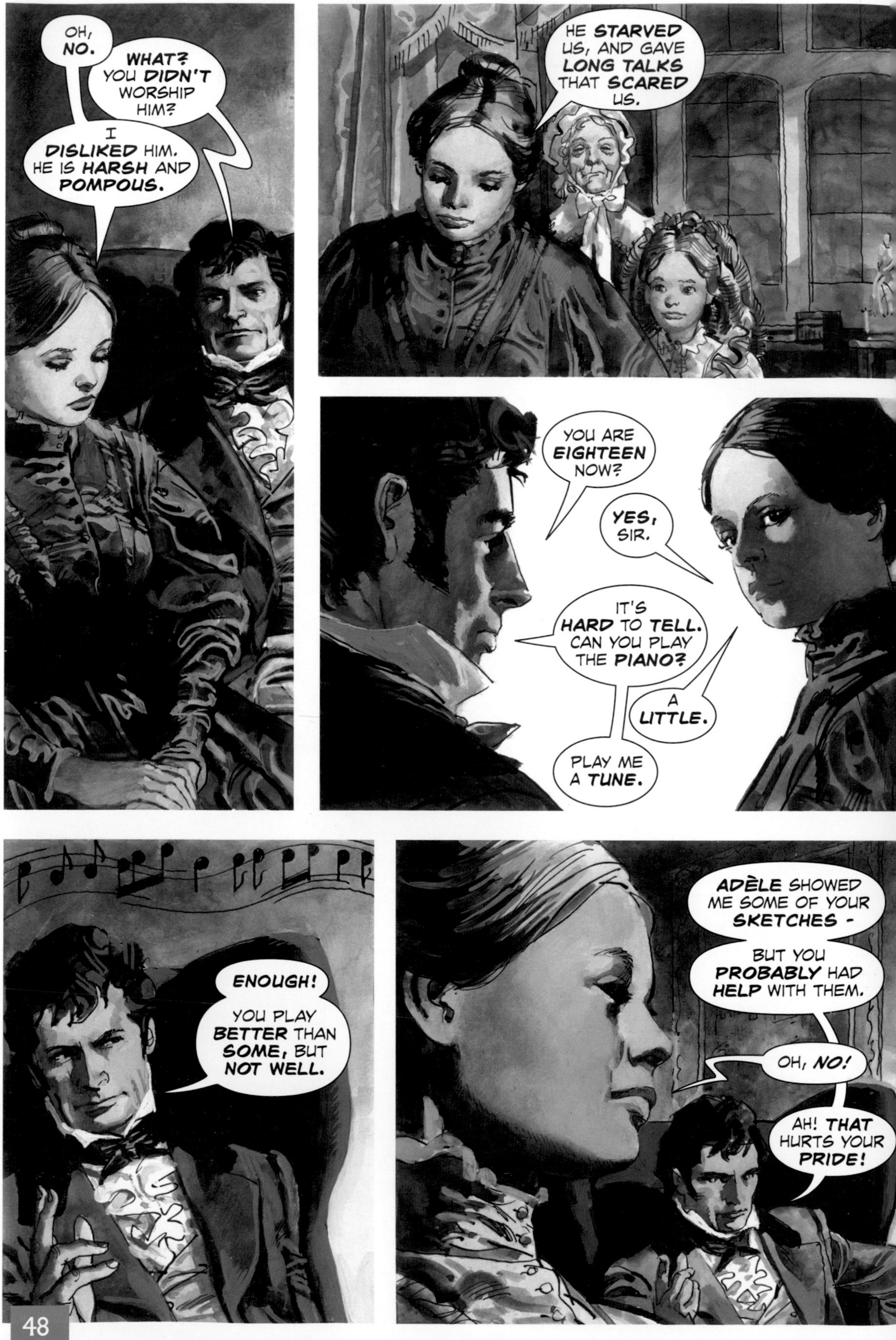

OH, NO.
WHAT? YOU DIDN'T WORSHIP HIM?
I DISLIKED HIM. HE IS HARSH AND POMPOUS.
HE STARVED US, AND GAVE LONG TALKS THAT SCARED US.
YOU ARE EIGHTEEN NOW?
YES, SIR.
IT'S HARD TO TELL. CAN YOU PLAY THE PIANO?
A LITTLE.
PLAY ME A TUNE.
ENOUGH!
YOU PLAY BETTER THAN SOME, BUT NOT WELL.
ADÈLE SHOWED ME SOME OF YOUR SKETCHES -
BUT YOU PROBABLY HAD HELP WITH THEM.
OH, NO!
AH! THAT HURTS YOUR PRIDE!

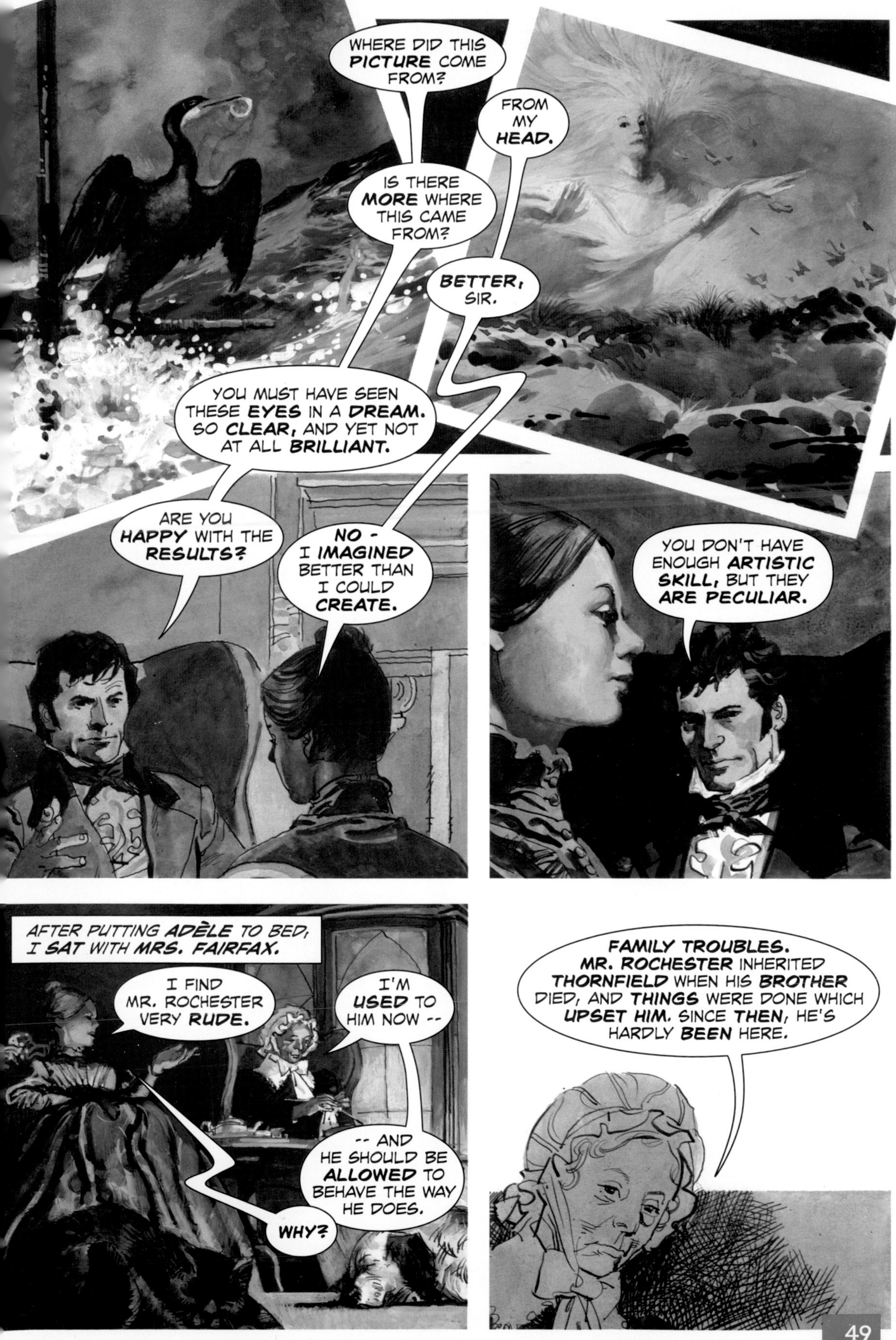
WHERE DID THIS PICTURE COME FROM?
FROM MY HEAD.
IS THERE MORE WHERE THIS CAME FROM?
BETTER, SIR.
YOU MUST HAVE SEEN THESE EYES IN A DREAM. SO CLEAR, AND YET NOT AT ALL BRILLIANT.
ARE YOU HAPPY WITH THE RESULTS?
NO - I IMAGINED BETTER THAN I COULD CREATE.
YOU DON'T HAVE ENOUGH ARTISTIC SKILL, BUT THEY ARE PECULIAR.
AFTER PUTTING ADÈLE TO BED, I SAT WITH MRS. FAIRFAX.
I FIND MR. ROCHESTER VERY RUDE.
I'M USED TO HIM NOW --
-- AND HE SHOULD BE ALLOWED TO BEHAVE THE WAY HE DOES.
WHY?
FAMILY TROUBLES. MR. ROCHESTER INHERITED THORNFIELD WHEN HIS BROTHER DIED, AND THINGS WERE DONE WHICH UPSET HIM. SINCE THEN, HE'S HARDLY BEEN HERE.

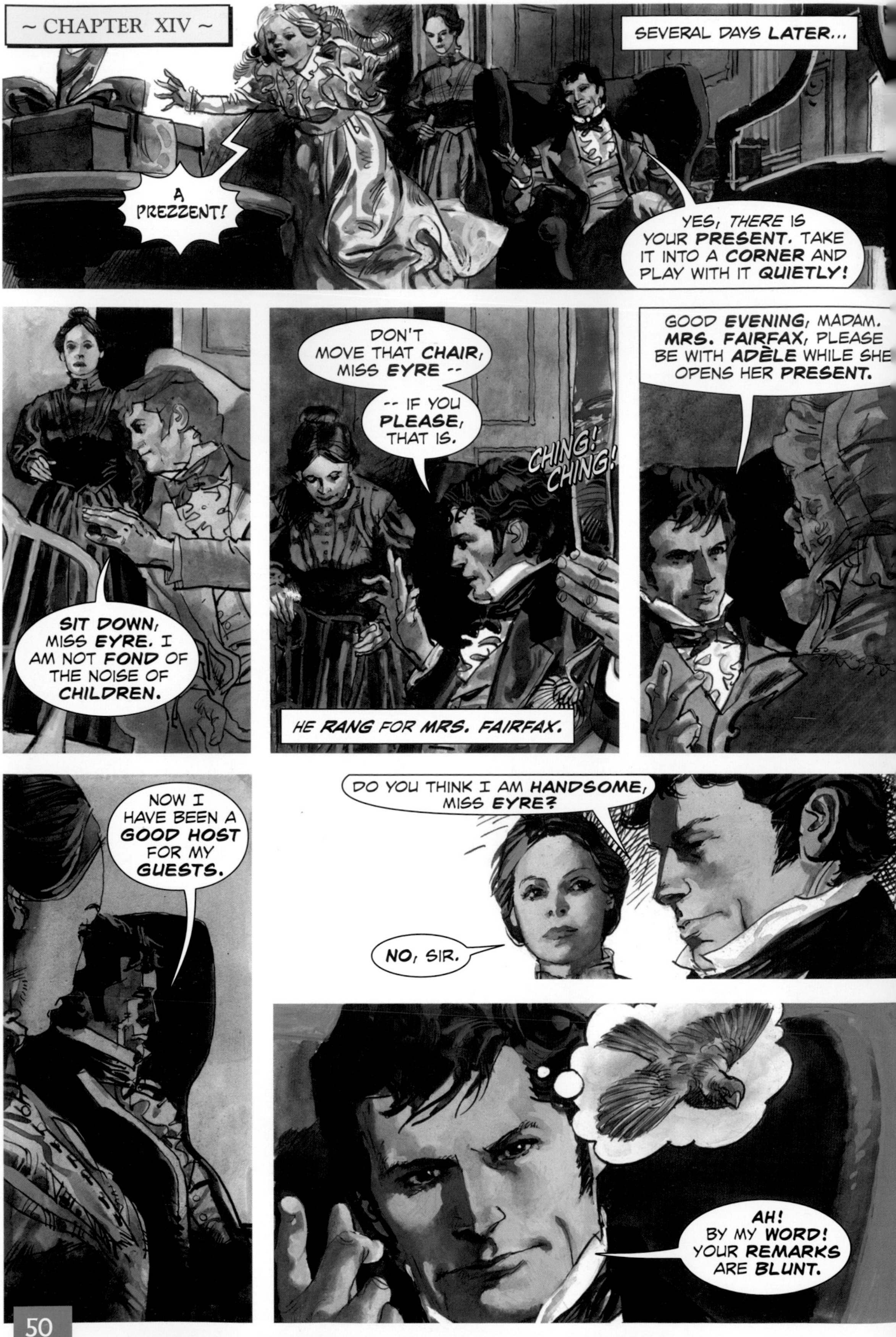
~ CHAPTER XIV ~
SEVERAL DAYS LATER...
A PREZZENT!
YES, THERE IS YOUR PRESENT. TAKE IT INTO A CORNER AND PLAY WITH IT QUIETLY!
SIT DOWN, MISS EYRE. I AM NOT FOND OF THE NOISE OF CHILDREN.
DON'T MOVE THAT CHAIR, MISS EYRE --
-- IF YOU PLEASE, THAT IS.
CHING! CHING!
HE RANG FOR MRS. FAIRFAX.
GOOD EVENING, MADAM. MRS. FAIRFAX, PLEASE BE WITH ADÈLE WHILE SHE OPENS HER PRESENT.
NOW I HAVE BEEN A GOOD HOST FOR MY GUESTS.
DO YOU THINK I AM HANDSOME, MISS EYRE?
NO, SIR.
AH! BY MY WORD! YOUR REMARKS ARE BLUNT.

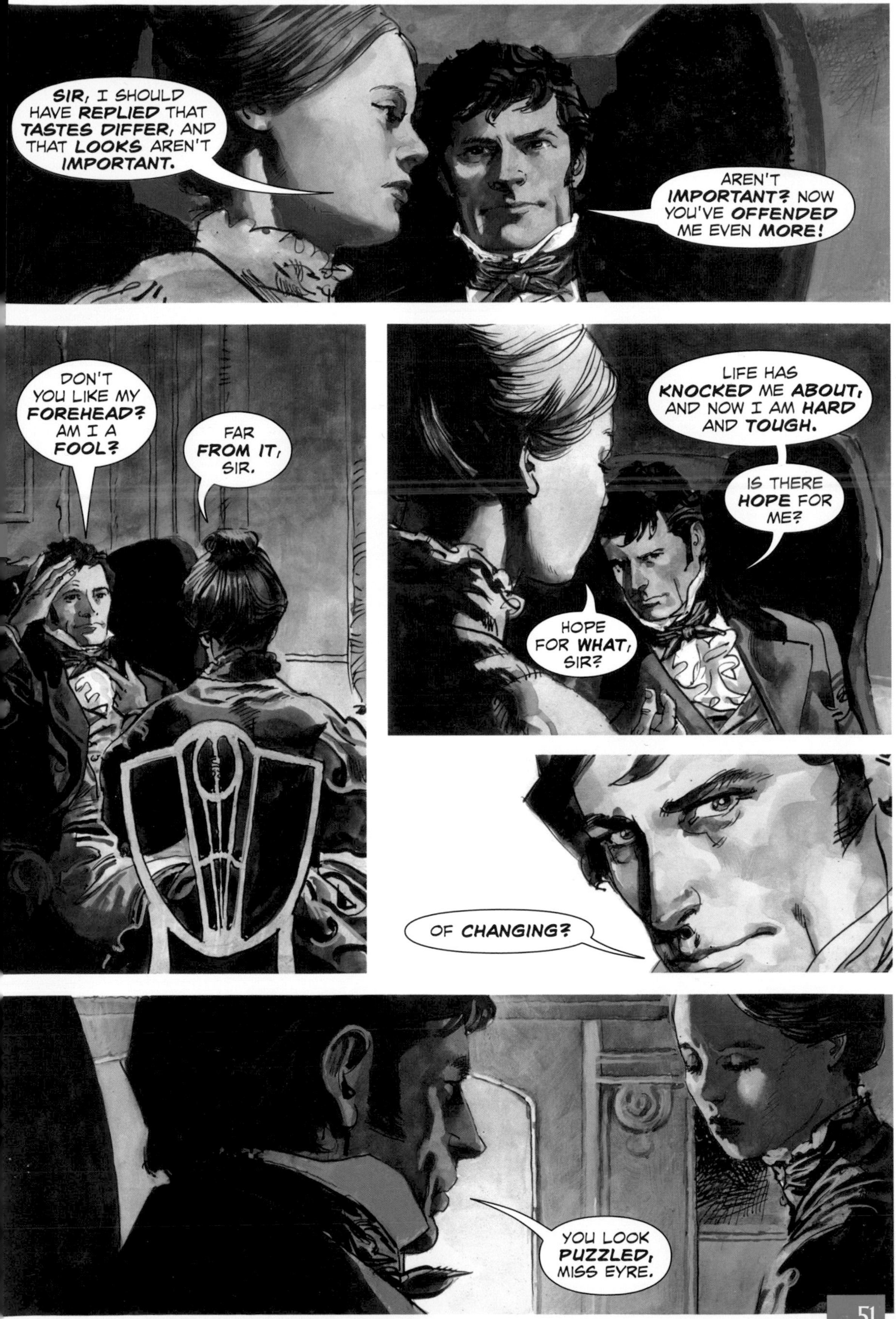
SIR, I SHOULD HAVE REPLIED THAT TASTES DIFFER, AND THAT LOOKS AREN'T IMPORTANT.
AREN'T IMPORTANT? NOW YOU'VE OFFENDED ME EVEN MORE!
DON'T YOU LIKE MY FOREHEAD? AM I A FOOL?
FAR FROM IT, SIR.
LIFE HAS KNOCKED ME ABOUT, AND NOW I AM HARD AND TOUGH.
IS THERE HOPE FOR ME?
HOPE FOR WHAT, SIR?
OF CHANGING?
YOU LOOK PUZZLED, MISS EYRE.

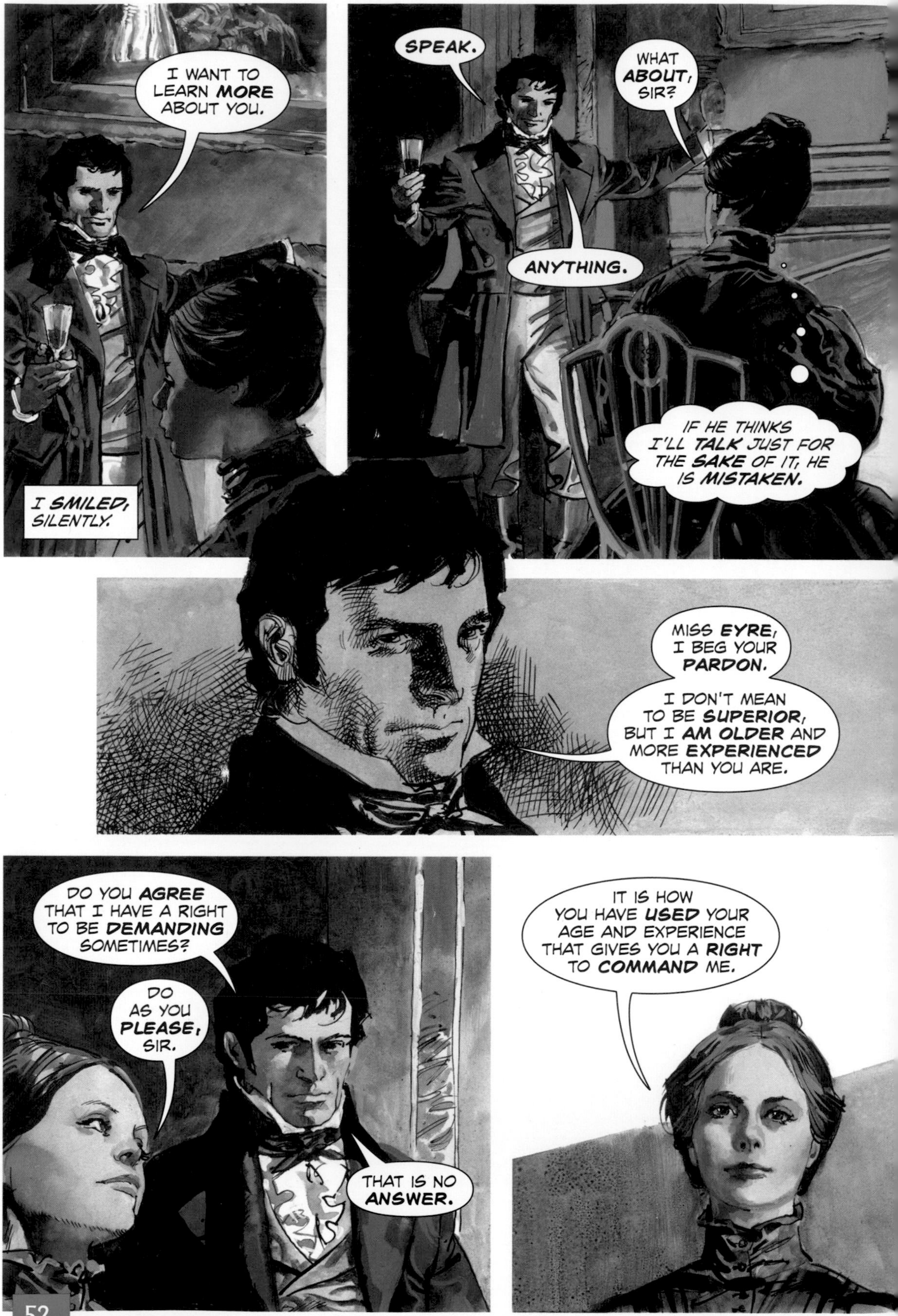
I WANT TO LEARN MORE ABOUT YOU.
I SMILED, SILENTLY.
SPEAK.
WHAT ABOUT, SIR?
ANYTHING.
IF HE THINKS I'LL TALK JUST FOR THE SAKE OF IT, HE IS MISTAKEN.
MISS EYRE, I BEG YOUR PARDON.
I DON'T MEAN TO BE SUPERIOR, BUT I AM OLDER AND MORE EXPERIENCED THAN YOU ARE.
DO YOU AGREE THAT I HAVE A RIGHT TO BE DEMANDING SOMETIMES?
DO AS YOU PLEASE, SIR.
THAT IS NO ANSWER.
IT IS HOW YOU HAVE USED YOUR AGE AND EXPERIENCE THAT GIVES YOU A RIGHT TO COMMAND ME.

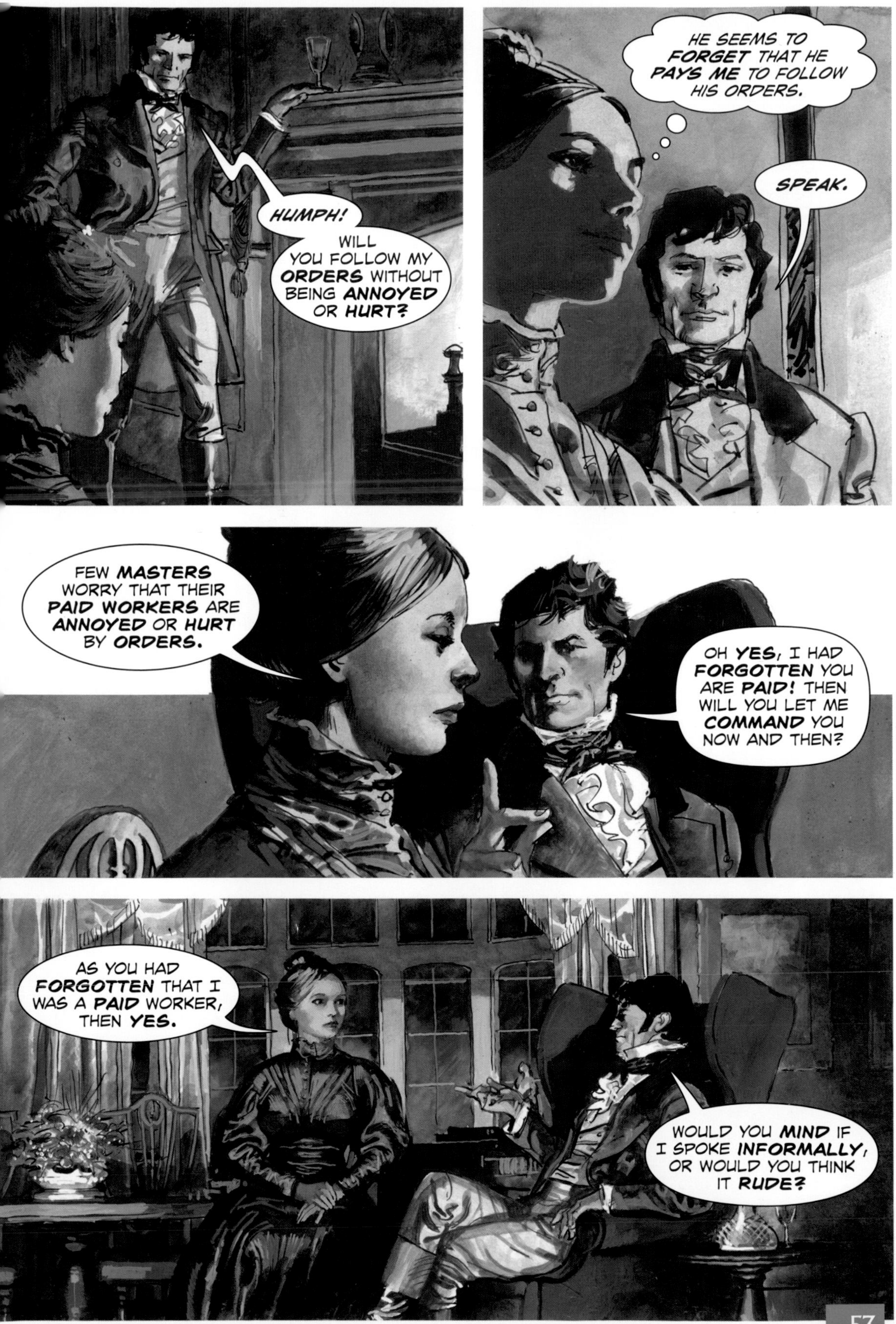
HUMPH!
WILL YOU FOLLOW MY ORDERS WITHOUT BEING ANNOYED OR HURT?
HE SEEMS TO FORGET THAT HE PAYS ME TO FOLLOW HIS ORDERS.
SPEAK.
FEW MASTERS WORRY THAT THEIR PAID WORKERS ARE ANNOYED OR HURT BY ORDERS.
OH YES, I HAD FORGOTTEN YOU ARE PAID! THEN WILL YOU LET ME COMMAND YOU NOW AND THEN?
AS YOU HAD FORGOTTEN THAT I WAS A PAID WORKER, THEN YES.
WOULD YOU MIND IF I SPOKE INFORMALLY, OR WOULD YOU THINK IT RUDE?

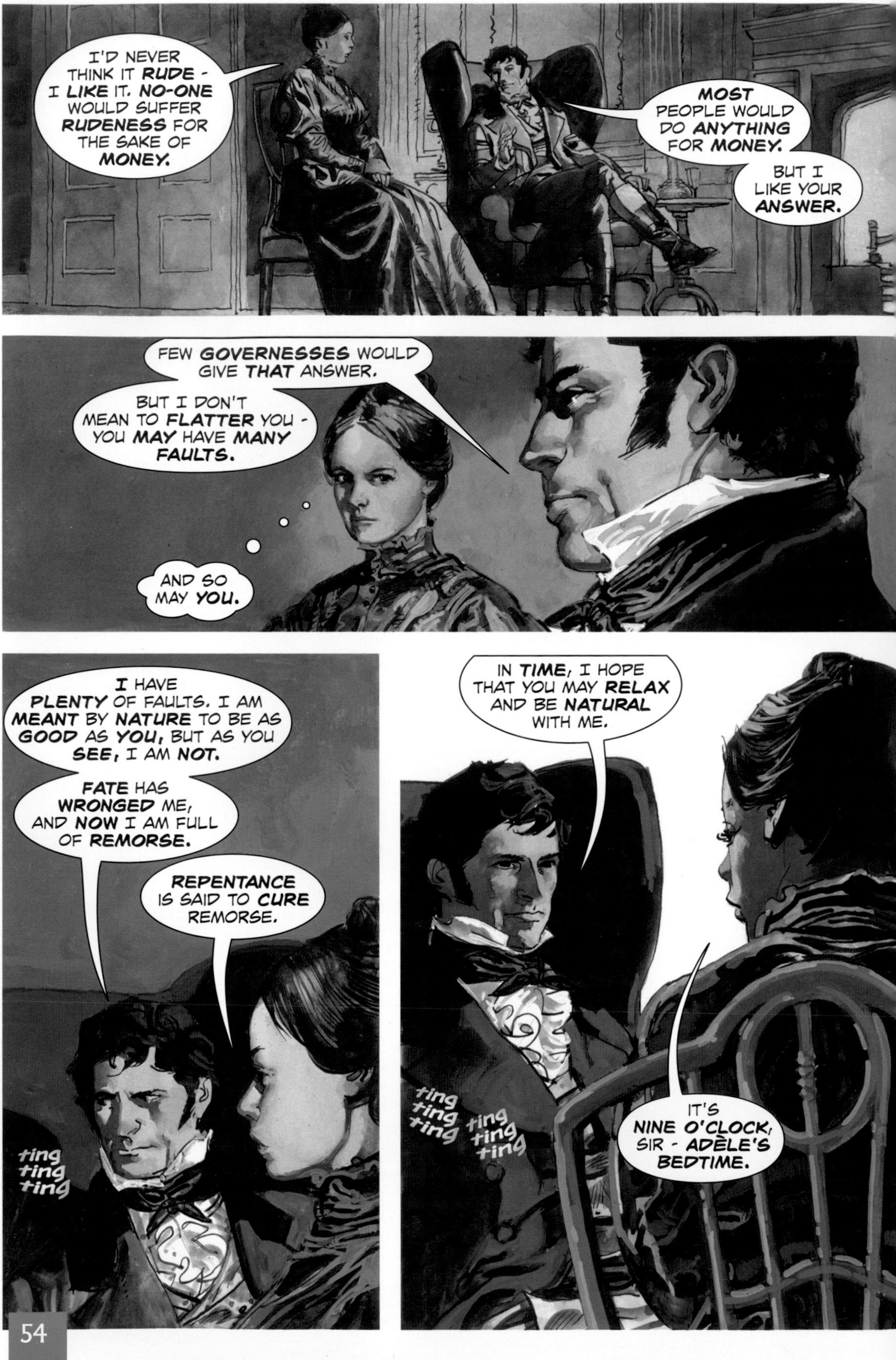
I'D NEVER THINK IT RUDE - I LIKE IT. NO-ONE WOULD SUFFER RUDENESS FOR THE SAKE OF MONEY.
MOST PEOPLE WOULD DO ANYTHING FOR MONEY.
BUT I LIKE YOUR ANSWER.
FEW GOVERNESSES WOULD GIVE THAT ANSWER.
BUT I DON'T MEAN TO FLATTER YOU - YOU MAY HAVE MANY FAULTS.
AND SO MAY YOU.
I HAVE PLENTY OF FAULTS. I AM MEANT BY NATURE TO BE AS GOOD AS YOU, BUT AS YOU SEE, I AM NOT.
FATE HAS WRONGED ME, AND NOW I AM FULL OF REMORSE.
REPENTANCE IS SAID TO CURE REMORSE.
ting ting ting
IN TIME, I HOPE THAT YOU MAY RELAX AND BE NATURAL WITH ME.
ting ting ting
ting ting ting
IT'S NINE O'CLOCK, SIR - ADÈLE'S BEDTIME.

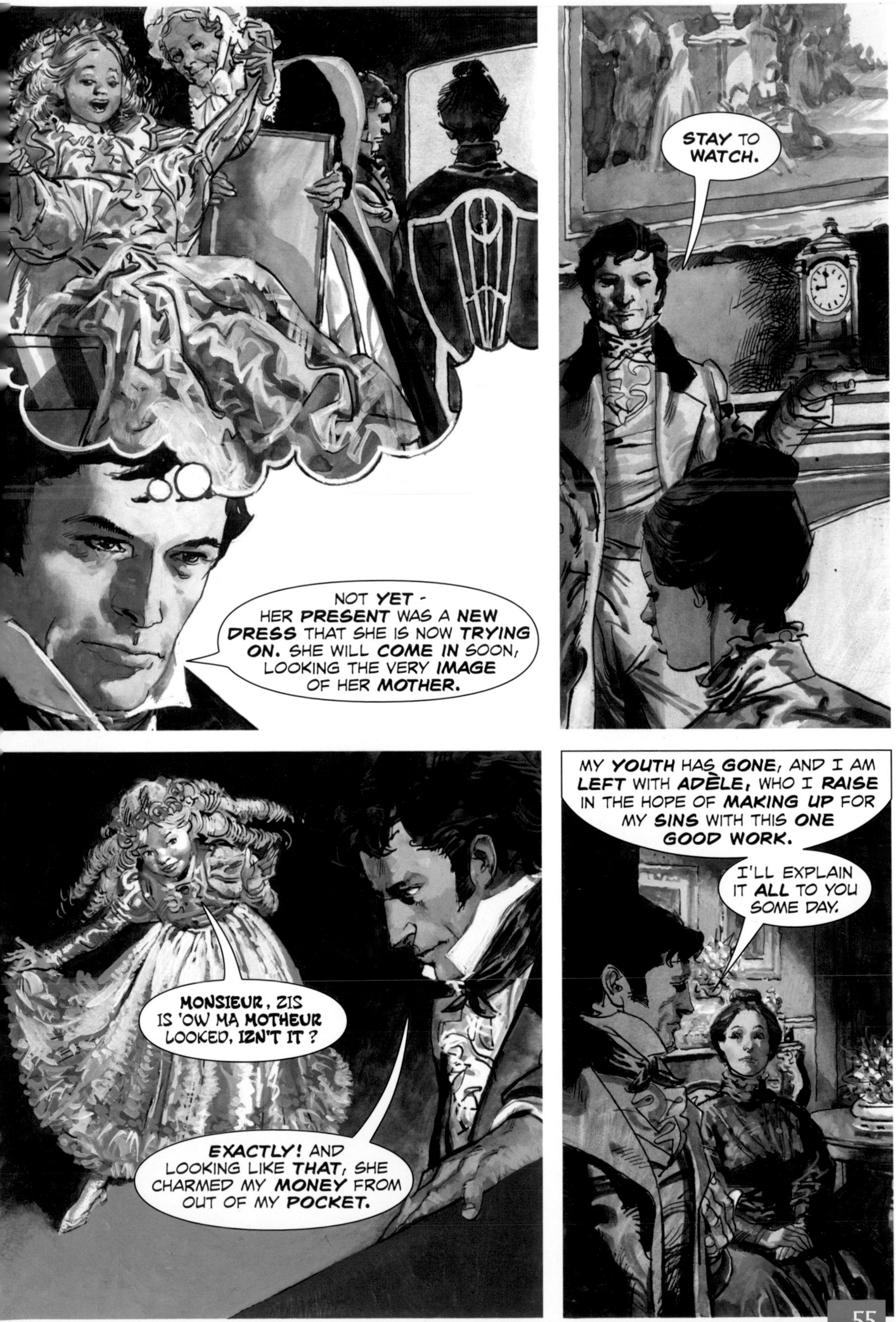
NOT YET - HER PRESENT WAS A NEW DRESS THAT SHE IS NOW TRYING ON. SHE WILL COME IN SOON, LOOKING THE VERY IMAGE OF HER MOTHER.
STAY TO WATCH.
MONSIEUR, ZIS IS 'OW MA MOTHEUR LOOKED, IZN'T IT ?
EXACTLY! AND LOOKING LIKE THAT, SHE CHARMED MY MONEY FROM OUT OF MY POCKET.
MY YOUTH HAS GONE, AND I AM LEFT WITH ADÈLE, WHO I RAISE IN THE HOPE OF MAKING UP FOR MY SINS WITH THIS ONE GOOD WORK.
I'LL EXPLAIN IT ALL TO YOU SOME DAY.

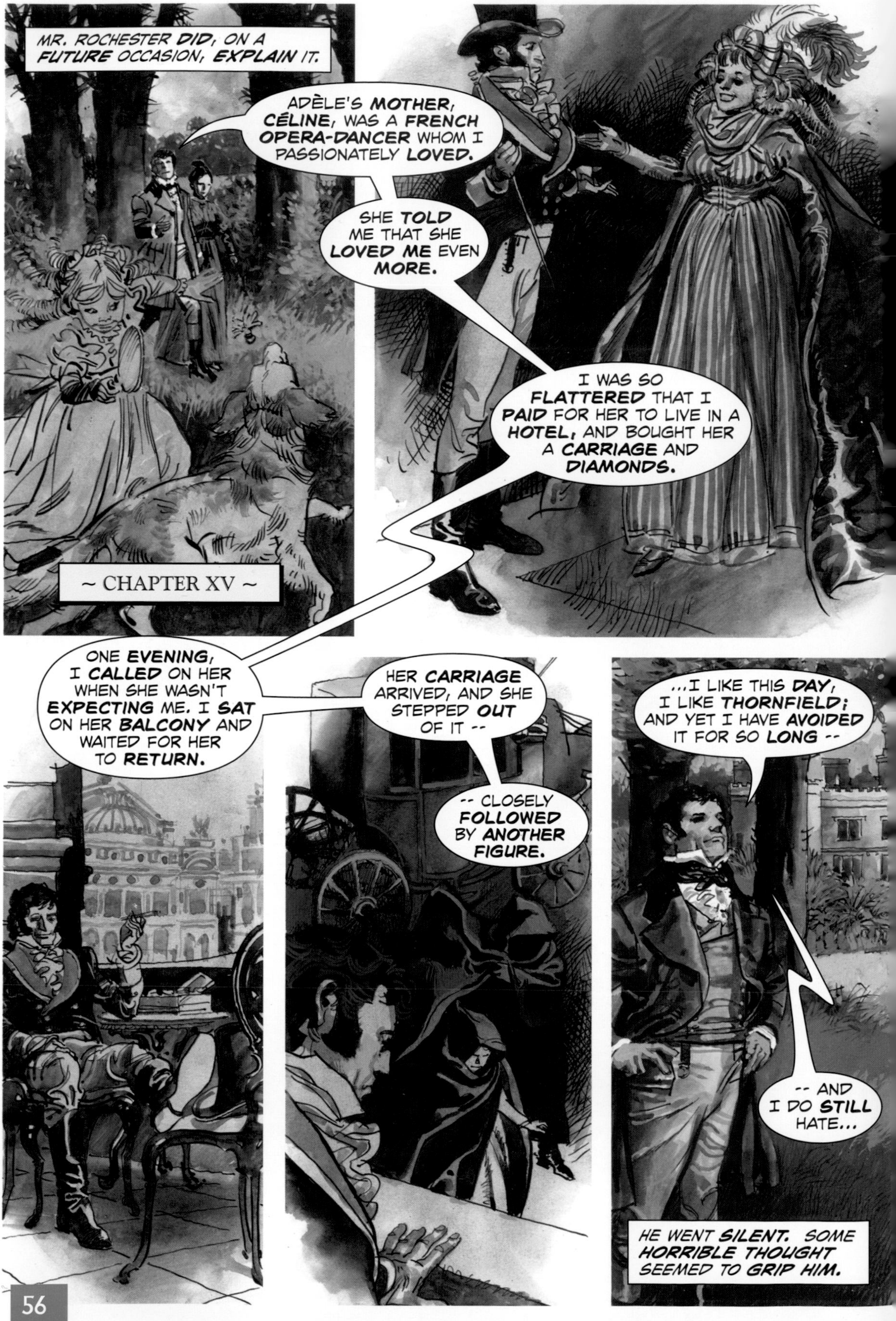
MR. ROCHESTER DID, ON A FUTURE OCCASION, EXPLAIN IT.
ADÈLE'S MOTHER, CÉLINE, WAS A FRENCH OPERA-DANCER WHOM I PASSIONATELY LOVED.
SHE TOLD ME THAT SHE LOVED ME EVEN MORE.
I WAS SO FLATTERED THAT I PAID FOR HER TO LIVE IN A HOTEL, AND BOUGHT HER A CARRIAGE AND DIAMONDS.
~ CHAPTER XV ~
ONE EVENING, I CALLED ON HER WHEN SHE WASN'T EXPECTING ME. I SAT ON HER BALCONY AND WAITED FOR HER TO RETURN.
HER CARRIAGE ARRIVED, AND SHE STEPPED OUT OF IT --
-- CLOSELY FOLLOWED BY ANOTHER FIGURE.
...I LIKE THIS DAY, I LIKE THORNFIELD; AND YET I HAVE AVOIDED IT FOR SO LONG --
-- AND I DO STILL HATE...
HE WENT SILENT. SOME HORRIBLE THOUGHT SEEMED TO GRIP HIM.

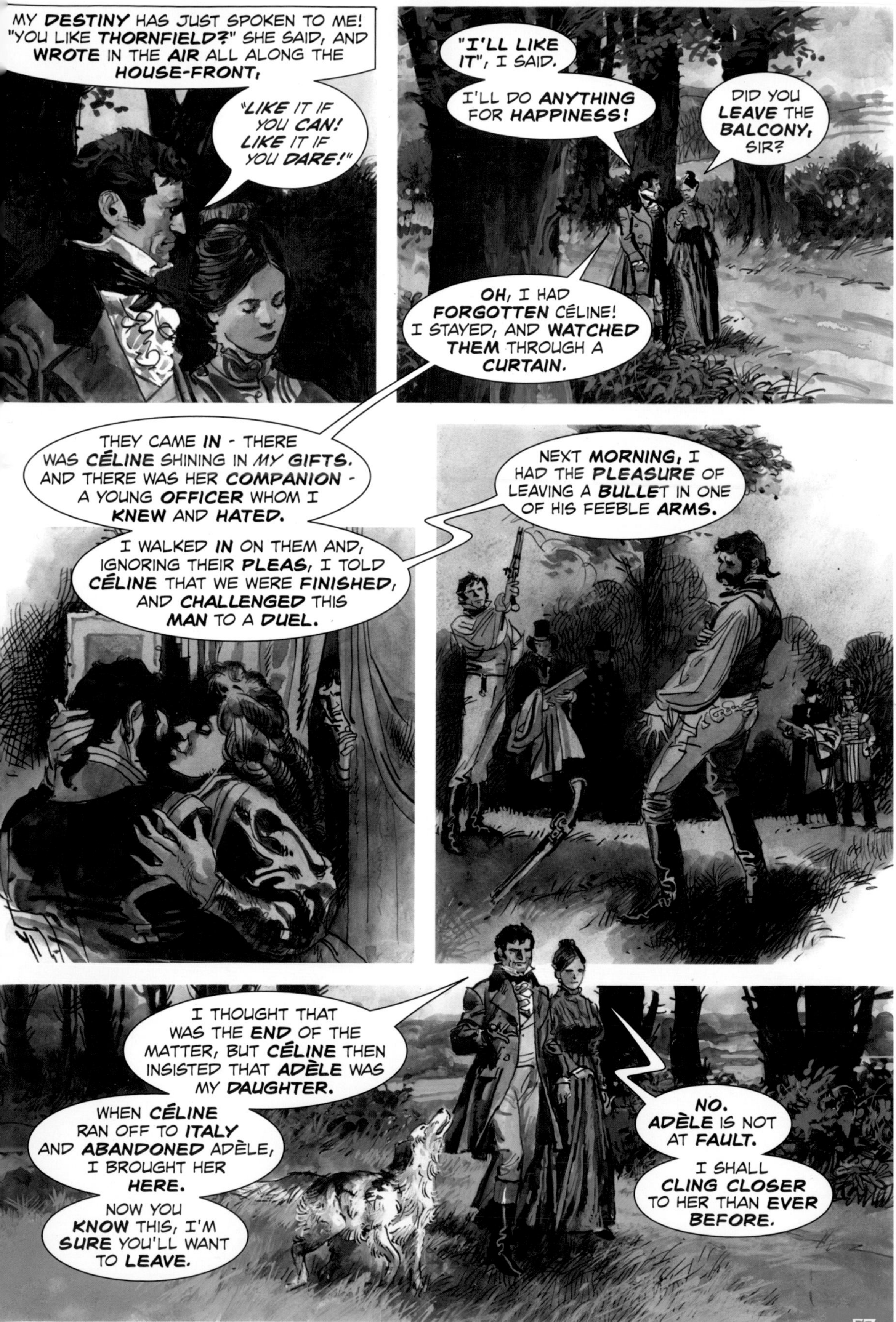
MY DESTINY HAS JUST SPOKEN TO ME! "YOU LIKE THORNFIELD?" SHE SAID, AND WROTE IN THE AIR ALL ALONG THE HOUSE-FRONT,
"LIKE IT IF YOU CAN! LIKE IT IF YOU DARE!"
"I'LL LIKE IT", I SAID.
I'LL DO ANYTHING FOR HAPPINESS!
DID YOU LEAVE THE BALCONY, SIR?
OH, I HAD FORGOTTEN CÉLINE! I STAYED, AND WATCHED THEM THROUGH A CURTAIN.
THEY CAME IN - THERE WAS CÉLINE SHINING IN MY GIFTS. AND THERE WAS HER COMPANION - A YOUNG OFFICER WHOM I KNEW AND HATED.
I WALKED IN ON THEM AND, IGNORING THEIR PLEAS, I TOLD CÉLINE THAT WE WERE FINISHED, AND CHALLENGED THIS MAN TO A DUEL.
NEXT MORNING, I HAD THE PLEASURE OF LEAVING A BULLET IN ONE OF HIS FEEBLE ARMS.
I THOUGHT THAT WAS THE END OF THE MATTER, BUT CÉLINE THEN INSISTED THAT ADÈLE WAS MY DAUGHTER.
WHEN CÉLINE RAN OFF TO ITALY AND ABANDONED ADÈLE, I BROUGHT HER HERE.
NOW YOU KNOW THIS, I'M SURE YOU'LL WANT TO LEAVE.
NO. ADÈLE IS NOT AT FAULT.
I SHALL CLING CLOSER TO HER THAN EVER BEFORE.

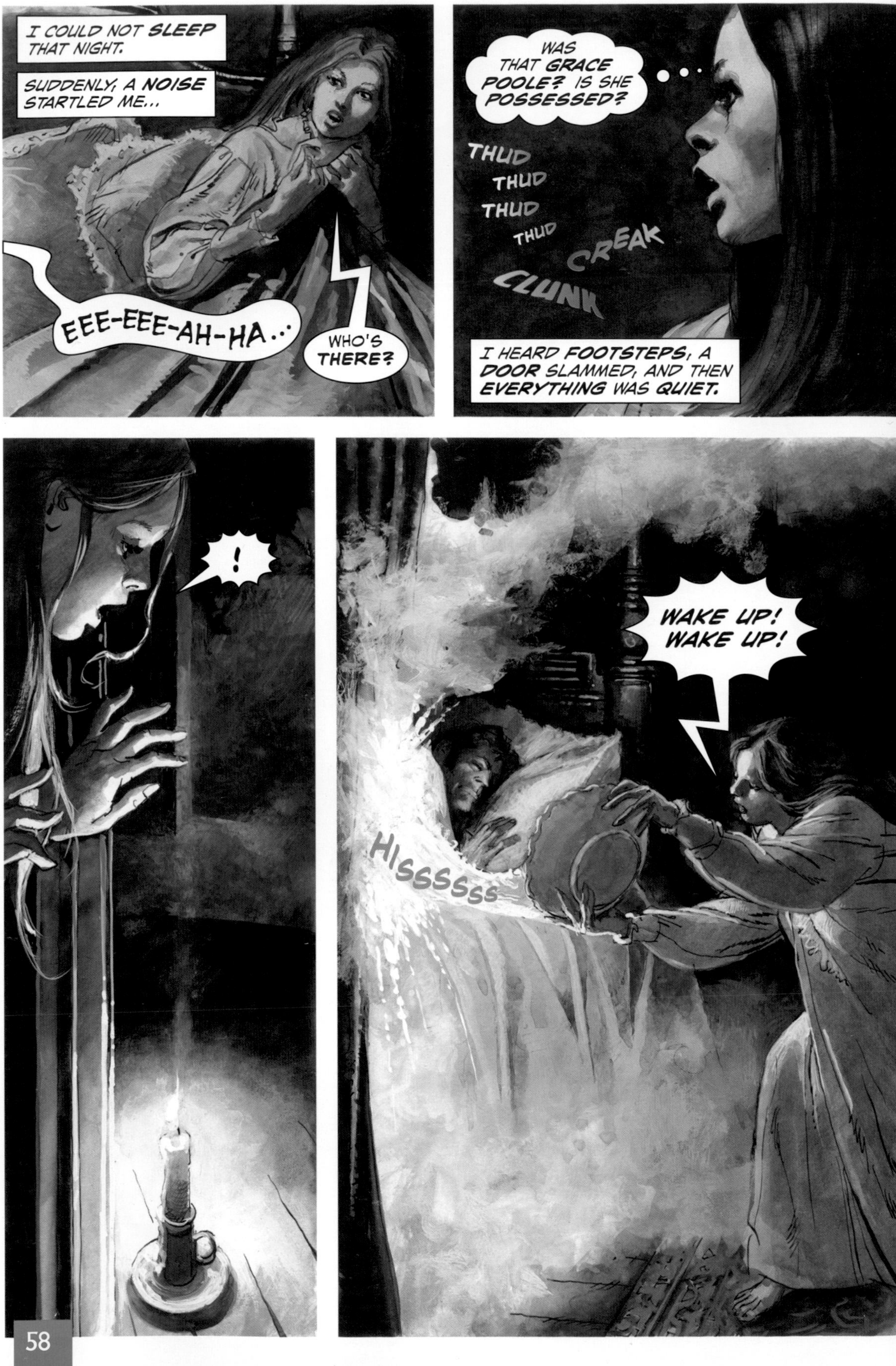
I COULD NOT SLEEP THAT NIGHT.
SUDDENLY, A NOISE STARTLED ME...
EEE-EEE-AH-HA...
WHO'S THERE?
WAS THAT GRACE POOLE? IS SHE POSSESSED?
THUD
THUD
THUD
THUD
CREAK
CLUNK
I HEARD FOOTSTEPS, A DOOR SLAMMED, AND THEN EVERYTHING WAS QUIET.
!
WAKE UP! WAKE UP!
HISSSSSS

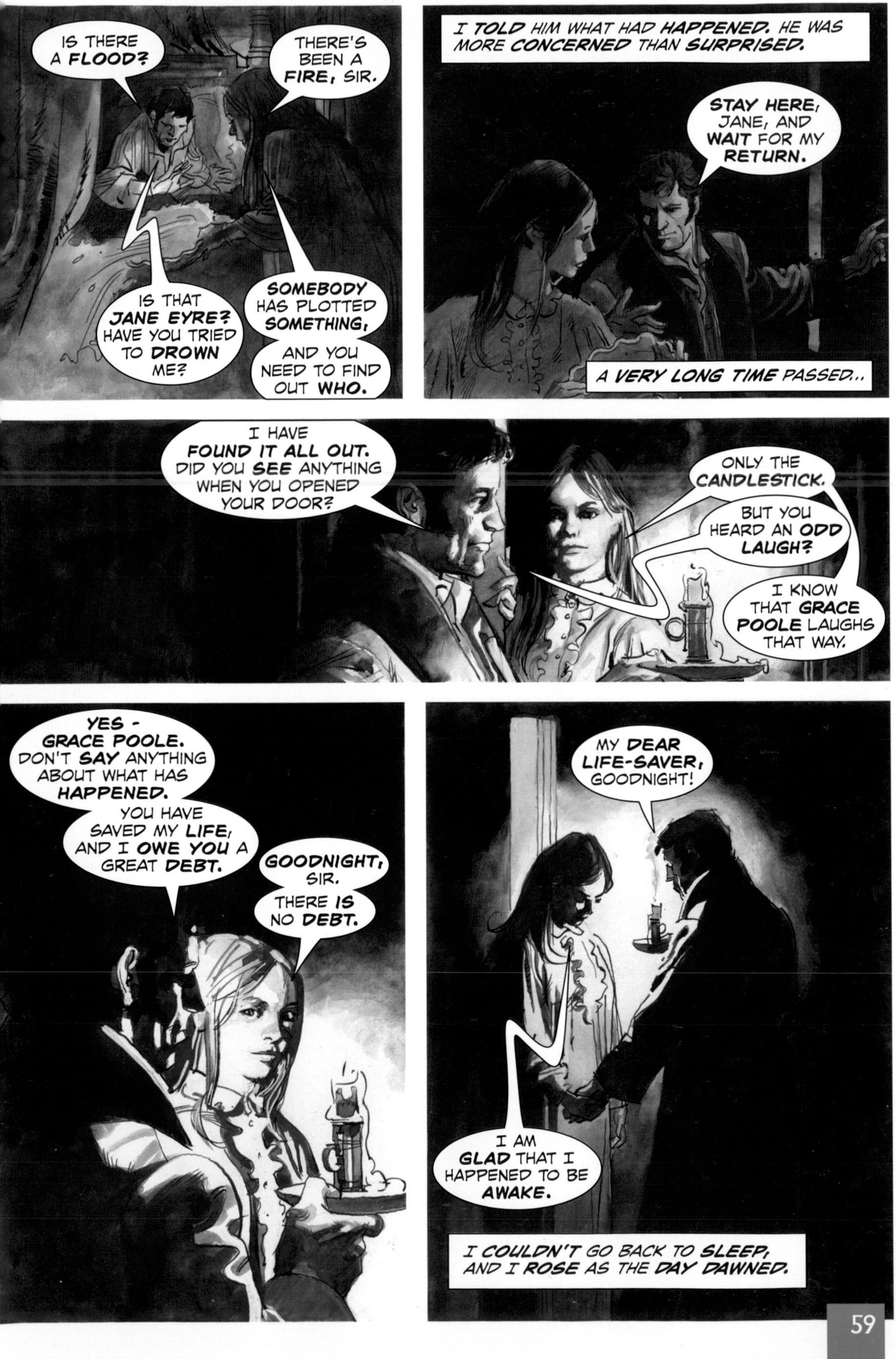
IS THERE A FLOOD?
THERE'S BEEN A FIRE, SIR.
IS THAT JANE EYRE? HAVE YOU TRIED TO DROWN ME?
SOMEBODY HAS PLOTTED SOMETHING,
AND YOU NEED TO FIND OUT WHO.
I TOLD HIM WHAT HAD HAPPENED. HE WAS MORE CONCERNED THAN SURPRISED.
STAY HERE, JANE, AND WAIT FOR MY RETURN.
A VERY LONG TIME PASSED...
I HAVE FOUND IT ALL OUT. DID YOU SEE ANYTHING WHEN YOU OPENED YOUR DOOR?
ONLY THE CANDLESTICK.
BUT YOU HEARD AN ODD LAUGH?
I KNOW THAT GRACE POOLE LAUGHS THAT WAY.
YES - GRACE POOLE. DON'T SAY ANYTHING ABOUT WHAT HAS HAPPENED.
YOU HAVE SAVED MY LIFE, AND I OWE YOU A GREAT DEBT.
GOODNIGHT, SIR.
THERE IS NO DEBT.
MY DEAR LIFE-SAVER, GOODNIGHT!
I AM GLAD THAT I HAPPENED TO BE AWAKE.
I COULDN'T GO BACK TO SLEEP, AND I ROSE AS THE DAY DAWNED.

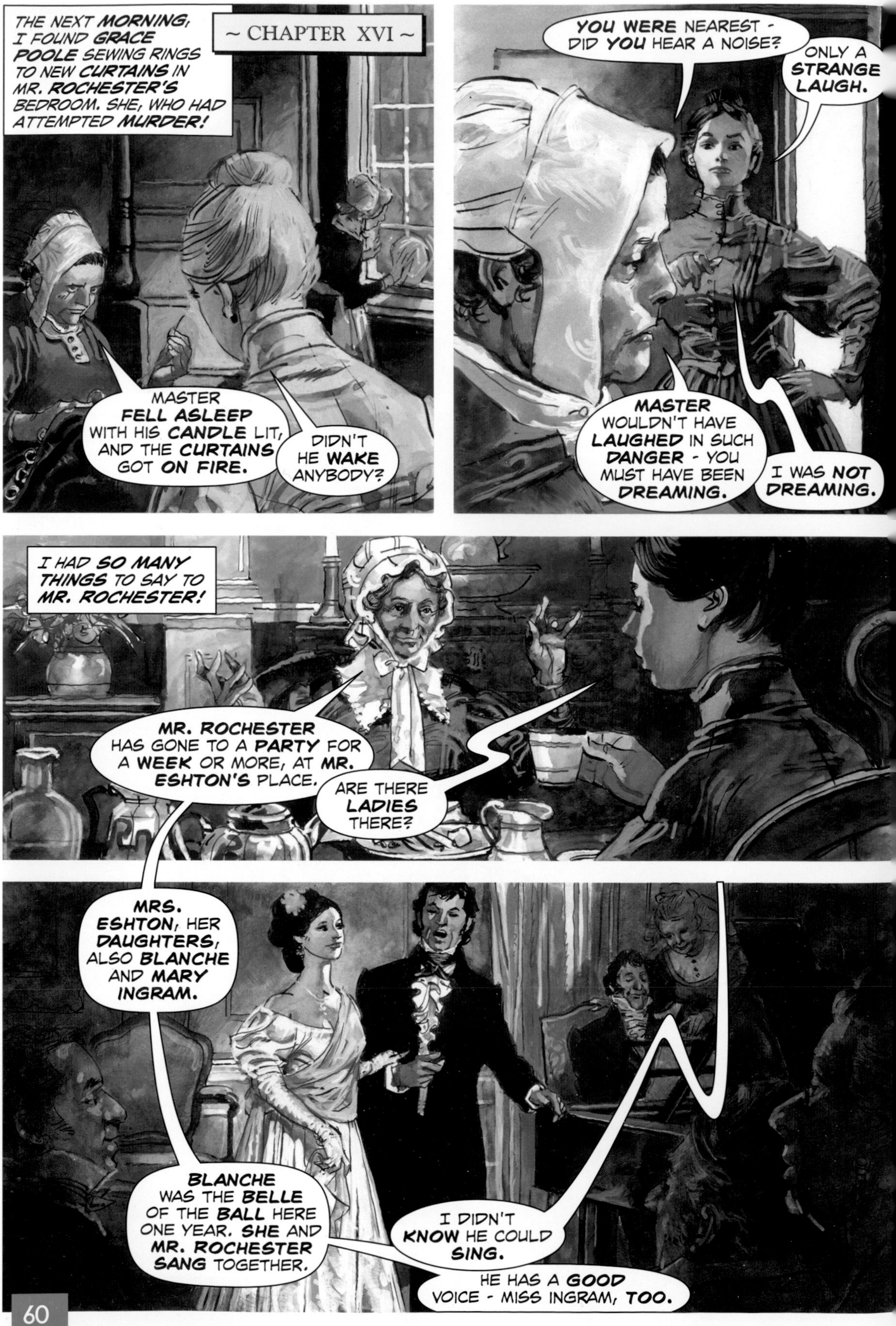
~ CHAPTER XVI ~
THE NEXT MORNING, I FOUND GRACE POOLE SEWING RINGS TO NEW CURTAINS IN MR. ROCHESTER'S BEDROOM. SHE, WHO HAD ATTEMPTED MURDER!
MASTER FELL ASLEEP WITH HIS CANDLE LIT, AND THE CURTAINS GOT ON FIRE.
DIDN'T HE WAKE ANYBODY?
YOU WERE NEAREST - DID YOU HEAR A NOISE?
ONLY A STRANGE LAUGH.
MASTER WOULDN'T HAVE LAUGHED IN SUCH DANGER - YOU MUST HAVE BEEN DREAMING.
I WAS NOT DREAMING.
I HAD SO MANY THINGS TO SAY TO MR. ROCHESTER!
MR. ROCHESTER HAS GONE TO A PARTY FOR A WEEK OR MORE, AT MR. ESHTON'S PLACE.
ARE THERE LADIES THERE?
MRS. ESHTON, HER DAUGHTERS, ALSO BLANCHE AND MARY INGRAM.
BLANCHE WAS THE BELLE OF THE BALL HERE ONE YEAR. SHE AND MR. ROCHESTER SANG TOGETHER.
I DIDN'T KNOW HE COULD SING.
HE HAS A GOOD VOICE - MISS INGRAM, TOO.

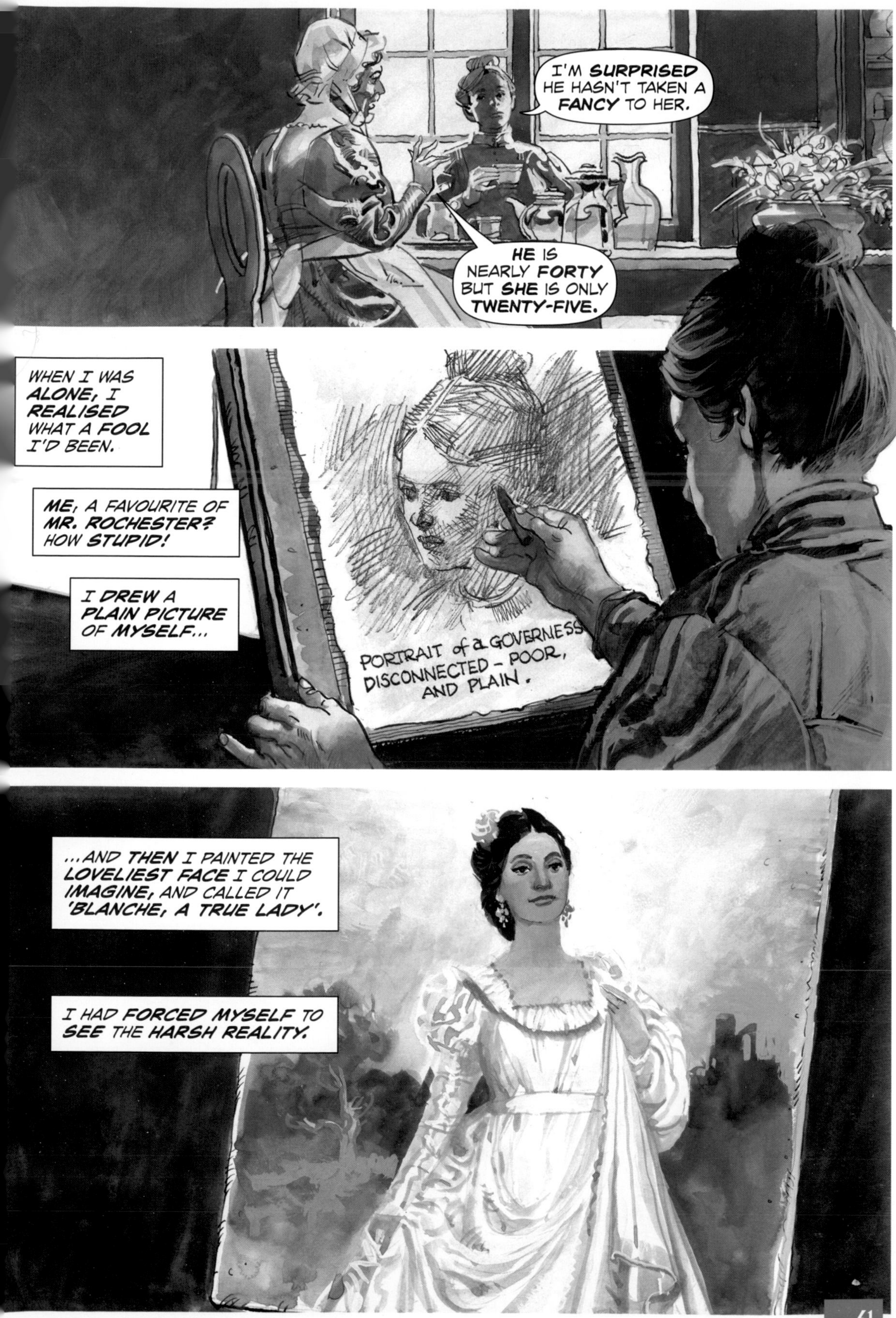
I'M SURPRISED HE HASN'T TAKEN A FANCY TO HER.
HE IS NEARLY FORTY BUT SHE IS ONLY TWENTY-FIVE.
WHEN I WAS ALONE, I REALISED WHAT A FOOL I'D BEEN.
ME, A FAVOURITE OF MR. ROCHESTER? HOW STUPID!
I DREW A PLAIN PICTURE OF MYSELF...
PORTRAIT of a GOVERNESS DISCONNECTED - POOR, AND PLAIN.
...AND THEN I PAINTED THE LOVELIEST FACE I COULD IMAGINE, AND CALLED IT 'BLANCHE, A TRUE LADY'.
I HAD FORCED MYSELF TO SEE THE HARSH REALITY.

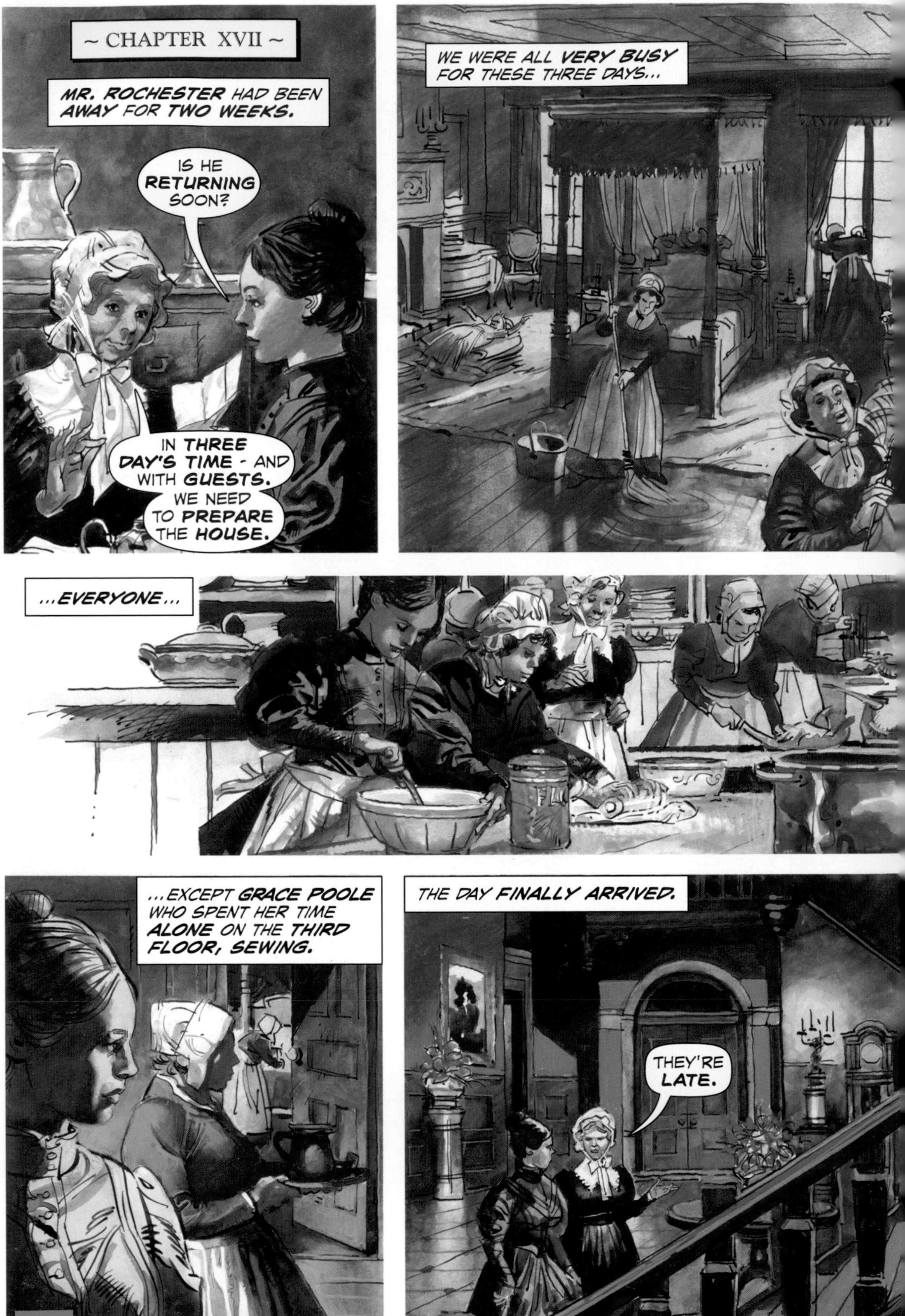
~ CHAPTER XVII ~
MR. ROCHESTER HAD BEEN AWAY FOR TWO WEEKS.
IS HE RETURNING SOON?
IN THREE DAY'S TIME - AND WITH GUESTS.
WE NEED TO PREPARE THE HOUSE.
WE WERE ALL VERY BUSY FOR THESE THREE DAYS...
...EVERYONE...
...EXCEPT GRACE POOLE WHO SPENT HER TIME ALONE ON THE THIRD FLOOR, SEWING.
THE DAY FINALLY ARRIVED.
THEY'RE LATE.

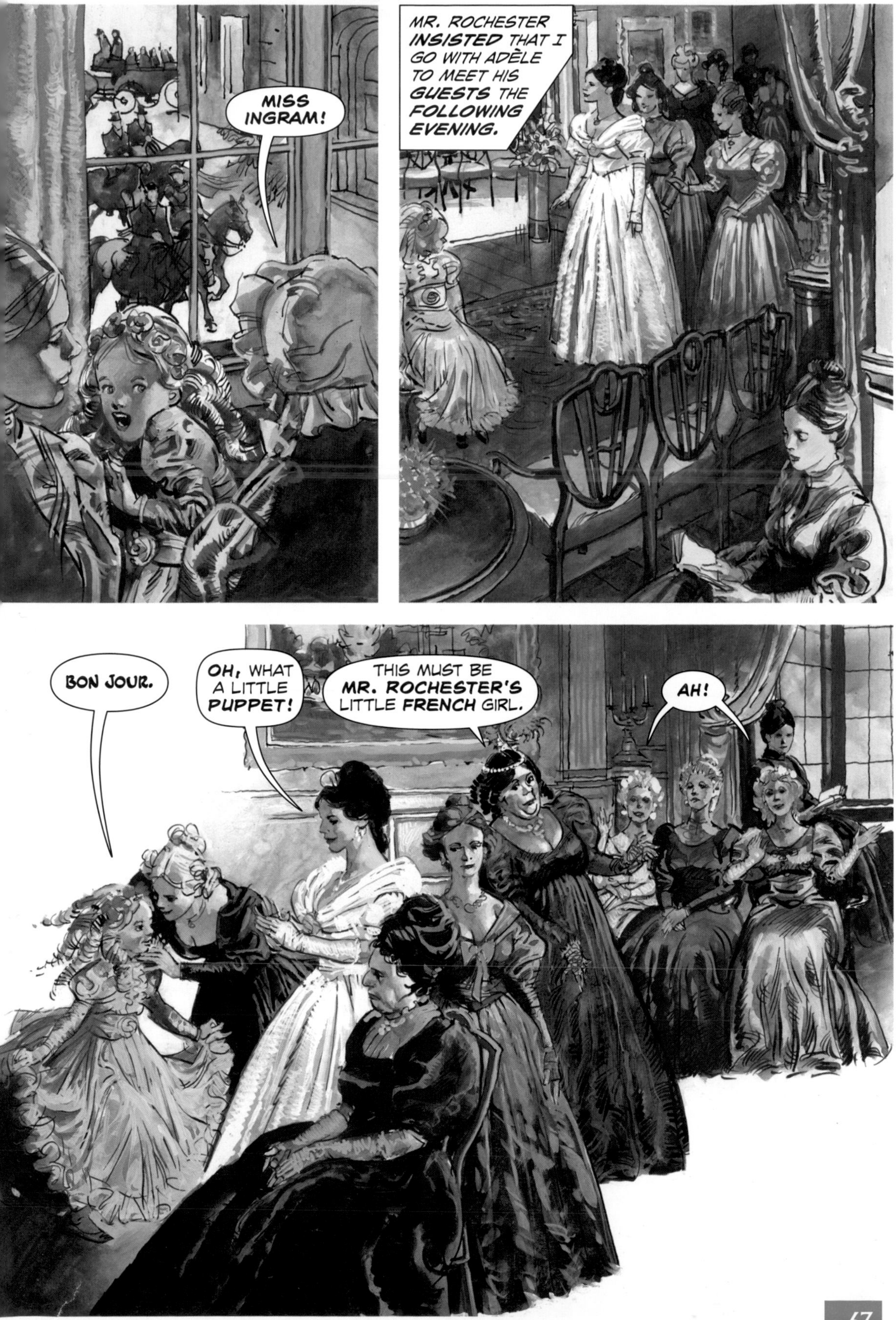
MISS INGRAM!
MR. ROCHESTER INSISTED THAT I GO WITH ADÈLE TO MEET HIS GUESTS THE FOLLOWING EVENING.
BON JOUR.
OH, WHAT A LITTLE PUPPET!
THIS MUST BE MR. ROCHESTER'S LITTLE FRENCH GIRL.
AH!

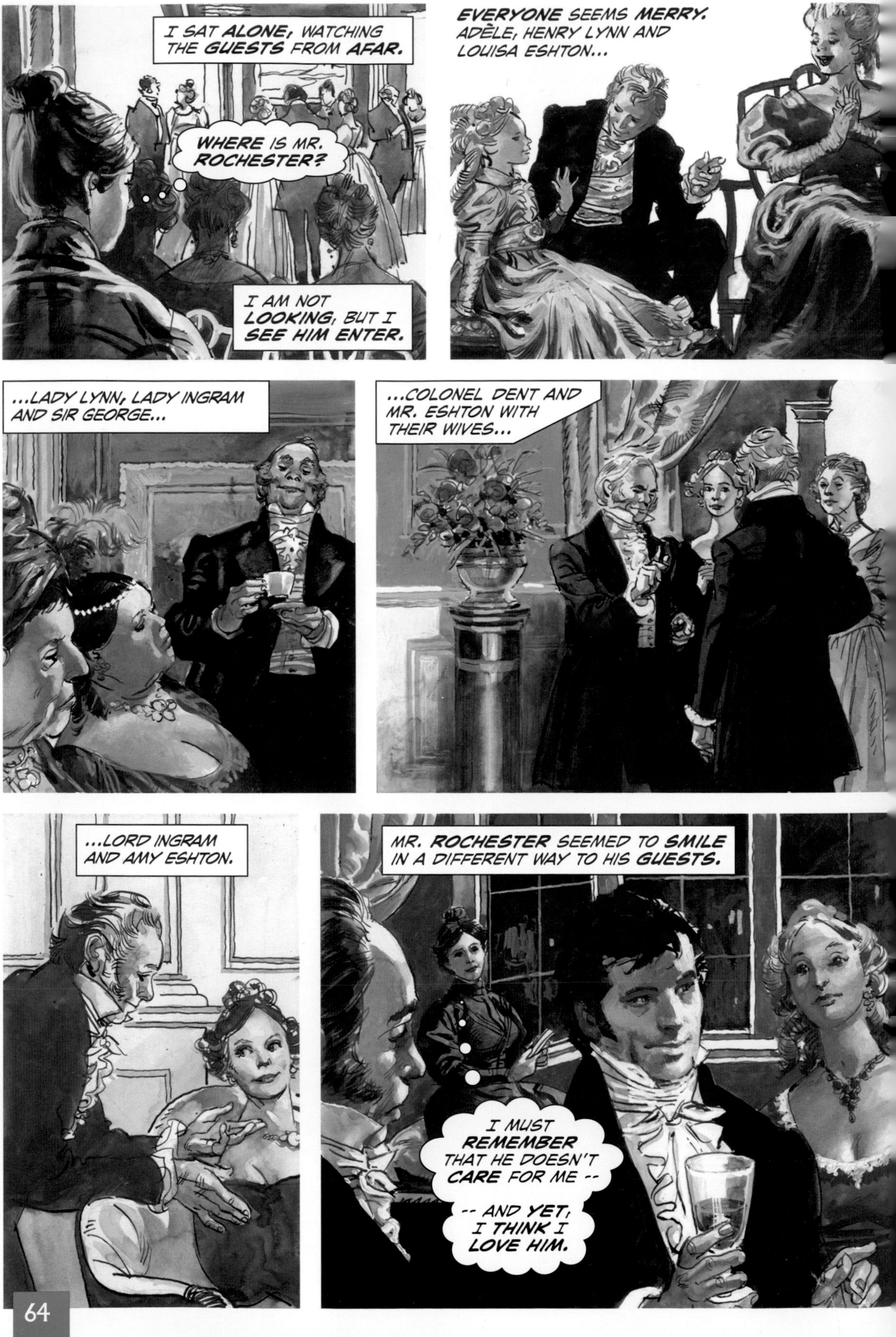
I SAT ALONE, WATCHING THE GUESTS FROM AFAR.
WHERE IS MR. ROCHESTER?
I AM NOT LOOKING, BUT I SEE HIM ENTER.
EVERYONE SEEMS MERRY. ADÈLE, HENRY LYNN AND LOUISA ESHTON...
...LADY LYNN, LADY INGRAM AND SIR GEORGE...
...COLONEL DENT AND MR. ESHTON WITH THEIR WIVES...
...LORD INGRAM AND AMY ESHTON.
MR. ROCHESTER SEEMED TO SMILE IN A DIFFERENT WAY TO HIS GUESTS.
I MUST REMEMBER THAT HE DOESN'T CARE FOR ME --
-- AND YET, I THINK I LOVE HIM.

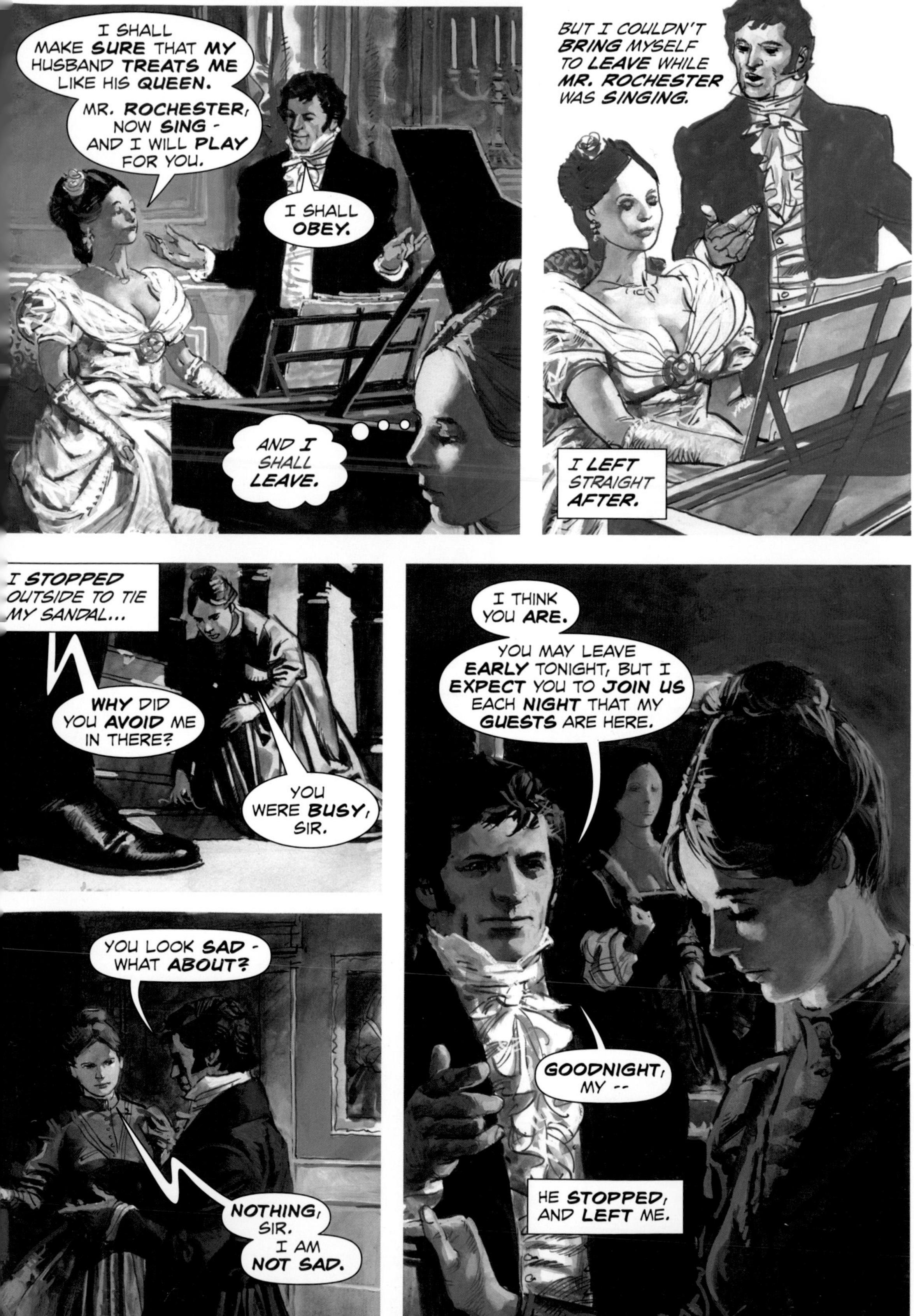
I SHALL MAKE SURE THAT MY HUSBAND TREATS ME LIKE HIS QUEEN.
MR. ROCHESTER, NOW SING - AND I WILL PLAY FOR YOU.
I SHALL OBEY.
AND I SHALL LEAVE.
BUT I COULDN'T BRING MYSELF TO LEAVE WHILE MR. ROCHESTER WAS SINGING.
I LEFT STRAIGHT AFTER.
I STOPPED OUTSIDE TO TIE MY SANDAL...
WHY DID YOU AVOID ME IN THERE?
YOU WERE BUSY, SIR.
YOU LOOK SAD - WHAT ABOUT?
NOTHING, SIR.
I AM NOT SAD.
I THINK YOU ARE.
YOU MAY LEAVE EARLY TONIGHT, BUT I EXPECT YOU TO JOIN US EACH NIGHT THAT MY GUESTS ARE HERE.
GOODNIGHT, MY --
HE STOPPED, AND LEFT ME.

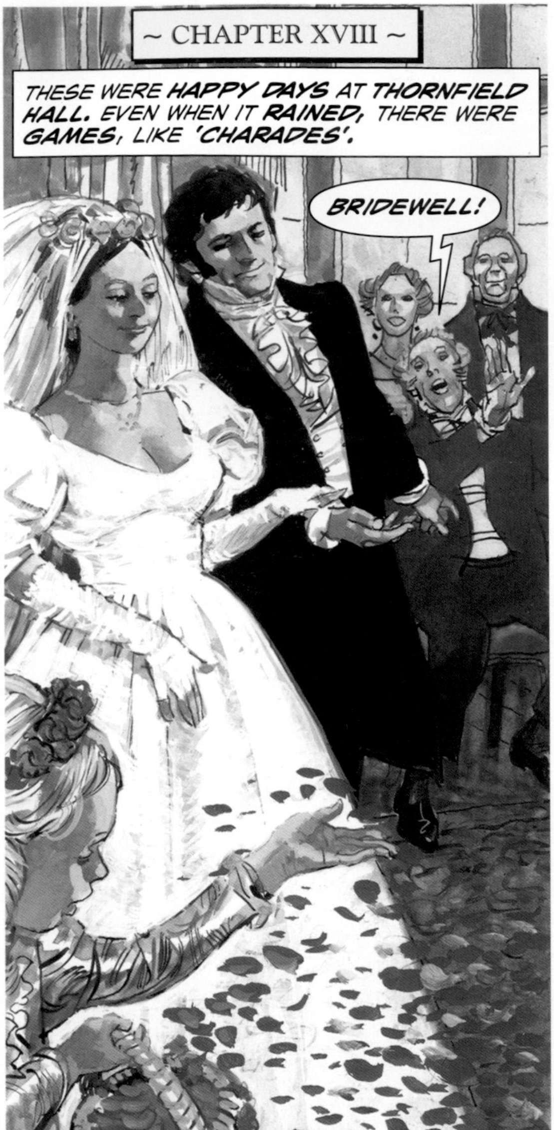
~ CHAPTER XVIII ~
THESE WERE HAPPY DAYS AT THORNFIELD HALL. EVEN WHEN IT RAINED, THERE WERE GAMES, LIKE 'CHARADES'.
BRIDEWELL!

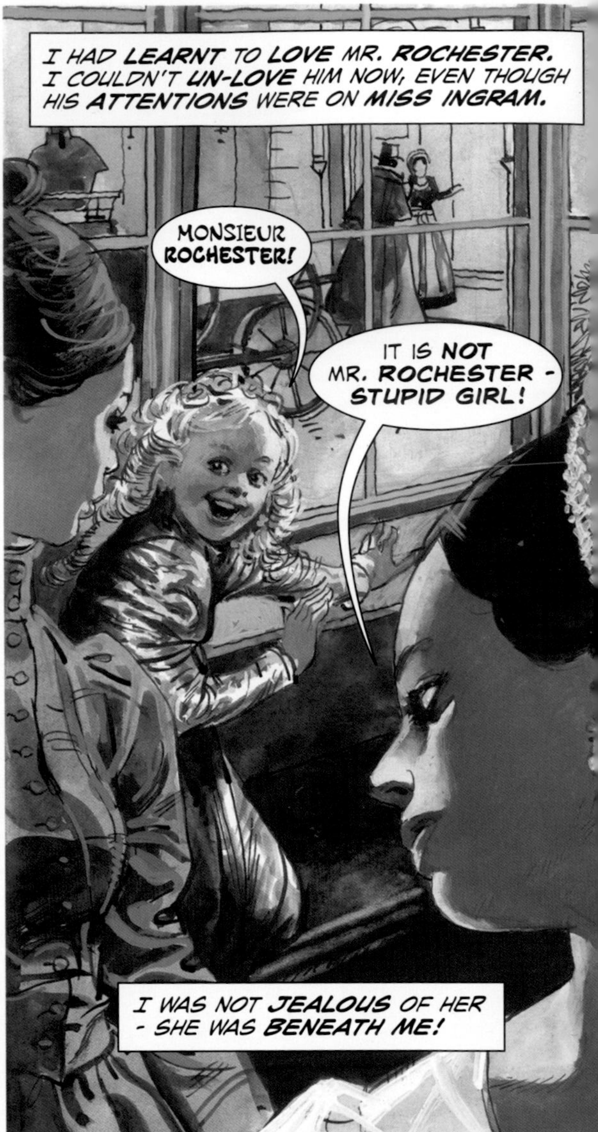
I HAD LEARNT TO LOVE MR. ROCHESTER. I COULDN'T UN-LOVE HIM NOW, EVEN THOUGH HIS ATTENTIONS WERE ON MISS INGRAM.
MONSIEUR ROCHESTER!
IT IS NOT MR. ROCHESTER - STUPID GIRL!
I WAS NOT JEALOUS OF HER - SHE WAS BENEATH ME!

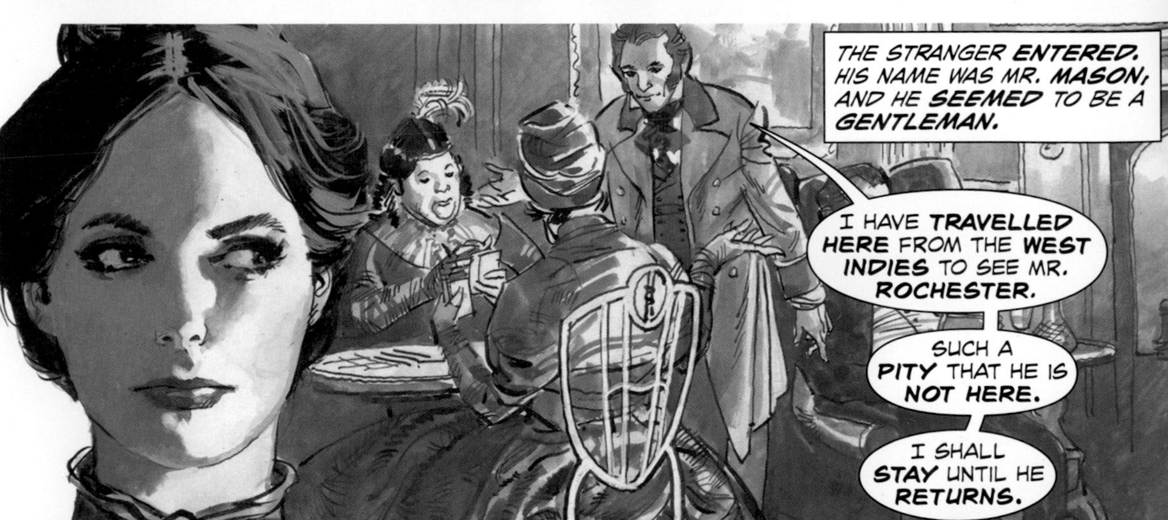
THE STRANGER ENTERED. HIS NAME WAS MR. MASON, AND HE SEEMED TO BE A GENTLEMAN.
I HAVE TRAVELLED HERE FROM THE WEST INDIES TO SEE MR. ROCHESTER.
SUCH A PITY THAT HE IS NOT HERE.
I SHALL STAY UNTIL HE RETURNS.

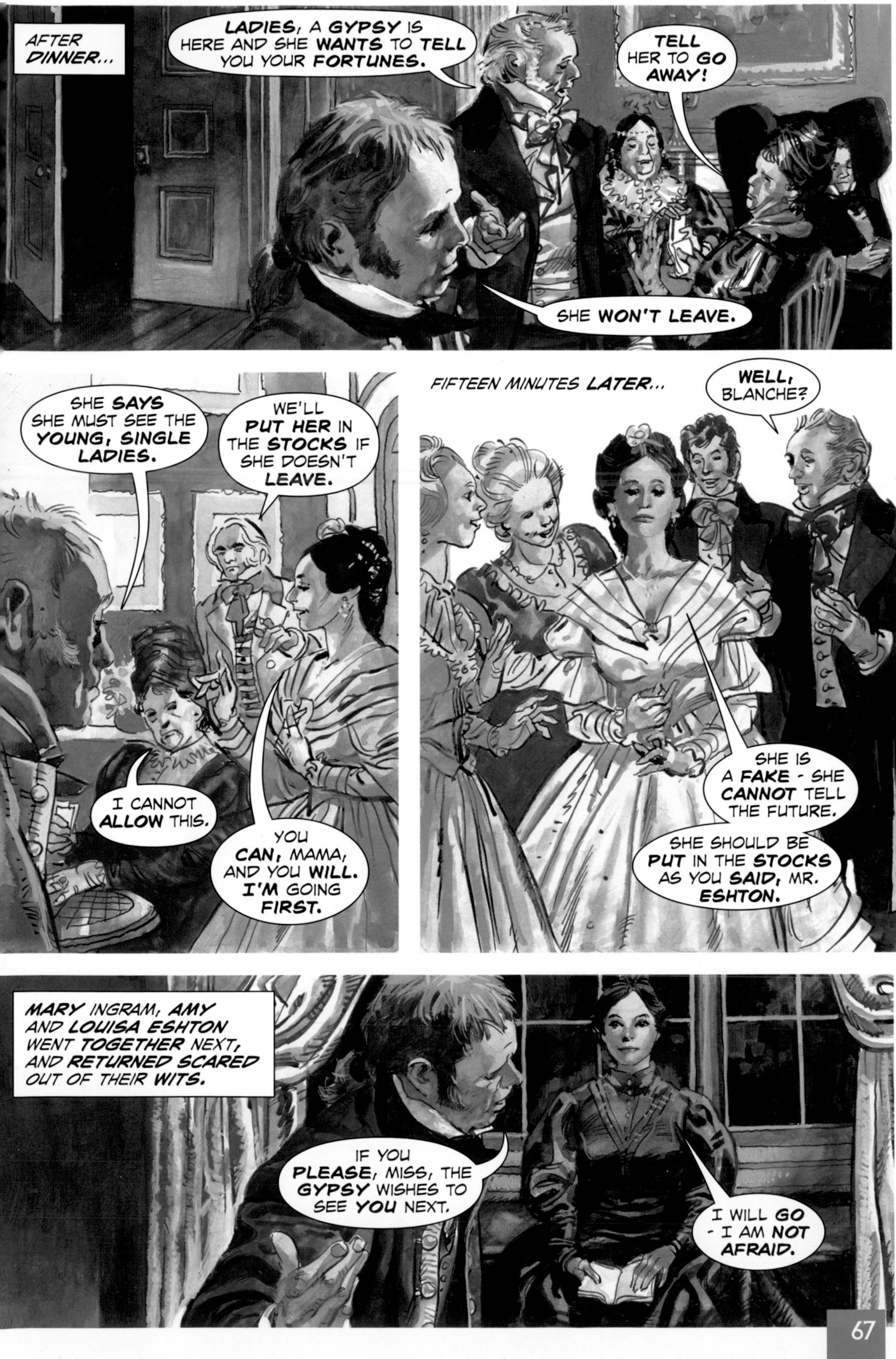
AFTER DINNER...
LADIES, A GYPSY IS HERE AND SHE WANTS TO TELL YOU YOUR FORTUNES.
TELL HER TO GO AWAY!
SHE WON'T LEAVE.
SHE SAYS SHE MUST SEE THE YOUNG, SINGLE LADIES.
WE'LL PUT HER IN THE STOCKS IF SHE DOESN'T LEAVE.
I CANNOT ALLOW THIS.
YOU CAN, MAMA, AND YOU WILL. I'M GOING FIRST.
FIFTEEN MINUTES LATER...
WELL, BLANCHE?
SHE IS A FAKE - SHE CANNOT TELL THE FUTURE.
SHE SHOULD BE PUT IN THE STOCKS AS YOU SAID, MR. ESHTON.
MARY INGRAM, AMY AND LOUISA ESHTON WENT TOGETHER NEXT, AND RETURNED SCARED OUT OF THEIR WITS.
IF YOU PLEASE, MISS, THE GYPSY WISHES TO SEE YOU NEXT.
I WILL GO - I AM NOT AFRAID.

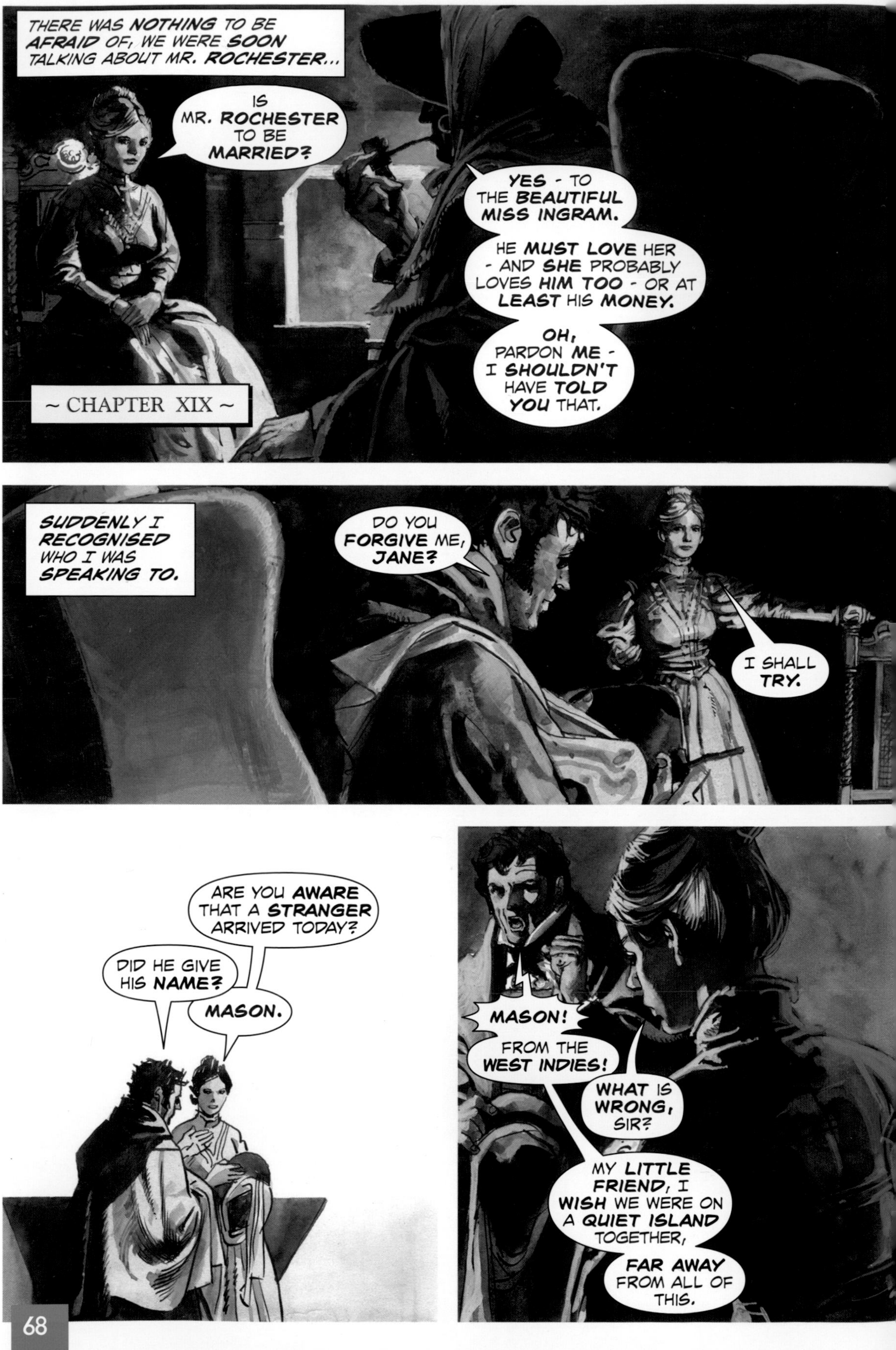
THERE WAS NOTHING TO BE AFRAID OF, WE WERE SOON TALKING ABOUT MR. ROCHESTER...
~ CHAPTER XIX ~
IS MR. ROCHESTER TO BE MARRIED?
YES - TO THE BEAUTIFUL MISS INGRAM.
HE MUST LOVE HER - AND SHE PROBABLY LOVES HIM TOO - OR AT LEAST HIS MONEY.
OH, PARDON ME - I SHOULDN'T HAVE TOLD YOU THAT.
SUDDENLY I RECOGNISED WHO I WAS SPEAKING TO.
DO YOU FORGIVE ME, JANE?
I SHALL TRY.
ARE YOU AWARE THAT A STRANGER ARRIVED TODAY?
DID HE GIVE HIS NAME?
MASON.
MASON!
FROM THE WEST INDIES!
WHAT IS WRONG, SIR?
MY LITTLE FRIEND, I WISH WE WERE ON A QUIET ISLAND TOGETHER,
FAR AWAY FROM ALL OF THIS.

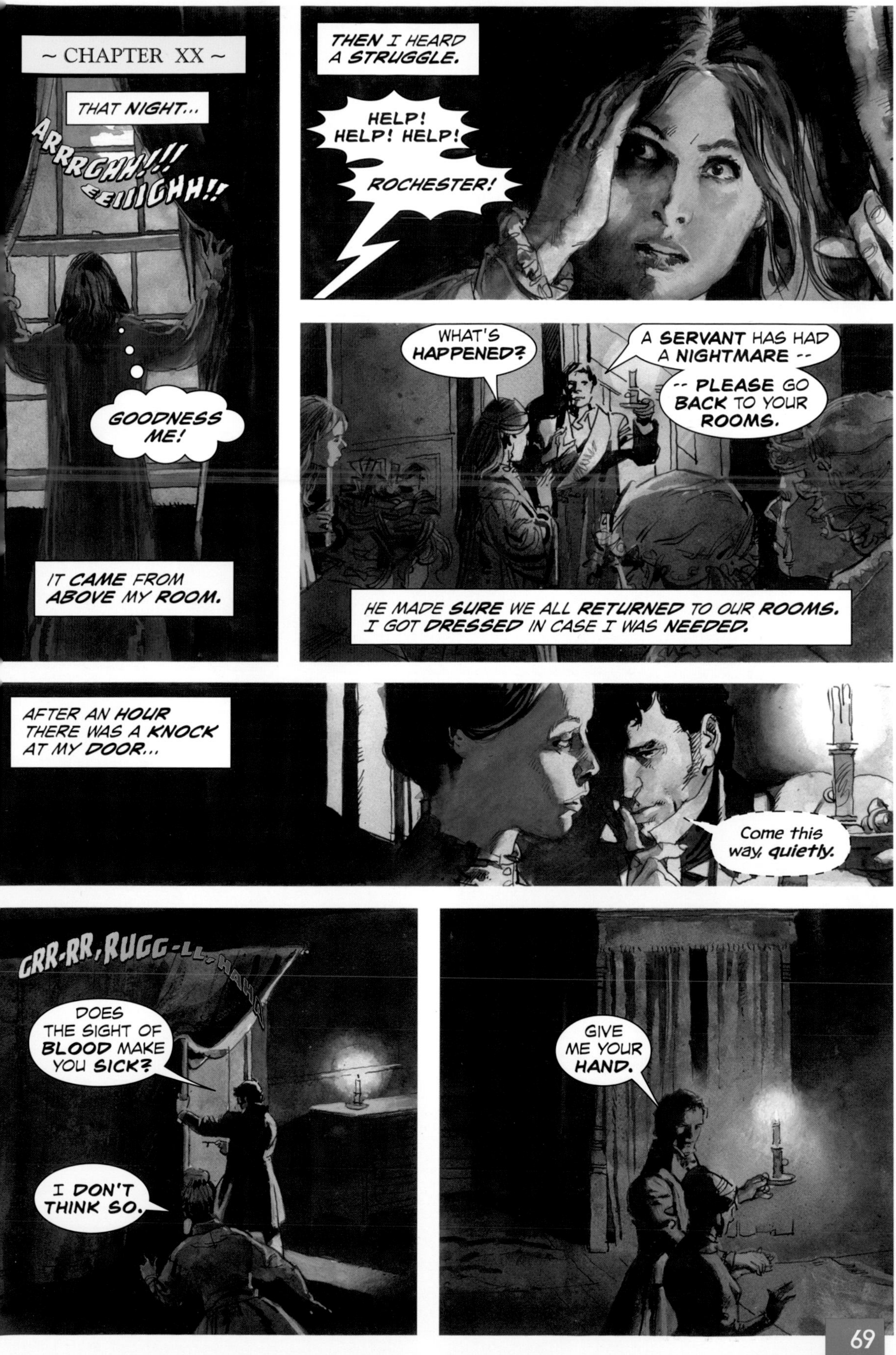
~ CHAPTER XX ~
THAT NIGHT...
ARRRGHH!!!
EEIIIGHH!!
GOODNESS ME!
IT CAME FROM ABOVE MY ROOM.
THEN I HEARD A STRUGGLE.
HELP! HELP! HELP!
ROCHESTER!
WHAT'S HAPPENED?
A SERVANT HAS HAD A NIGHTMARE --
-- PLEASE GO BACK TO YOUR ROOMS.
HE MADE SURE WE ALL RETURNED TO OUR ROOMS. I GOT DRESSED IN CASE I WAS NEEDED.
AFTER AN HOUR THERE WAS A KNOCK AT MY DOOR...
Come this way, quietly.
GRR-RR, RUGG-LL, HAHA!
DOES THE SIGHT OF BLOOD MAKE YOU SICK?
I DON'T THINK SO.
GIVE ME YOUR HAND.

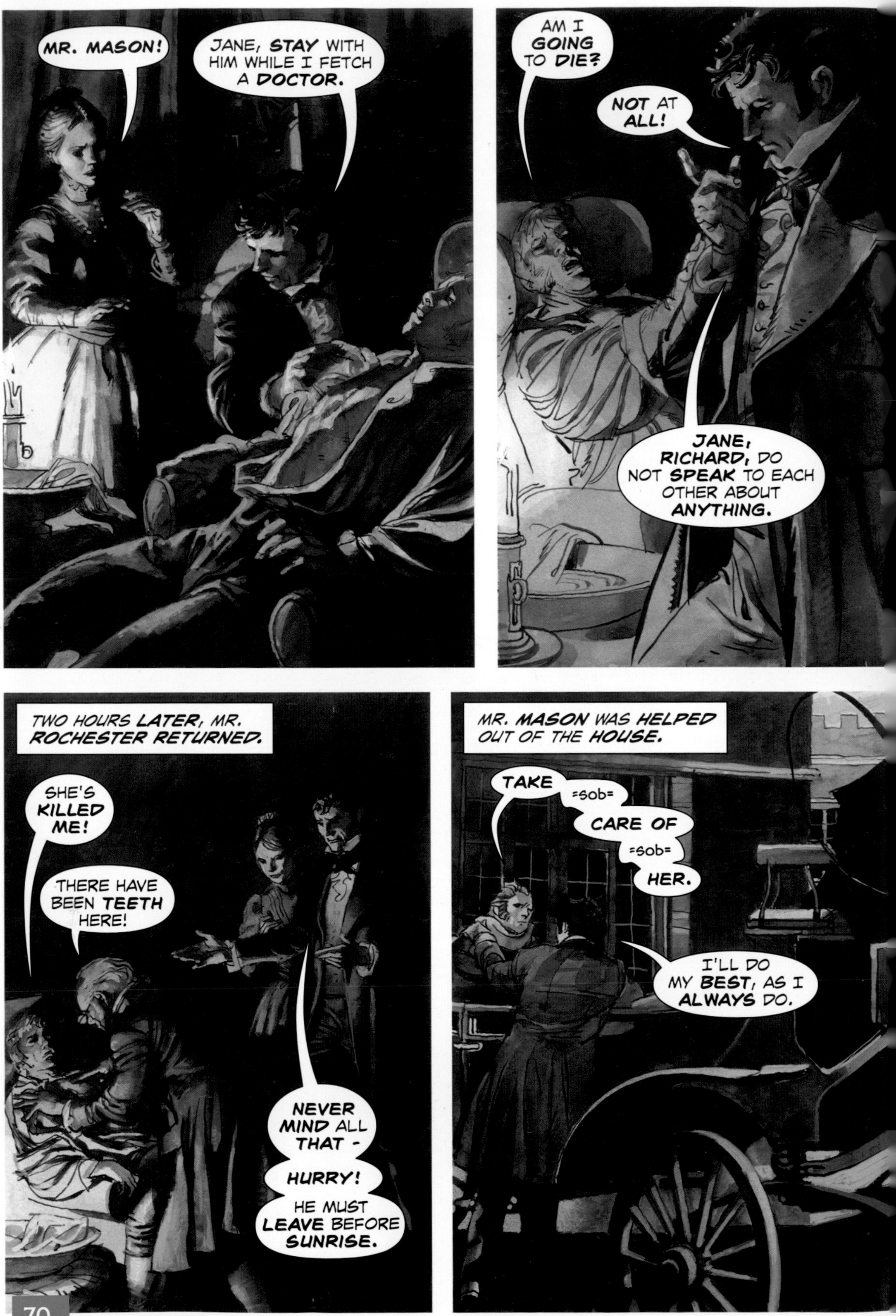
MR. MASON!
JANE, STAY WITH HIM WHILE I FETCH A DOCTOR.
AM I GOING TO DIE?
NOT AT ALL!
JANE, RICHARD, DO NOT SPEAK TO EACH OTHER ABOUT ANYTHING.
TWO HOURS LATER, MR. ROCHESTER RETURNED.
SHE'S KILLED ME!
THERE HAVE BEEN TEETH HERE!
NEVER MIND ALL THAT -
HURRY!
HE MUST LEAVE BEFORE SUNRISE.
MR. MASON WAS HELPED OUT OF THE HOUSE.
TAKE
=sob=
CARE OF
=sob=
HER.
I'LL DO MY BEST, AS I ALWAYS DO.

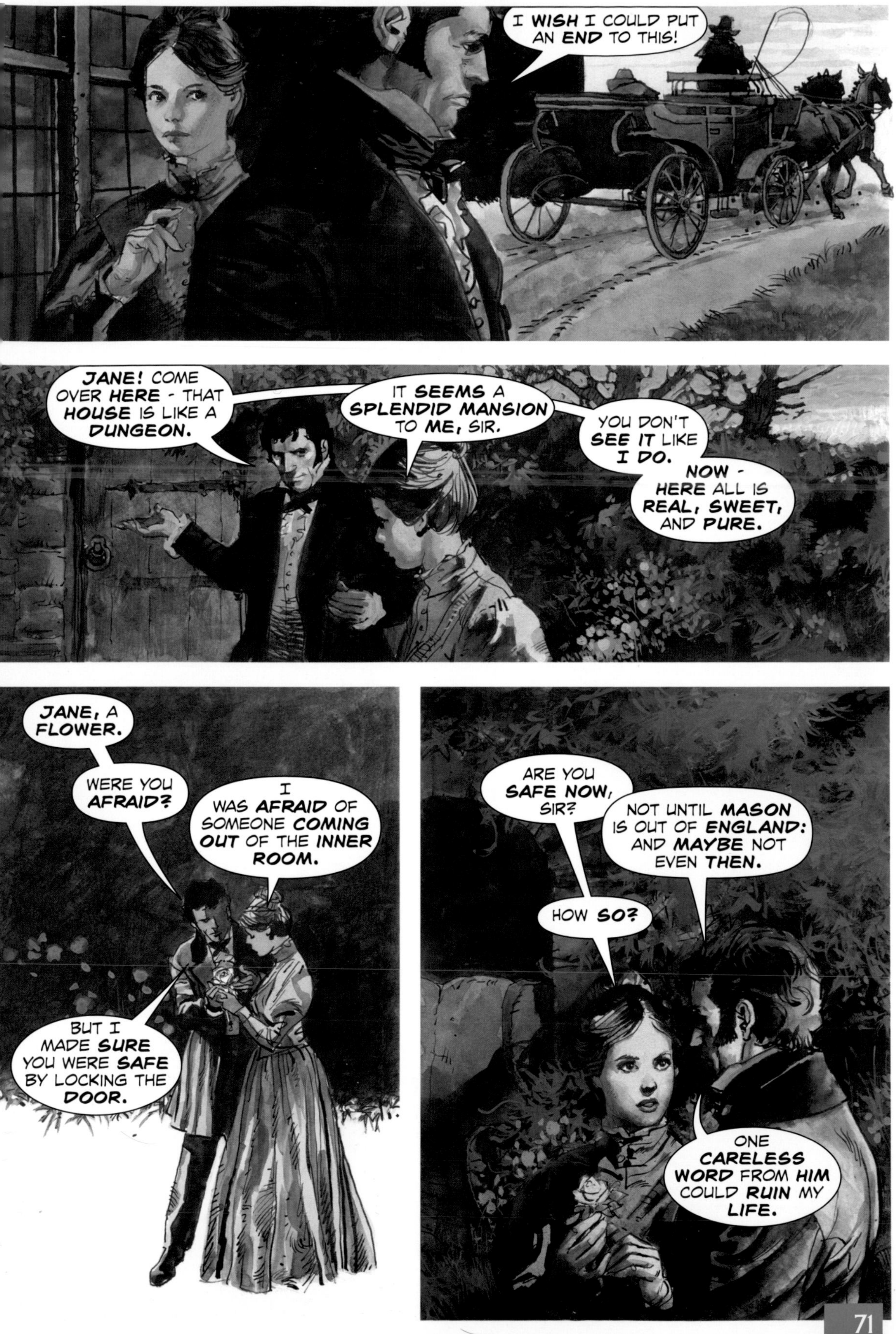
I WISH I COULD PUT AN END TO THIS!
JANE! COME OVER HERE - THAT HOUSE IS LIKE A DUNGEON.
IT SEEMS A SPLENDID MANSION TO ME, SIR.
YOU DON'T SEE IT LIKE I DO.
NOW - HERE ALL IS REAL, SWEET, AND PURE.
JANE, A FLOWER.
WERE YOU AFRAID?
I WAS AFRAID OF SOMEONE COMING OUT OF THE INNER ROOM.
BUT I MADE SURE YOU WERE SAFE BY LOCKING THE DOOR.
ARE YOU SAFE NOW, SIR?
NOT UNTIL MASON IS OUT OF ENGLAND: AND MAYBE NOT EVEN THEN.
HOW SO?
ONE CARELESS WORD FROM HIM COULD RUIN MY LIFE.

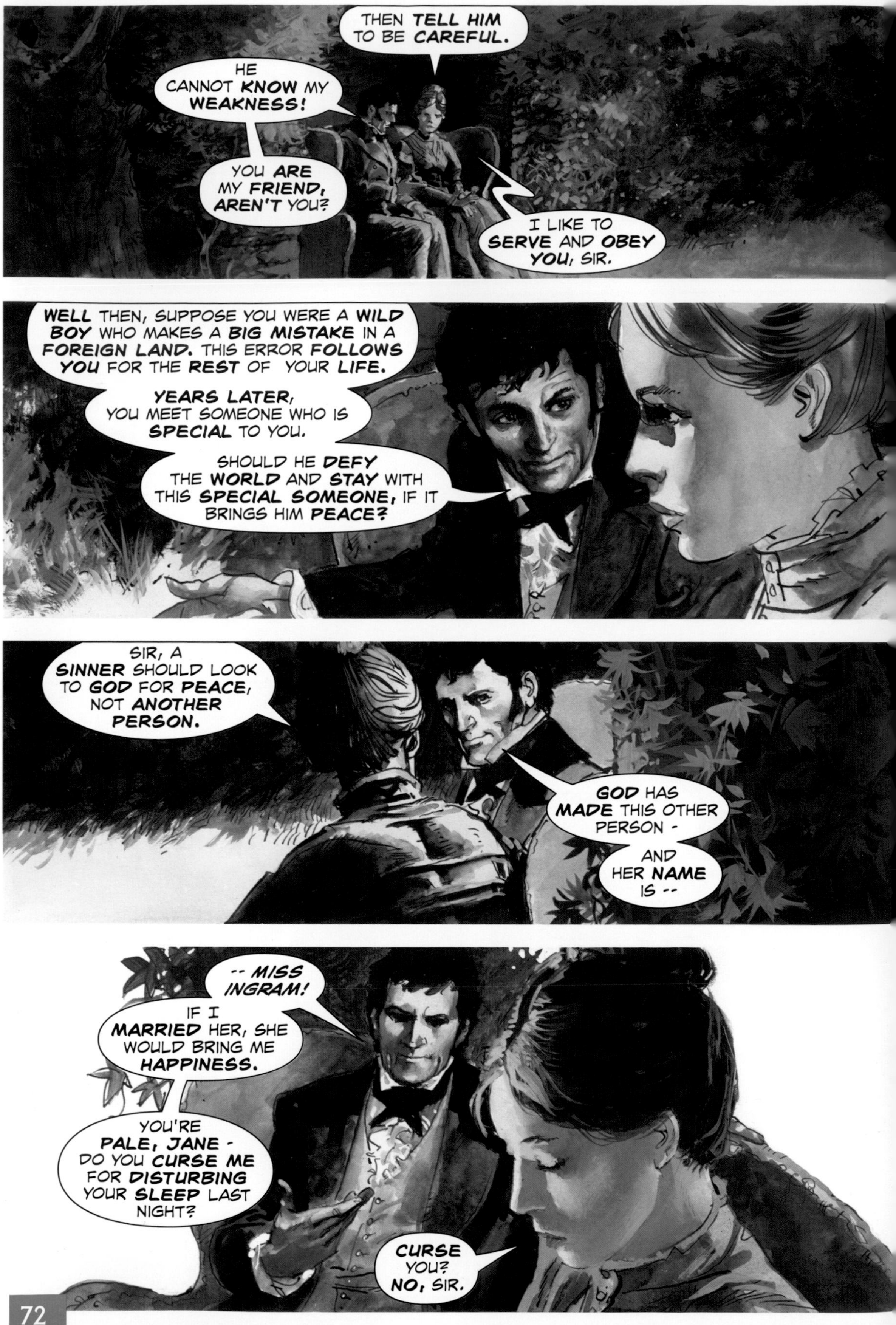
THEN TELL HIM TO BE CAREFUL.
HE CANNOT KNOW MY WEAKNESS!
YOU ARE MY FRIEND, AREN'T YOU?
I LIKE TO SERVE AND OBEY YOU, SIR.
WELL THEN, SUPPOSE YOU WERE A WILD BOY WHO MAKES A BIG MISTAKE IN A FOREIGN LAND. THIS ERROR FOLLOWS YOU FOR THE REST OF YOUR LIFE.
YEARS LATER, YOU MEET SOMEONE WHO IS SPECIAL TO YOU.
SHOULD HE DEFY THE WORLD AND STAY WITH THIS SPECIAL SOMEONE, IF IT BRINGS HIM PEACE?
SIR, A SINNER SHOULD LOOK TO GOD FOR PEACE, NOT ANOTHER PERSON.
GOD HAS MADE THIS OTHER PERSON -
AND HER NAME IS --
-- MISS INGRAM!
IF I MARRIED HER, SHE WOULD BRING ME HAPPINESS.
YOU'RE PALE, JANE - DO YOU CURSE ME FOR DISTURBING YOUR SLEEP LAST NIGHT?
CURSE YOU? NO, SIR.

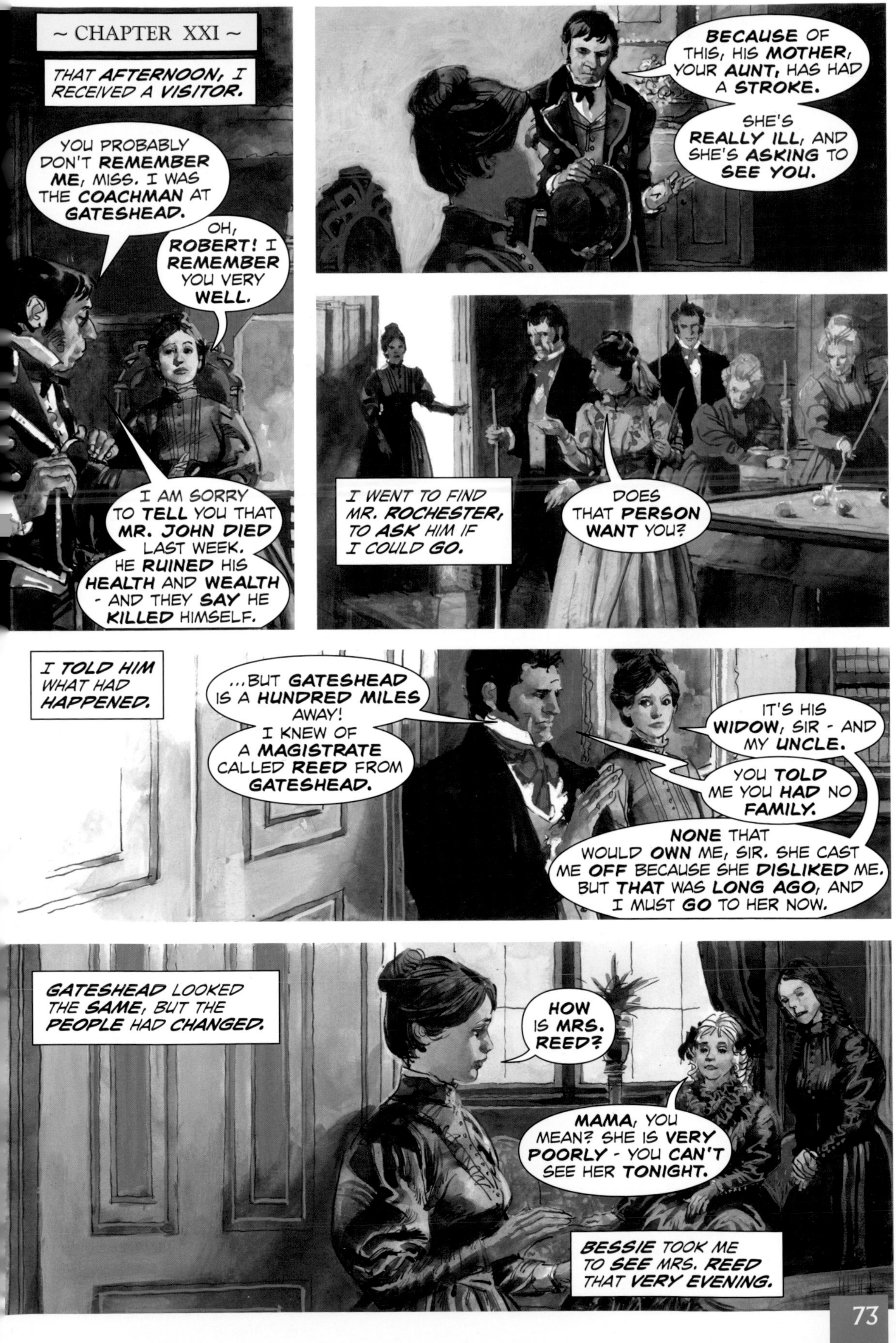
~ CHAPTER XXI ~
THAT AFTERNOON, I RECEIVED A VISITOR.
YOU PROBABLY DON'T REMEMBER ME, MISS. I WAS THE COACHMAN AT GATESHEAD.
OH, ROBERT! I REMEMBER YOU VERY WELL.
I AM SORRY TO TELL YOU THAT MR. JOHN DIED LAST WEEK.
HE RUINED HIS HEALTH AND WEALTH - AND THEY SAY HE KILLED HIMSELF.
BECAUSE OF THIS, HIS MOTHER, YOUR AUNT, HAS HAD A STROKE.
SHE'S REALLY ILL, AND SHE'S ASKING TO SEE YOU.
I WENT TO FIND MR. ROCHESTER, TO ASK HIM IF I COULD GO.
DOES THAT PERSON WANT YOU?
I TOLD HIM WHAT HAD HAPPENED.
...BUT GATESHEAD IS A HUNDRED MILES AWAY!
I KNEW OF A MAGISTRATE CALLED REED FROM GATESHEAD.
IT'S HIS WIDOW, SIR - AND MY UNCLE.
YOU TOLD ME YOU HAD NO FAMILY.
NONE THAT WOULD OWN ME, SIR. SHE CAST ME OFF BECAUSE SHE DISLIKED ME. BUT THAT WAS LONG AGO, AND I MUST GO TO HER NOW.
GATESHEAD LOOKED THE SAME, BUT THE PEOPLE HAD CHANGED.
HOW IS MRS. REED?
MAMA, YOU MEAN? SHE IS VERY POORLY - YOU CAN'T SEE HER TONIGHT.
BESSIE TOOK ME TO SEE MRS. REED THAT VERY EVENING.

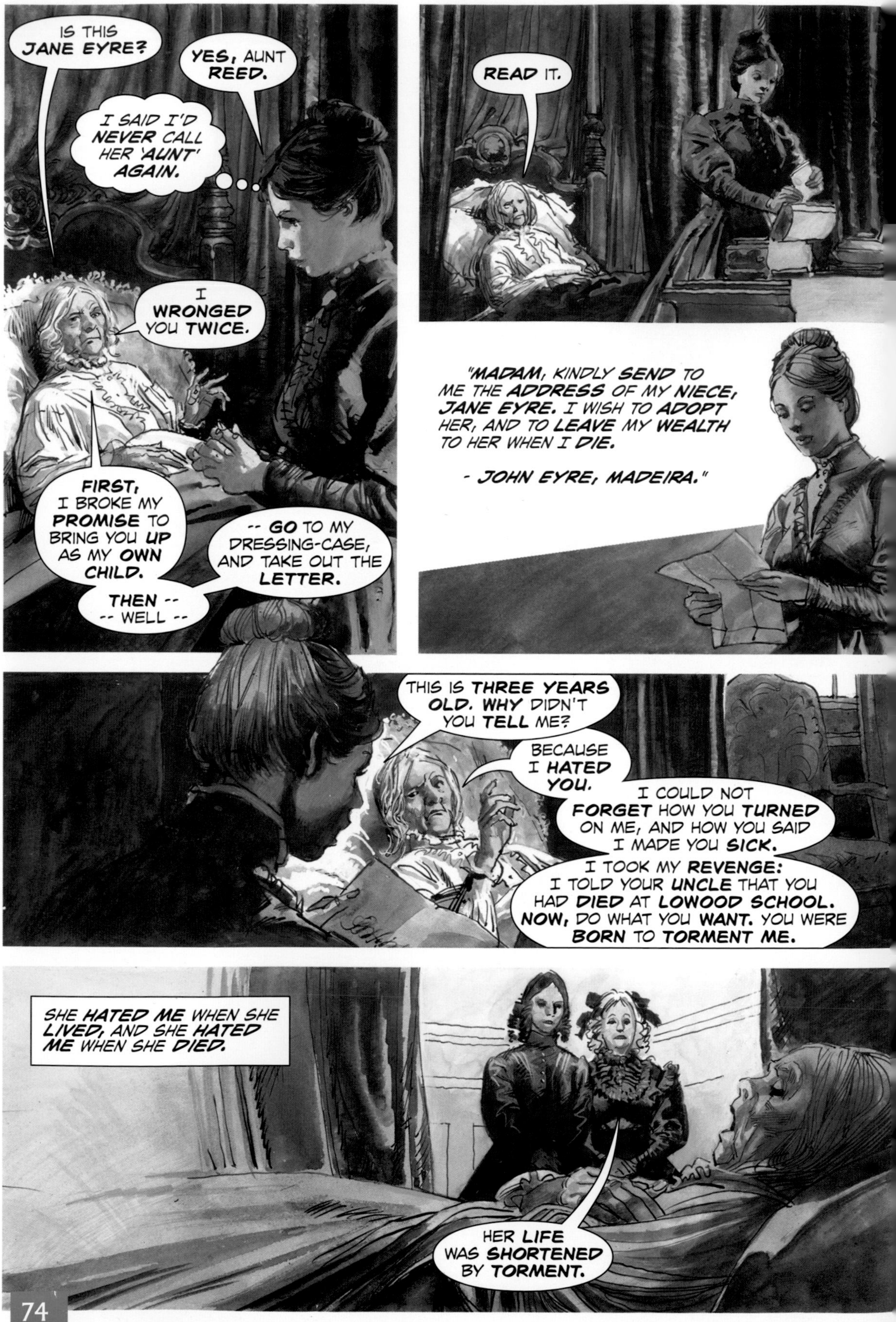
IS THIS JANE EYRE?
YES, AUNT REED.
I SAID I'D NEVER CALL HER 'AUNT' AGAIN.
I WRONGED YOU TWICE.
FIRST, I BROKE MY PROMISE TO BRING YOU UP AS MY OWN CHILD.
THEN -- -- WELL --
-- GO TO MY DRESSING-CASE, AND TAKE OUT THE LETTER.
READ IT.
"MADAM, KINDLY SEND TO ME THE ADDRESS OF MY NIECE, JANE EYRE. I WISH TO ADOPT HER, AND TO LEAVE MY WEALTH TO HER WHEN I DIE.
- JOHN EYRE, MADEIRA."
THIS IS THREE YEARS OLD. WHY DIDN'T YOU TELL ME?
BECAUSE I HATED YOU.
I COULD NOT FORGET HOW YOU TURNED ON ME, AND HOW YOU SAID I MADE YOU SICK.
I TOOK MY REVENGE: I TOLD YOUR UNCLE THAT YOU HAD DIED AT LOWOOD SCHOOL. NOW, DO WHAT YOU WANT. YOU WERE BORN TO TORMENT ME.
SHE HATED ME WHEN SHE LIVED, AND SHE HATED ME WHEN SHE DIED.
HER LIFE WAS SHORTENED BY TORMENT.

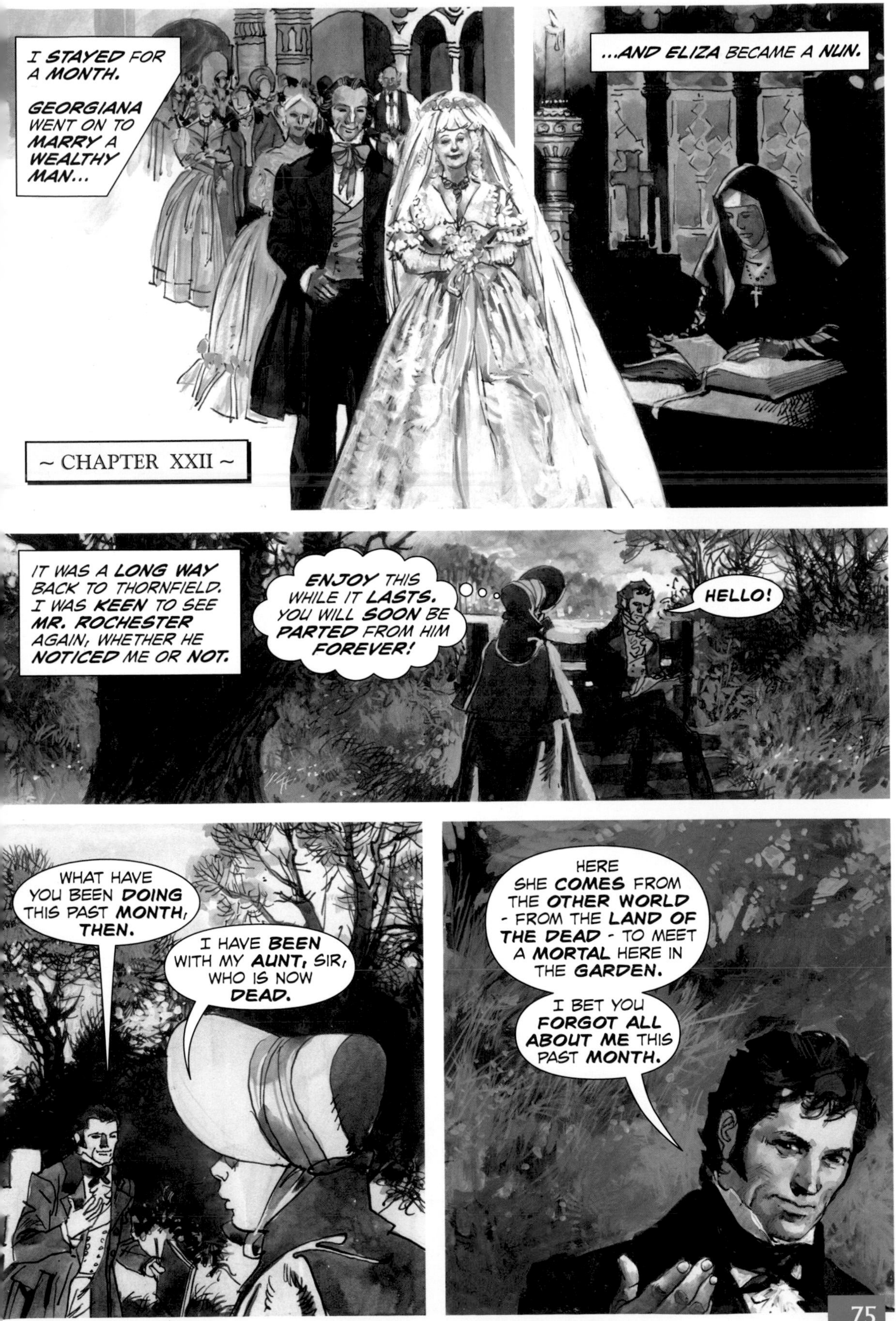
I STAYED FOR A MONTH.
GEORGIANA WENT ON TO MARRY A WEALTHY MAN...
~ CHAPTER XXII ~
...AND ELIZA BECAME A NUN.
IT WAS A LONG WAY BACK TO THORNFIELD. I WAS KEEN TO SEE MR. ROCHESTER AGAIN, WHETHER HE NOTICED ME OR NOT.
ENJOY THIS WHILE IT LASTS. YOU WILL SOON BE PARTED FROM HIM FOREVER!
HELLO!
WHAT HAVE YOU BEEN DOING THIS PAST MONTH, THEN.
I HAVE BEEN WITH MY AUNT, SIR, WHO IS NOW DEAD.
HERE SHE COMES FROM THE OTHER WORLD - FROM THE LAND OF THE DEAD - TO MEET A MORTAL HERE IN THE GARDEN.
I BET YOU FORGOT ALL ABOUT ME THIS PAST MONTH.

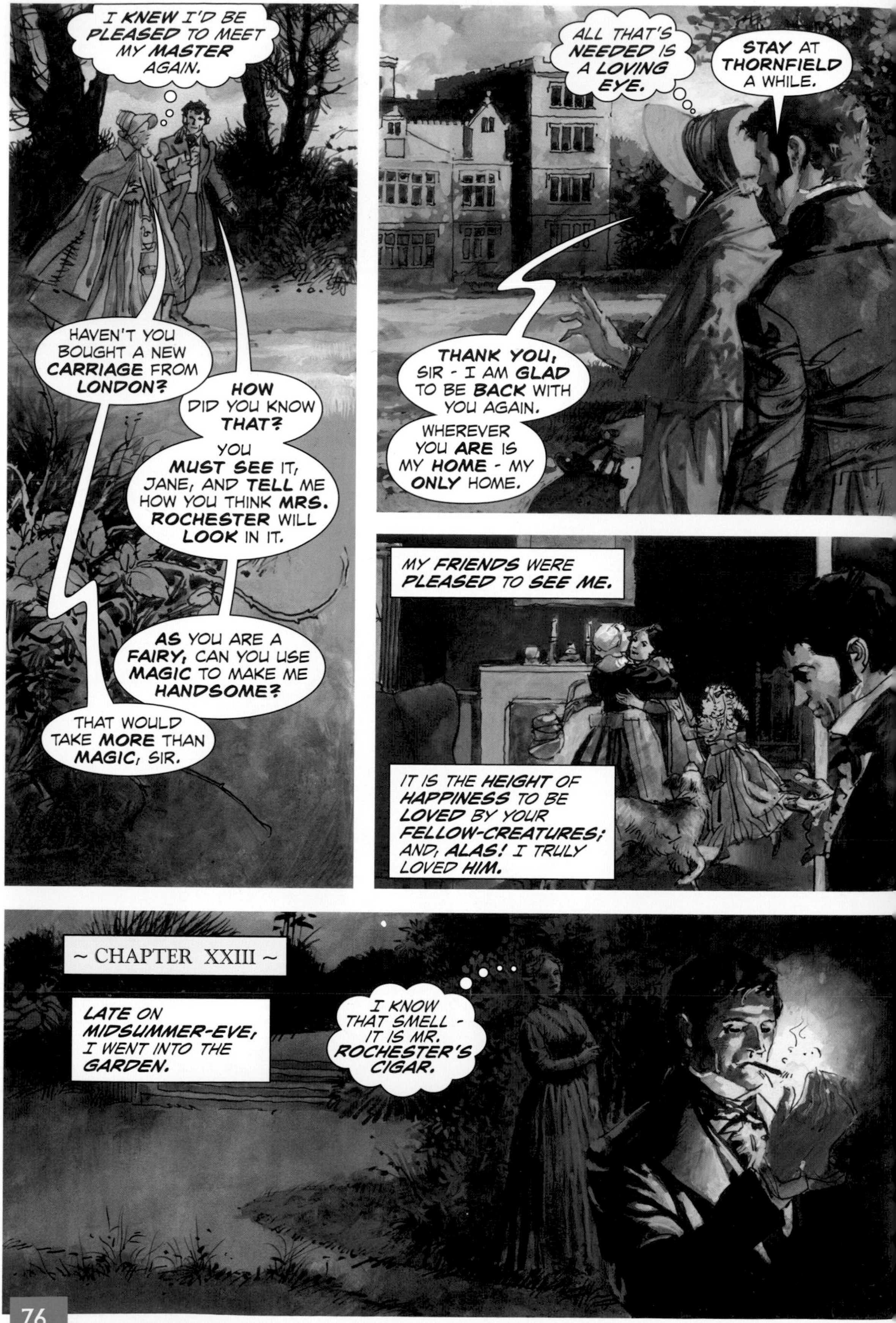
I KNEW I'D BE PLEASED TO MEET MY MASTER AGAIN.
HAVEN'T YOU BOUGHT A NEW CARRIAGE FROM LONDON?
HOW DID YOU KNOW THAT?
YOU MUST SEE IT, JANE, AND TELL ME HOW YOU THINK MRS. ROCHESTER WILL LOOK IN IT.
AS YOU ARE A FAIRY, CAN YOU USE MAGIC TO MAKE ME HANDSOME?
THAT WOULD TAKE MORE THAN MAGIC, SIR.
ALL THAT'S NEEDED IS A LOVING EYE.
STAY AT THORNFIELD A WHILE.
THANK YOU, SIR - I AM GLAD TO BE BACK WITH YOU AGAIN.
WHEREVER YOU ARE IS MY HOME - MY ONLY HOME.
MY FRIENDS WERE PLEASED TO SEE ME.
IT IS THE HEIGHT OF HAPPINESS TO BE LOVED BY YOUR FELLOW-CREATURES; AND, ALAS! I TRULY LOVED HIM.
~ CHAPTER XXIII ~
LATE ON MIDSUMMER-EVE, I WENT INTO THE GARDEN.
I KNOW THAT SMELL - IT IS MR. ROCHESTER'S CIGAR.

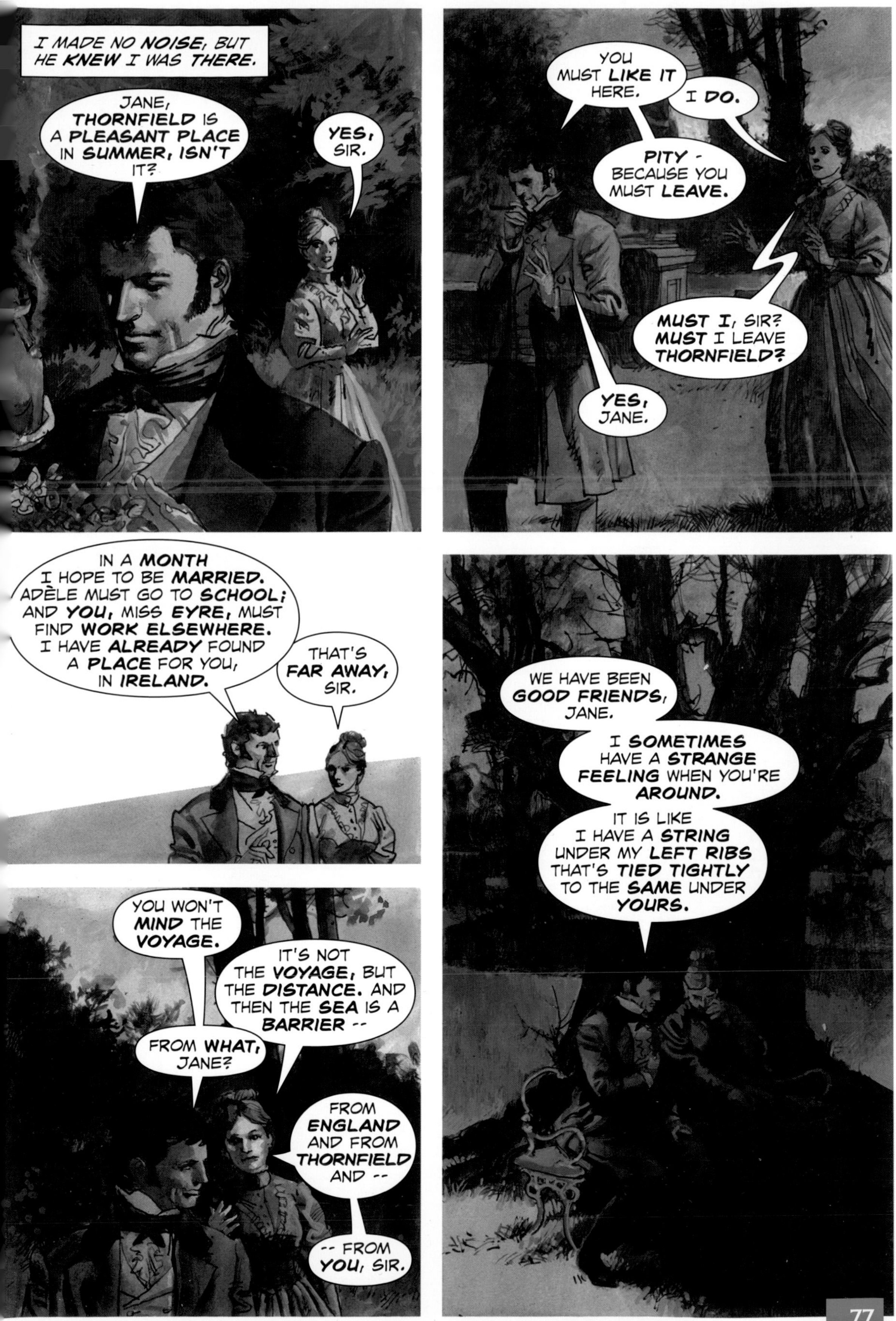
I MADE NO NOISE; BUT HE KNEW I WAS THERE.
JANE, THORNFIELD IS A PLEASANT PLACE IN SUMMER, ISN'T IT?
YES, SIR.
YOU MUST LIKE IT HERE.
I DO.
PITY - BECAUSE YOU MUST LEAVE.
MUST I, SIR? MUST I LEAVE THORNFIELD?
YES, JANE.
IN A MONTH I HOPE TO BE MARRIED. ADÈLE MUST GO TO SCHOOL; AND YOU, MISS EYRE, MUST FIND WORK ELSEWHERE. I HAVE ALREADY FOUND A PLACE FOR YOU, IN IRELAND.
THAT'S FAR AWAY, SIR.
YOU WON'T MIND THE VOYAGE.
IT'S NOT THE VOYAGE, BUT THE DISTANCE. AND THEN THE SEA IS A BARRIER --
FROM WHAT, JANE?
FROM ENGLAND AND FROM THORNFIELD AND --
-- FROM YOU, SIR.
WE HAVE BEEN GOOD FRIENDS, JANE.
I SOMETIMES HAVE A STRANGE FEELING WHEN YOU'RE AROUND.
IT IS LIKE I HAVE A STRING UNDER MY LEFT RIBS THAT'S TIED TIGHTLY TO THE SAME UNDER YOURS.

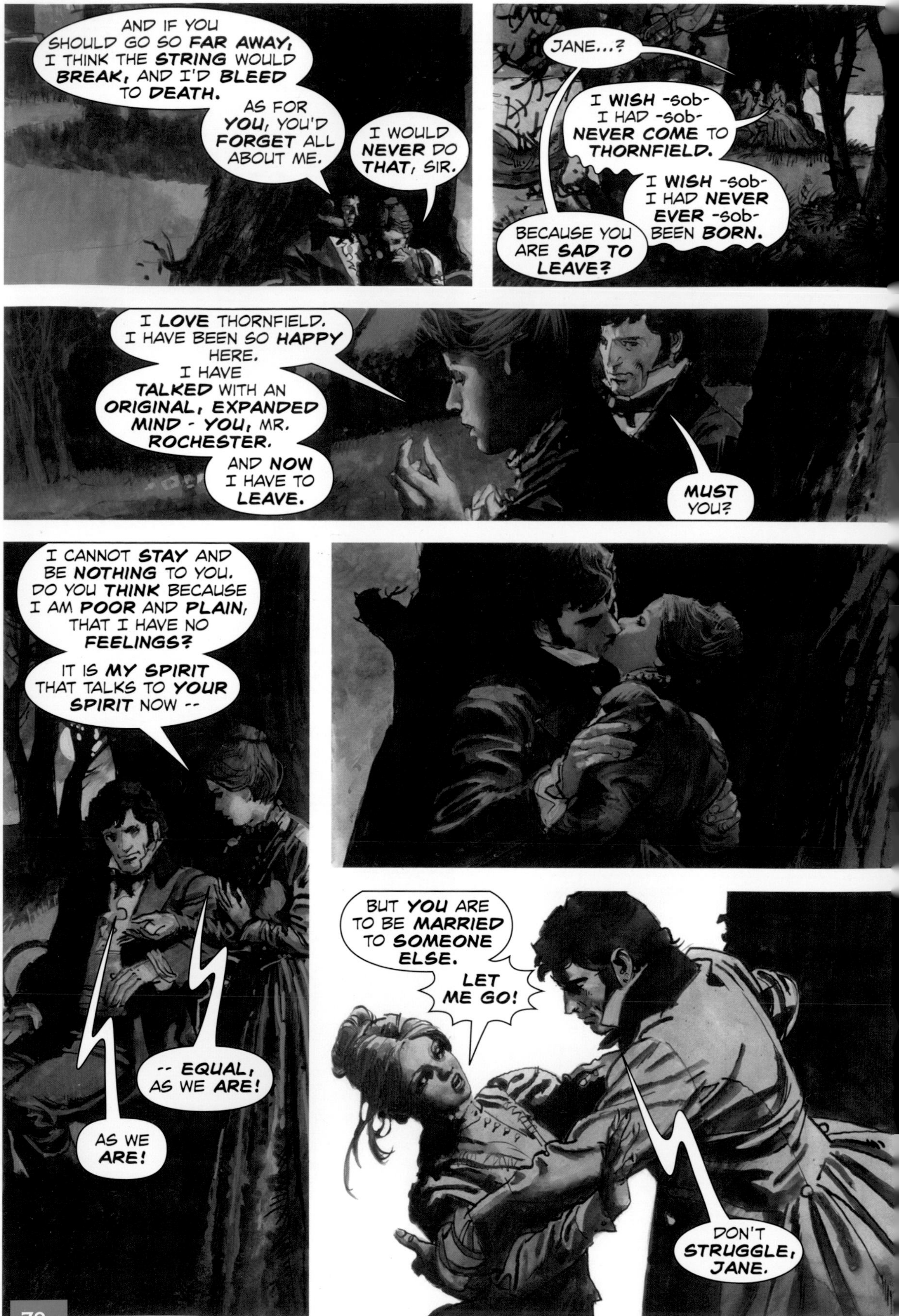
AND IF YOU SHOULD GO SO FAR AWAY, I THINK THE STRING WOULD BREAK, AND I'D BLEED TO DEATH.
AS FOR YOU, YOU'D FORGET ALL ABOUT ME.
I WOULD NEVER DO THAT, SIR.
JANE...?
I WISH -sob- I HAD -sob- NEVER COME TO THORNFIELD.
I WISH -sob- I HAD NEVER EVER -sob- BEEN BORN.
BECAUSE YOU ARE SAD TO LEAVE?
I LOVE THORNFIELD. I HAVE BEEN SO HAPPY HERE.
I HAVE TALKED WITH AN ORIGINAL, EXPANDED MIND - YOU, MR. ROCHESTER.
AND NOW I HAVE TO LEAVE.
MUST YOU?
I CANNOT STAY AND BE NOTHING TO YOU. DO YOU THINK BECAUSE I AM POOR AND PLAIN, THAT I HAVE NO FEELINGS?
IT IS MY SPIRIT THAT TALKS TO YOUR SPIRIT NOW --
-- EQUAL, AS WE ARE!
AS WE ARE!
BUT YOU ARE TO BE MARRIED TO SOMEONE ELSE.
LET ME GO!
DON'T STRUGGLE, JANE.

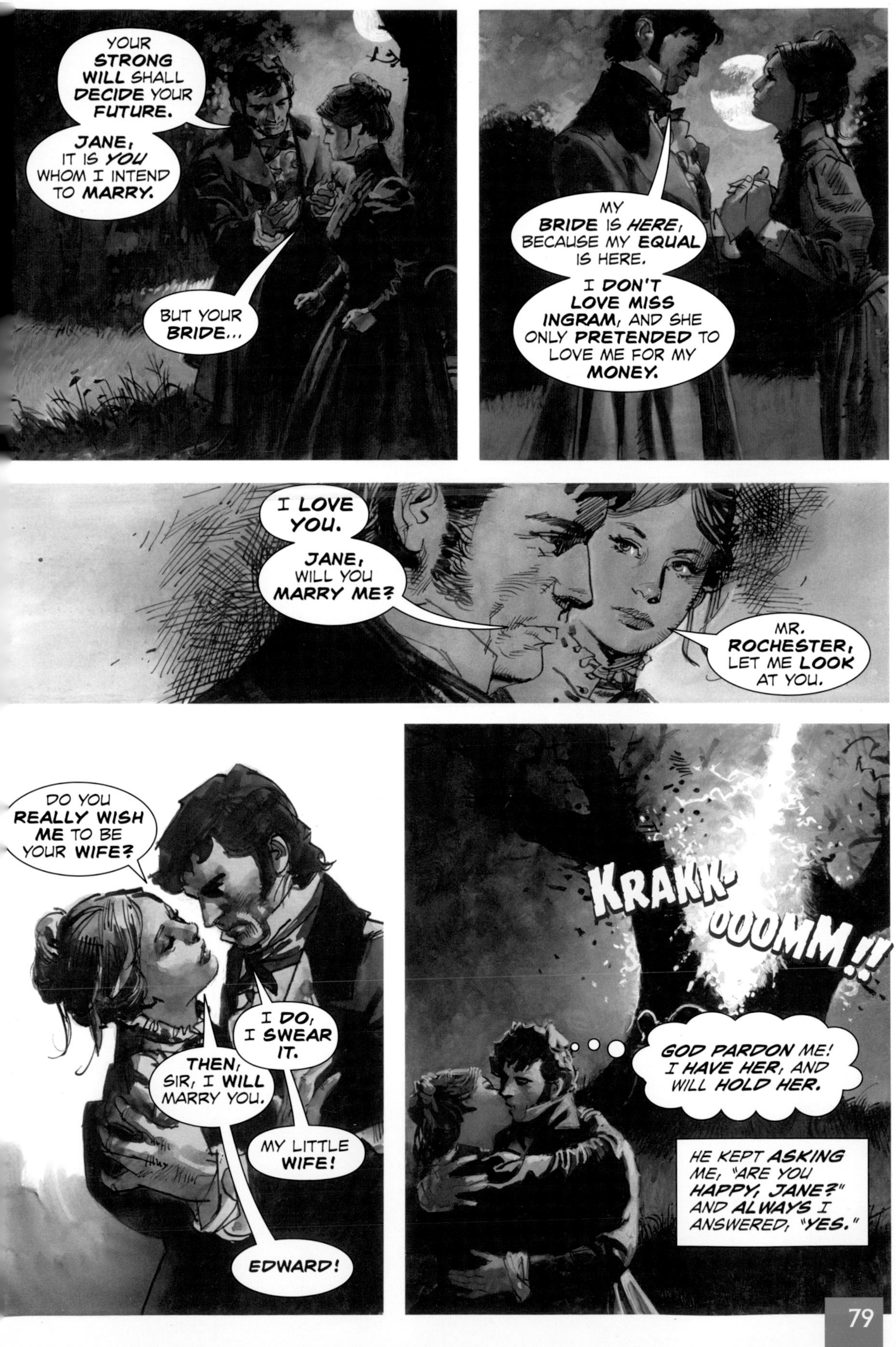
YOUR STRONG WILL SHALL DECIDE YOUR FUTURE.
JANE, IT IS YOU WHOM I INTEND TO MARRY.
BUT YOUR BRIDE...
MY BRIDE IS HERE, BECAUSE MY EQUAL IS HERE.
I DON'T LOVE MISS INGRAM, AND SHE ONLY PRETENDED TO LOVE ME FOR MY MONEY.
I LOVE YOU.
JANE, WILL YOU MARRY ME?
MR. ROCHESTER, LET ME LOOK AT YOU.
DO YOU REALLY WISH ME TO BE YOUR WIFE?
I DO, I SWEAR IT.
THEN, SIR, I WILL MARRY YOU.
MY LITTLE WIFE!
EDWARD!
KRAKK-OOOOMM!!
GOD PARDON ME! I HAVE HER, AND WILL HOLD HER.
HE KEPT ASKING ME, "ARE YOU HAPPY, JANE?" AND ALWAYS I ANSWERED, "YES."

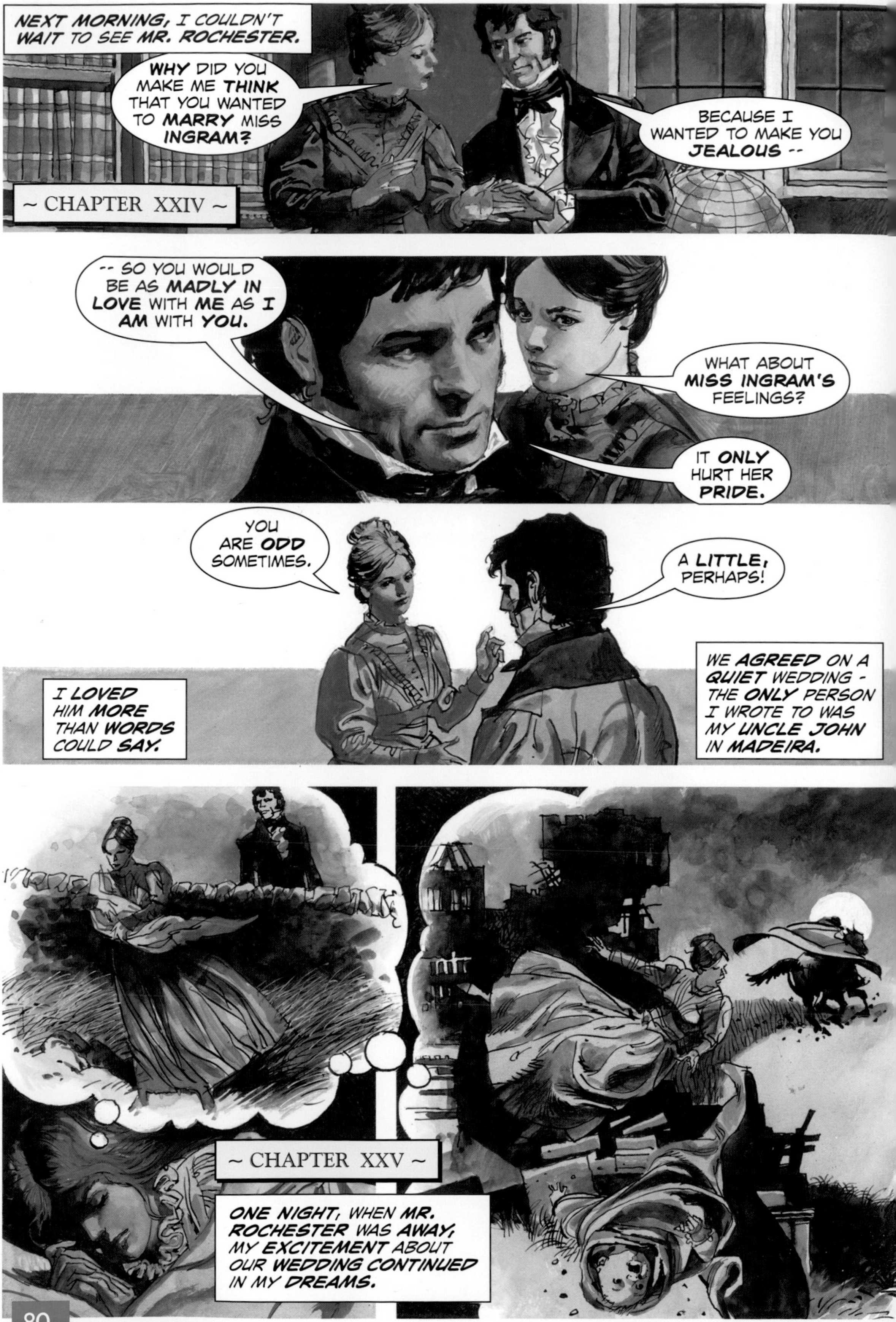
NEXT MORNING, I COULDN'T WAIT TO SEE MR. ROCHESTER.
WHY DID YOU MAKE ME THINK THAT YOU WANTED TO MARRY MISS INGRAM?
BECAUSE I WANTED TO MAKE YOU JEALOUS --
~ CHAPTER XXIV ~
-- SO YOU WOULD BE AS MADLY IN LOVE WITH ME AS I AM WITH YOU.
WHAT ABOUT MISS INGRAM'S FEELINGS?
IT ONLY HURT HER PRIDE.
YOU ARE ODD SOMETIMES.
A LITTLE, PERHAPS!
I LOVED HIM MORE THAN WORDS COULD SAY.
WE AGREED ON A QUIET WEDDING - THE ONLY PERSON I WROTE TO WAS MY UNCLE JOHN IN MADEIRA.
~ CHAPTER XXV ~
ONE NIGHT, WHEN MR. ROCHESTER WAS AWAY, MY EXCITEMENT ABOUT OUR WEDDING CONTINUED IN MY DREAMS.

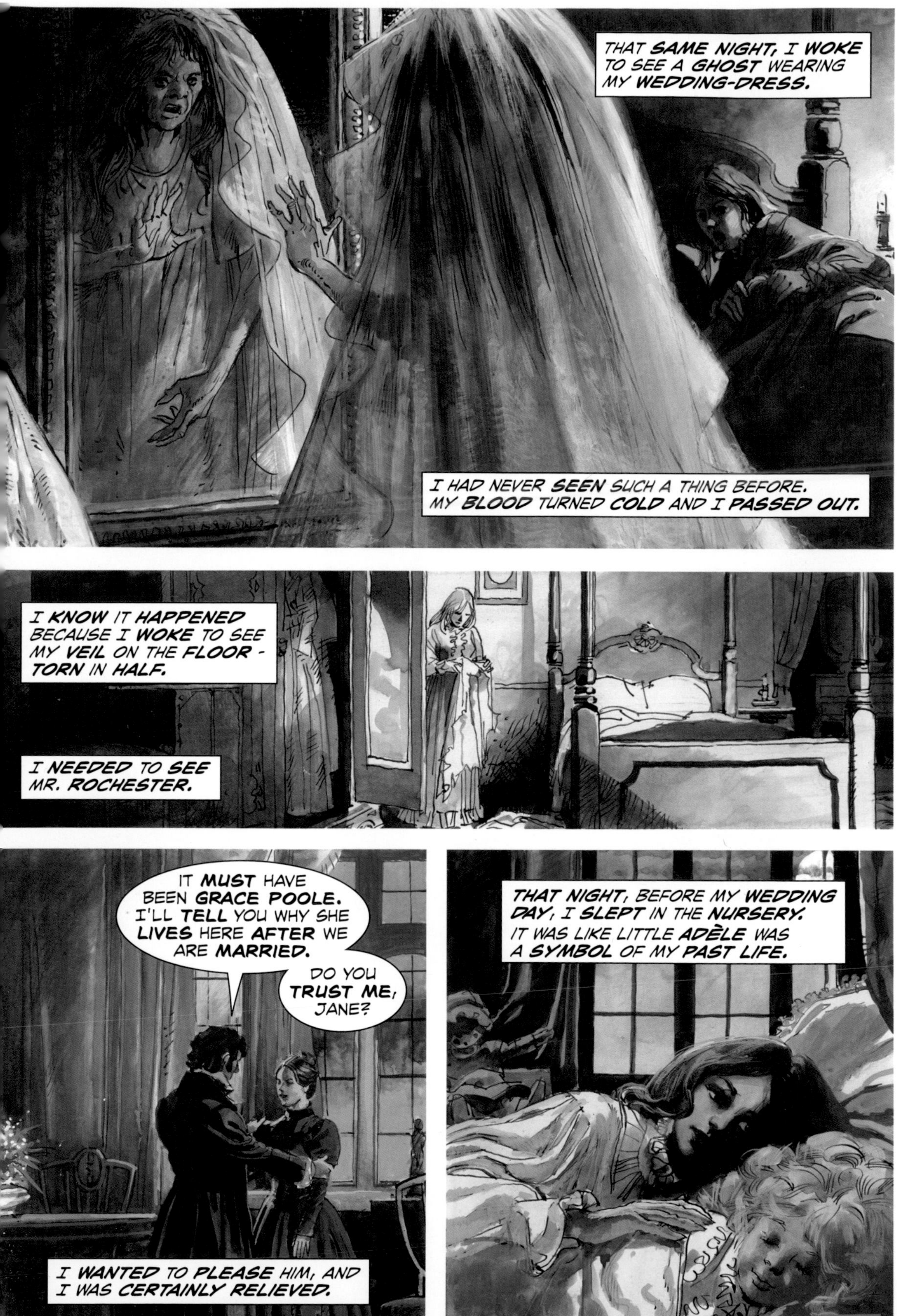
THAT SAME NIGHT, I WOKE TO SEE A GHOST WEARING MY WEDDING-DRESS.
I HAD NEVER SEEN SUCH A THING BEFORE. MY BLOOD TURNED COLD AND I PASSED OUT.
I KNOW IT HAPPENED BECAUSE I WOKE TO SEE MY VEIL ON THE FLOOR - TORN IN HALF.
I NEEDED TO SEE MR. ROCHESTER.
IT MUST HAVE BEEN GRACE POOLE. I'LL TELL YOU WHY SHE LIVES HERE AFTER WE ARE MARRIED.
DO YOU TRUST ME, JANE?
I WANTED TO PLEASE HIM, AND I WAS CERTAINLY RELIEVED.
THAT NIGHT, BEFORE MY WEDDING DAY, I SLEPT IN THE NURSERY. IT WAS LIKE LITTLE ADÈLE WAS A SYMBOL OF MY PAST LIFE.

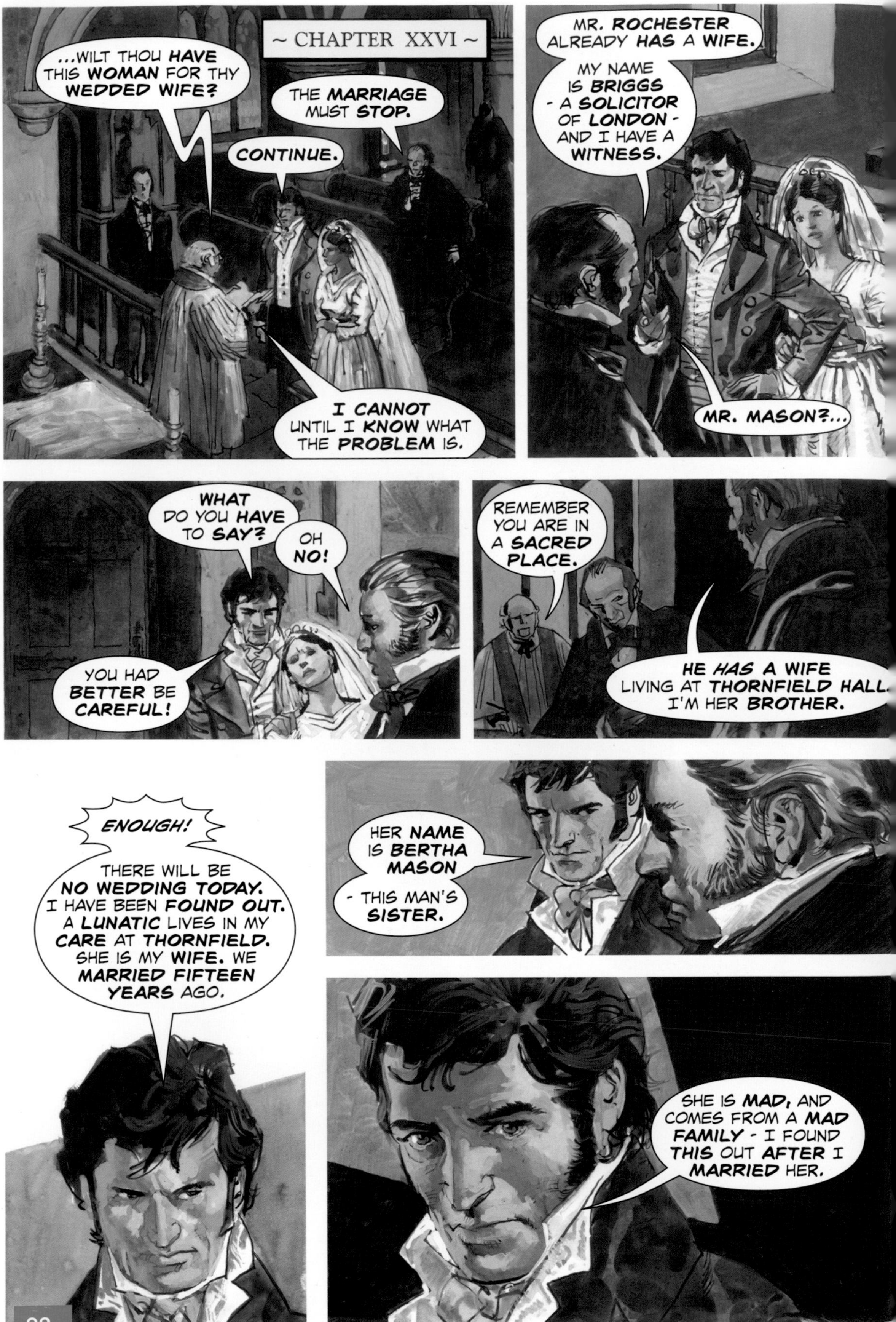
~ CHAPTER XXVI ~
...WILT THOU HAVE THIS WOMAN FOR THY WEDDED WIFE?
THE MARRIAGE MUST STOP.
CONTINUE.
I CANNOT UNTIL I KNOW WHAT THE PROBLEM IS.
MR. ROCHESTER ALREADY HAS A WIFE.
MY NAME IS BRIGGS - A SOLICITOR OF LONDON - AND I HAVE A WITNESS.
MR. MASON?...
WHAT DO YOU HAVE TO SAY?
OH NO!
YOU HAD BETTER BE CAREFUL!
REMEMBER YOU ARE IN A SACRED PLACE.
HE HAS A WIFE LIVING AT THORNFIELD HALL. I'M HER BROTHER.
HER NAME IS BERTHA MASON
- THIS MAN'S SISTER.
ENOUGH!
THERE WILL BE NO WEDDING TODAY. I HAVE BEEN FOUND OUT. A LUNATIC LIVES IN MY CARE AT THORNFIELD. SHE IS MY WIFE. WE MARRIED FIFTEEN YEARS AGO.
SHE IS MAD, AND COMES FROM A MAD FAMILY - I FOUND THIS OUT AFTER I MARRIED HER.

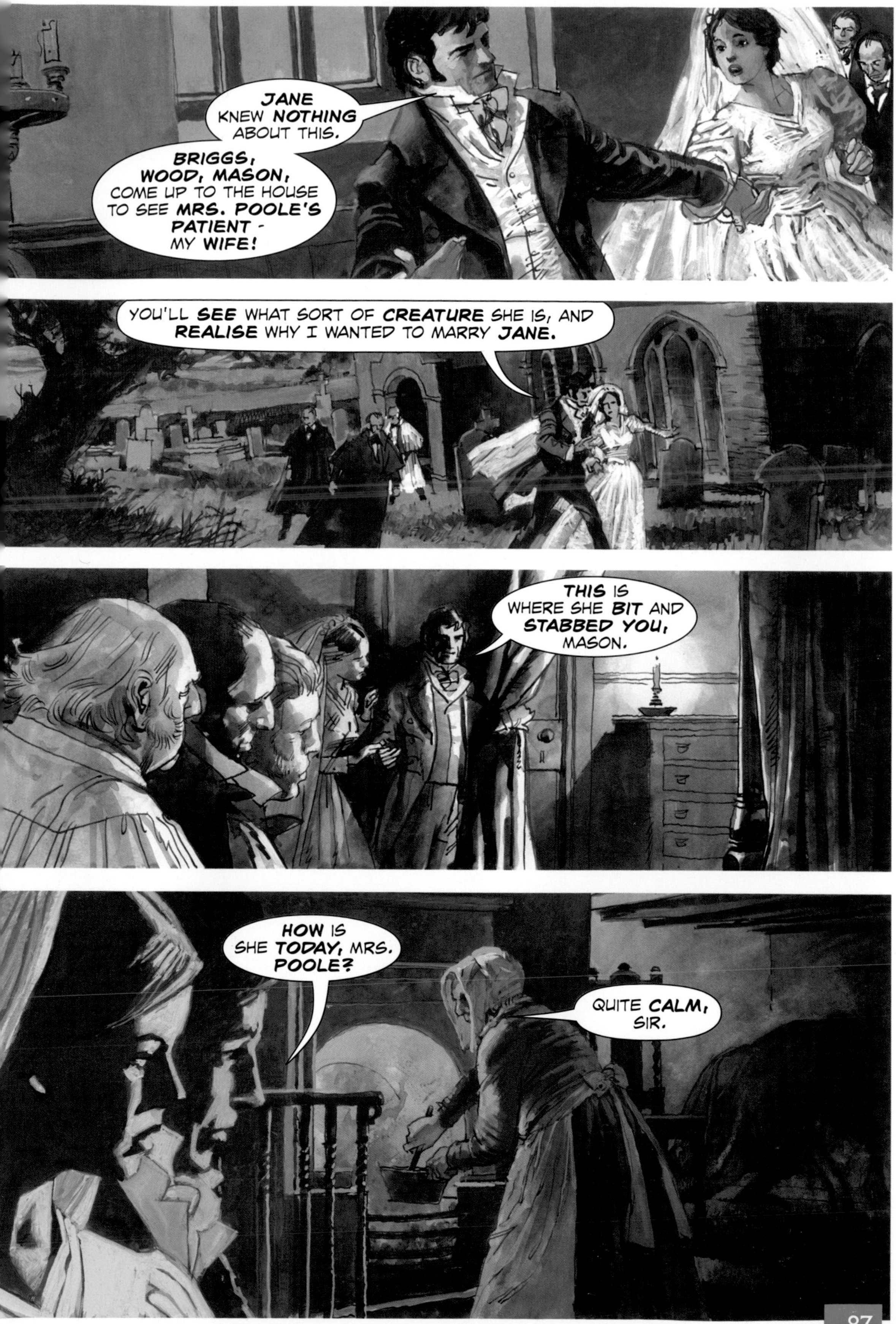
JANE KNEW NOTHING ABOUT THIS.
BRIGGS, WOOD, MASON, COME UP TO THE HOUSE TO SEE MRS. POOLE'S PATIENT - MY WIFE!
YOU'LL SEE WHAT SORT OF CREATURE SHE IS, AND REALISE WHY I WANTED TO MARRY JANE.
THIS IS WHERE SHE BIT AND STABBED YOU, MASON.
HOW IS SHE TODAY, MRS. POOLE?
QUITE CALM, SIR.

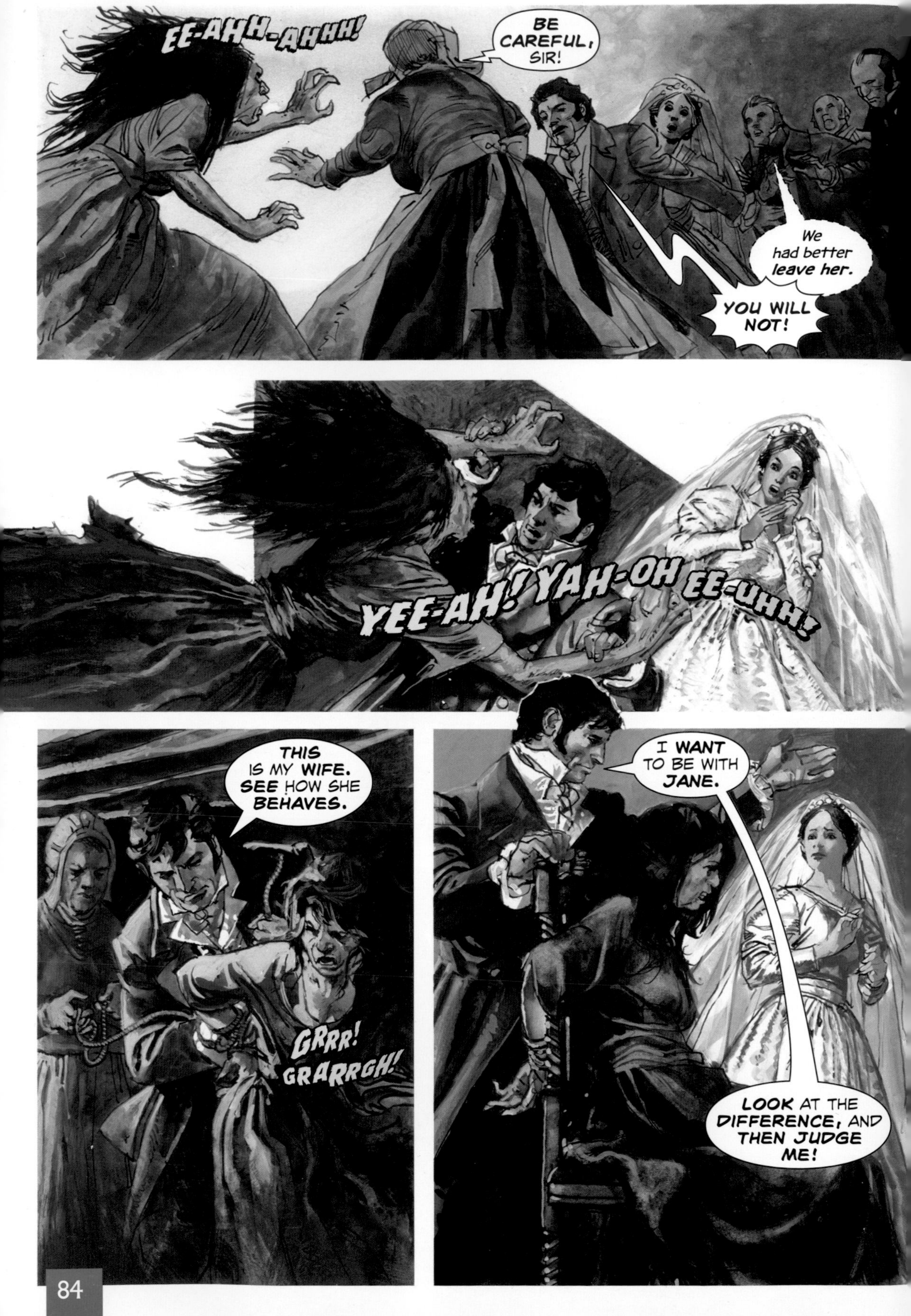
EE-AHH-AHHH!
BE CAREFUL, SIR!
We had better leave her.
YOU WILL NOT!
YEE-AH! YAH-OH EE-UHH!
THIS IS MY WIFE. SEE HOW SHE BEHAVES.
GRRR! GRARRGH!
I WANT TO BE WITH JANE.
LOOK AT THE DIFFERENCE, AND THEN JUDGE ME!

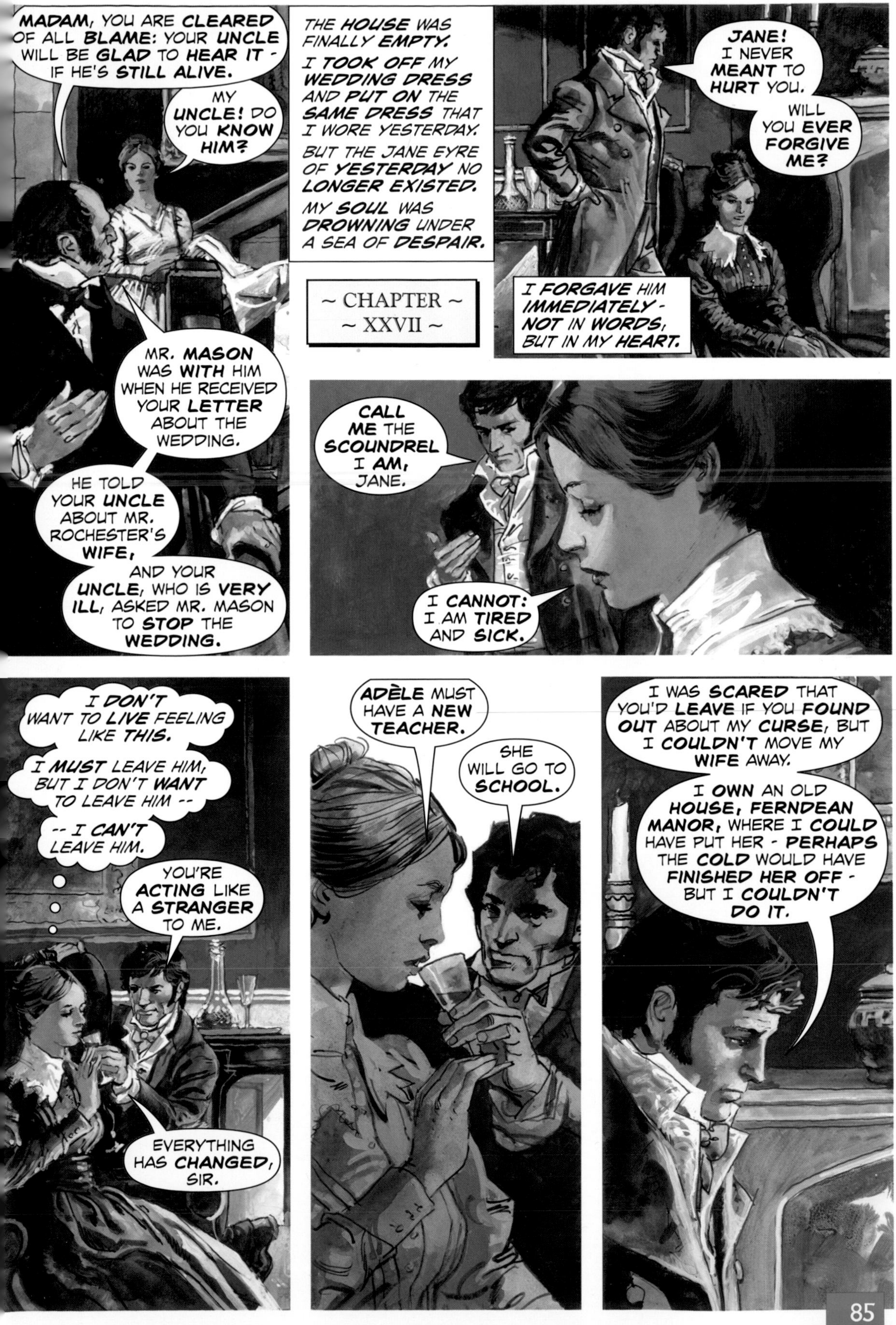
MADAM, YOU ARE CLEARED OF ALL BLAME: YOUR UNCLE WILL BE GLAD TO HEAR IT - IF HE'S STILL ALIVE.
MY UNCLE! DO YOU KNOW HIM?
MR. MASON WAS WITH HIM WHEN HE RECEIVED YOUR LETTER ABOUT THE WEDDING.
HE TOLD YOUR UNCLE ABOUT MR. ROCHESTER'S WIFE,
AND YOUR UNCLE, WHO IS VERY ILL, ASKED MR. MASON TO STOP THE WEDDING.
THE HOUSE WAS FINALLY EMPTY.
I TOOK OFF MY WEDDING DRESS AND PUT ON THE SAME DRESS THAT I WORE YESTERDAY.
BUT THE JANE EYRE OF YESTERDAY NO LONGER EXISTED.
MY SOUL WAS DROWNING UNDER A SEA OF DESPAIR.
~ CHAPTER ~
~ XXVII ~
JANE! I NEVER MEANT TO HURT YOU.
WILL YOU EVER FORGIVE ME?
I FORGAVE HIM IMMEDIATELY - NOT IN WORDS, BUT IN MY HEART.
CALL ME THE SCOUNDREL I AM, JANE.
I CANNOT: I AM TIRED AND SICK.
I DON'T WANT TO LIVE FEELING LIKE THIS.
I MUST LEAVE HIM, BUT I DON'T WANT TO LEAVE HIM --
-- I CAN'T LEAVE HIM.
YOU'RE ACTING LIKE A STRANGER TO ME.
EVERYTHING HAS CHANGED, SIR.
ADÈLE MUST HAVE A NEW TEACHER.
SHE WILL GO TO SCHOOL.
I WAS SCARED THAT YOU'D LEAVE IF YOU FOUND OUT ABOUT MY CURSE, BUT I COULDN'T MOVE MY WIFE AWAY.
I OWN AN OLD HOUSE, FERNDEAN MANOR, WHERE I COULD HAVE PUT HER - PERHAPS THE COLD WOULD HAVE FINISHED HER OFF - BUT I COULDN'T DO IT.

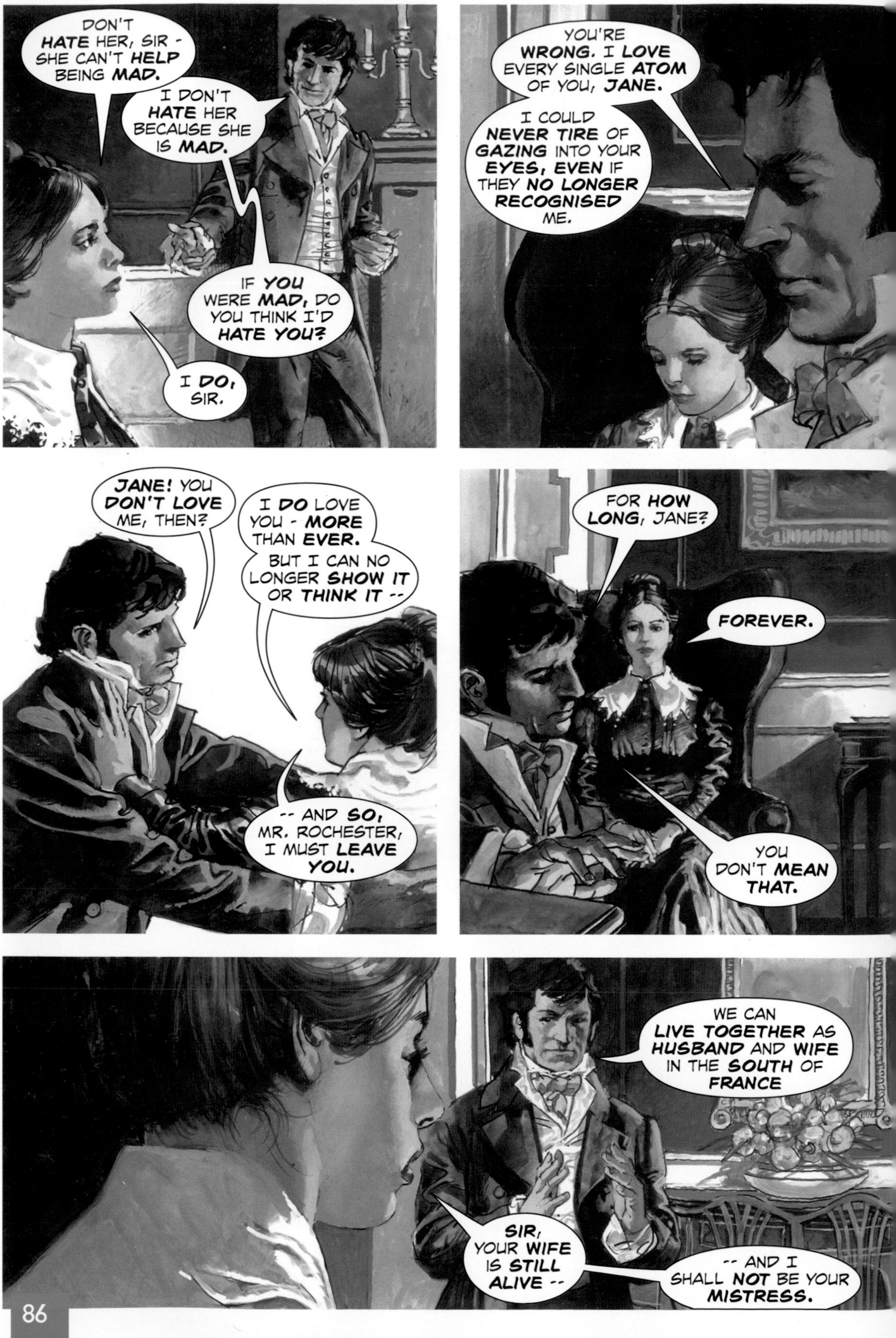
DON'T HATE HER, SIR - SHE CAN'T HELP BEING MAD.
I DON'T HATE HER BECAUSE SHE IS MAD.
IF YOU WERE MAD, DO YOU THINK I'D HATE YOU?
I DO, SIR.
YOU'RE WRONG. I LOVE EVERY SINGLE ATOM OF YOU, JANE.
I COULD NEVER TIRE OF GAZING INTO YOUR EYES, EVEN IF THEY NO LONGER RECOGNISED ME.
JANE! YOU DON'T LOVE ME, THEN?
I DO LOVE YOU - MORE THAN EVER.
BUT I CAN NO LONGER SHOW IT OR THINK IT --
-- AND SO, MR. ROCHESTER, I MUST LEAVE YOU.
FOR HOW LONG, JANE?
FOREVER.
YOU DON'T MEAN THAT.
WE CAN LIVE TOGETHER AS HUSBAND AND WIFE IN THE SOUTH OF FRANCE
SIR, YOUR WIFE IS STILL ALIVE --
-- AND I SHALL NOT BE YOUR MISTRESS.

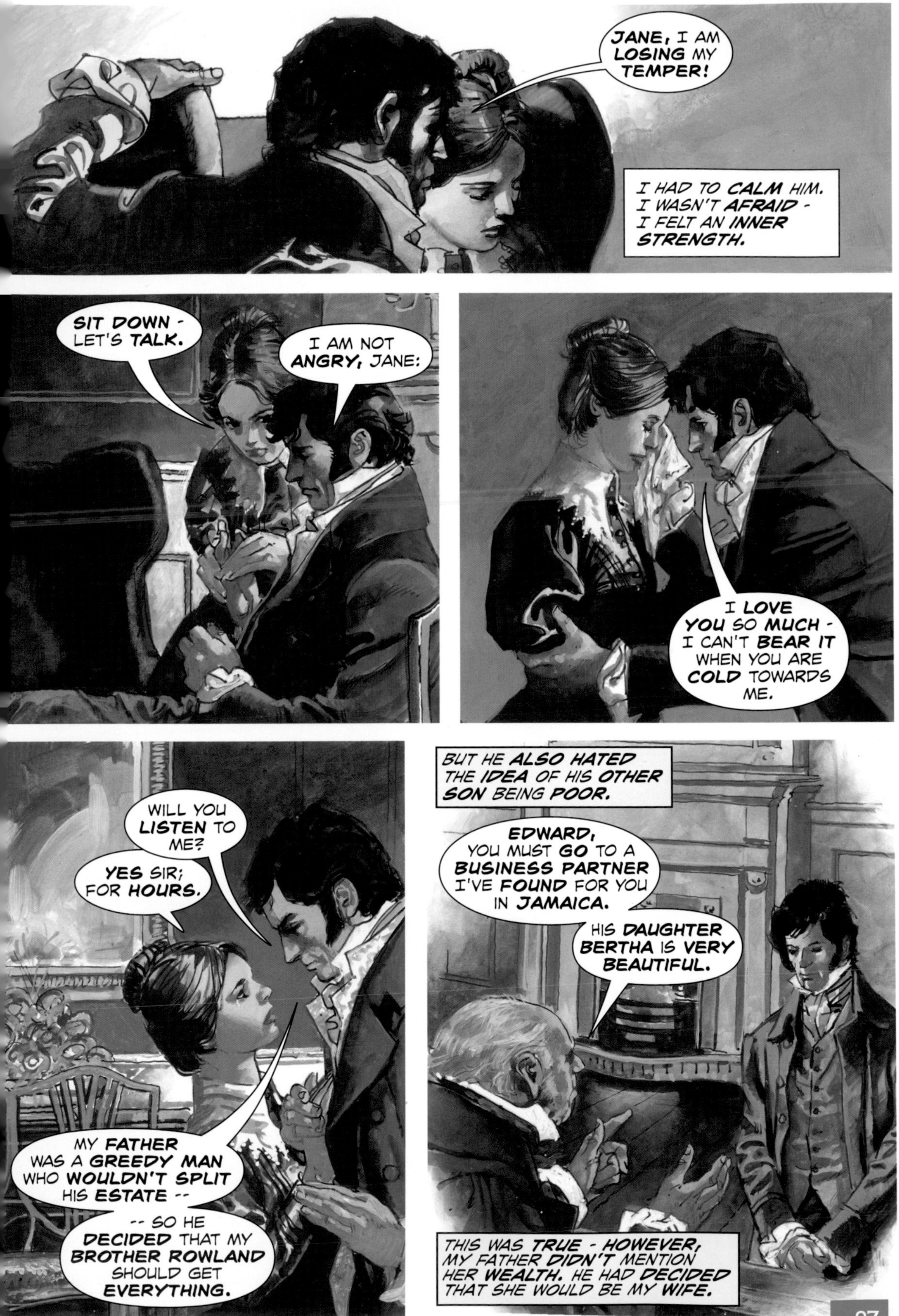
JANE, I AM LOSING MY TEMPER!
I HAD TO CALM HIM. I WASN'T AFRAID - I FELT AN INNER STRENGTH.
SIT DOWN - LET'S TALK.
I AM NOT ANGRY, JANE:
I LOVE YOU SO MUCH - I CAN'T BEAR IT WHEN YOU ARE COLD TOWARDS ME.
WILL YOU LISTEN TO ME?
YES SIR; FOR HOURS.
MY FATHER WAS A GREEDY MAN WHO WOULDN'T SPLIT HIS ESTATE --
-- SO HE DECIDED THAT MY BROTHER ROWLAND SHOULD GET EVERYTHING.
BUT HE ALSO HATED THE IDEA OF HIS OTHER SON BEING POOR.
EDWARD, YOU MUST GO TO A BUSINESS PARTNER I'VE FOUND FOR YOU IN JAMAICA.
HIS DAUGHTER BERTHA IS VERY BEAUTIFUL.
THIS WAS TRUE - HOWEVER, MY FATHER DIDN'T MENTION HER WEALTH. HE HAD DECIDED THAT SHE WOULD BE MY WIFE.

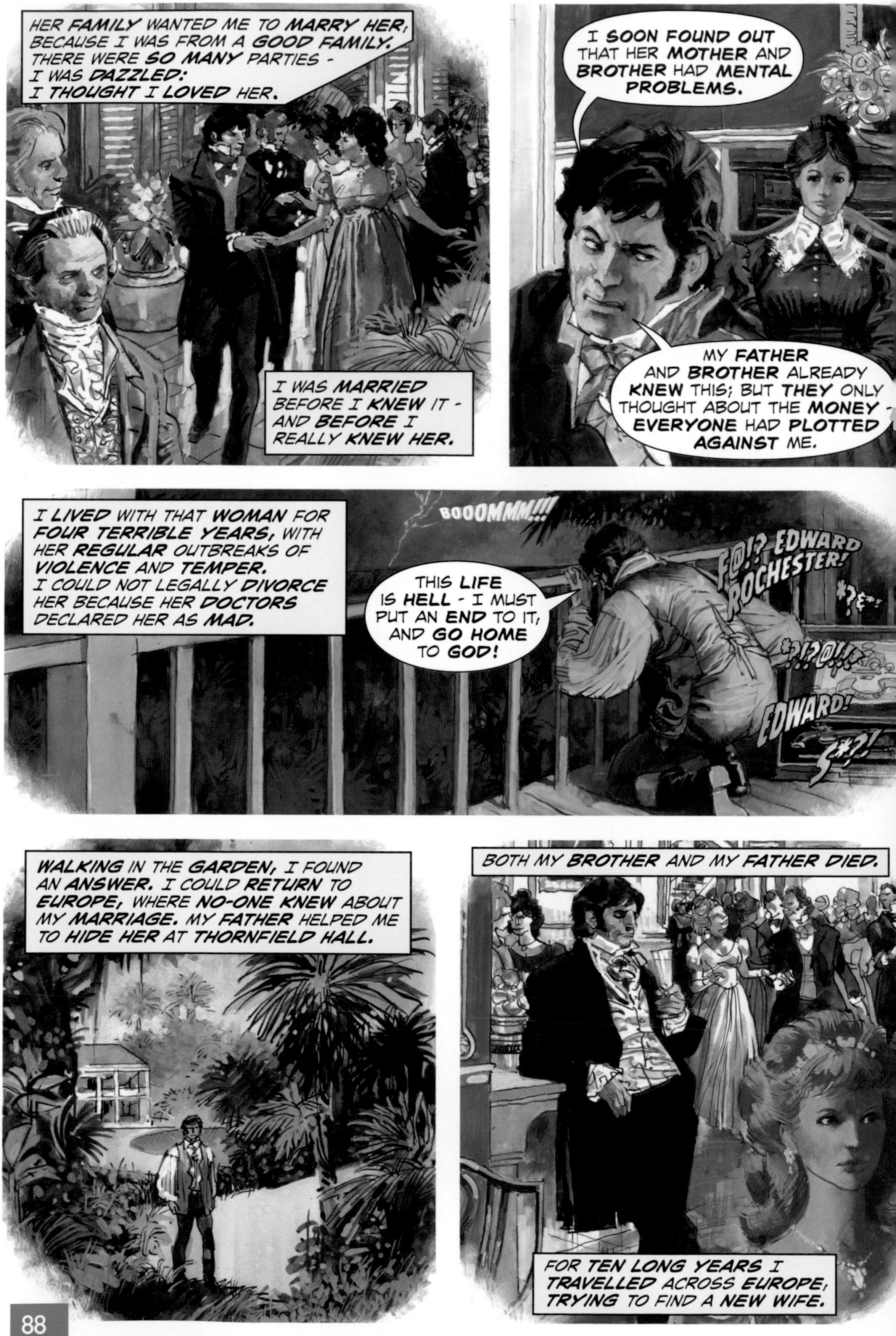
HER FAMILY WANTED ME TO MARRY HER, BECAUSE I WAS FROM A GOOD FAMILY. THERE WERE SO MANY PARTIES - I WAS DAZZLED: I THOUGHT I LOVED HER.
I WAS MARRIED BEFORE I KNEW IT - AND BEFORE I REALLY KNEW HER.
I SOON FOUND OUT THAT HER MOTHER AND BROTHER HAD MENTAL PROBLEMS.
MY FATHER AND BROTHER ALREADY KNEW THIS; BUT THEY ONLY THOUGHT ABOUT THE MONEY - EVERYONE HAD PLOTTED AGAINST ME.
I LIVED WITH THAT WOMAN FOR FOUR TERRIBLE YEARS, WITH HER REGULAR OUTBREAKS OF VIOLENCE AND TEMPER. I COULD NOT LEGALLY DIVORCE HER BECAUSE HER DOCTORS DECLARED HER AS MAD.
BOOOMMM!!!
THIS LIFE IS HELL - I MUST PUT AN END TO IT, AND GO HOME TO GOD!
F@!? EDWARD ROCHESTER!
EDWARD!
WALKING IN THE GARDEN, I FOUND AN ANSWER. I COULD RETURN TO EUROPE, WHERE NO-ONE KNEW ABOUT MY MARRIAGE. MY FATHER HELPED ME TO HIDE HER AT THORNFIELD HALL.
BOTH MY BROTHER AND MY FATHER DIED.
FOR TEN LONG YEARS I TRAVELLED ACROSS EUROPE, TRYING TO FIND A NEW WIFE.

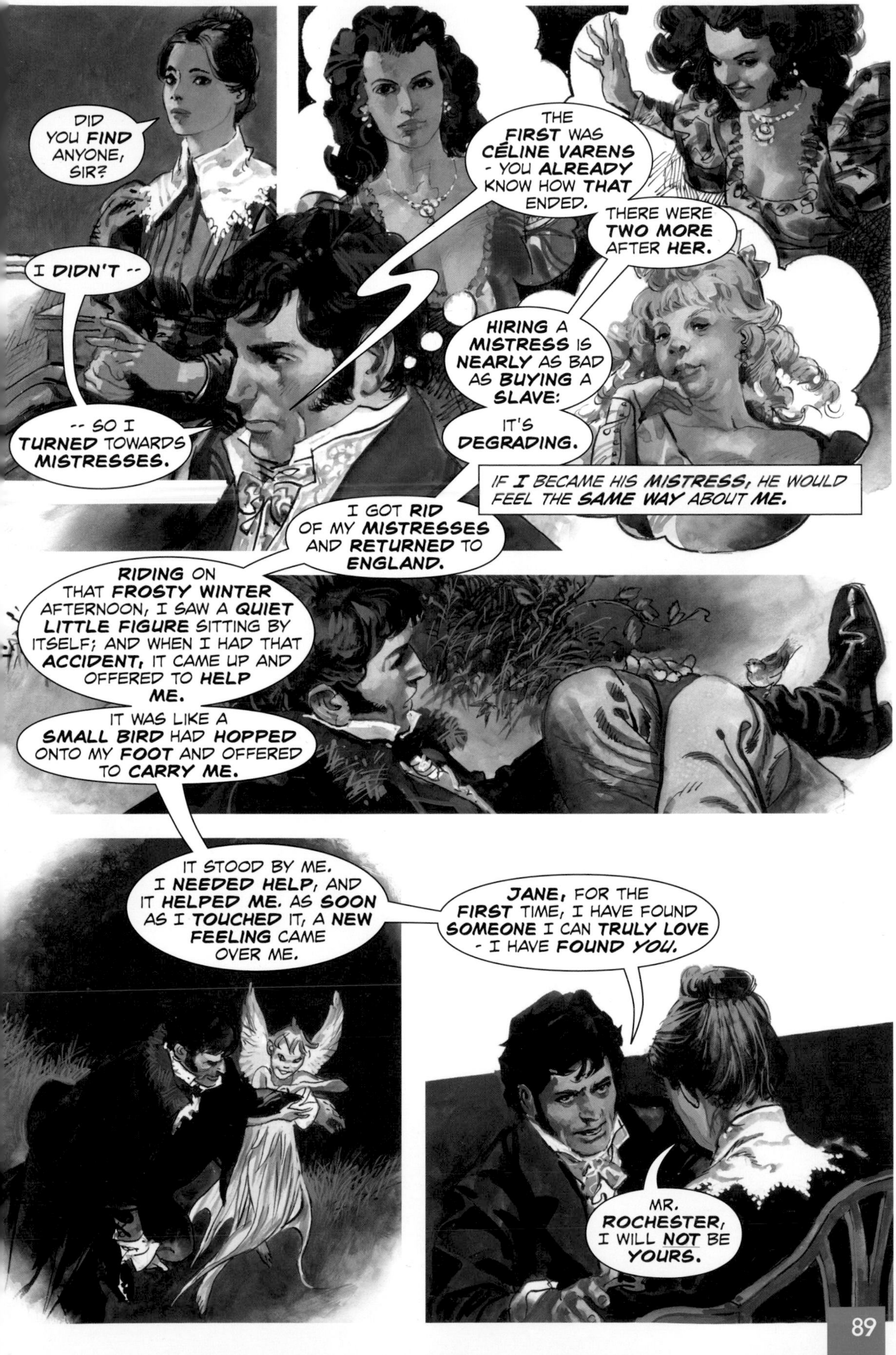
DID YOU FIND ANYONE, SIR?
I DIDN'T --
-- SO I TURNED TOWARDS MISTRESSES.
THE FIRST WAS CÉLINE VARENS - YOU ALREADY KNOW HOW THAT ENDED.
THERE WERE TWO MORE AFTER HER.
HIRING A MISTRESS IS NEARLY AS BAD AS BUYING A SLAVE:
IT'S DEGRADING.
IF I BECAME HIS MISTRESS, HE WOULD FEEL THE SAME WAY ABOUT ME.
I GOT RID OF MY MISTRESSES AND RETURNED TO ENGLAND.
RIDING ON THAT FROSTY WINTER AFTERNOON, I SAW A QUIET LITTLE FIGURE SITTING BY ITSELF; AND WHEN I HAD THAT ACCIDENT, IT CAME UP AND OFFERED TO HELP ME.
IT WAS LIKE A SMALL BIRD HAD HOPPED ONTO MY FOOT AND OFFERED TO CARRY ME.
IT STOOD BY ME. I NEEDED HELP, AND IT HELPED ME. AS SOON AS I TOUCHED IT, A NEW FEELING CAME OVER ME.
JANE, FOR THE FIRST TIME, I HAVE FOUND SOMEONE I CAN TRULY LOVE - I HAVE FOUND YOU.
MR. ROCHESTER, I WILL NOT BE YOURS.

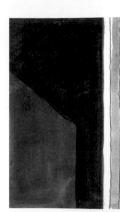

JANE, ARE WE TO PART?

WE ARE.

BUT JANE - IT WOULD **NOT** BE WICKED TO LOVE ME.

IT WOULD BE **WICKED** TO **OBEY** YOU.

WHAT SHALL I DO, JANE?

DO AS I DO: TRUST IN **GOD**.

NO MATTER WHAT I DO, I CAN'T HAVE YOU.

YOU WILL NOT **FREELY** BE **MINE** - AND IF I **FORCE** YOU, I DON'T GET YOUR **SPIRIT** -

I GET **NOTHING**.

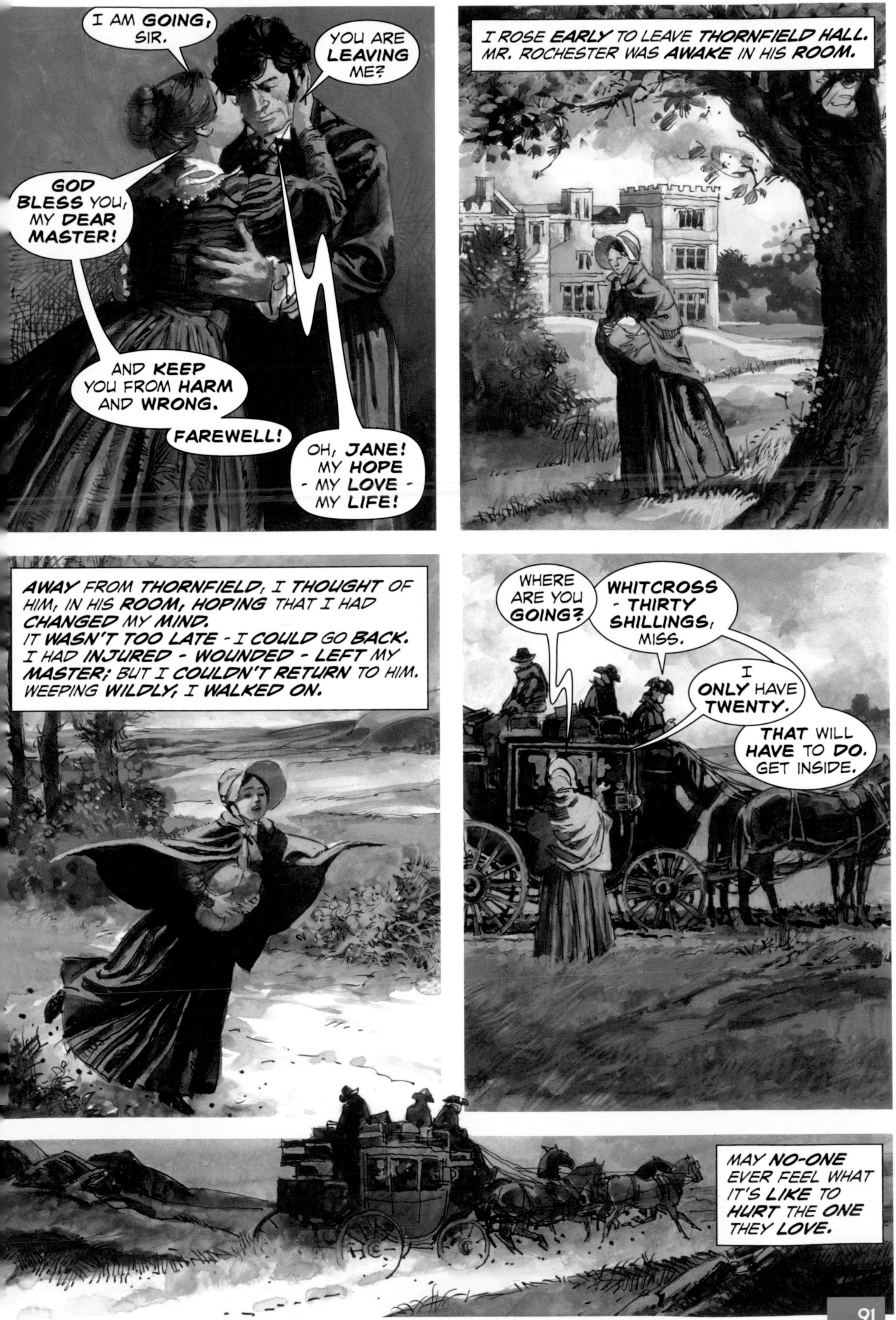
I AM GOING, SIR.
YOU ARE LEAVING ME?
GOD BLESS YOU, MY DEAR MASTER!
AND KEEP YOU FROM HARM AND WRONG.
FAREWELL!
OH, JANE! MY HOPE - MY LOVE - MY LIFE!
I ROSE EARLY TO LEAVE THORNFIELD HALL. MR. ROCHESTER WAS AWAKE IN HIS ROOM.
AWAY FROM THORNFIELD, I THOUGHT OF HIM, IN HIS ROOM, HOPING THAT I HAD CHANGED MY MIND. IT WASN'T TOO LATE - I COULD GO BACK. I HAD INJURED - WOUNDED - LEFT MY MASTER; BUT I COULDN'T RETURN TO HIM. WEEPING WILDLY, I WALKED ON.
WHERE ARE YOU GOING?
WHITCROSS - THIRTY SHILLINGS, MISS.
I ONLY HAVE TWENTY.
THAT WILL HAVE TO DO. GET INSIDE.
MAY NO-ONE EVER FEEL WHAT IT'S LIKE TO HURT THE ONE THEY LOVE.

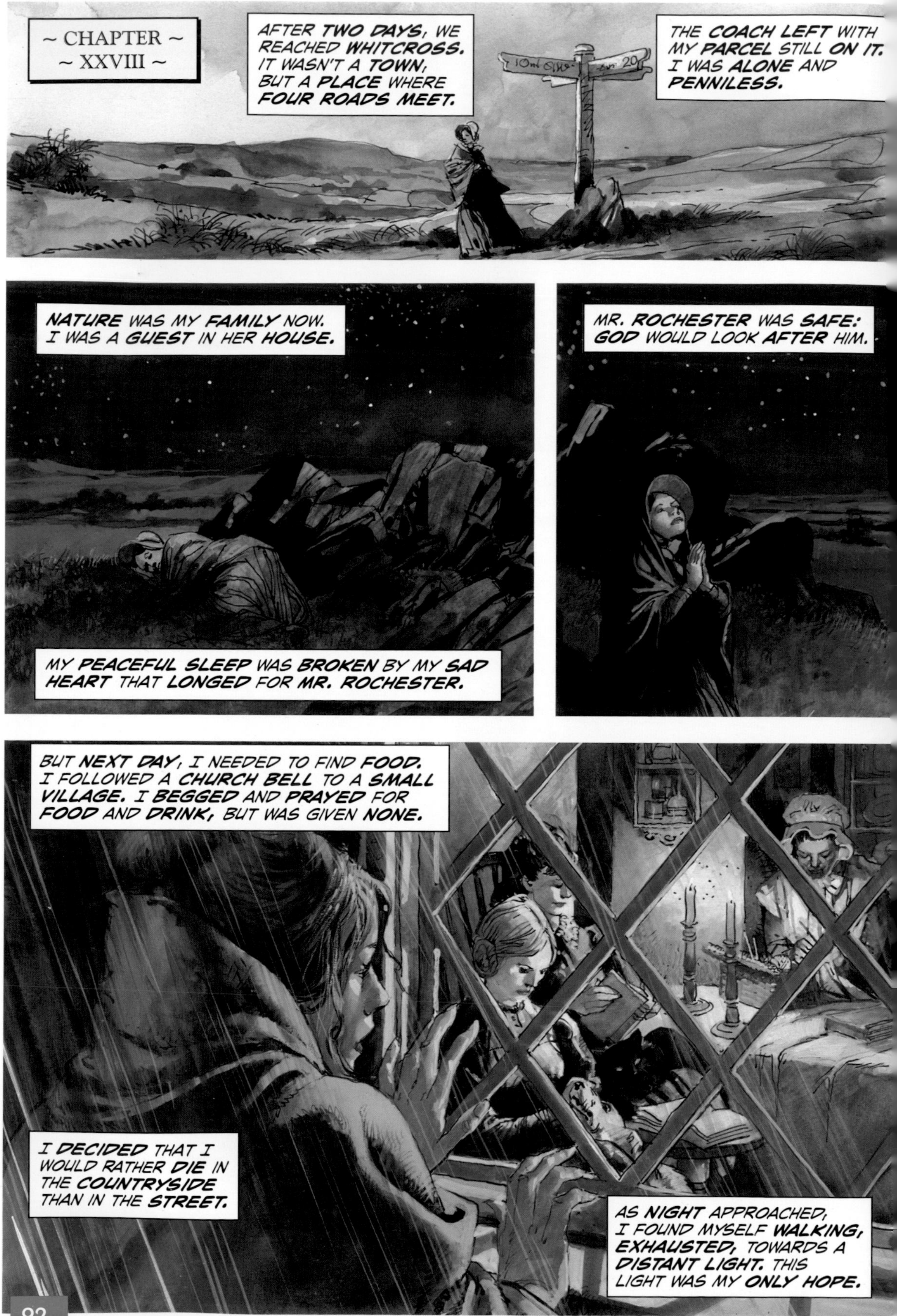
~ CHAPTER ~
~ XXVIII ~
AFTER TWO DAYS, WE REACHED WHITCROSS. IT WASN'T A TOWN, BUT A PLACE WHERE FOUR ROADS MEET.
THE COACH LEFT WITH MY PARCEL STILL ON IT. I WAS ALONE AND PENNILESS.
NATURE WAS MY FAMILY NOW. I WAS A GUEST IN HER HOUSE.
MY PEACEFUL SLEEP WAS BROKEN BY MY SAD HEART THAT LONGED FOR MR. ROCHESTER.
MR. ROCHESTER WAS SAFE: GOD WOULD LOOK AFTER HIM.
BUT NEXT DAY, I NEEDED TO FIND FOOD. I FOLLOWED A CHURCH BELL TO A SMALL VILLAGE. I BEGGED AND PRAYED FOR FOOD AND DRINK, BUT WAS GIVEN NONE.
I DECIDED THAT I WOULD RATHER DIE IN THE COUNTRYSIDE THAN IN THE STREET.
AS NIGHT APPROACHED, I FOUND MYSELF WALKING, EXHAUSTED, TOWARDS A DISTANT LIGHT. THIS LIGHT WAS MY ONLY HOPE.

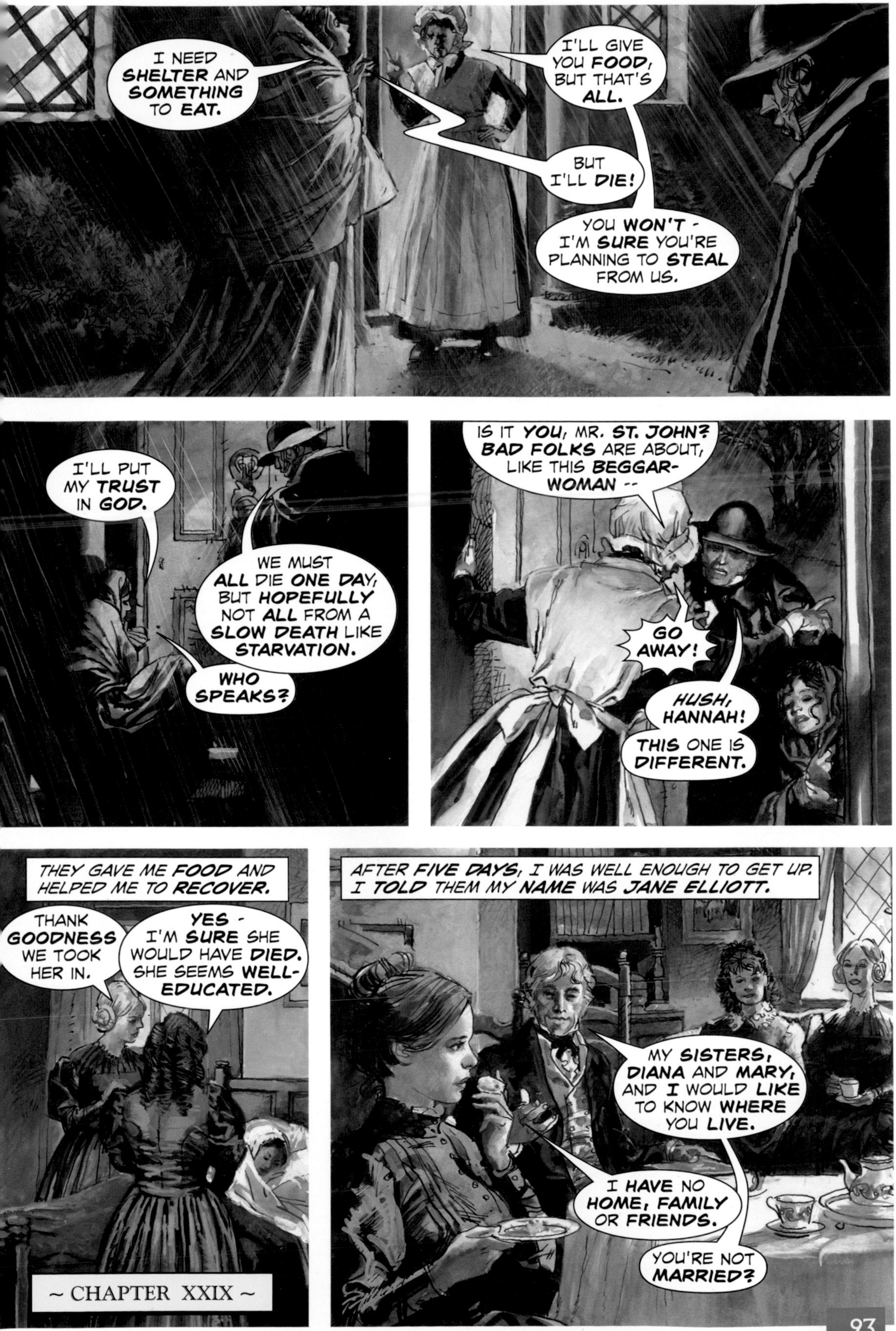
I NEED SHELTER AND SOMETHING TO EAT.
I'LL GIVE YOU FOOD, BUT THAT'S ALL.
BUT I'LL DIE!
YOU WON'T - I'M SURE YOU'RE PLANNING TO STEAL FROM US.
I'LL PUT MY TRUST IN GOD.
WE MUST ALL DIE ONE DAY, BUT HOPEFULLY NOT ALL FROM A SLOW DEATH LIKE STARVATION.
WHO SPEAKS?
IS IT YOU, MR. ST. JOHN? BAD FOLKS ARE ABOUT, LIKE THIS BEGGAR-WOMAN --
GO AWAY!
HUSH, HANNAH!
THIS ONE IS DIFFERENT.
THEY GAVE ME FOOD AND HELPED ME TO RECOVER.
THANK GOODNESS WE TOOK HER IN.
YES - I'M SURE SHE WOULD HAVE DIED. SHE SEEMS WELL-EDUCATED.
~ CHAPTER XXIX ~
AFTER FIVE DAYS, I WAS WELL ENOUGH TO GET UP. I TOLD THEM MY NAME WAS JANE ELLIOTT.
MY SISTERS, DIANA AND MARY, AND I WOULD LIKE TO KNOW WHERE YOU LIVE.
I HAVE NO HOME, FAMILY OR FRIENDS.
YOU'RE NOT MARRIED?

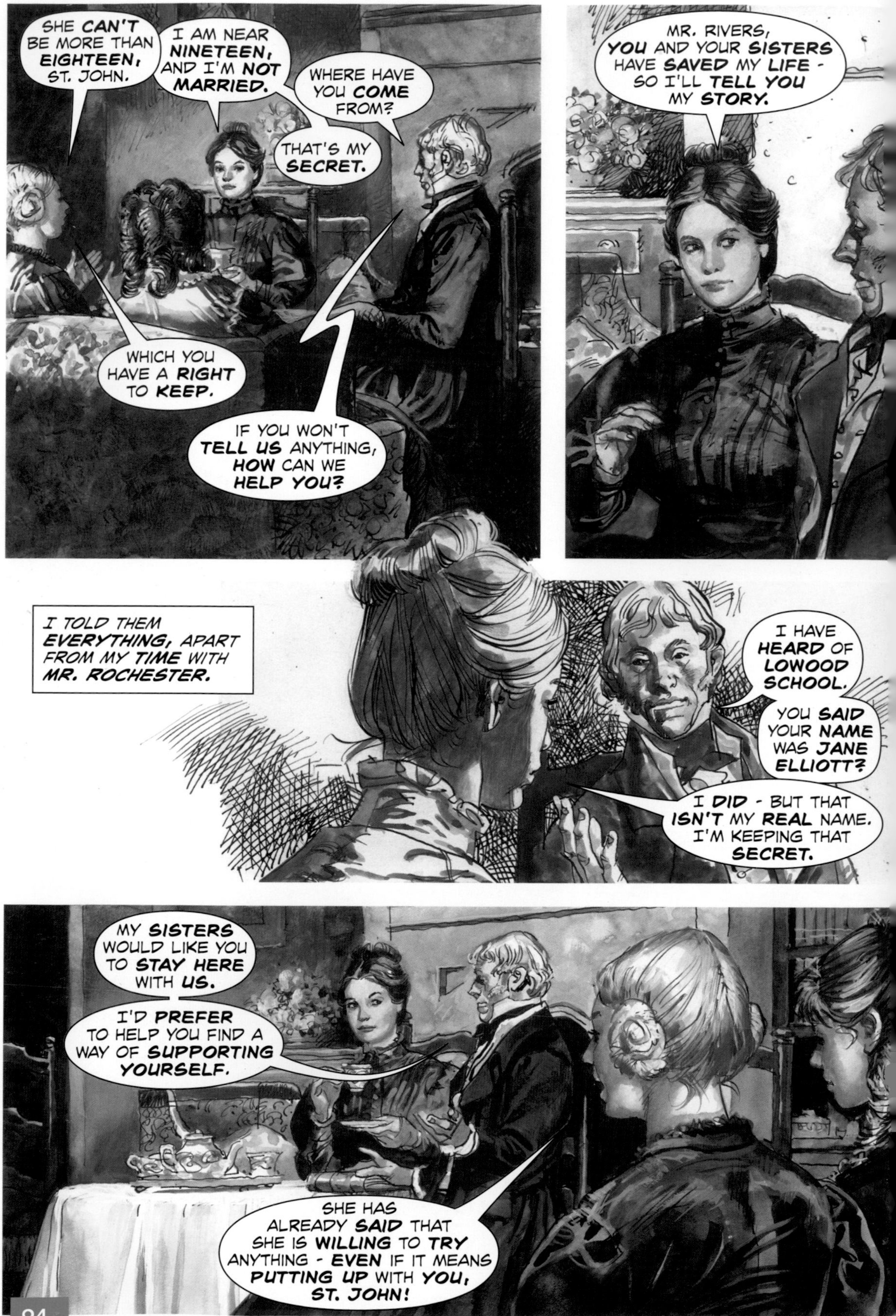
SHE CAN'T BE MORE THAN EIGHTEEN, ST. JOHN.
I AM NEAR NINETEEN, AND I'M NOT MARRIED.
WHERE HAVE YOU COME FROM?
THAT'S MY SECRET.
WHICH YOU HAVE A RIGHT TO KEEP.
IF YOU WON'T TELL US ANYTHING, HOW CAN WE HELP YOU?
MR. RIVERS, YOU AND YOUR SISTERS HAVE SAVED MY LIFE - SO I'LL TELL YOU MY STORY.
I TOLD THEM EVERYTHING, APART FROM MY TIME WITH MR. ROCHESTER.
I HAVE HEARD OF LOWOOD SCHOOL.
YOU SAID YOUR NAME WAS JANE ELLIOTT?
I DID - BUT THAT ISN'T MY REAL NAME. I'M KEEPING THAT SECRET.
MY SISTERS WOULD LIKE YOU TO STAY HERE WITH US.
I'D PREFER TO HELP YOU FIND A WAY OF SUPPORTING YOURSELF.
SHE HAS ALREADY SAID THAT SHE IS WILLING TO TRY ANYTHING - EVEN IF IT MEANS PUTTING UP WITH YOU, ST. JOHN!

~ CHAPTER XXX ~

I FELT *MUCH BETTER* NOW, AND *ENJOYED* THE *COMPANY* OF *DIANA* AND *MARY.*

THEY *LENT* ME *BOOKS* THAT I *EAGERLY* READ; AND WE ENJOYED DISCUSSING THEM IN THE *EVENINGS.*

WE HAD *SO MUCH* IN *COMMON.*

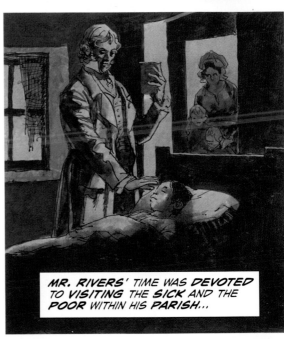

MR. RIVERS' TIME WAS *DEVOTED* TO *VISITING* THE *SICK* AND THE *POOR* WITHIN HIS *PARISH...*

...AS WELL AS *PREACHING* IN HIS *OWN* CHURCH - BUT HIS *SERMONS* MADE ME FEEL *SAD* RATHER THAN *HAPPY.*

MARY AND DIANA WILL SOON *LEAVE HERE* TO WORK AS *GOVERNESSES* FOR *POMPOUS FAMILIES* WHO WON'T *APPRECIATE* THEM FOR THE PEOPLE THEY *ARE.*

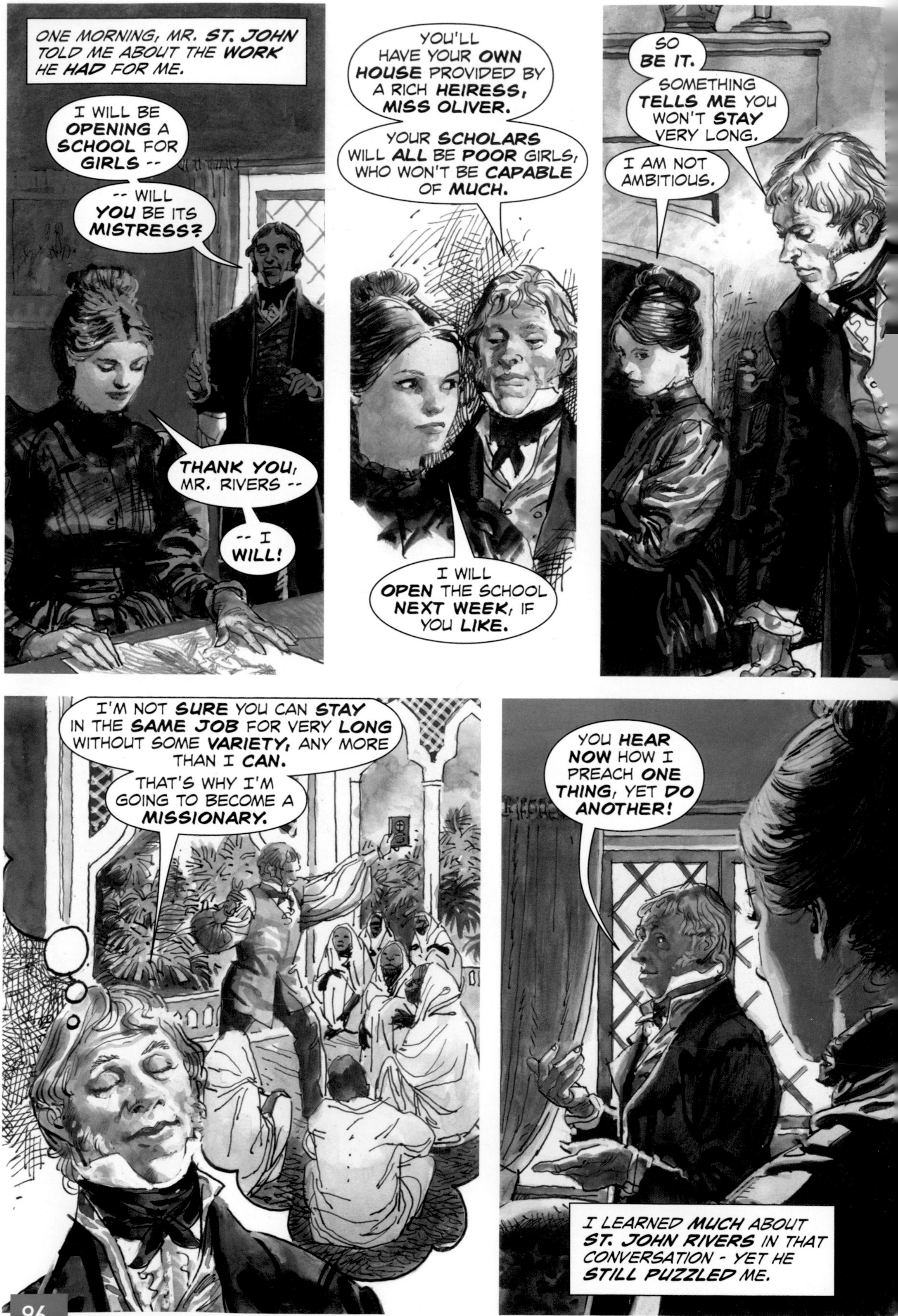
ONE MORNING, MR. ST. JOHN TOLD ME ABOUT THE WORK HE HAD FOR ME.
I WILL BE OPENING A SCHOOL FOR GIRLS --
-- WILL YOU BE ITS MISTRESS?
THANK YOU, MR. RIVERS --
-- I WILL!
YOU'LL HAVE YOUR OWN HOUSE PROVIDED BY A RICH HEIRESS, MISS OLIVER.
YOUR SCHOLARS WILL ALL BE POOR GIRLS, WHO WON'T BE CAPABLE OF MUCH.
I WILL OPEN THE SCHOOL NEXT WEEK, IF YOU LIKE.
SO BE IT.
SOMETHING TELLS ME YOU WON'T STAY VERY LONG.
I AM NOT AMBITIOUS.
I'M NOT SURE YOU CAN STAY IN THE SAME JOB FOR VERY LONG WITHOUT SOME VARIETY, ANY MORE THAN I CAN.
THAT'S WHY I'M GOING TO BECOME A MISSIONARY.
YOU HEAR NOW HOW I PREACH ONE THING, YET DO ANOTHER!
I LEARNED MUCH ABOUT ST. JOHN RIVERS IN THAT CONVERSATION - YET HE STILL PUZZLED ME.

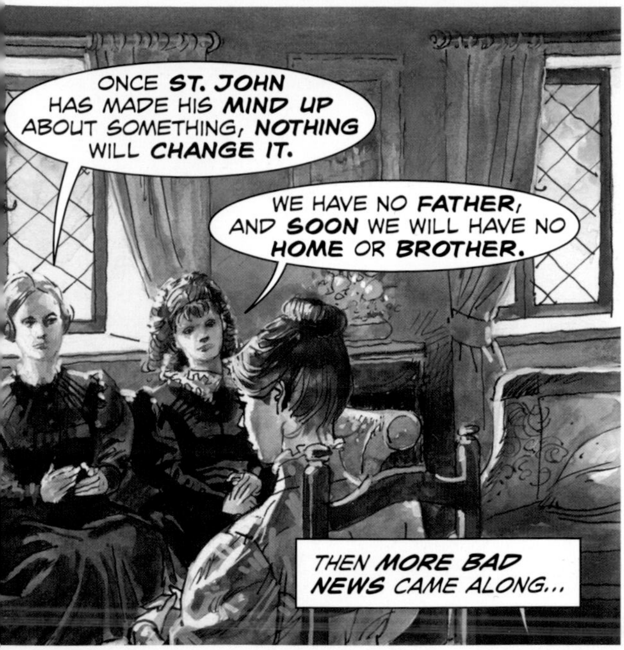
ONCE ST. JOHN HAS MADE HIS MIND UP ABOUT SOMETHING, NOTHING WILL CHANGE IT.
WE HAVE NO FATHER, AND SOON WE WILL HAVE NO HOME OR BROTHER.
THEN MORE BAD NEWS CAME ALONG...

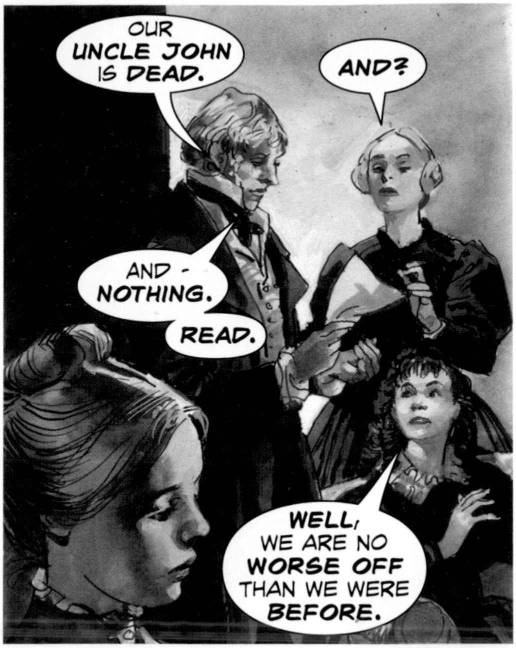
OUR UNCLE JOHN IS DEAD.
AND?
AND - NOTHING.
READ.
WELL, WE ARE NO WORSE OFF THAN WE WERE BEFORE.

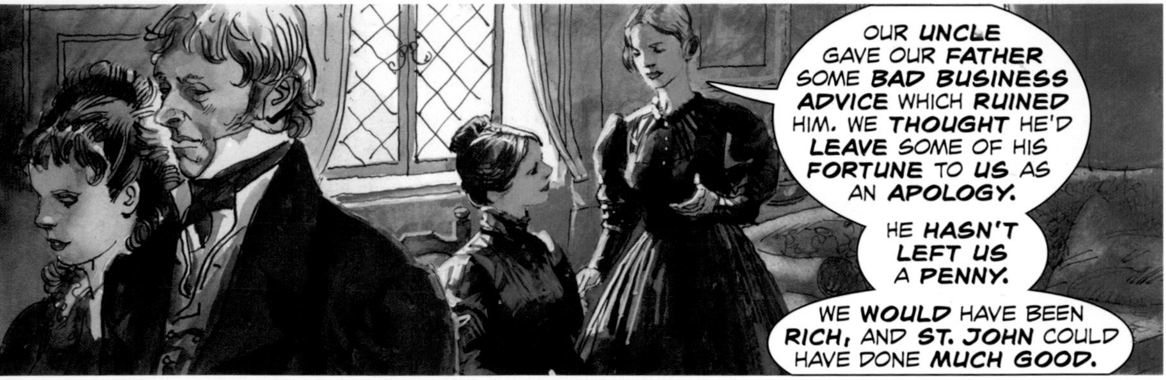
OUR UNCLE GAVE OUR FATHER SOME BAD BUSINESS ADVICE WHICH RUINED HIM. WE THOUGHT HE'D LEAVE SOME OF HIS FORTUNE TO US AS AN APOLOGY.
HE HASN'T LEFT US A PENNY.
WE WOULD HAVE BEEN RICH, AND ST. JOHN COULD HAVE DONE MUCH GOOD.

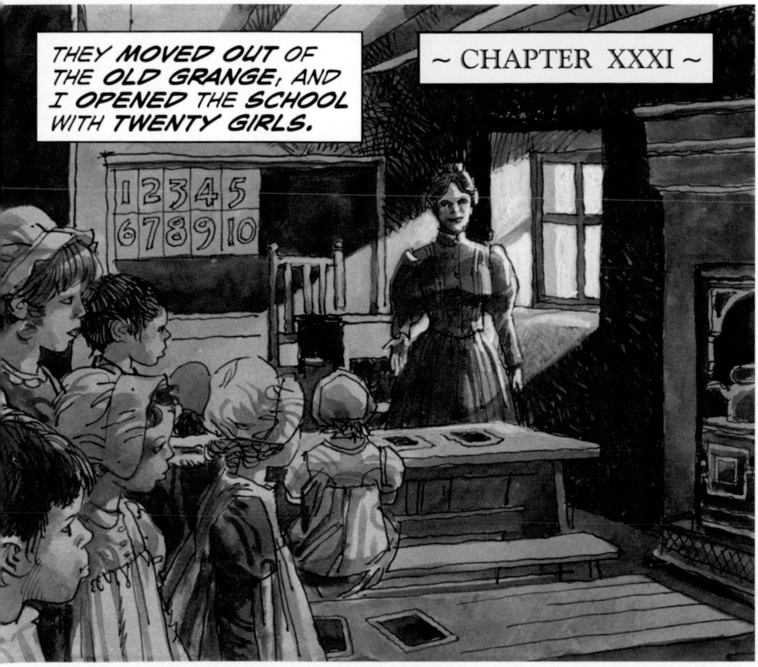
THEY MOVED OUT OF THE OLD GRANGE, AND I OPENED THE SCHOOL WITH TWENTY GIRLS.
~ CHAPTER XXXI ~
12345
678910

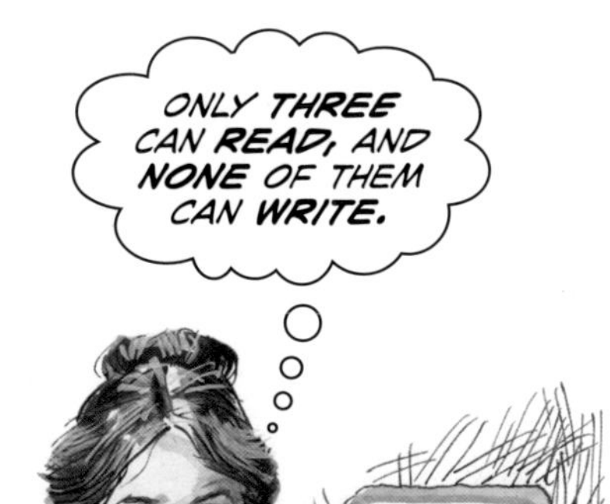
ONLY THREE CAN READ, AND NONE OF THEM CAN WRITE.
A

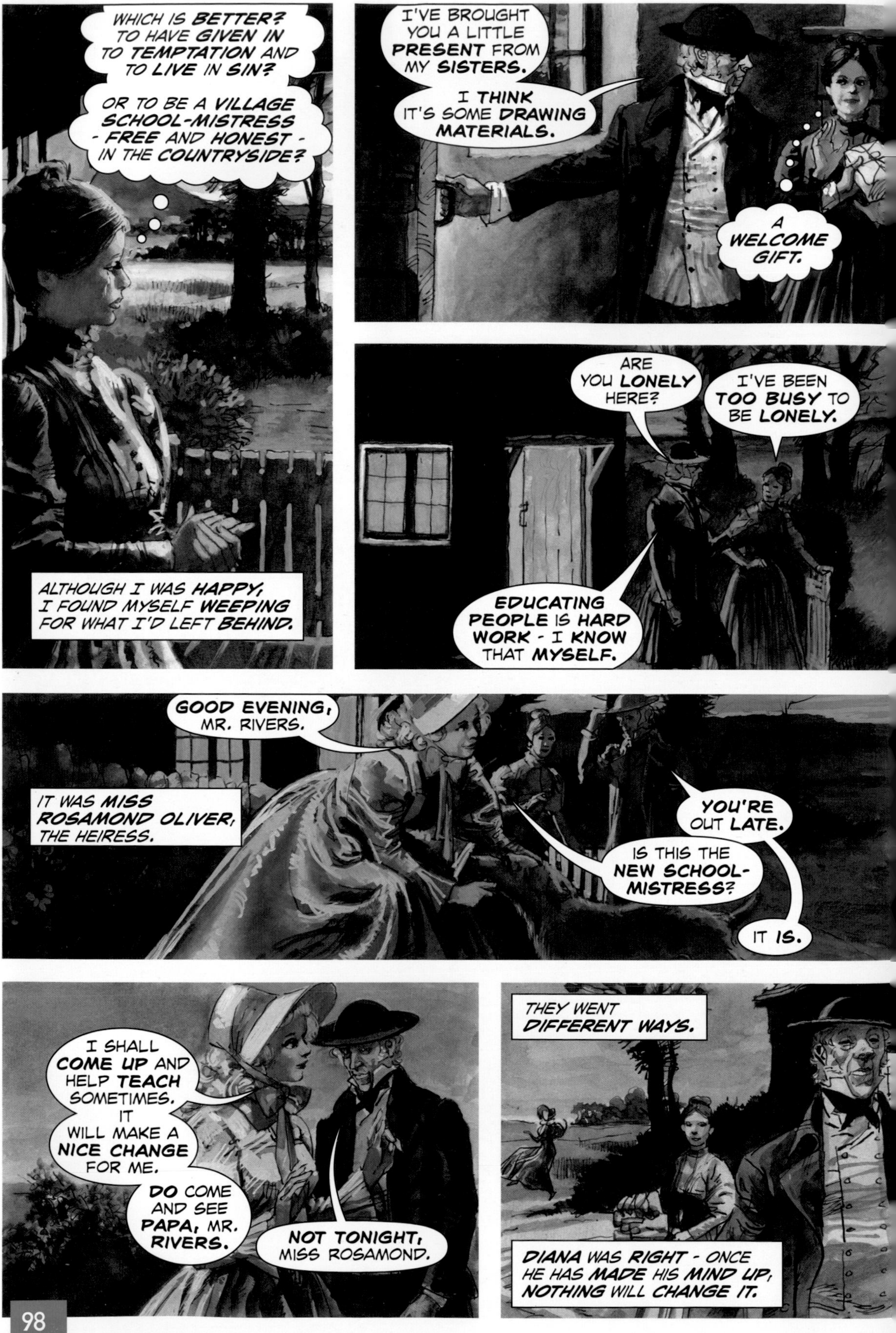
WHICH IS BETTER? TO HAVE GIVEN IN TO TEMPTATION AND TO LIVE IN SIN?
OR TO BE A VILLAGE SCHOOL-MISTRESS - FREE AND HONEST - IN THE COUNTRYSIDE?
ALTHOUGH I WAS HAPPY, I FOUND MYSELF WEEPING FOR WHAT I'D LEFT BEHIND.
I'VE BROUGHT YOU A LITTLE PRESENT FROM MY SISTERS.
I THINK IT'S SOME DRAWING MATERIALS.
A WELCOME GIFT.
ARE YOU LONELY HERE?
I'VE BEEN TOO BUSY TO BE LONELY.
EDUCATING PEOPLE IS HARD WORK - I KNOW THAT MYSELF.
GOOD EVENING, MR. RIVERS.
IT WAS MISS ROSAMOND OLIVER, THE HEIRESS.
YOU'RE OUT LATE.
IS THIS THE NEW SCHOOL-MISTRESS?
IT IS.
I SHALL COME UP AND HELP TEACH SOMETIMES. IT WILL MAKE A NICE CHANGE FOR ME.
DO COME AND SEE PAPA, MR. RIVERS.
NOT TONIGHT, MISS ROSAMOND.
THEY WENT DIFFERENT WAYS.
DIANA WAS RIGHT - ONCE HE HAS MADE HIS MIND UP, NOTHING WILL CHANGE IT.

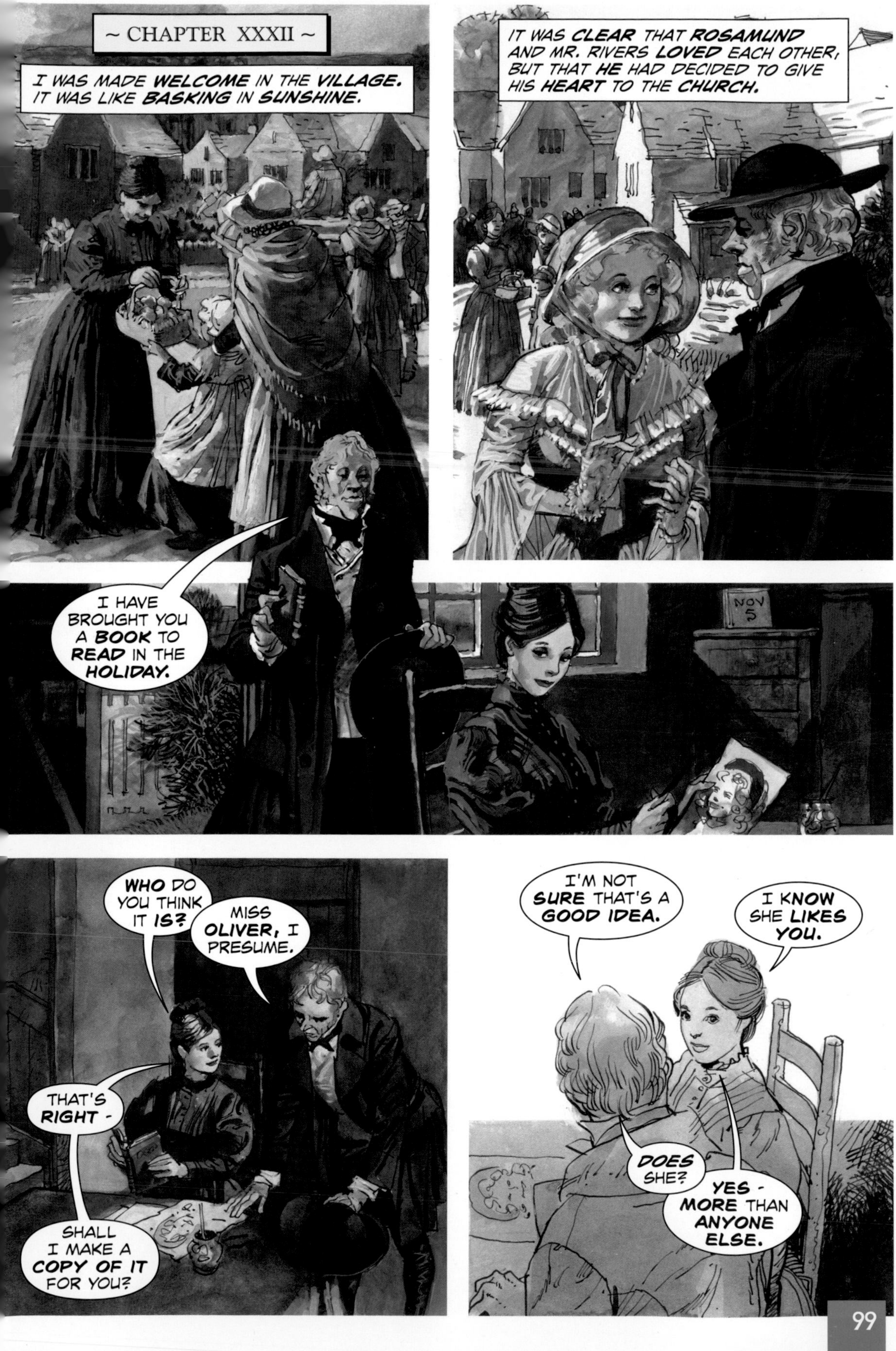
~ CHAPTER XXXII ~
I WAS MADE WELCOME IN THE VILLAGE. IT WAS LIKE BASKING IN SUNSHINE.
IT WAS CLEAR THAT ROSAMUND AND MR. RIVERS LOVED EACH OTHER, BUT THAT HE HAD DECIDED TO GIVE HIS HEART TO THE CHURCH.
I HAVE BROUGHT YOU A BOOK TO READ IN THE HOLIDAY.
NOV 5
WHO DO YOU THINK IT IS?
MISS OLIVER, I PRESUME.
THAT'S RIGHT -
SHALL I MAKE A COPY OF IT FOR YOU?
I'M NOT SURE THAT'S A GOOD IDEA.
I KNOW SHE LIKES YOU.
DOES SHE?
YES - MORE THAN ANYONE ELSE.

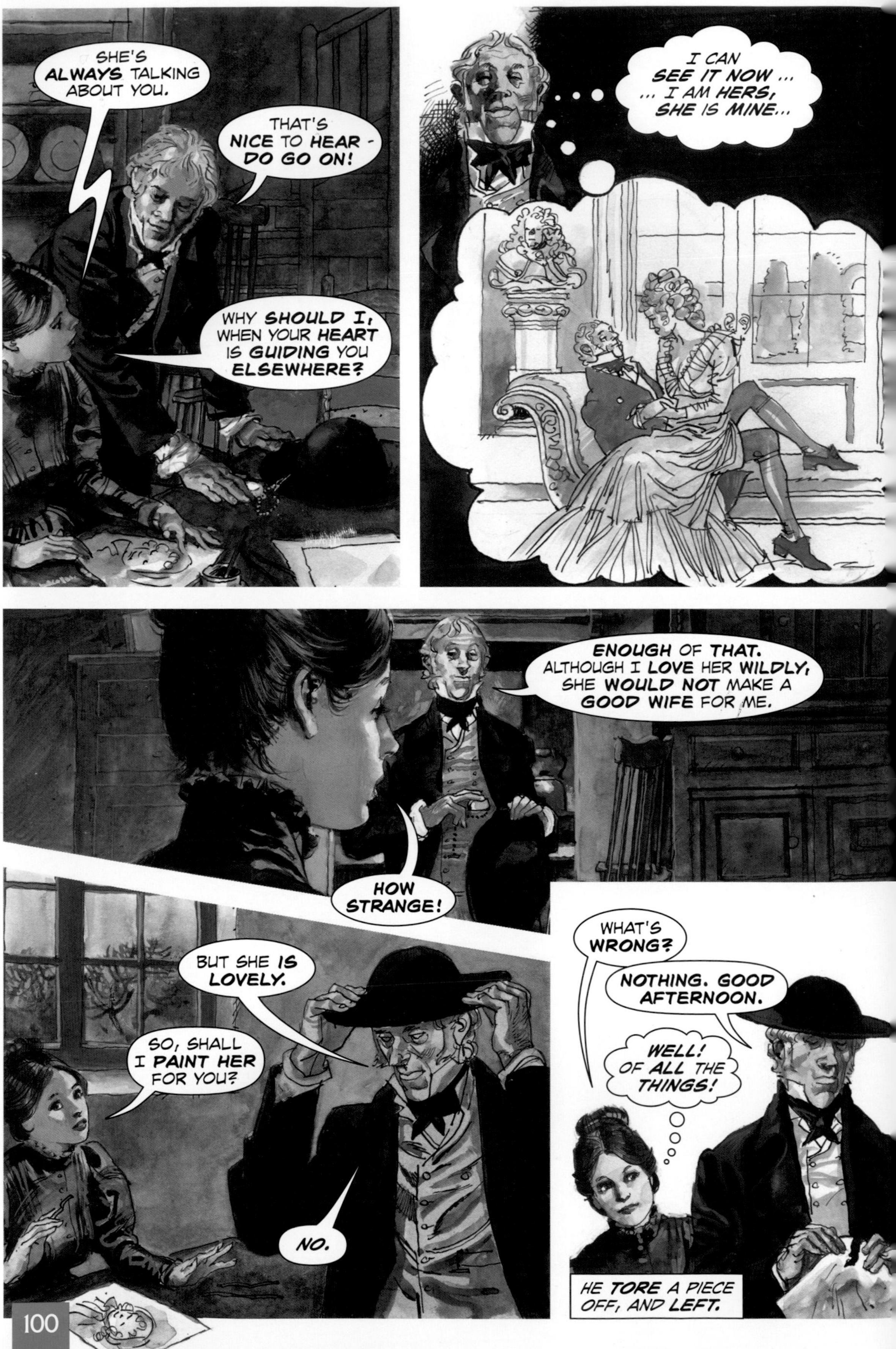
SHE'S ALWAYS TALKING ABOUT YOU.
THAT'S NICE TO HEAR - DO GO ON!
WHY SHOULD I, WHEN YOUR HEART IS GUIDING YOU ELSEWHERE?
I CAN SEE IT NOW ... ... I AM HERS, SHE IS MINE...
ENOUGH OF THAT. ALTHOUGH I LOVE HER WILDLY, SHE WOULD NOT MAKE A GOOD WIFE FOR ME.
HOW STRANGE!
BUT SHE IS LOVELY.
SO, SHALL I PAINT HER FOR YOU?
NO.
WHAT'S WRONG?
NOTHING. GOOD AFTERNOON.
WELL! OF ALL THE THINGS!
HE TORE A PIECE OFF, AND LEFT.

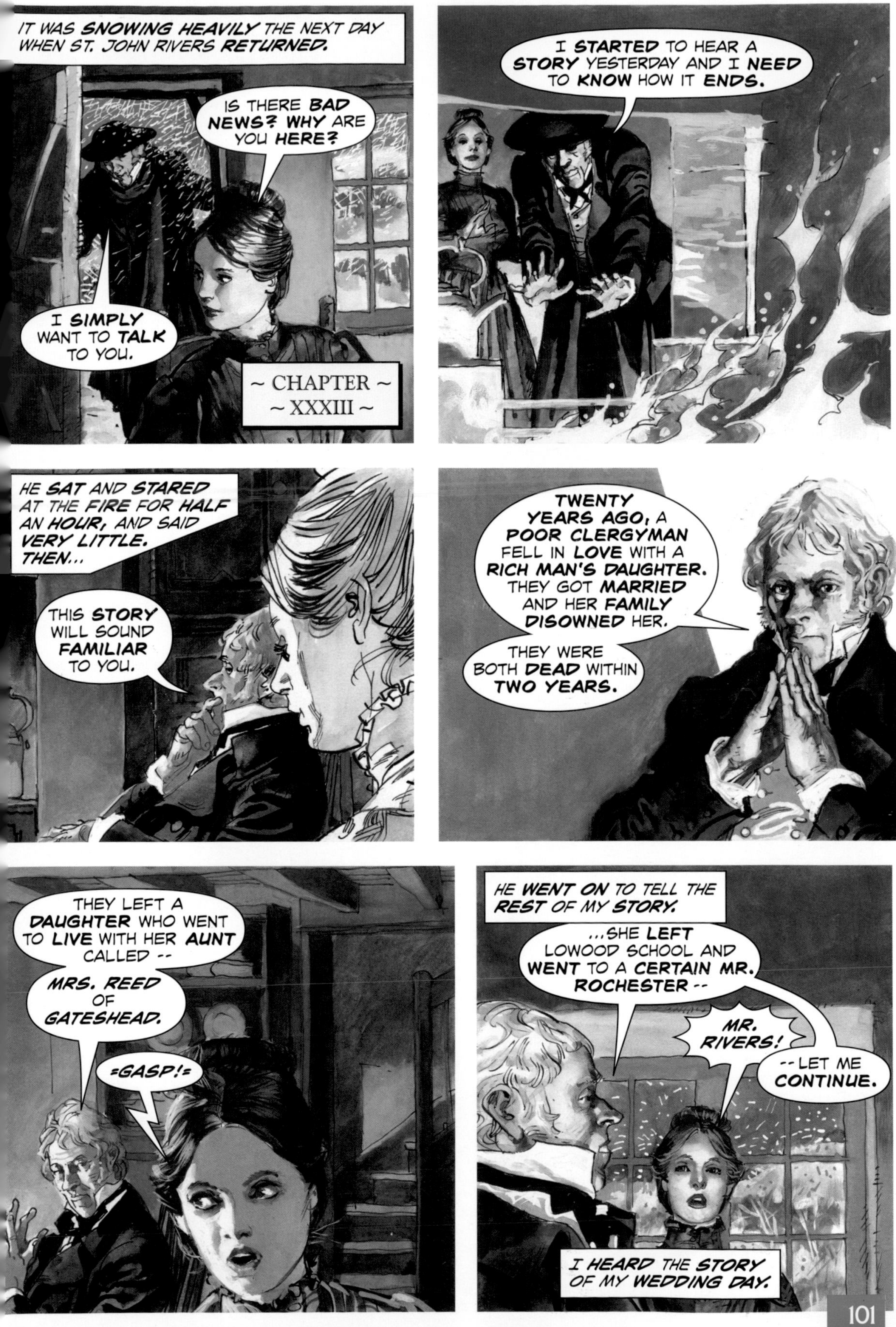
IT WAS SNOWING HEAVILY THE NEXT DAY WHEN ST. JOHN RIVERS RETURNED.
IS THERE BAD NEWS? WHY ARE YOU HERE?
I SIMPLY WANT TO TALK TO YOU.
~ CHAPTER ~ ~ XXXIII ~
I STARTED TO HEAR A STORY YESTERDAY AND I NEED TO KNOW HOW IT ENDS.
HE SAT AND STARED AT THE FIRE FOR HALF AN HOUR, AND SAID VERY LITTLE. THEN...
THIS STORY WILL SOUND FAMILIAR TO YOU.
TWENTY YEARS AGO, A POOR CLERGYMAN FELL IN LOVE WITH A RICH MAN'S DAUGHTER. THEY GOT MARRIED AND HER FAMILY DISOWNED HER.
THEY WERE BOTH DEAD WITHIN TWO YEARS.
THEY LEFT A DAUGHTER WHO WENT TO LIVE WITH HER AUNT CALLED --
MRS. REED OF GATESHEAD.
=GASP!=
HE WENT ON TO TELL THE REST OF MY STORY.
...SHE LEFT LOWOOD SCHOOL AND WENT TO A CERTAIN MR. ROCHESTER --
MR. RIVERS!
-- LET ME CONTINUE.
I HEARD THE STORY OF MY WEDDING DAY.

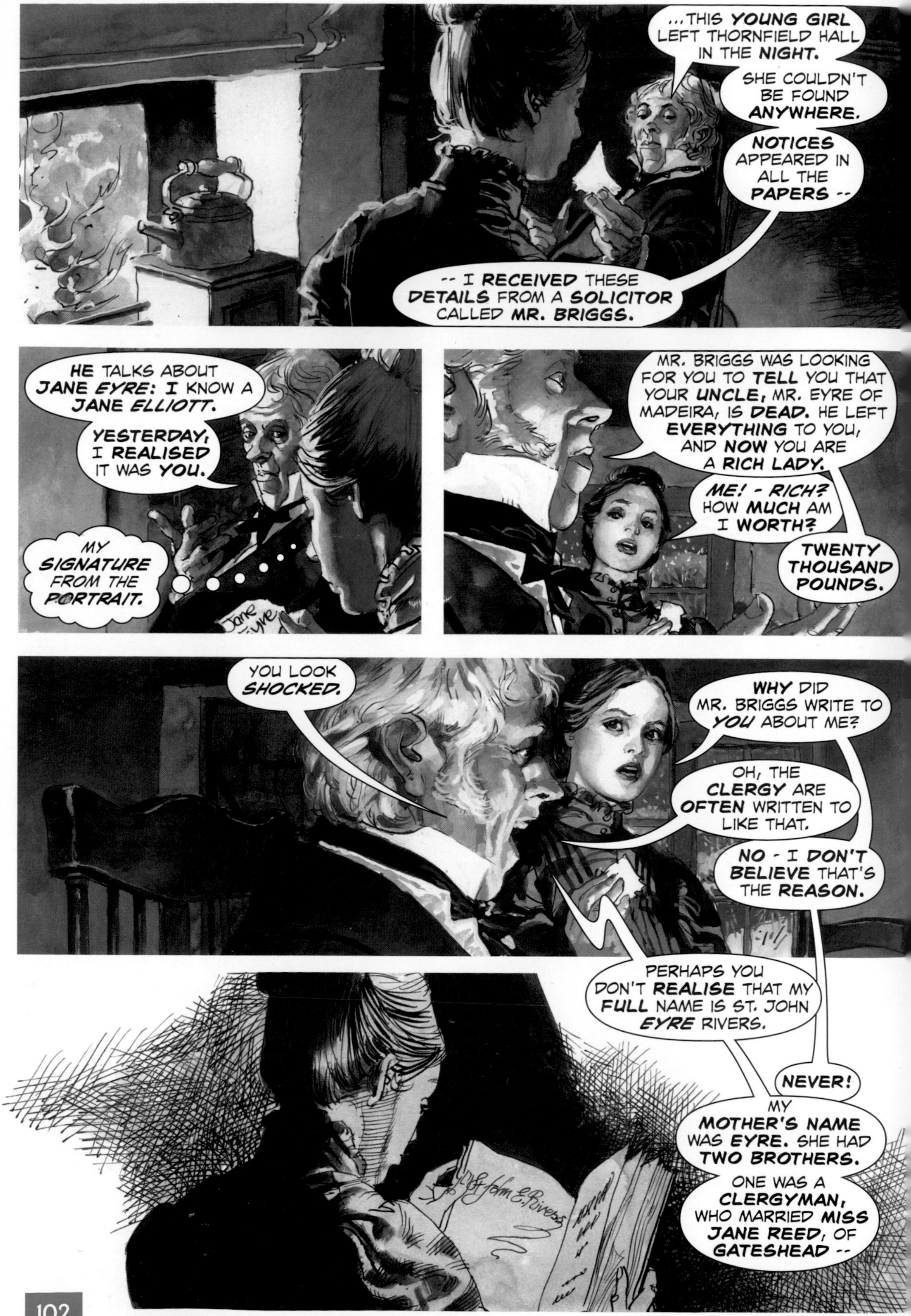
...THIS YOUNG GIRL LEFT THORNFIELD HALL IN THE NIGHT.
SHE COULDN'T BE FOUND ANYWHERE.
NOTICES APPEARED IN ALL THE PAPERS --
-- I RECEIVED THESE DETAILS FROM A SOLICITOR CALLED MR. BRIGGS.
HE TALKS ABOUT JANE EYRE: I KNOW A JANE ELLIOTT.
YESTERDAY, I REALISED IT WAS YOU.
MY SIGNATURE FROM THE PORTRAIT.
Jane Eyre
MR. BRIGGS WAS LOOKING FOR YOU TO TELL YOU THAT YOUR UNCLE, MR. EYRE OF MADEIRA, IS DEAD. HE LEFT EVERYTHING TO YOU, AND NOW YOU ARE A RICH LADY.
ME! - RICH? HOW MUCH AM I WORTH?
TWENTY THOUSAND POUNDS.
YOU LOOK SHOCKED.
WHY DID MR. BRIGGS WRITE TO YOU ABOUT ME?
OH, THE CLERGY ARE OFTEN WRITTEN TO LIKE THAT.
NO - I DON'T BELIEVE THAT'S THE REASON.
PERHAPS YOU DON'T REALISE THAT MY FULL NAME IS ST. JOHN EYRE RIVERS.
NEVER!
MY MOTHER'S NAME WAS EYRE. SHE HAD TWO BROTHERS.
ONE WAS A CLERGYMAN, WHO MARRIED MISS JANE REED, OF GATESHEAD --
St John E. Rivers

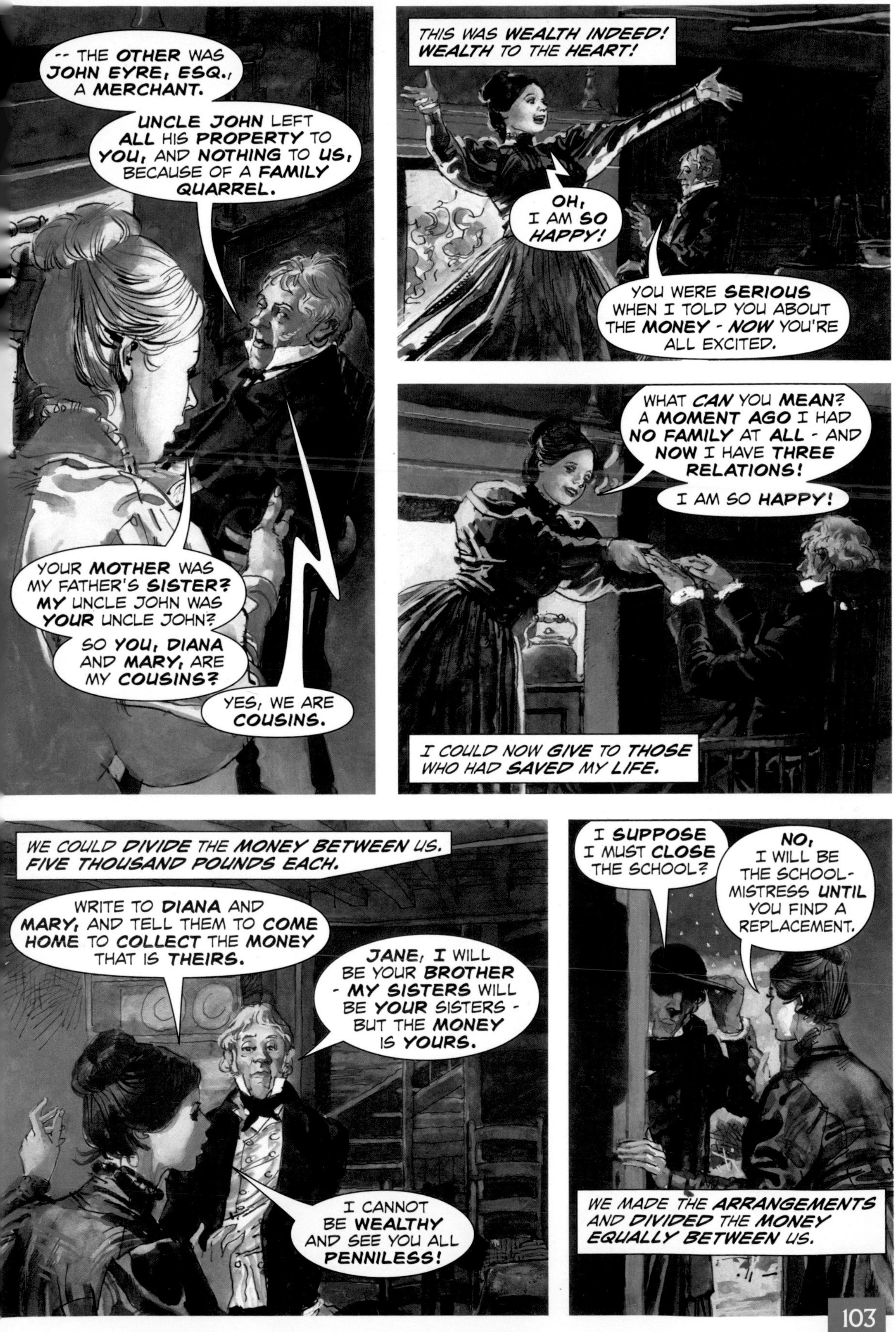
-- THE OTHER WAS JOHN EYRE, ESQ., A MERCHANT.
UNCLE JOHN LEFT ALL HIS PROPERTY TO YOU, AND NOTHING TO US, BECAUSE OF A FAMILY QUARREL.
YOUR MOTHER WAS MY FATHER'S SISTER? MY UNCLE JOHN WAS YOUR UNCLE JOHN?
SO YOU, DIANA AND MARY, ARE MY COUSINS?
YES, WE ARE COUSINS.
THIS WAS WEALTH INDEED! WEALTH TO THE HEART!
OH, I AM SO HAPPY!
YOU WERE SERIOUS WHEN I TOLD YOU ABOUT THE MONEY - NOW YOU'RE ALL EXCITED.
WHAT CAN YOU MEAN? A MOMENT AGO I HAD NO FAMILY AT ALL - AND NOW I HAVE THREE RELATIONS!
I AM SO HAPPY!
I COULD NOW GIVE TO THOSE WHO HAD SAVED MY LIFE.
WE COULD DIVIDE THE MONEY BETWEEN US. FIVE THOUSAND POUNDS EACH.
WRITE TO DIANA AND MARY, AND TELL THEM TO COME HOME TO COLLECT THE MONEY THAT IS THEIRS.
JANE, I WILL BE YOUR BROTHER - MY SISTERS WILL BE YOUR SISTERS - BUT THE MONEY IS YOURS.
I CANNOT BE WEALTHY AND SEE YOU ALL PENNILESS!
I SUPPOSE I MUST CLOSE THE SCHOOL?
NO, I WILL BE THE SCHOOL-MISTRESS UNTIL YOU FIND A REPLACEMENT.
WE MADE THE ARRANGEMENTS AND DIVIDED THE MONEY EQUALLY BETWEEN US.

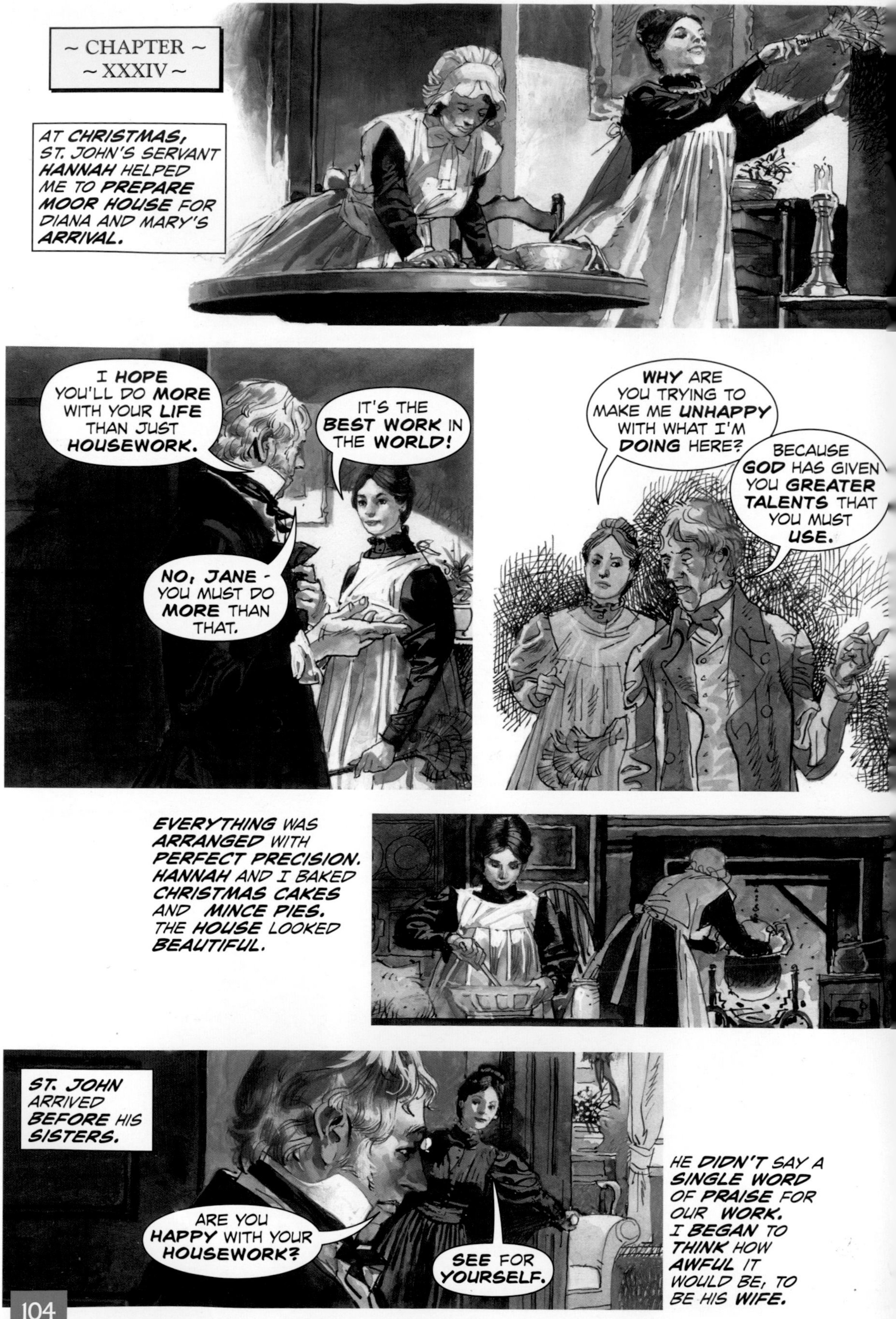
~ CHAPTER ~
~ XXXIV ~
AT CHRISTMAS, ST. JOHN'S SERVANT HANNAH HELPED ME TO PREPARE MOOR HOUSE FOR DIANA AND MARY'S ARRIVAL.
I HOPE YOU'LL DO MORE WITH YOUR LIFE THAN JUST HOUSEWORK.
IT'S THE BEST WORK IN THE WORLD!
NO, JANE - YOU MUST DO MORE THAN THAT.
WHY ARE YOU TRYING TO MAKE ME UNHAPPY WITH WHAT I'M DOING HERE?
BECAUSE GOD HAS GIVEN YOU GREATER TALENTS THAT YOU MUST USE.
EVERYTHING WAS ARRANGED WITH PERFECT PRECISION. HANNAH AND I BAKED CHRISTMAS CAKES AND MINCE PIES. THE HOUSE LOOKED BEAUTIFUL.
ST. JOHN ARRIVED BEFORE HIS SISTERS.
ARE YOU HAPPY WITH YOUR HOUSEWORK?
SEE FOR YOURSELF.
HE DIDN'T SAY A SINGLE WORD OF PRAISE FOR OUR WORK. I BEGAN TO THINK HOW AWFUL IT WOULD BE, TO BE HIS WIFE.

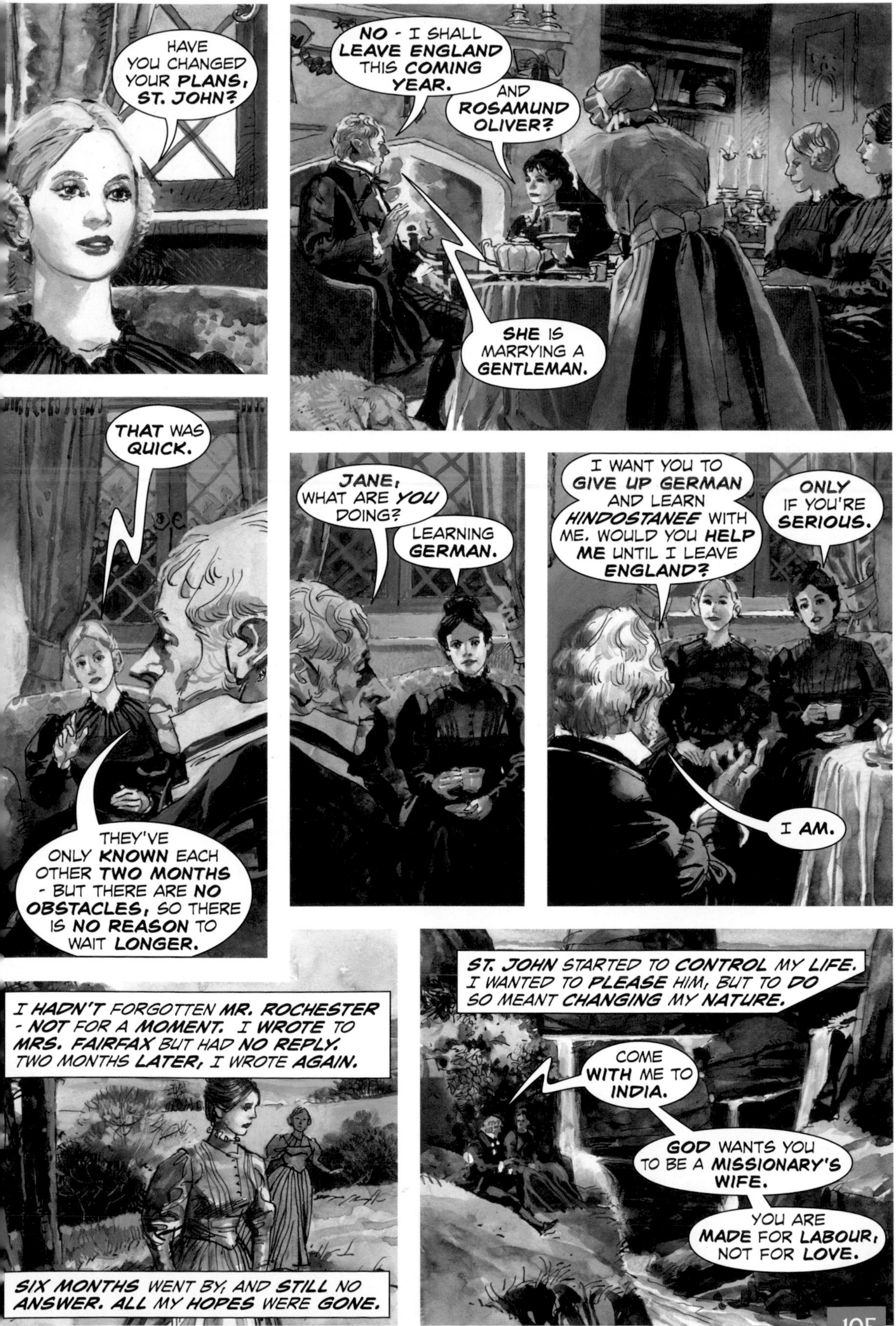
HAVE YOU CHANGED YOUR PLANS, ST. JOHN?
NO - I SHALL LEAVE ENGLAND THIS COMING YEAR.
AND ROSAMUND OLIVER?
SHE IS MARRYING A GENTLEMAN.
THAT WAS QUICK.
THEY'VE ONLY KNOWN EACH OTHER TWO MONTHS - BUT THERE ARE NO OBSTACLES, SO THERE IS NO REASON TO WAIT LONGER.
JANE, WHAT ARE YOU DOING?
LEARNING GERMAN.
I WANT YOU TO GIVE UP GERMAN AND LEARN HINDOSTANEE WITH ME. WOULD YOU HELP ME UNTIL I LEAVE ENGLAND?
ONLY IF YOU'RE SERIOUS.
I AM.
I HADN'T FORGOTTEN MR. ROCHESTER - NOT FOR A MOMENT. I WROTE TO MRS. FAIRFAX BUT HAD NO REPLY. TWO MONTHS LATER, I WROTE AGAIN.
SIX MONTHS WENT BY, AND STILL NO ANSWER. ALL MY HOPES WERE GONE.
ST. JOHN STARTED TO CONTROL MY LIFE. I WANTED TO PLEASE HIM, BUT TO DO SO MEANT CHANGING MY NATURE.
COME WITH ME TO INDIA.
GOD WANTS YOU TO BE A MISSIONARY'S WIFE.
YOU ARE MADE FOR LABOUR, NOT FOR LOVE.

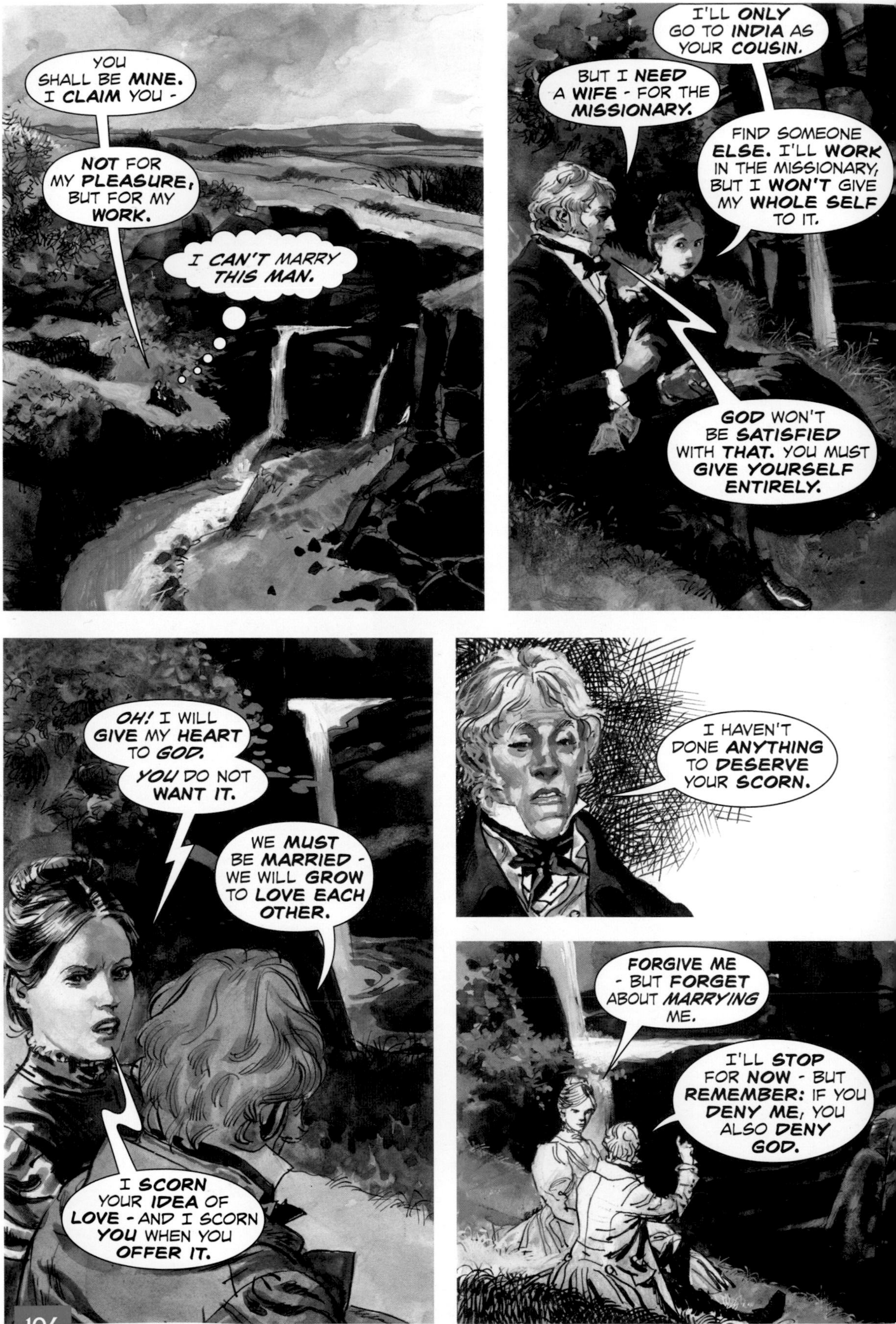
YOU SHALL BE MINE. I CLAIM YOU -
NOT FOR MY PLEASURE, BUT FOR MY WORK.
I CAN'T MARRY THIS MAN.
I'LL ONLY GO TO INDIA AS YOUR COUSIN.
BUT I NEED A WIFE - FOR THE MISSIONARY.
FIND SOMEONE ELSE. I'LL WORK IN THE MISSIONARY, BUT I WON'T GIVE MY WHOLE SELF TO IT.
GOD WON'T BE SATISFIED WITH THAT. YOU MUST GIVE YOURSELF ENTIRELY.
OH! I WILL GIVE MY HEART TO GOD.
YOU DO NOT WANT IT.
WE MUST BE MARRIED - WE WILL GROW TO LOVE EACH OTHER.
I SCORN YOUR IDEA OF LOVE - AND I SCORN YOU WHEN YOU OFFER IT.
I HAVEN'T DONE ANYTHING TO DESERVE YOUR SCORN.
FORGIVE ME - BUT FORGET ABOUT MARRYING ME.
I'LL STOP FOR NOW - BUT REMEMBER: IF YOU DENY ME, YOU ALSO DENY GOD.

~ CHAPTER ~ ~ XXXV ~

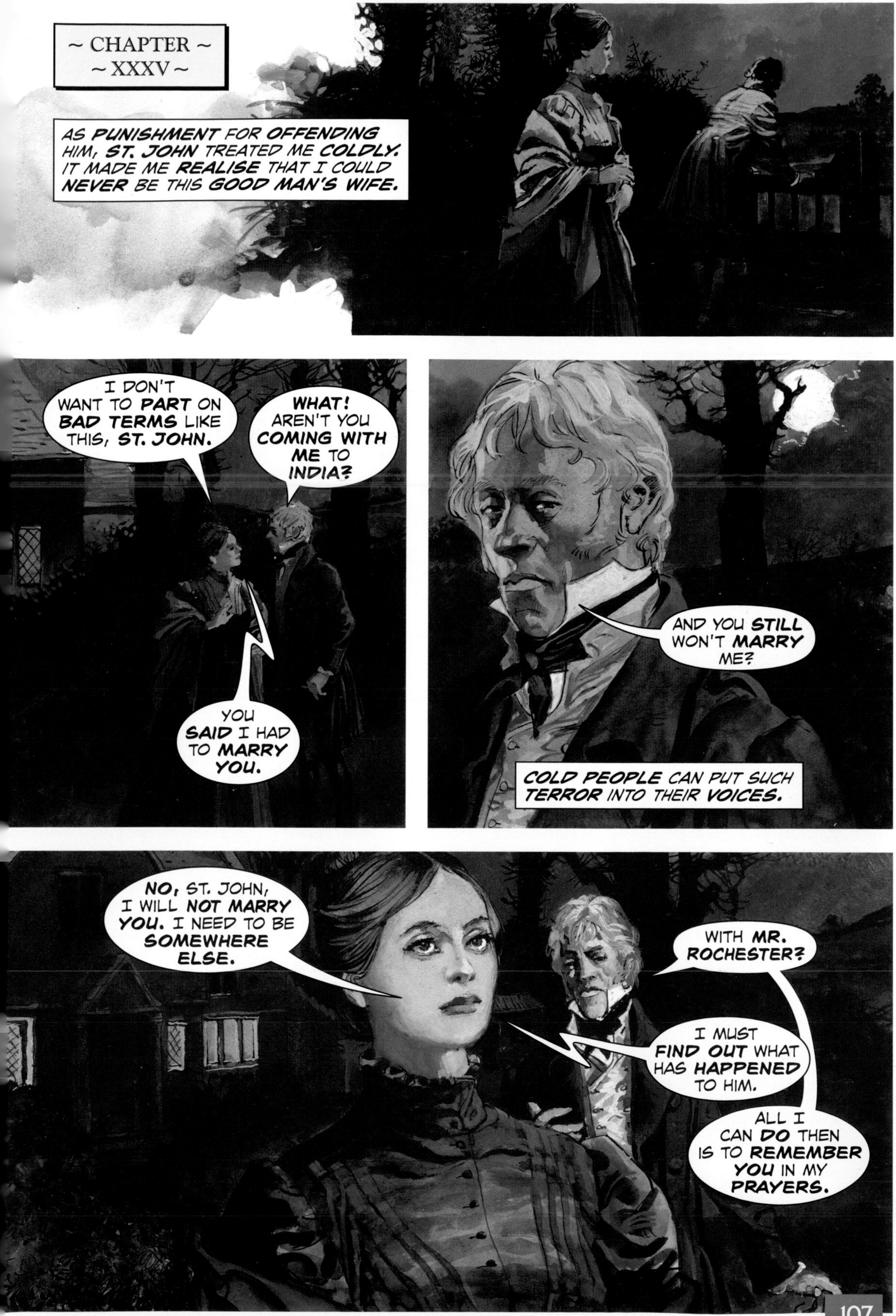
AS PUNISHMENT FOR OFFENDING HIM, ST. JOHN TREATED ME COLDLY. IT MADE ME REALISE THAT I COULD NEVER BE THIS GOOD MAN'S WIFE.
I DON'T WANT TO PART ON BAD TERMS LIKE THIS, ST. JOHN.
WHAT! AREN'T YOU COMING WITH ME TO INDIA?
YOU SAID I HAD TO MARRY YOU.
AND YOU STILL WON'T MARRY ME?
COLD PEOPLE CAN PUT SUCH TERROR INTO THEIR VOICES.
NO, ST. JOHN, I WILL NOT MARRY YOU. I NEED TO BE SOMEWHERE ELSE.
WITH MR. ROCHESTER?
I MUST FIND OUT WHAT HAS HAPPENED TO HIM.
ALL I CAN DO THEN IS TO REMEMBER YOU IN MY PRAYERS.

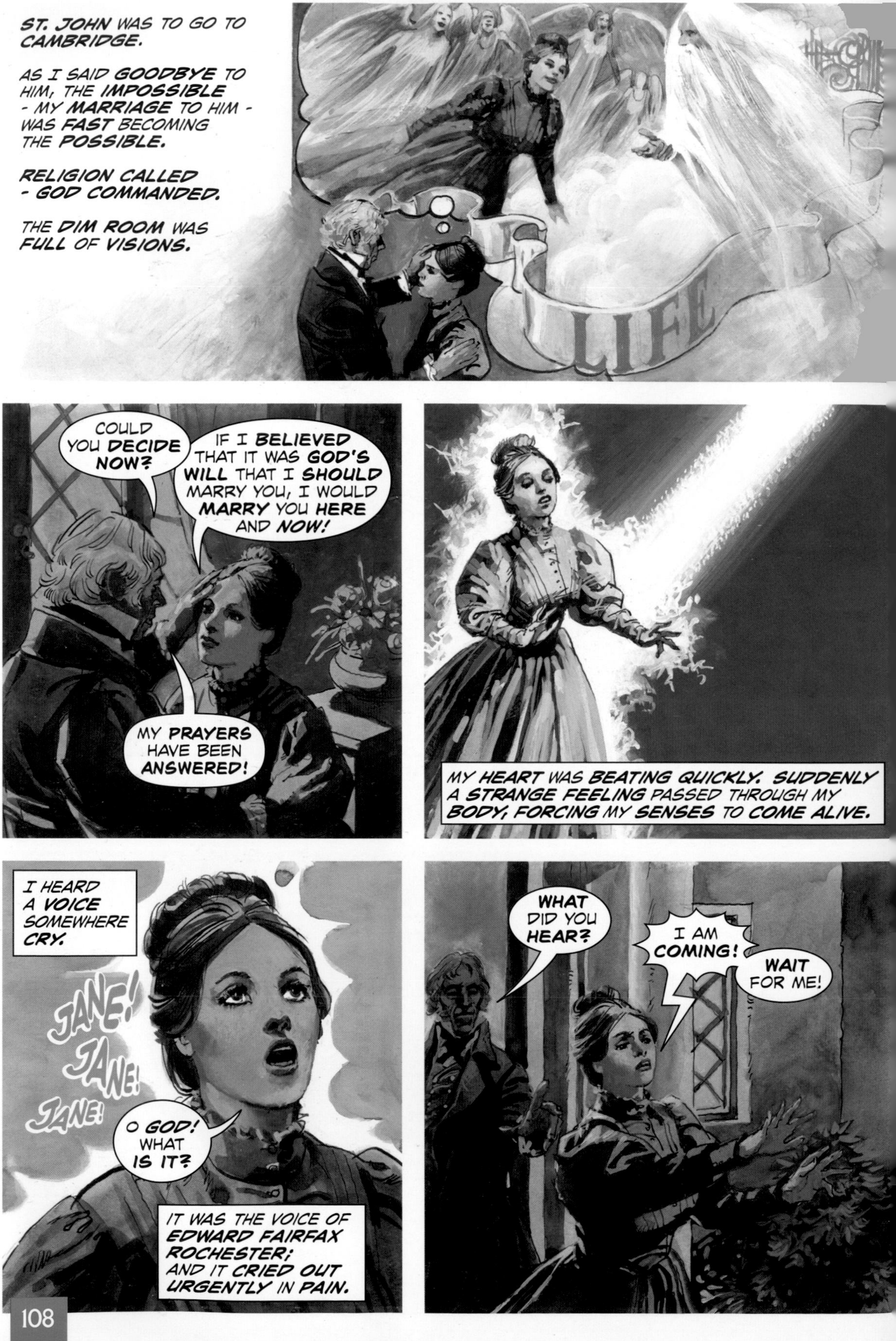
ST. JOHN WAS TO GO TO CAMBRIDGE.
AS I SAID GOODBYE TO HIM, THE IMPOSSIBLE - MY MARRIAGE TO HIM - WAS FAST BECOMING THE POSSIBLE.
RELIGION CALLED - GOD COMMANDED.
THE DIM ROOM WAS FULL OF VISIONS.
LIFE
COULD YOU DECIDE NOW?
IF I BELIEVED THAT IT WAS GOD'S WILL THAT I SHOULD MARRY YOU, I WOULD MARRY YOU HERE AND NOW!
MY PRAYERS HAVE BEEN ANSWERED!
MY HEART WAS BEATING QUICKLY. SUDDENLY A STRANGE FEELING PASSED THROUGH MY BODY, FORCING MY SENSES TO COME ALIVE.
I HEARD A VOICE SOMEWHERE CRY.
JANE!
JANE!
JANE!
O GOD! WHAT IS IT?
IT WAS THE VOICE OF EDWARD FAIRFAX ROCHESTER; AND IT CRIED OUT URGENTLY IN PAIN.
WHAT DID YOU HEAR?
I AM COMING!
WAIT FOR ME!

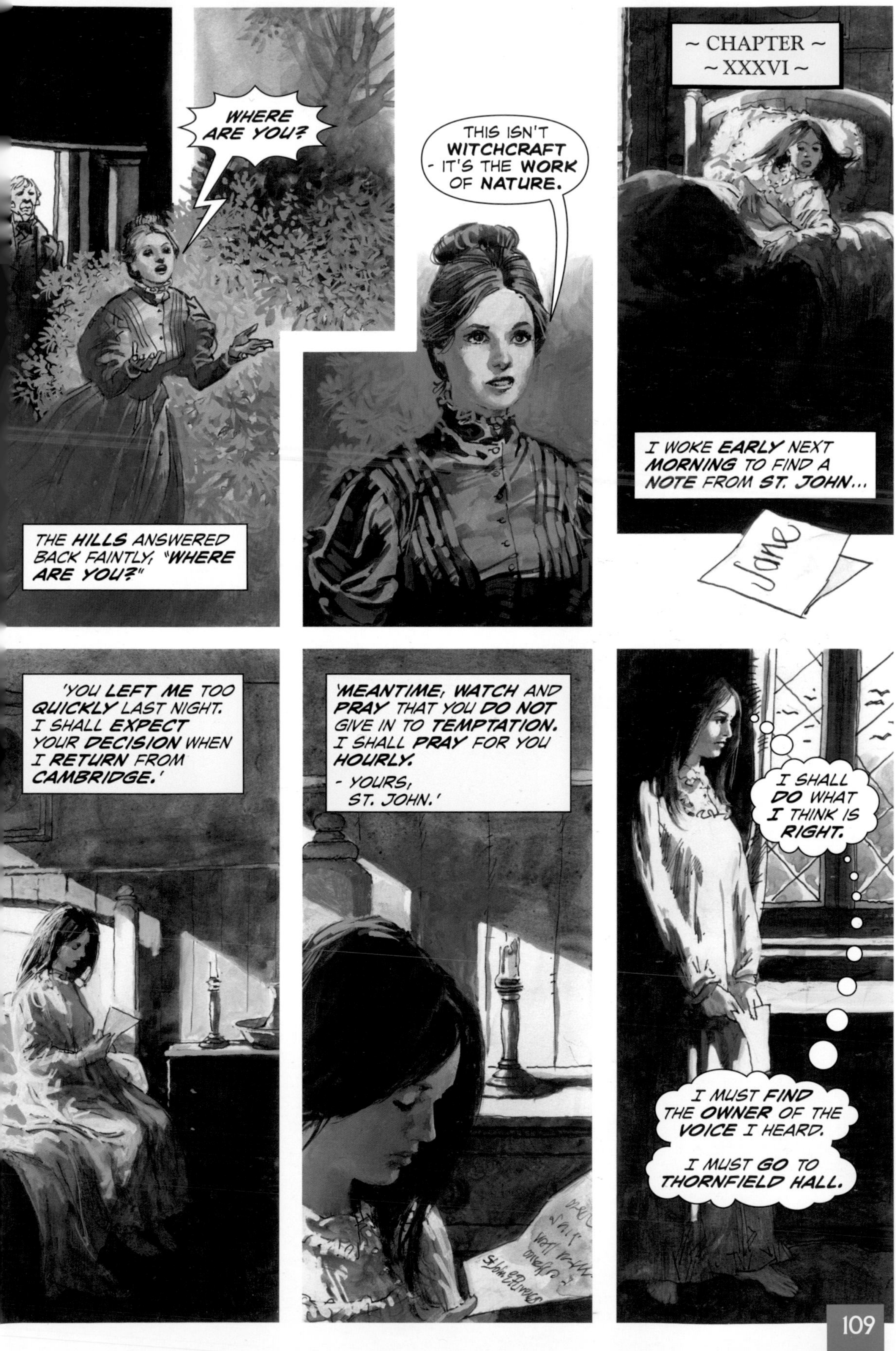
WHERE ARE YOU?
THE HILLS ANSWERED BACK FAINTLY, "WHERE ARE YOU?"
THIS ISN'T WITCHCRAFT - IT'S THE WORK OF NATURE.
~ CHAPTER ~
~ XXXVI ~
I WOKE EARLY NEXT MORNING TO FIND A NOTE FROM ST. JOHN...
Jane
'YOU LEFT ME TOO QUICKLY LAST NIGHT. I SHALL EXPECT YOUR DECISION WHEN I RETURN FROM CAMBRIDGE.'
'MEANTIME, WATCH AND PRAY THAT YOU DO NOT GIVE IN TO TEMPTATION. I SHALL PRAY FOR YOU HOURLY.
- YOURS, ST. JOHN.'
I SHALL DO WHAT I THINK IS RIGHT.
I MUST FIND THE OWNER OF THE VOICE I HEARD.
I MUST GO TO THORNFIELD HALL.

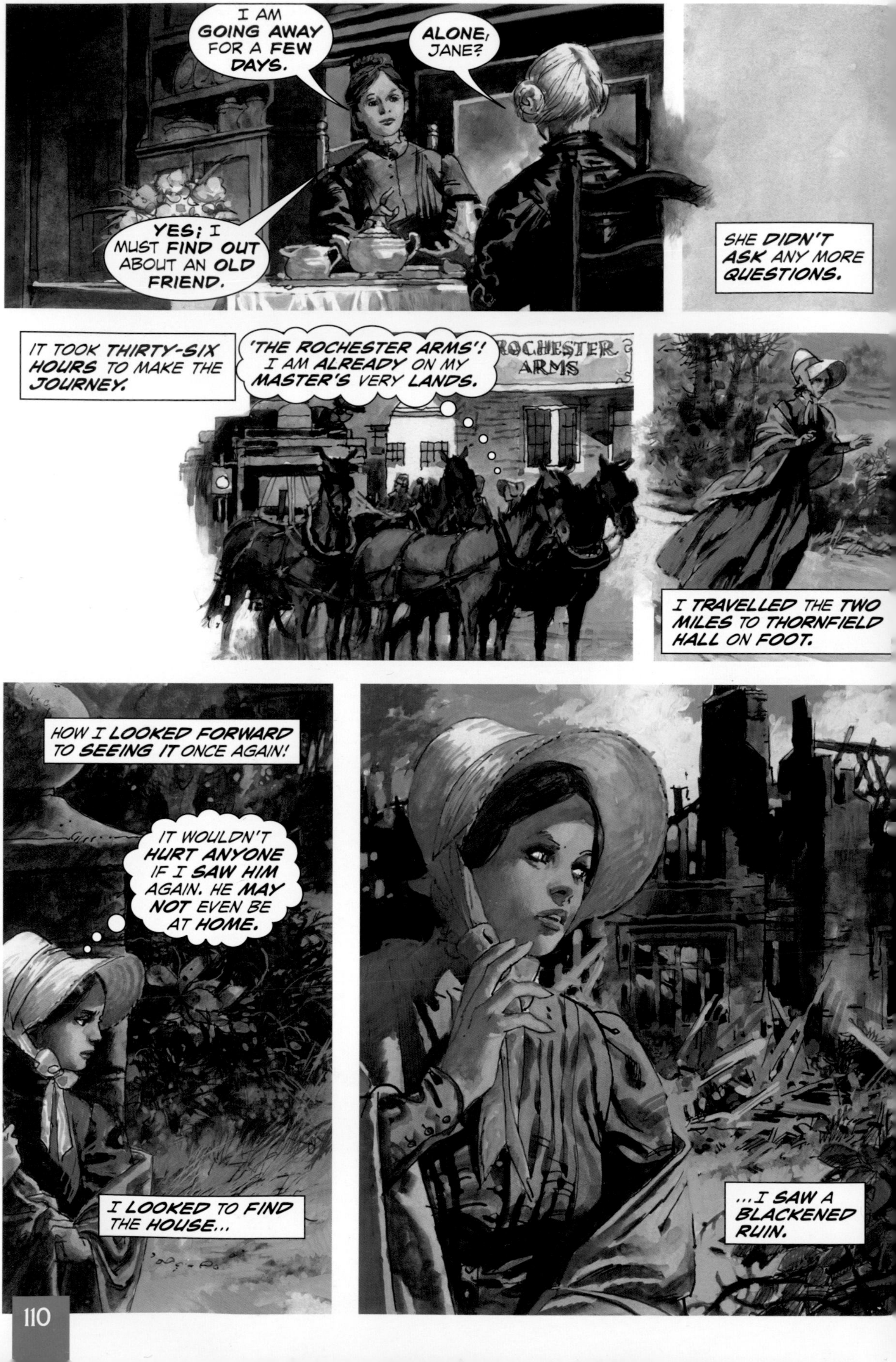

I AM GOING AWAY FOR A FEW DAYS.
ALONE, JANE?
YES; I MUST FIND OUT ABOUT AN OLD FRIEND.
SHE DIDN'T ASK ANY MORE QUESTIONS.
IT TOOK THIRTY-SIX HOURS TO MAKE THE JOURNEY.
'THE ROCHESTER ARMS'! I AM ALREADY ON MY MASTER'S VERY LANDS.
ROCHESTER ARMS
I TRAVELLED THE TWO MILES TO THORNFIELD HALL ON FOOT.
HOW I LOOKED FORWARD TO SEEING IT ONCE AGAIN!
IT WOULDN'T HURT ANYONE IF I SAW HIM AGAIN. HE MAY NOT EVEN BE AT HOME.
I LOOKED TO FIND THE HOUSE...
...I SAW A BLACKENED RUIN.

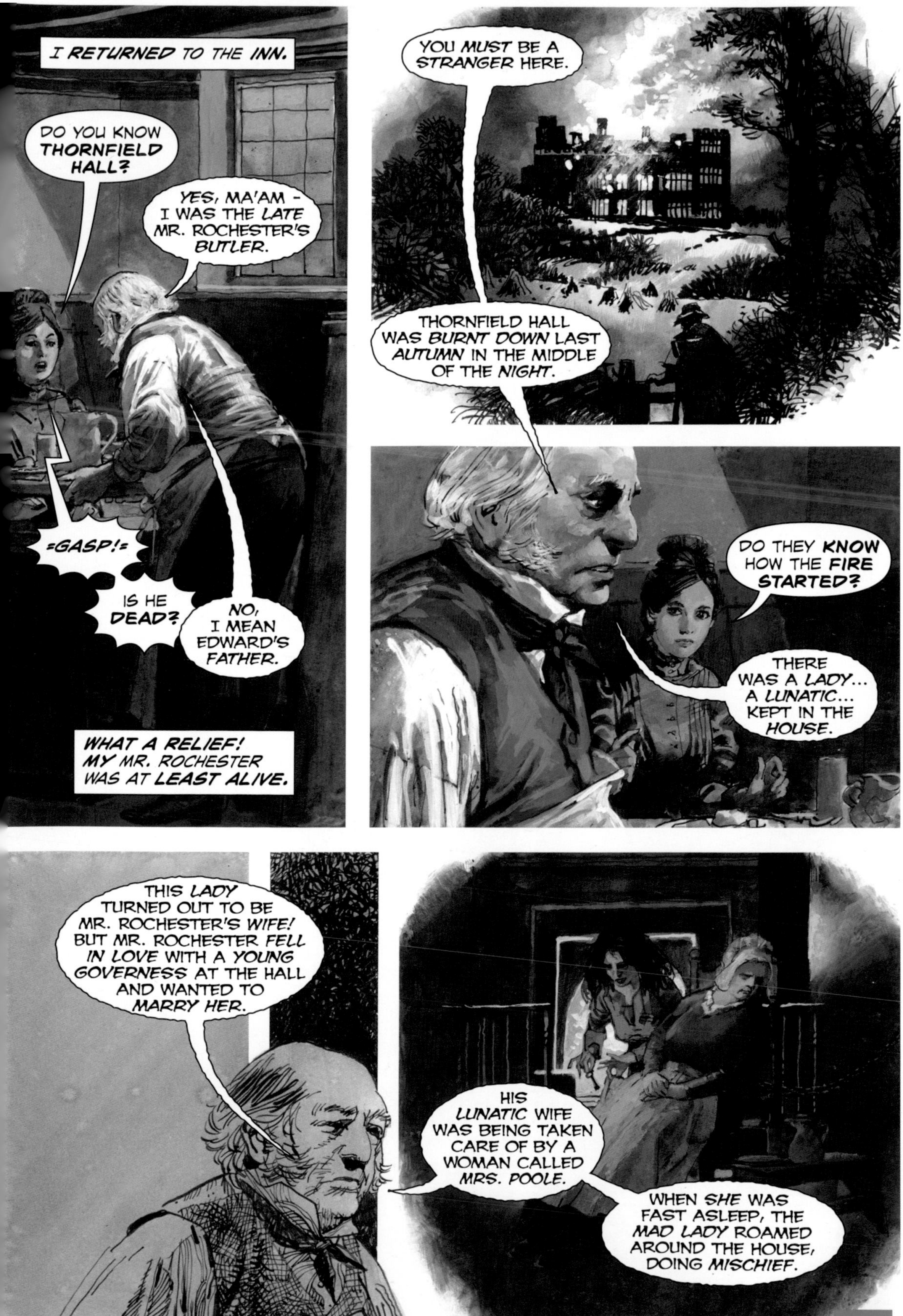
I RETURNED TO THE INN.
DO YOU KNOW THORNFIELD HALL?
YES, MA'AM - I WAS THE LATE MR. ROCHESTER'S BUTLER.
=GASP!=
IS HE DEAD?
NO, I MEAN EDWARD'S FATHER.
WHAT A RELIEF! MY MR. ROCHESTER WAS AT LEAST ALIVE.
YOU MUST BE A STRANGER HERE.
THORNFIELD HALL WAS BURNT DOWN LAST AUTUMN IN THE MIDDLE OF THE NIGHT.
DO THEY KNOW HOW THE FIRE STARTED?
THERE WAS A LADY... A LUNATIC... KEPT IN THE HOUSE.
THIS LADY TURNED OUT TO BE MR. ROCHESTER'S WIFE! BUT MR. ROCHESTER FELL IN LOVE WITH A YOUNG GOVERNESS AT THE HALL AND WANTED TO MARRY HER.
HIS LUNATIC WIFE WAS BEING TAKEN CARE OF BY A WOMAN CALLED MRS. POOLE.
WHEN SHE WAS FAST ASLEEP, THE MAD LADY ROAMED AROUND THE HOUSE, DOING MISCHIEF.

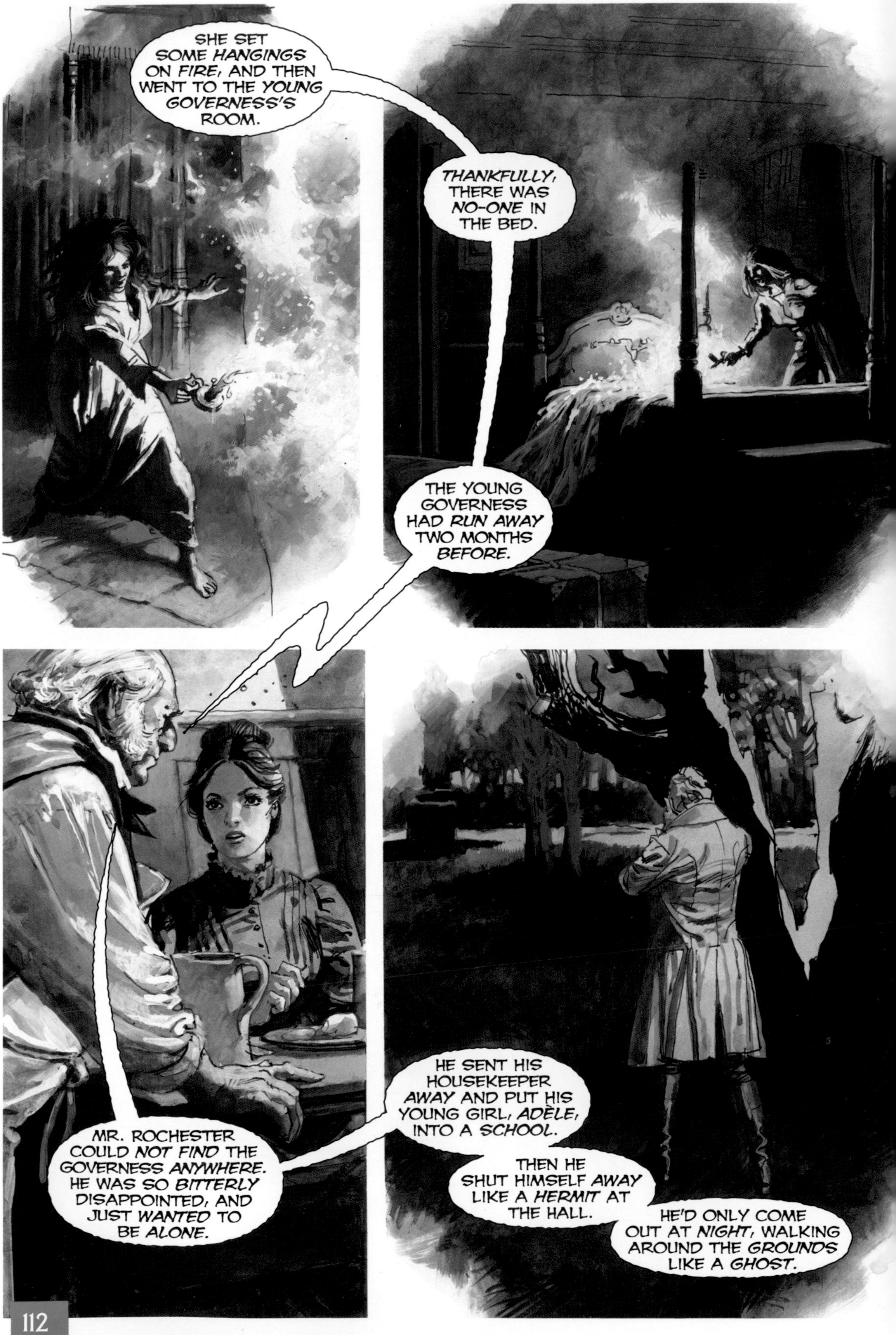
SHE SET SOME HANGINGS ON FIRE, AND THEN WENT TO THE YOUNG GOVERNESS'S ROOM.
THANKFULLY, THERE WAS NO-ONE IN THE BED.
THE YOUNG GOVERNESS HAD RUN AWAY TWO MONTHS BEFORE.
MR. ROCHESTER COULD NOT FIND THE GOVERNESS ANYWHERE. HE WAS SO BITTERLY DISAPPOINTED, AND JUST WANTED TO BE ALONE.
HE SENT HIS HOUSEKEEPER AWAY AND PUT HIS YOUNG GIRL, ADÈLE, INTO A SCHOOL.
THEN HE SHUT HIMSELF AWAY LIKE A HERMIT AT THE HALL.
HE'D ONLY COME OUT AT NIGHT, WALKING AROUND THE GROUNDS LIKE A GHOST.

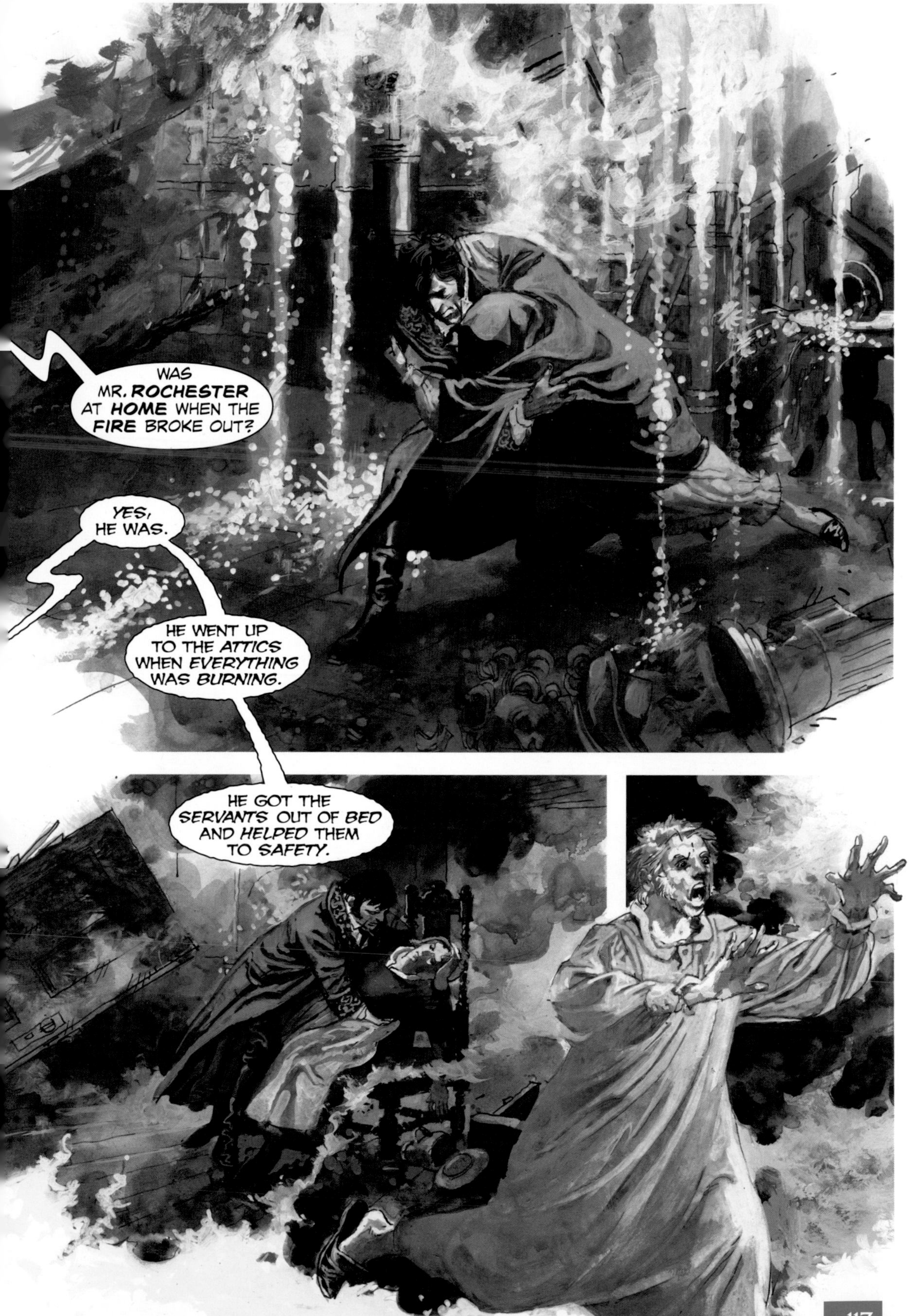
WAS MR. ROCHESTER AT HOME WHEN THE FIRE BROKE OUT?
YES, HE WAS.
HE WENT UP TO THE ATTICS WHEN EVERYTHING WAS BURNING.
HE GOT THE SERVANTS OUT OF BED AND HELPED THEM TO SAFETY.

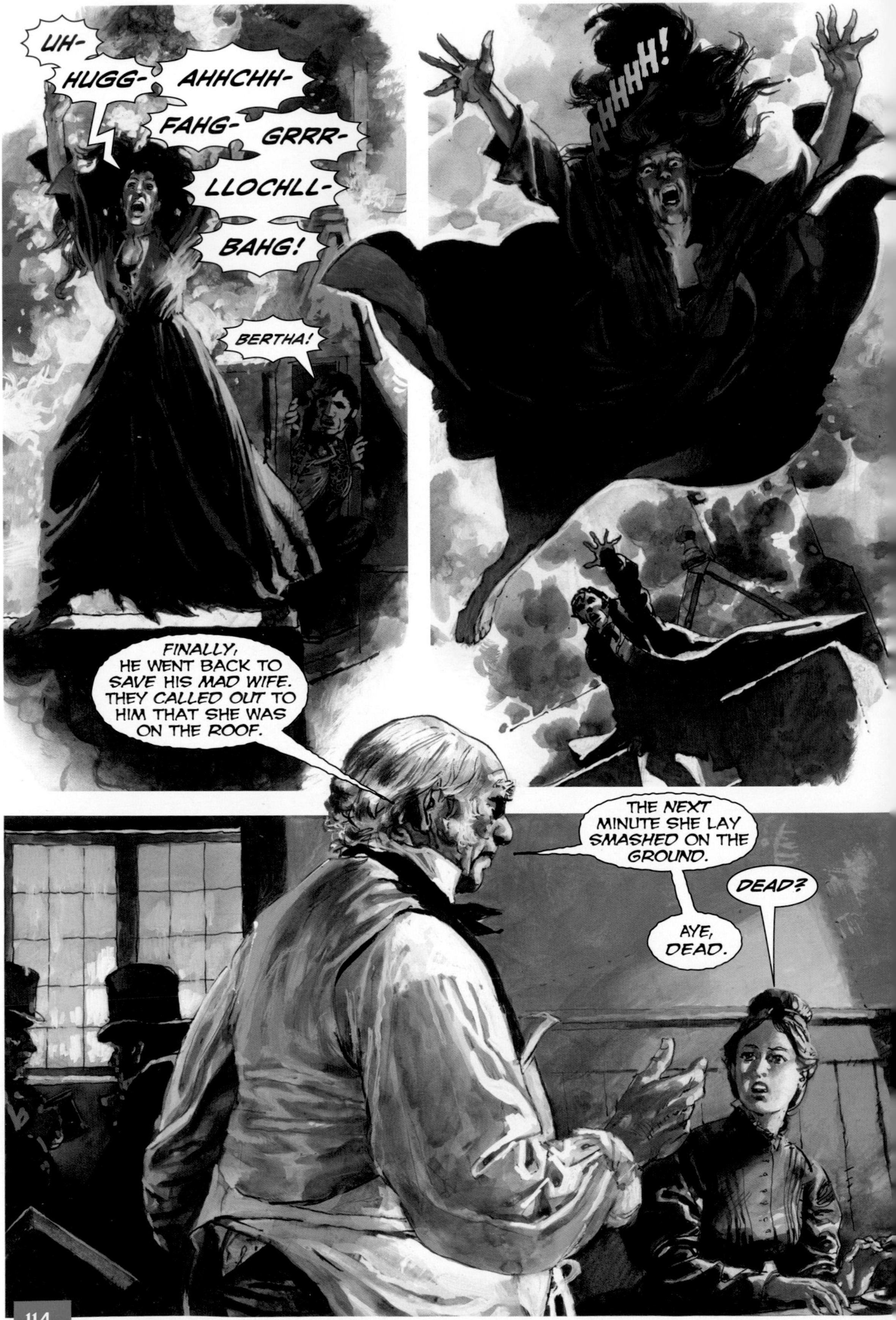
UH- HUGG- AHHCHH- FAHG- GRRR- LLOCHLL- BAHG!
BERTHA!
AHHHH!
FINALLY, HE WENT BACK TO SAVE HIS MAD WIFE. THEY CALLED OUT TO HIM THAT SHE WAS ON THE ROOF.
THE NEXT MINUTE SHE LAY SMASHED ON THE GROUND.
DEAD?
AYE, DEAD.

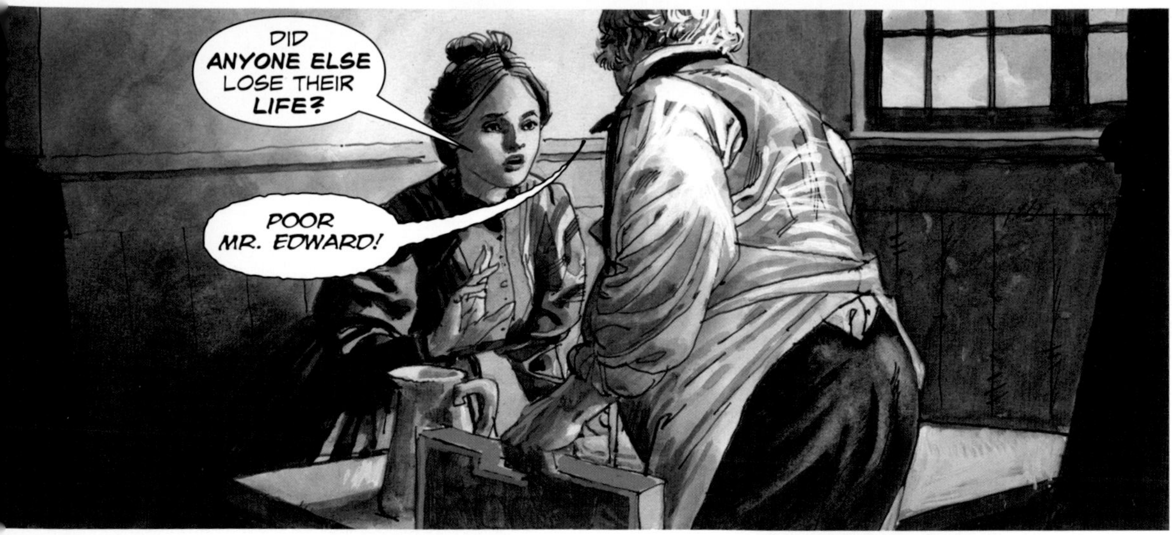

DID ANYONE ELSE LOSE THEIR LIFE?
POOR MR. EDWARD!

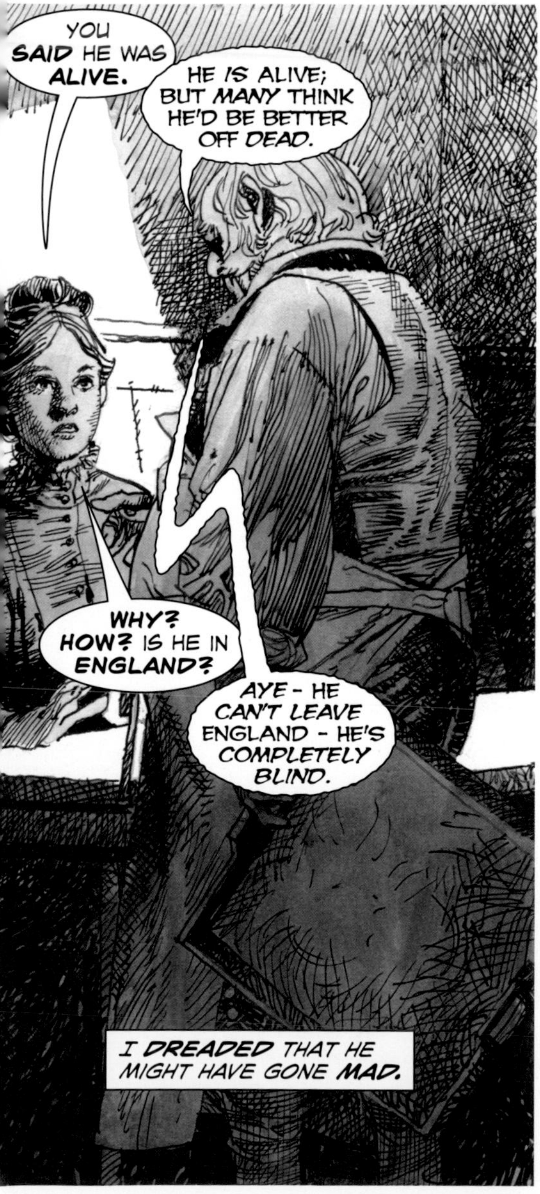

YOU SAID HE WAS ALIVE.
HE IS ALIVE; BUT MANY THINK HE'D BE BETTER OFF DEAD.
WHY? HOW? IS HE IN ENGLAND?
AYE - HE CAN'T LEAVE ENGLAND - HE'S COMPLETELY BLIND.
I DREADED THAT HE MIGHT HAVE GONE MAD.

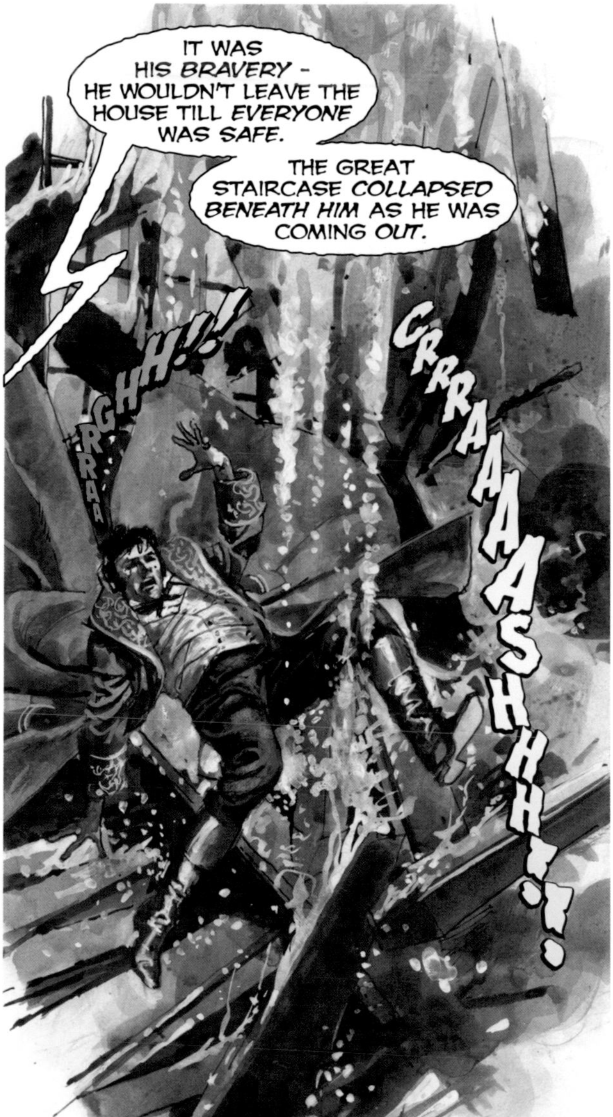

IT WAS HIS BRAVERY - HE WOULDN'T LEAVE THE HOUSE TILL EVERYONE WAS SAFE.
THE GREAT STAIRCASE COLLAPSED BENEATH HIM AS HE WAS COMING OUT.
AARRGHH!!!
CRRRAAAAASHHH!!

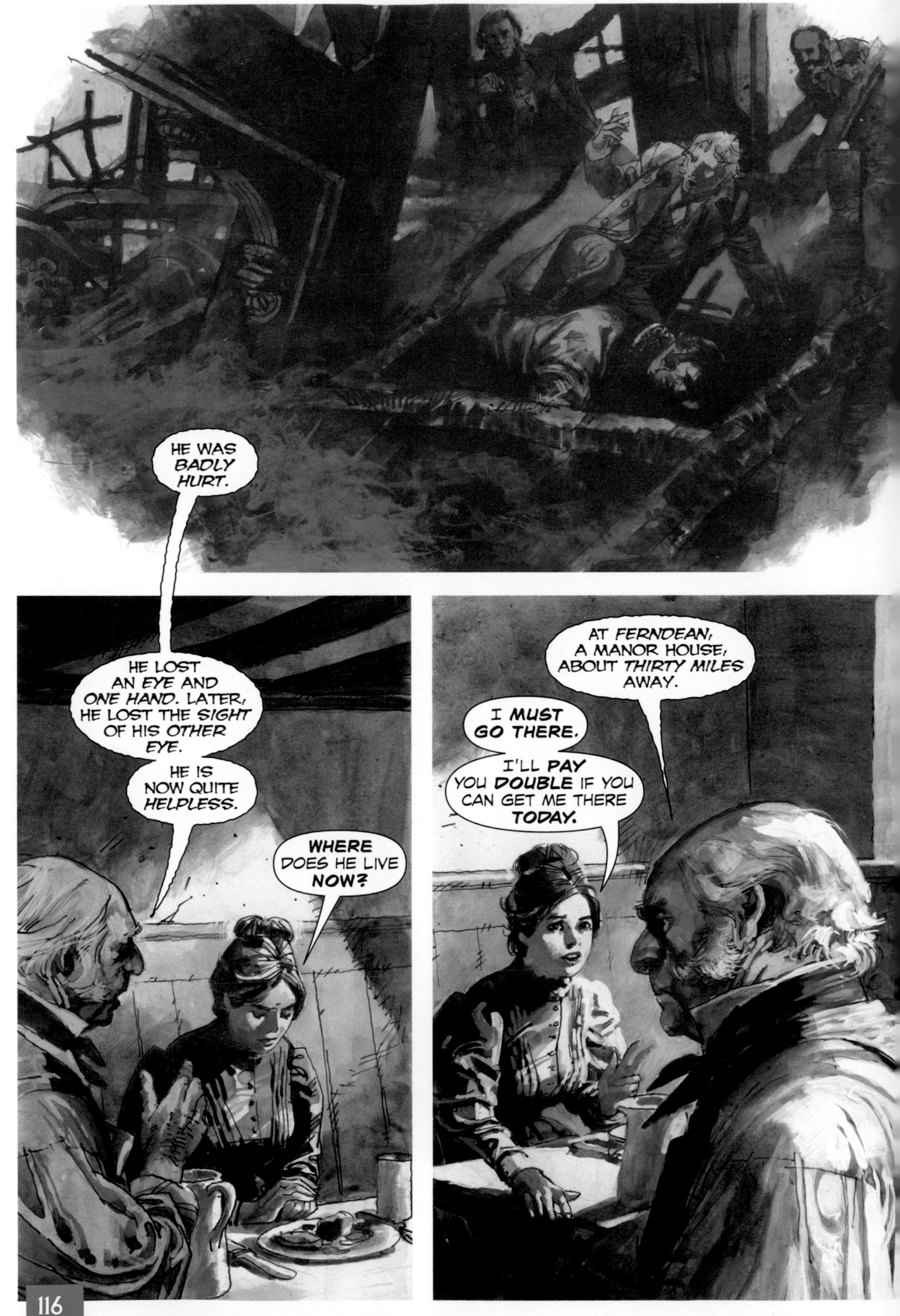
HE WAS BADLY HURT.
HE LOST AN EYE AND ONE HAND. LATER, HE LOST THE SIGHT OF HIS OTHER EYE.
HE IS NOW QUITE HELPLESS.
WHERE DOES HE LIVE NOW?
AT FERNDEAN, A MANOR HOUSE, ABOUT THIRTY MILES AWAY.
I MUST GO THERE.
I'LL PAY YOU DOUBLE IF YOU CAN GET ME THERE TODAY.

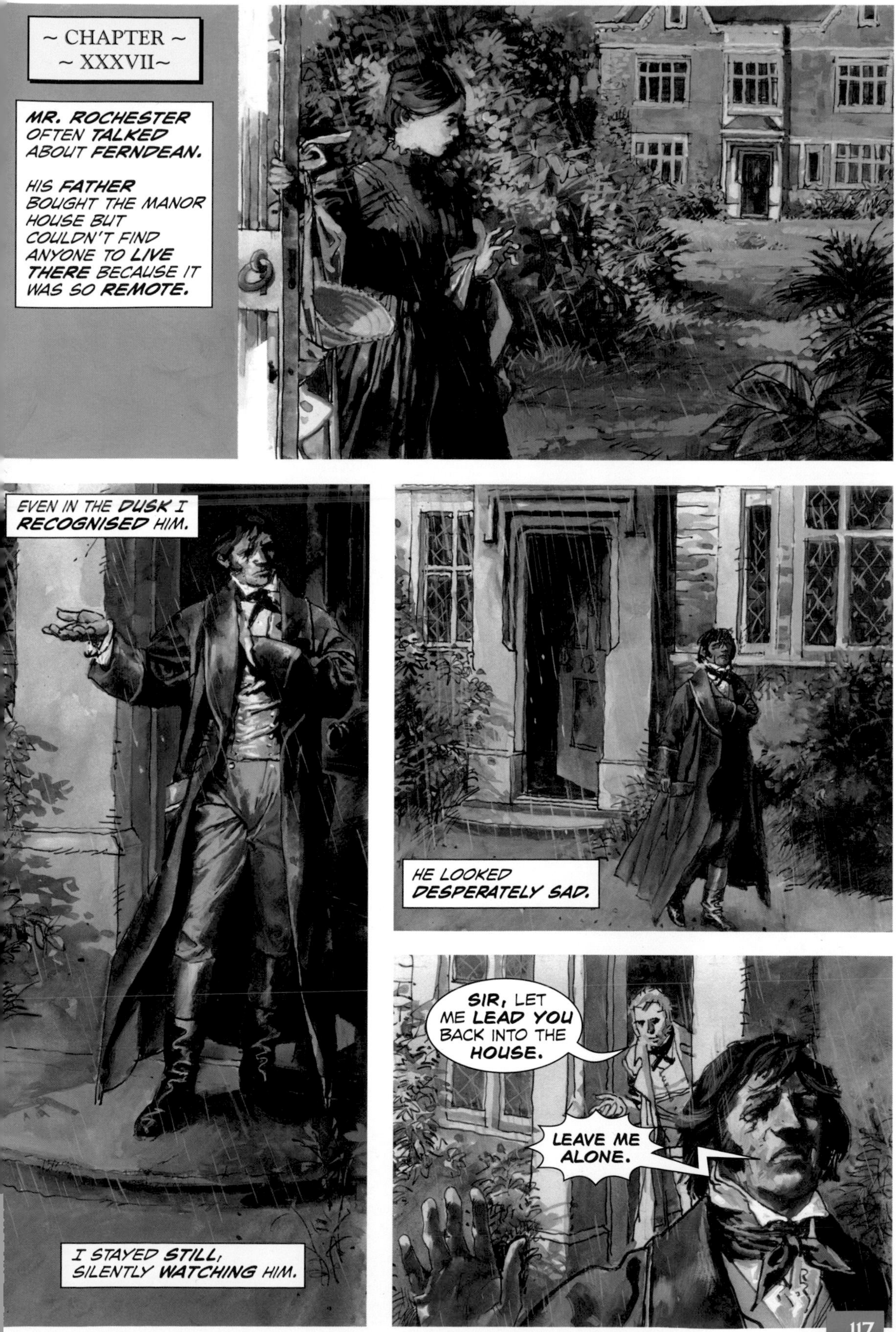
~ CHAPTER ~
~ XXXVII ~
MR. ROCHESTER OFTEN TALKED ABOUT FERNDEAN.
HIS FATHER BOUGHT THE MANOR HOUSE BUT COULDN'T FIND ANYONE TO LIVE THERE BECAUSE IT WAS SO REMOTE.
EVEN IN THE DUSK I RECOGNISED HIM.
I STAYED STILL, SILENTLY WATCHING HIM.
HE LOOKED DESPERATELY SAD.
SIR, LET ME LEAD YOU BACK INTO THE HOUSE.
LEAVE ME ALONE.

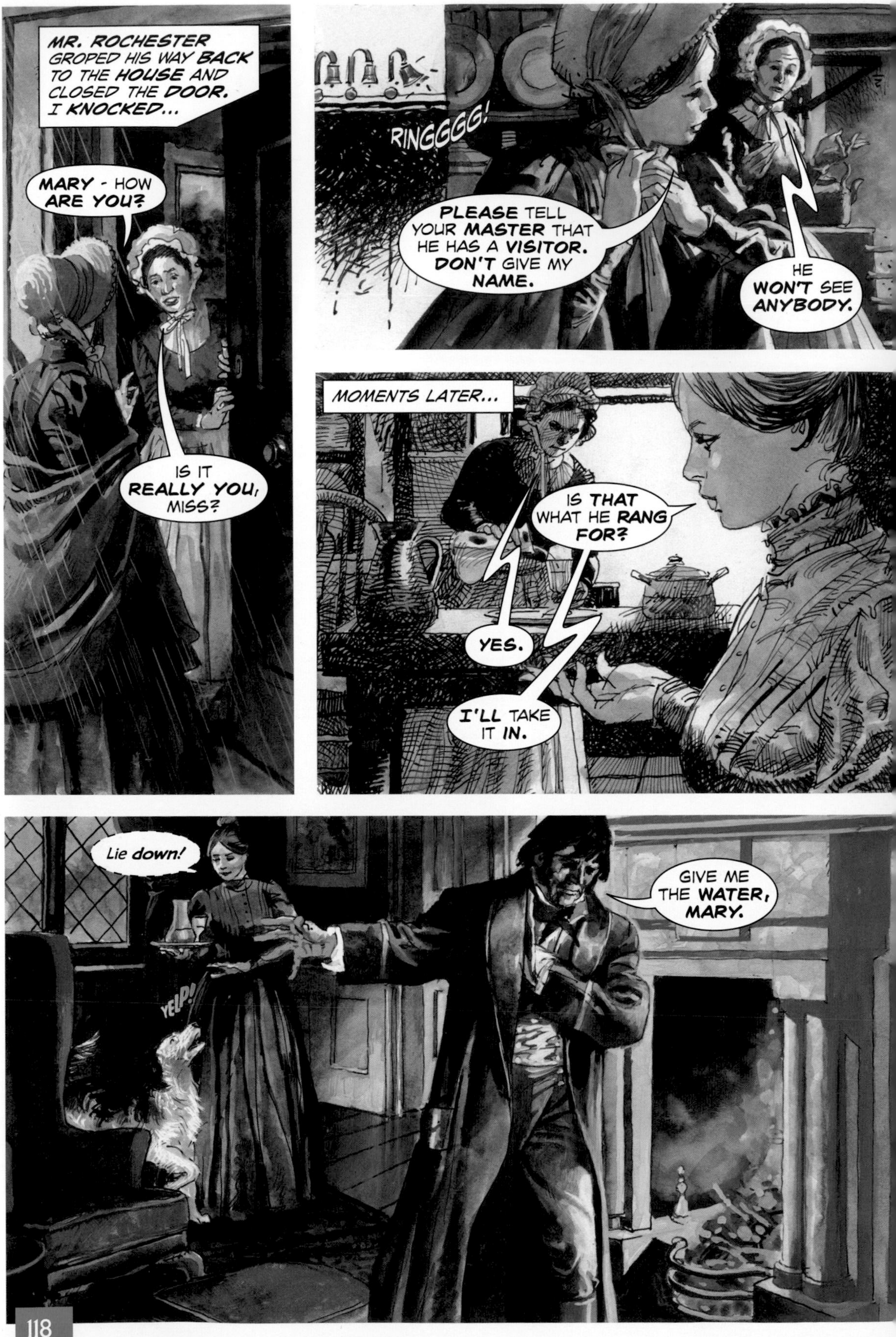

MR. ROCHESTER GROPED HIS WAY BACK TO THE HOUSE AND CLOSED THE DOOR. I KNOCKED...
MARY - HOW ARE YOU?
IS IT REALLY YOU, MISS?
RINGGGG!
PLEASE TELL YOUR MASTER THAT HE HAS A VISITOR. DON'T GIVE MY NAME.
HE WON'T SEE ANYBODY.
MOMENTS LATER...
IS THAT WHAT HE RANG FOR?
YES.
I'LL TAKE IT IN.
Lie down!
GIVE ME THE WATER, MARY.
YELP!

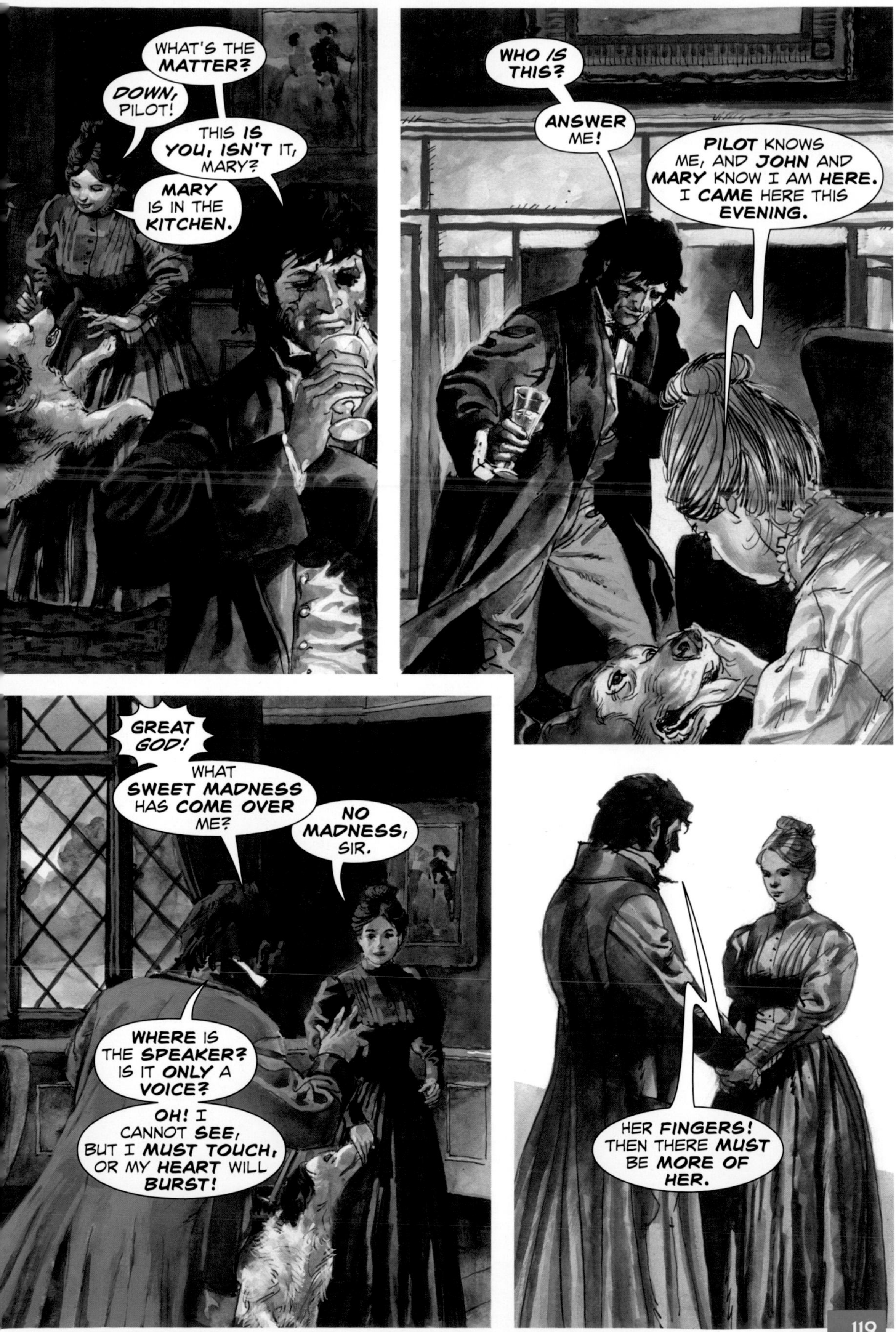
WHAT'S THE MATTER?
DOWN, PILOT!
THIS IS YOU, ISN'T IT, MARY?
MARY IS IN THE KITCHEN.
WHO IS THIS?
ANSWER ME!
PILOT KNOWS ME, AND JOHN AND MARY KNOW I AM HERE. I CAME HERE THIS EVENING.
GREAT GOD!
WHAT SWEET MADNESS HAS COME OVER ME?
NO MADNESS, SIR.
WHERE IS THE SPEAKER? IS IT ONLY A VOICE?
OH! I CANNOT SEE, BUT I MUST TOUCH, OR MY HEART WILL BURST!
HER FINGERS! THEN THERE MUST BE MORE OF HER.

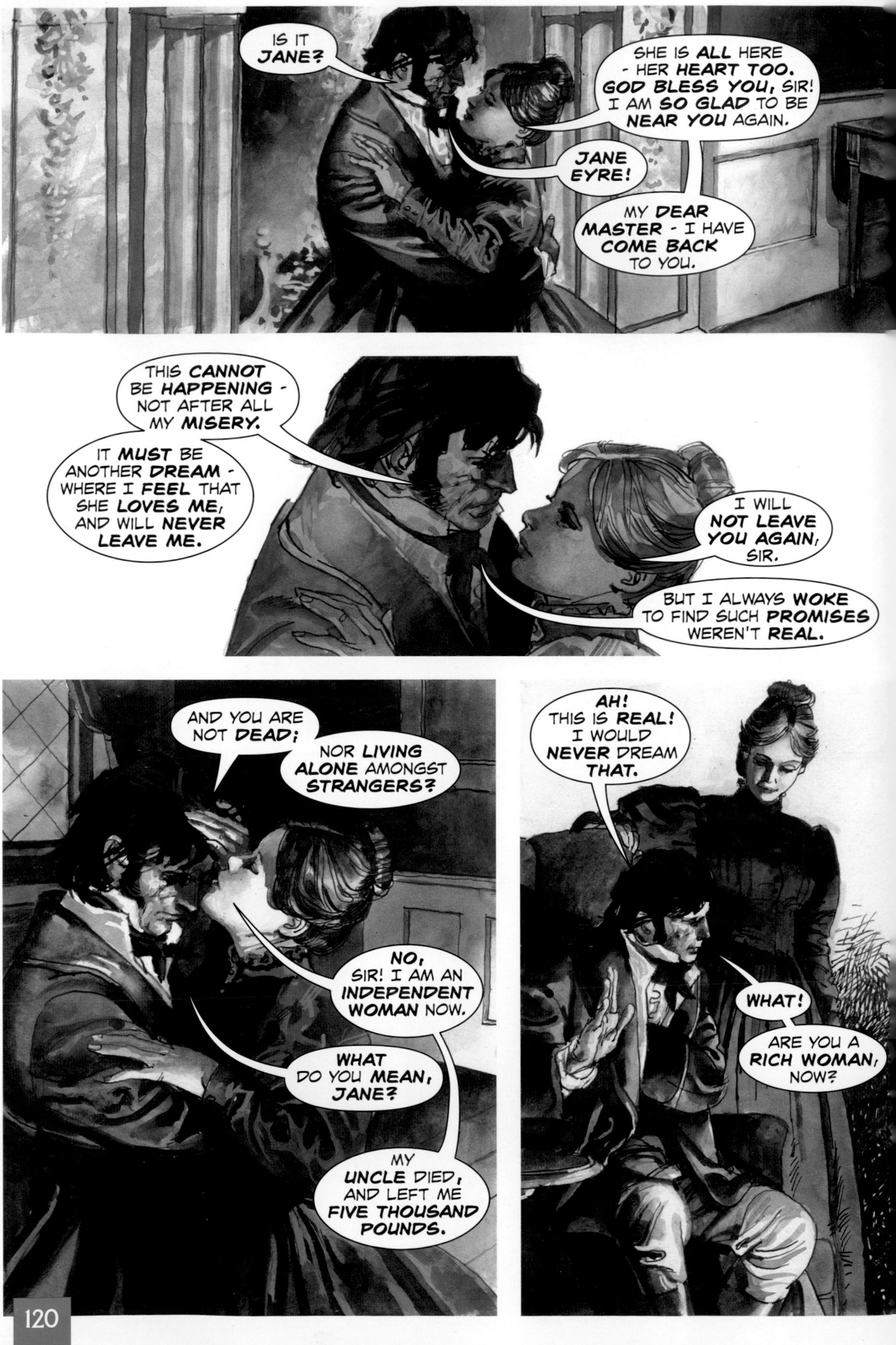
IS IT JANE?
SHE IS ALL HERE - HER HEART TOO. GOD BLESS YOU, SIR! I AM SO GLAD TO BE NEAR YOU AGAIN.
JANE EYRE!
MY DEAR MASTER - I HAVE COME BACK TO YOU.
THIS CANNOT BE HAPPENING - NOT AFTER ALL MY MISERY.
IT MUST BE ANOTHER DREAM - WHERE I FEEL THAT SHE LOVES ME, AND WILL NEVER LEAVE ME.
I WILL NOT LEAVE YOU AGAIN, SIR.
BUT I ALWAYS WOKE TO FIND SUCH PROMISES WEREN'T REAL.
AND YOU ARE NOT DEAD;
NOR LIVING ALONE AMONGST STRANGERS?
NO, SIR! I AM AN INDEPENDENT WOMAN NOW.
WHAT DO YOU MEAN, JANE?
MY UNCLE DIED, AND LEFT ME FIVE THOUSAND POUNDS.
AH! THIS IS REAL! I WOULD NEVER DREAM THAT.
WHAT!
ARE YOU A RICH WOMAN, NOW?

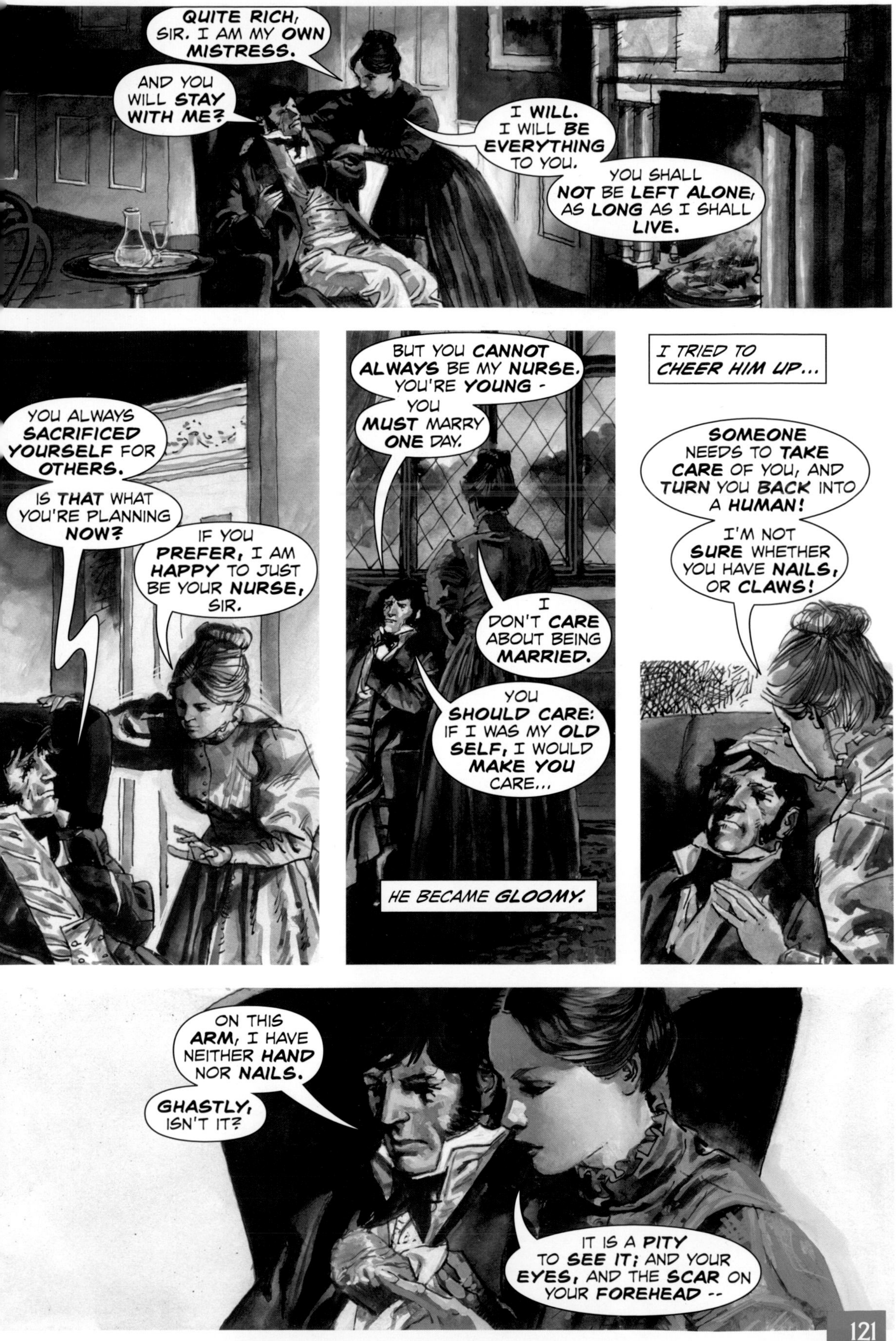
QUITE RICH, SIR. I AM MY OWN MISTRESS.
AND YOU WILL STAY WITH ME?
I WILL. I WILL BE EVERYTHING TO YOU.
YOU SHALL NOT BE LEFT ALONE, AS LONG AS I SHALL LIVE.
YOU ALWAYS SACRIFICED YOURSELF FOR OTHERS.
IS THAT WHAT YOU'RE PLANNING NOW?
IF YOU PREFER, I AM HAPPY TO JUST BE YOUR NURSE, SIR.
BUT YOU CANNOT ALWAYS BE MY NURSE. YOU'RE YOUNG - YOU MUST MARRY ONE DAY.
I DON'T CARE ABOUT BEING MARRIED.
YOU SHOULD CARE: IF I WAS MY OLD SELF, I WOULD MAKE YOU CARE...
HE BECAME GLOOMY.
I TRIED TO CHEER HIM UP...
SOMEONE NEEDS TO TAKE CARE OF YOU, AND TURN YOU BACK INTO A HUMAN!
I'M NOT SURE WHETHER YOU HAVE NAILS, OR CLAWS!
ON THIS ARM, I HAVE NEITHER HAND NOR NAILS.
GHASTLY, ISN'T IT?
IT IS A PITY TO SEE IT; AND YOUR EYES, AND THE SCAR ON YOUR FOREHEAD --

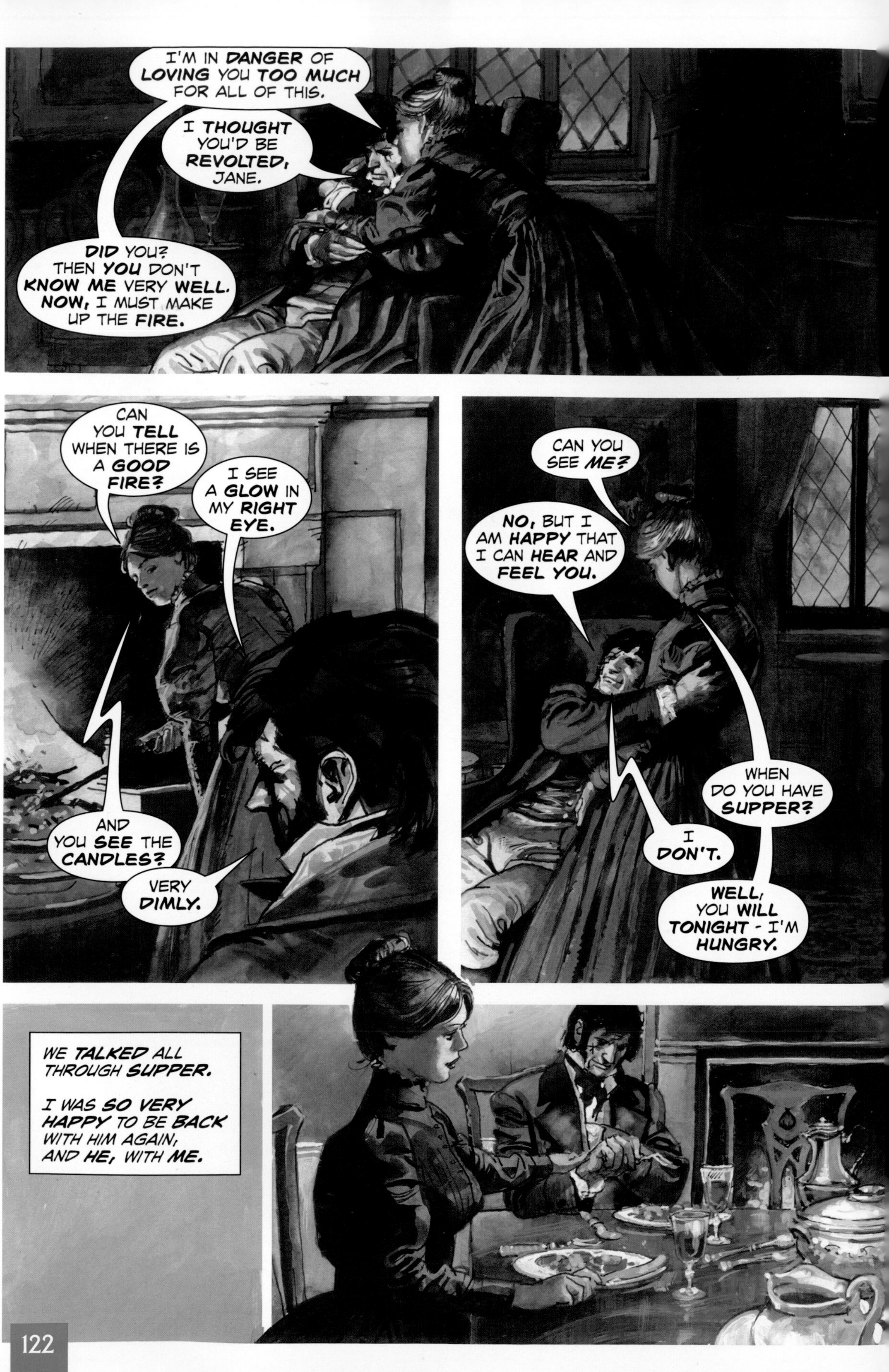
I'M IN **DANGER** OF **LOVING** YOU **TOO MUCH** FOR ALL OF THIS.
I **THOUGHT** YOU'D BE **REVOLTED,** JANE.
DID YOU? THEN **YOU** DON'T **KNOW ME** VERY **WELL. NOW,** I MUST MAKE UP THE **FIRE.**
CAN YOU **TELL** WHEN THERE IS A **GOOD FIRE?**
I SEE A **GLOW** IN MY **RIGHT EYE.**
AND YOU **SEE** THE **CANDLES?**
VERY **DIMLY.**
CAN YOU SEE ***ME?***
NO, BUT I AM **HAPPY** THAT I CAN **HEAR** AND **FEEL YOU.**
WHEN DO YOU HAVE **SUPPER?**
I **DON'T.**
WELL, YOU **WILL TONIGHT** - I'M **HUNGRY.**
*WE **TALKED** ALL THROUGH **SUPPER.***
*I WAS **SO VERY HAPPY** TO BE **BACK** WITH HIM AGAIN, AND **HE,** WITH **ME.***

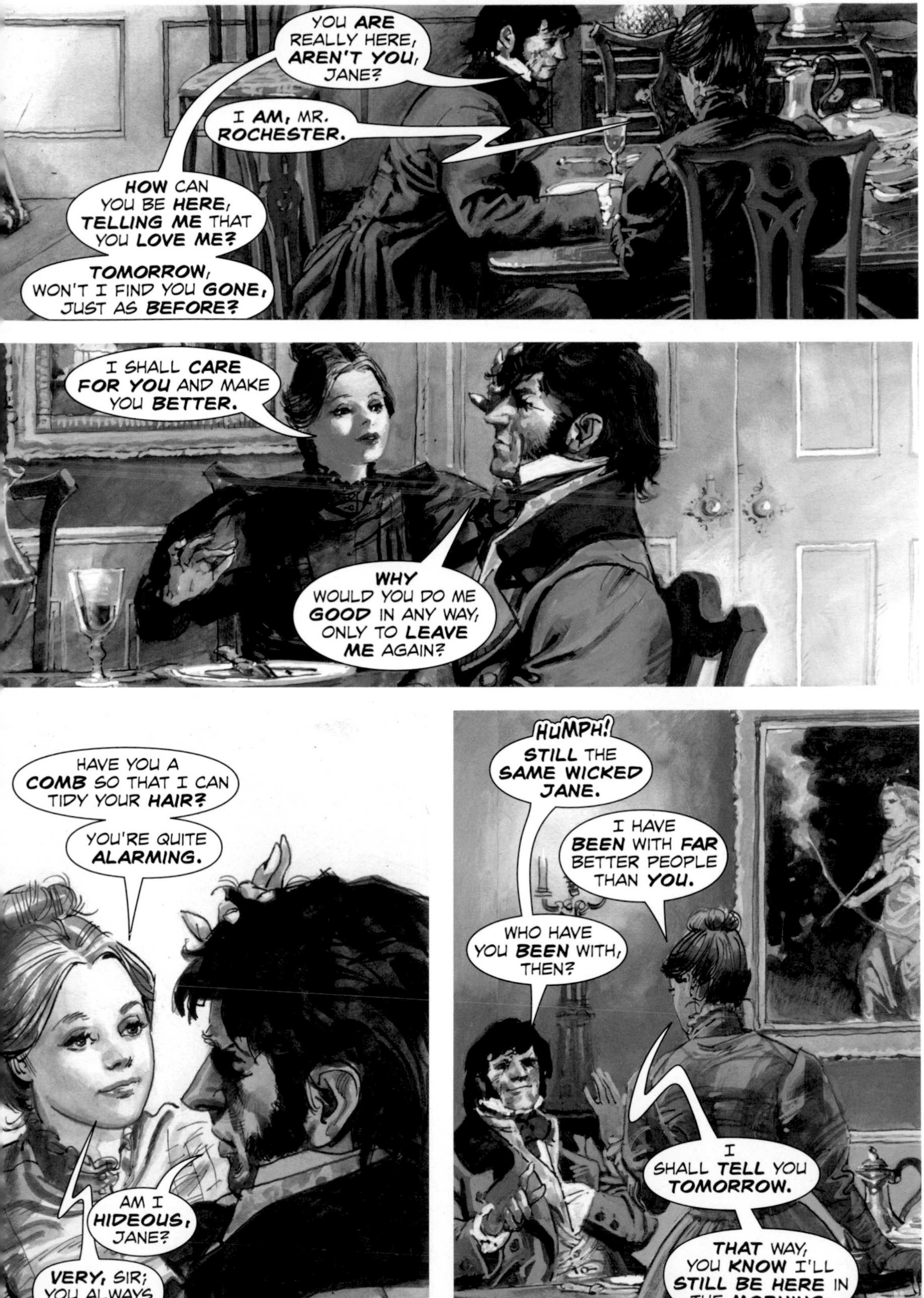
YOU ARE REALLY HERE, AREN'T YOU, JANE?
I AM, MR. ROCHESTER.
HOW CAN YOU BE HERE, TELLING ME THAT YOU LOVE ME?
TOMORROW, WON'T I FIND YOU GONE, JUST AS BEFORE?
I SHALL CARE FOR YOU AND MAKE YOU BETTER.
WHY WOULD YOU DO ME GOOD IN ANY WAY, ONLY TO LEAVE ME AGAIN?
HAVE YOU A COMB SO THAT I CAN TIDY YOUR HAIR?
YOU'RE QUITE ALARMING.
AM I HIDEOUS, JANE?
VERY, SIR; YOU ALWAYS WERE.
HUMPH! STILL THE SAME WICKED JANE.
I HAVE BEEN WITH FAR BETTER PEOPLE THAN YOU.
WHO HAVE YOU BEEN WITH, THEN?
I SHALL TELL YOU TOMORROW.
THAT WAY, YOU KNOW I'LL STILL BE HERE IN THE MORNING.

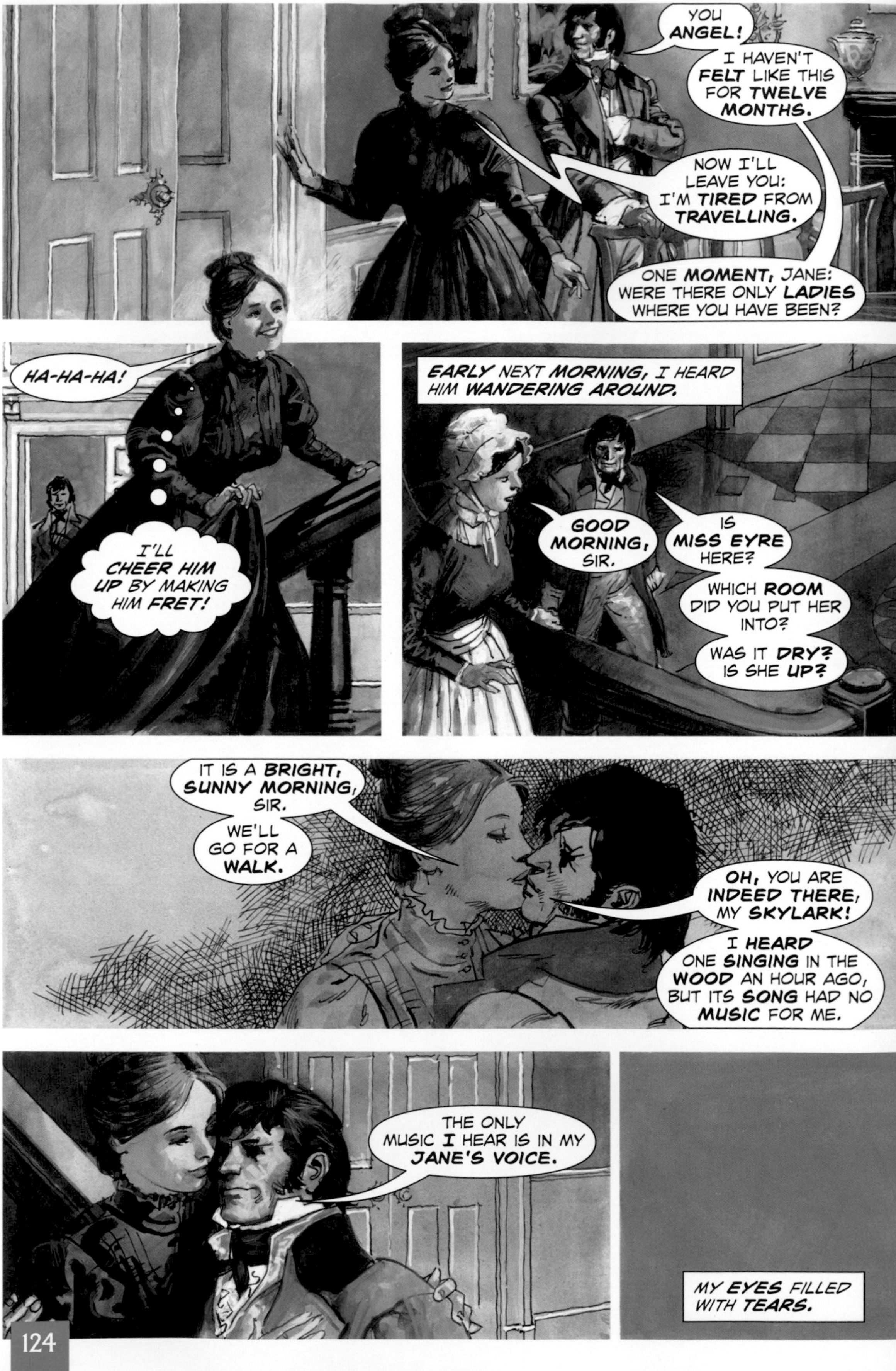
YOU ANGEL!
I HAVEN'T FELT LIKE THIS FOR TWELVE MONTHS.
NOW I'LL LEAVE YOU: I'M TIRED FROM TRAVELLING.
ONE MOMENT, JANE: WERE THERE ONLY LADIES WHERE YOU HAVE BEEN?
HA-HA-HA!
I'LL CHEER HIM UP BY MAKING HIM FRET!
EARLY NEXT MORNING, I HEARD HIM WANDERING AROUND.
GOOD MORNING, SIR.
IS MISS EYRE HERE?
WHICH ROOM DID YOU PUT HER INTO?
WAS IT DRY? IS SHE UP?
IT IS A BRIGHT, SUNNY MORNING, SIR.
WE'LL GO FOR A WALK.
OH, YOU ARE INDEED THERE, MY SKYLARK!
I HEARD ONE SINGING IN THE WOOD AN HOUR AGO, BUT ITS SONG HAD NO MUSIC FOR ME.
THE ONLY MUSIC I HEAR IS IN MY JANE'S VOICE.
MY EYES FILLED WITH TEARS.

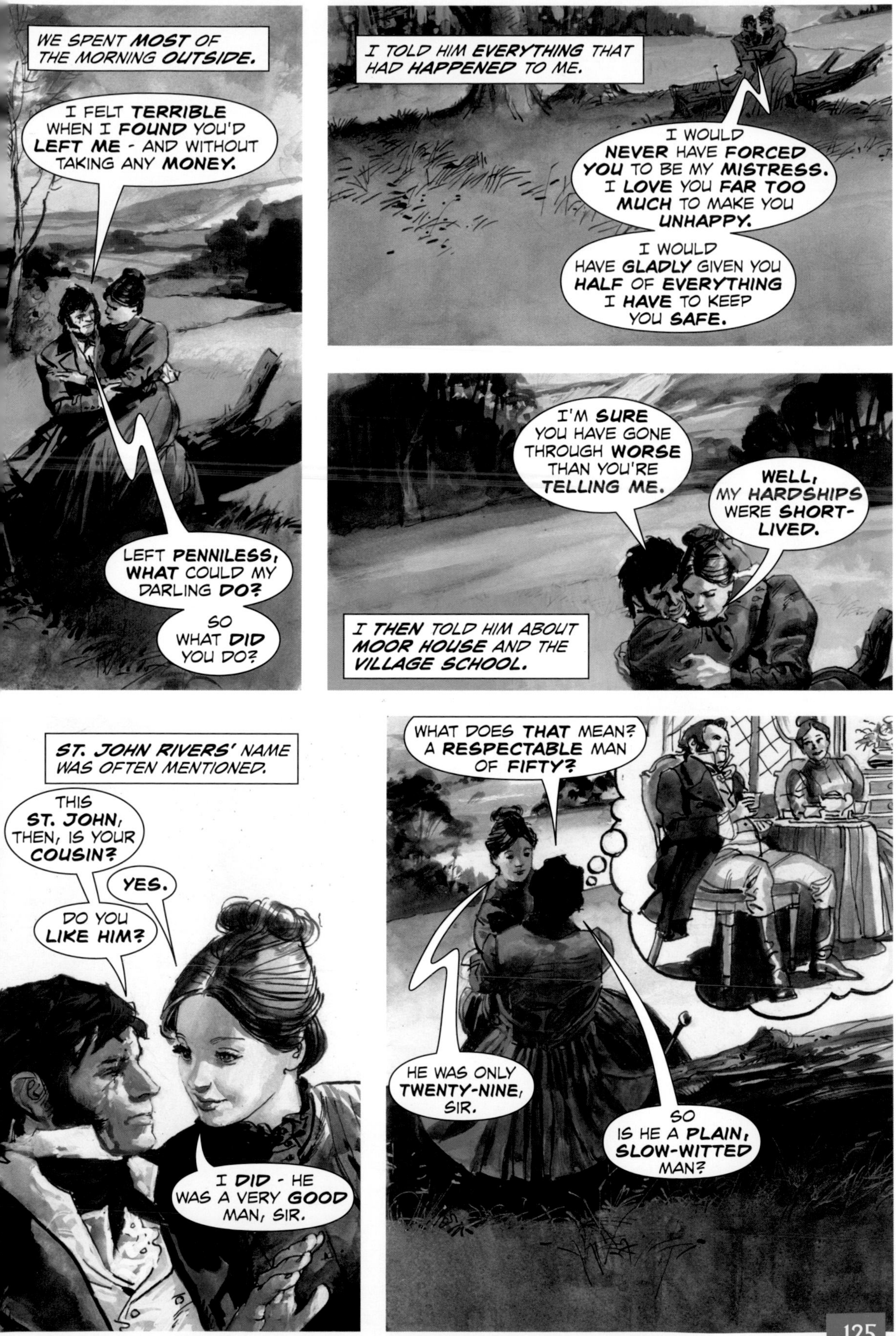
WE SPENT MOST OF THE MORNING OUTSIDE.
I FELT TERRIBLE WHEN I FOUND YOU'D LEFT ME - AND WITHOUT TAKING ANY MONEY.
LEFT PENNILESS, WHAT COULD MY DARLING DO?
SO WHAT DID YOU DO?
I TOLD HIM EVERYTHING THAT HAD HAPPENED TO ME.
I WOULD NEVER HAVE FORCED YOU TO BE MY MISTRESS. I LOVE YOU FAR TOO MUCH TO MAKE YOU UNHAPPY.
I WOULD HAVE GLADLY GIVEN YOU HALF OF EVERYTHING I HAVE TO KEEP YOU SAFE.
I'M SURE YOU HAVE GONE THROUGH WORSE THAN YOU'RE TELLING ME.
WELL, MY HARDSHIPS WERE SHORT-LIVED.
I THEN TOLD HIM ABOUT MOOR HOUSE AND THE VILLAGE SCHOOL.
ST. JOHN RIVERS' NAME WAS OFTEN MENTIONED.
THIS ST. JOHN, THEN, IS YOUR COUSIN?
YES.
DO YOU LIKE HIM?
I DID - HE WAS A VERY GOOD MAN, SIR.
WHAT DOES THAT MEAN? A RESPECTABLE MAN OF FIFTY?
HE WAS ONLY TWENTY-NINE, SIR.
SO IS HE A PLAIN, SLOW-WITTED MAN?

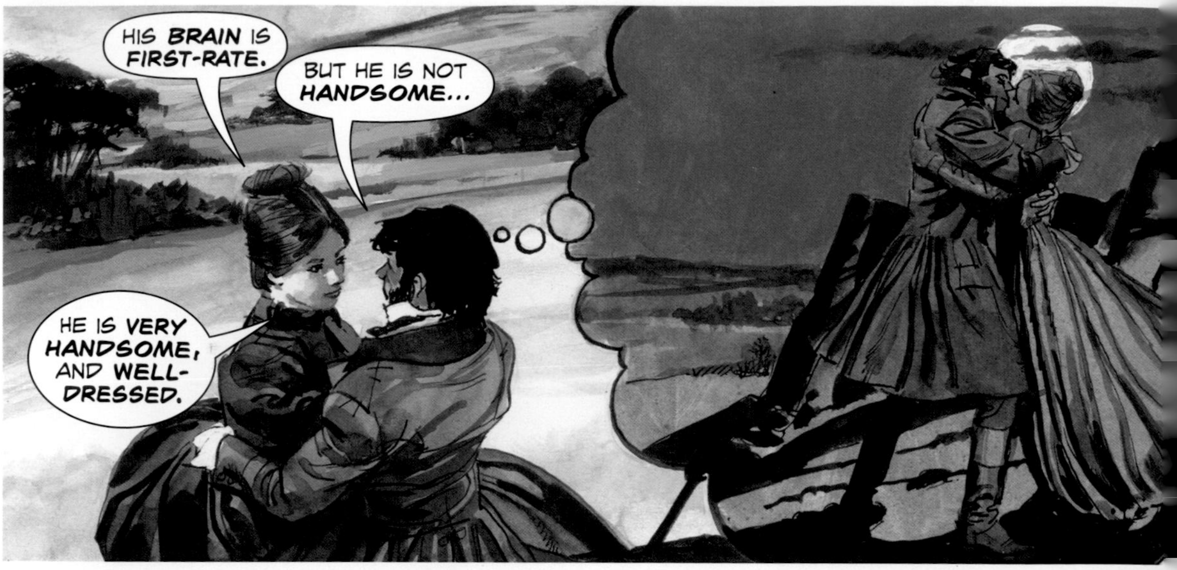
HIS BRAIN IS FIRST-RATE.
BUT HE IS NOT HANDSOME...
HE IS VERY HANDSOME, AND WELL-DRESSED.

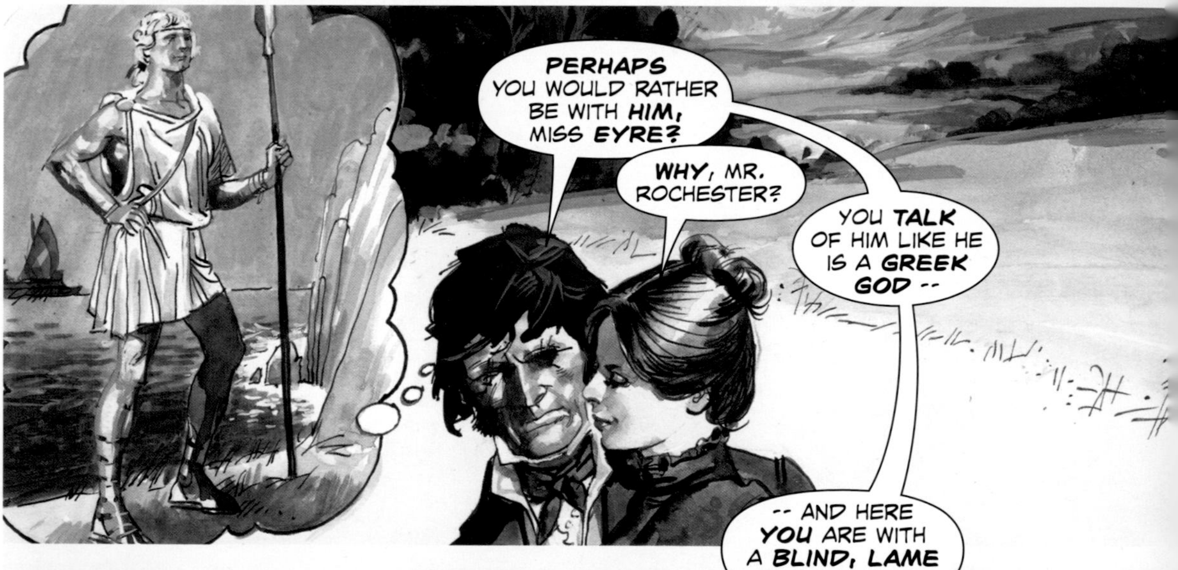
PERHAPS YOU WOULD RATHER BE WITH HIM, MISS EYRE?
WHY, MR. ROCHESTER?
YOU TALK OF HIM LIKE HE IS A GREEK GOD --
-- AND HERE YOU ARE WITH A BLIND, LAME BLACKSMITH.

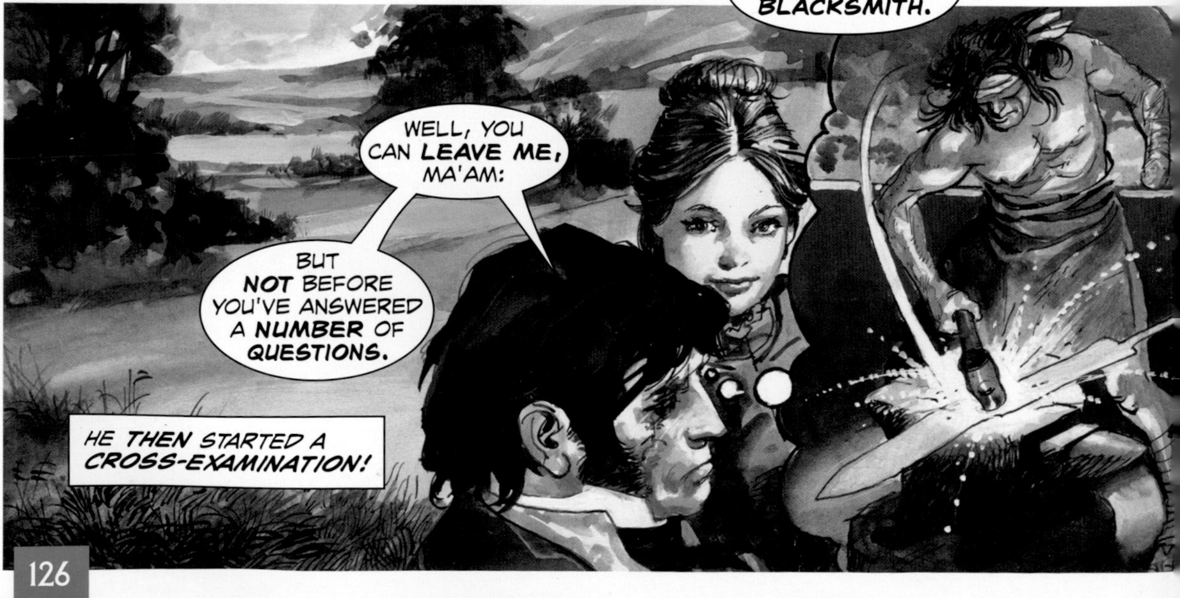
WELL, YOU CAN LEAVE ME, MA'AM:
BUT NOT BEFORE YOU'VE ANSWERED A NUMBER OF QUESTIONS.
HE THEN STARTED A CROSS-EXAMINATION!

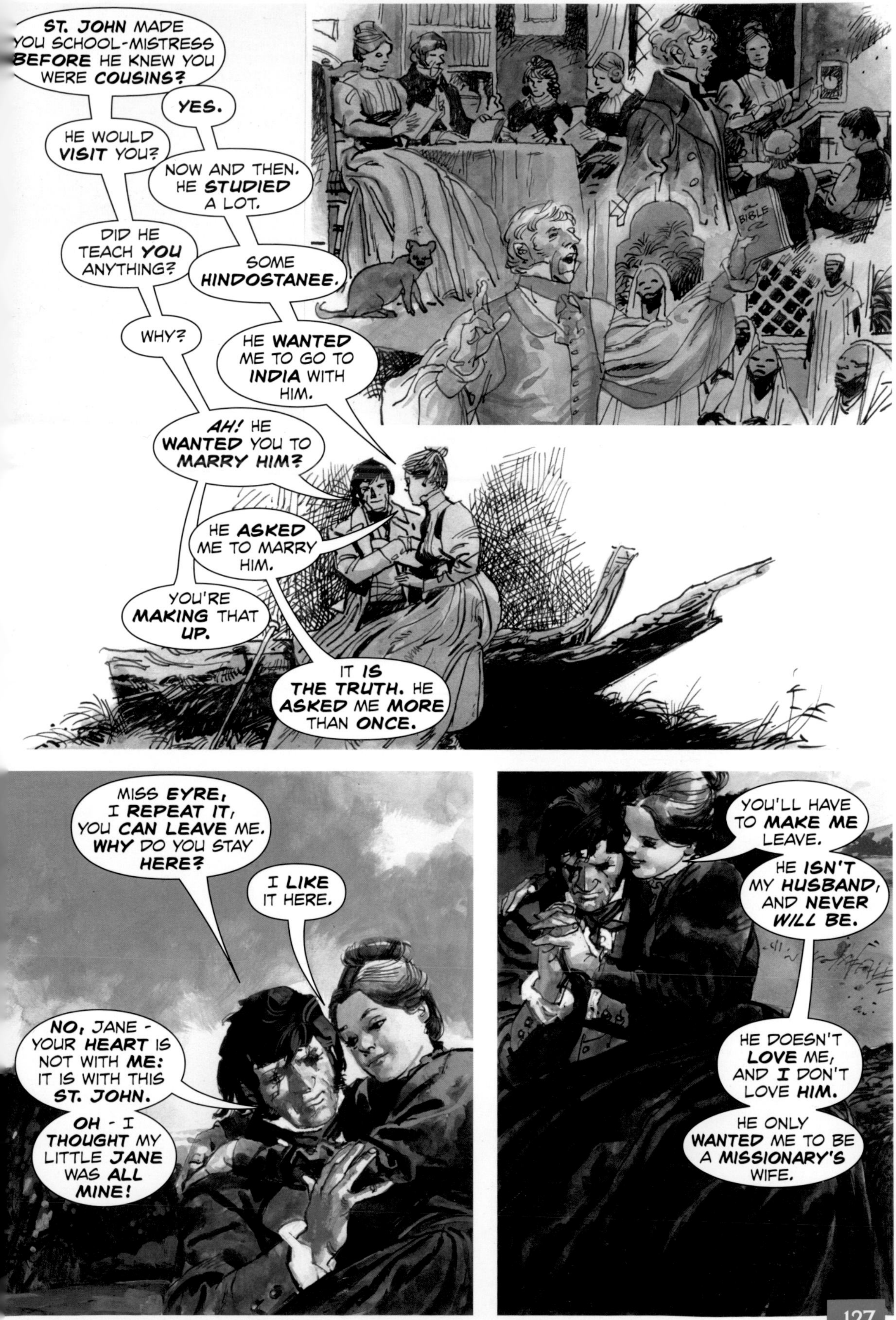

ST. JOHN MADE YOU SCHOOL-MISTRESS BEFORE HE KNEW YOU WERE COUSINS?
YES.
HE WOULD VISIT YOU?
NOW AND THEN. HE STUDIED A LOT.
DID HE TEACH YOU ANYTHING?
SOME HINDOSTANEE.
WHY?
HE WANTED ME TO GO TO INDIA WITH HIM.
AH! HE WANTED YOU TO MARRY HIM?
HE ASKED ME TO MARRY HIM.
YOU'RE MAKING THAT UP.
IT IS THE TRUTH. HE ASKED ME MORE THAN ONCE.
MISS EYRE, I REPEAT IT, YOU CAN LEAVE ME. WHY DO YOU STAY HERE?
I LIKE IT HERE.
NO, JANE - YOUR HEART IS NOT WITH ME: IT IS WITH THIS ST. JOHN.
OH - I THOUGHT MY LITTLE JANE WAS ALL MINE!
YOU'LL HAVE TO MAKE ME LEAVE.
HE ISN'T MY HUSBAND, AND NEVER WILL BE.
HE DOESN'T LOVE ME, AND I DON'T LOVE HIM.
HE ONLY WANTED ME TO BE A MISSIONARY'S WIFE.

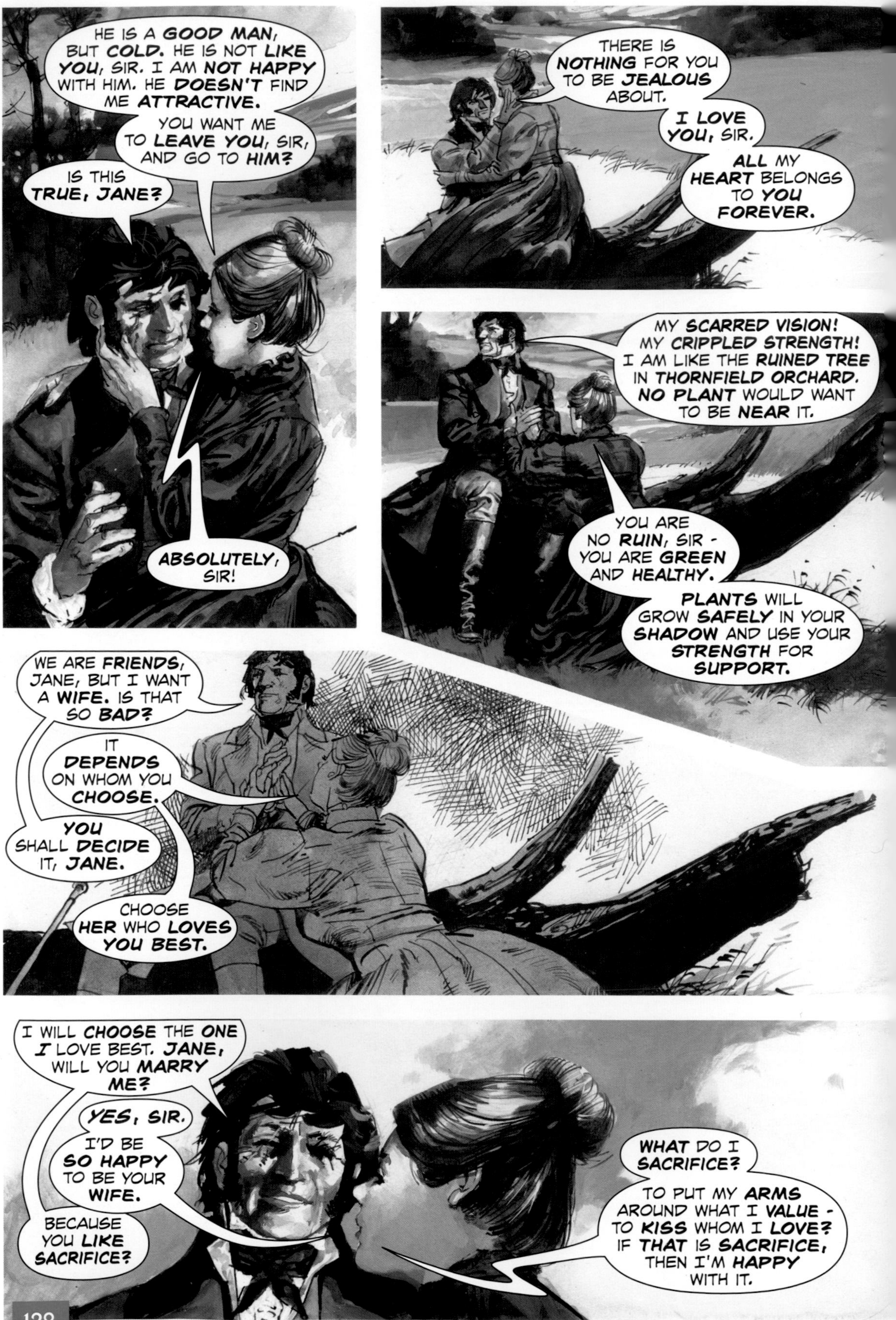

HE IS A GOOD MAN, BUT COLD. HE IS NOT LIKE YOU, SIR. I AM NOT HAPPY WITH HIM. HE DOESN'T FIND ME ATTRACTIVE.
YOU WANT ME TO LEAVE YOU, SIR, AND GO TO HIM?
IS THIS TRUE, JANE?
ABSOLUTELY, SIR!
THERE IS NOTHING FOR YOU TO BE JEALOUS ABOUT.
I LOVE YOU, SIR.
ALL MY HEART BELONGS TO YOU FOREVER.
MY SCARRED VISION! MY CRIPPLED STRENGTH! I AM LIKE THE RUINED TREE IN THORNFIELD ORCHARD. NO PLANT WOULD WANT TO BE NEAR IT.
YOU ARE NO RUIN, SIR - YOU ARE GREEN AND HEALTHY.
PLANTS WILL GROW SAFELY IN YOUR SHADOW AND USE YOUR STRENGTH FOR SUPPORT.
WE ARE FRIENDS, JANE, BUT I WANT A WIFE. IS THAT SO BAD?
IT DEPENDS ON WHOM YOU CHOOSE.
YOU SHALL DECIDE IT, JANE.
CHOOSE HER WHO LOVES YOU BEST.
I WILL CHOOSE THE ONE I LOVE BEST. JANE, WILL YOU MARRY ME?
YES, SIR.
I'D BE SO HAPPY TO BE YOUR WIFE.
BECAUSE YOU LIKE SACRIFICE?
WHAT DO I SACRIFICE?
TO PUT MY ARMS AROUND WHAT I VALUE - TO KISS WHOM I LOVE? IF THAT IS SACRIFICE, THEN I'M HAPPY WITH IT.

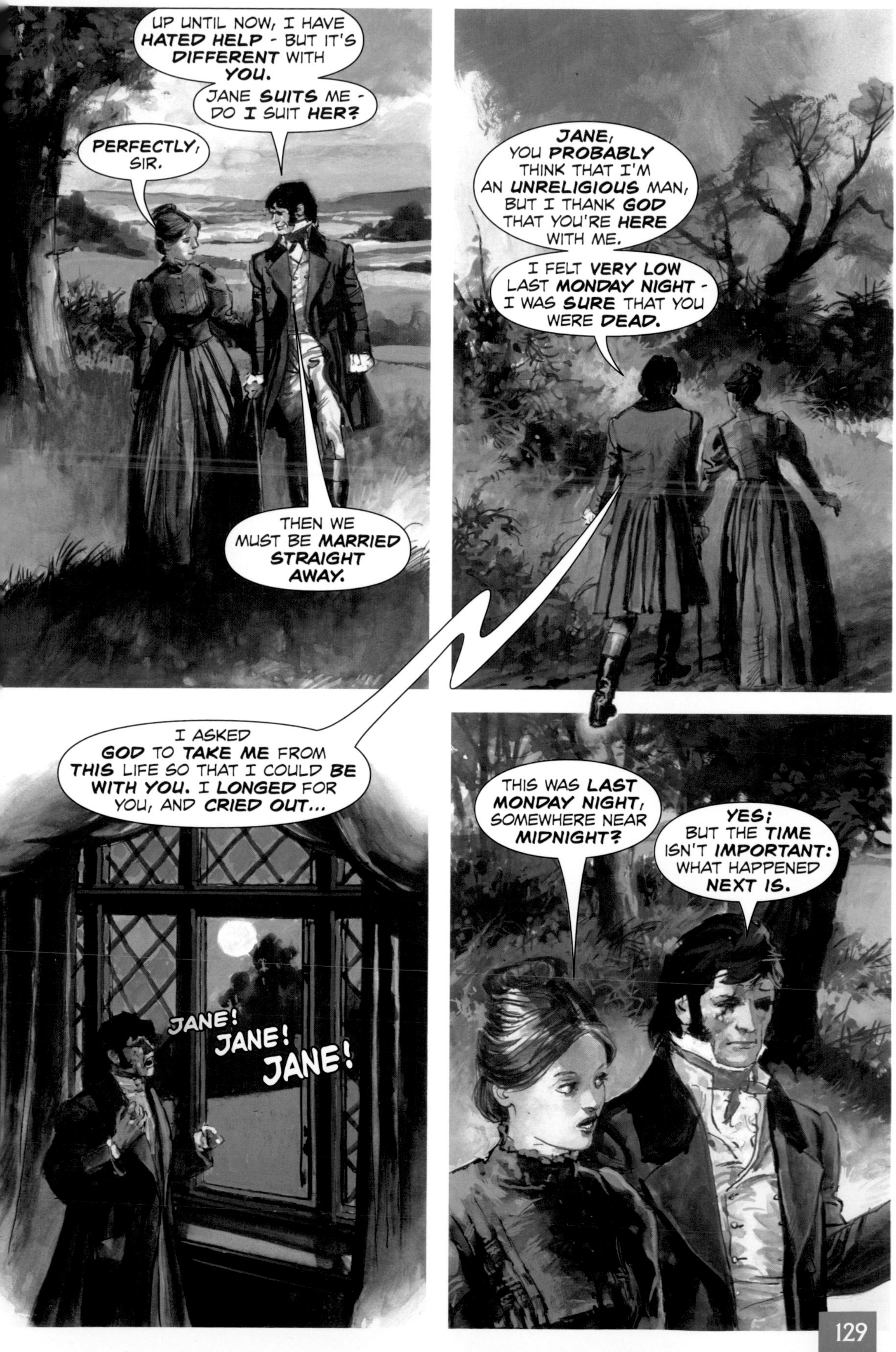
UP UNTIL NOW, I HAVE HATED HELP - BUT IT'S DIFFERENT WITH YOU.
JANE SUITS ME - DO I SUIT HER?
PERFECTLY, SIR.
THEN WE MUST BE MARRIED STRAIGHT AWAY.
JANE, YOU PROBABLY THINK THAT I'M AN UNRELIGIOUS MAN, BUT I THANK GOD THAT YOU'RE HERE WITH ME.
I FELT VERY LOW LAST MONDAY NIGHT - I WAS SURE THAT YOU WERE DEAD.
I ASKED GOD TO TAKE ME FROM THIS LIFE SO THAT I COULD BE WITH YOU. I LONGED FOR YOU, AND CRIED OUT...
JANE! JANE! JANE!
THIS WAS LAST MONDAY NIGHT, SOMEWHERE NEAR MIDNIGHT?
YES; BUT THE TIME ISN'T IMPORTANT: WHAT HAPPENED NEXT IS.

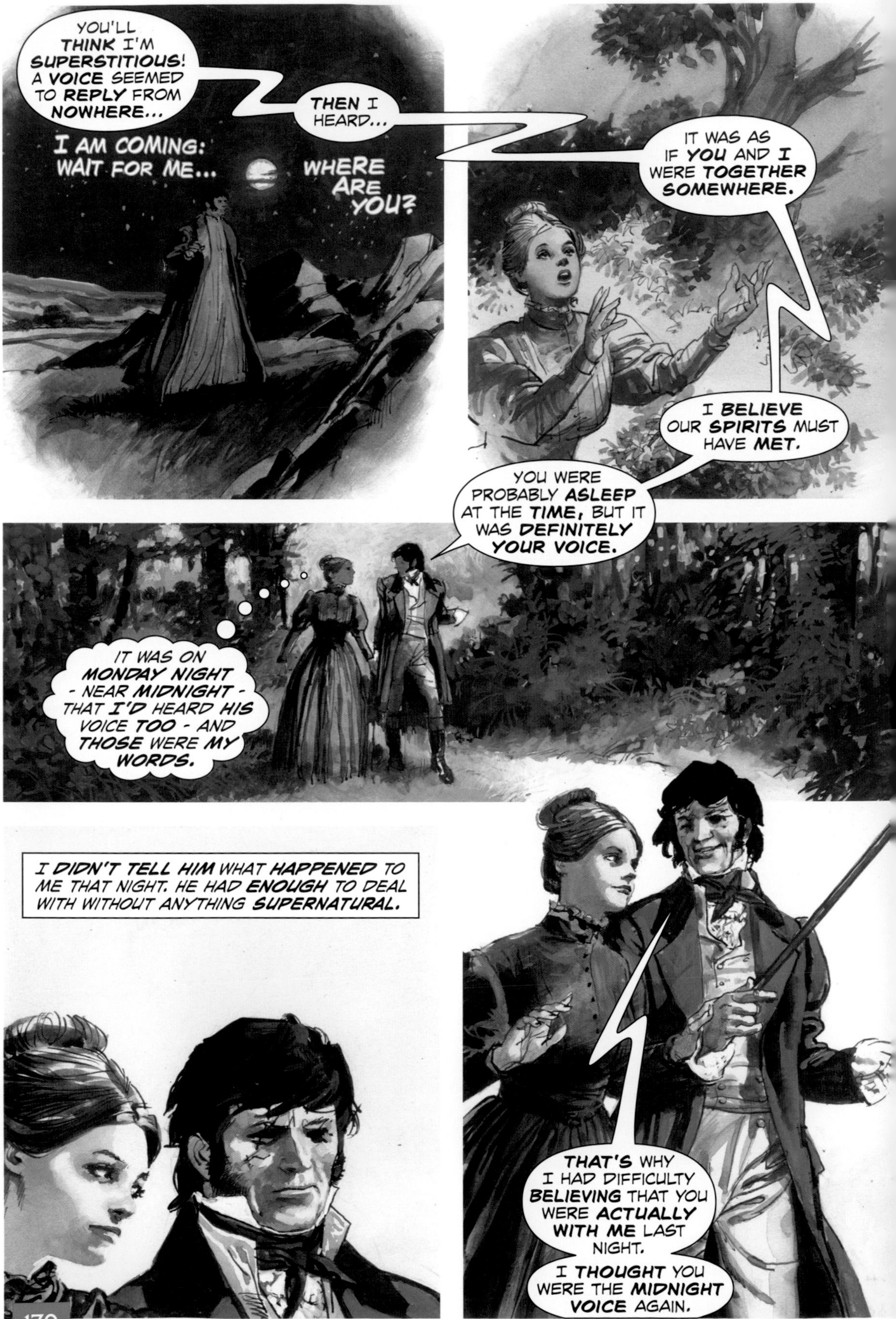
YOU'LL THINK I'M SUPERSTITIOUS! A VOICE SEEMED TO REPLY FROM NOWHERE...
I AM COMING: WAIT FOR ME...
WHERE ARE YOU?
THEN I HEARD...
IT WAS AS IF YOU AND I WERE TOGETHER SOMEWHERE.
I BELIEVE OUR SPIRITS MUST HAVE MET.
YOU WERE PROBABLY ASLEEP AT THE TIME, BUT IT WAS DEFINITELY YOUR VOICE.
IT WAS ON MONDAY NIGHT - NEAR MIDNIGHT - THAT I'D HEARD HIS VOICE TOO - AND THOSE WERE MY WORDS.
I DIDN'T TELL HIM WHAT HAPPENED TO ME THAT NIGHT. HE HAD ENOUGH TO DEAL WITH WITHOUT ANYTHING SUPERNATURAL.
THAT'S WHY I HAD DIFFICULTY BELIEVING THAT YOU WERE ACTUALLY WITH ME LAST NIGHT.
I THOUGHT YOU WERE THE MIDNIGHT VOICE AGAIN.

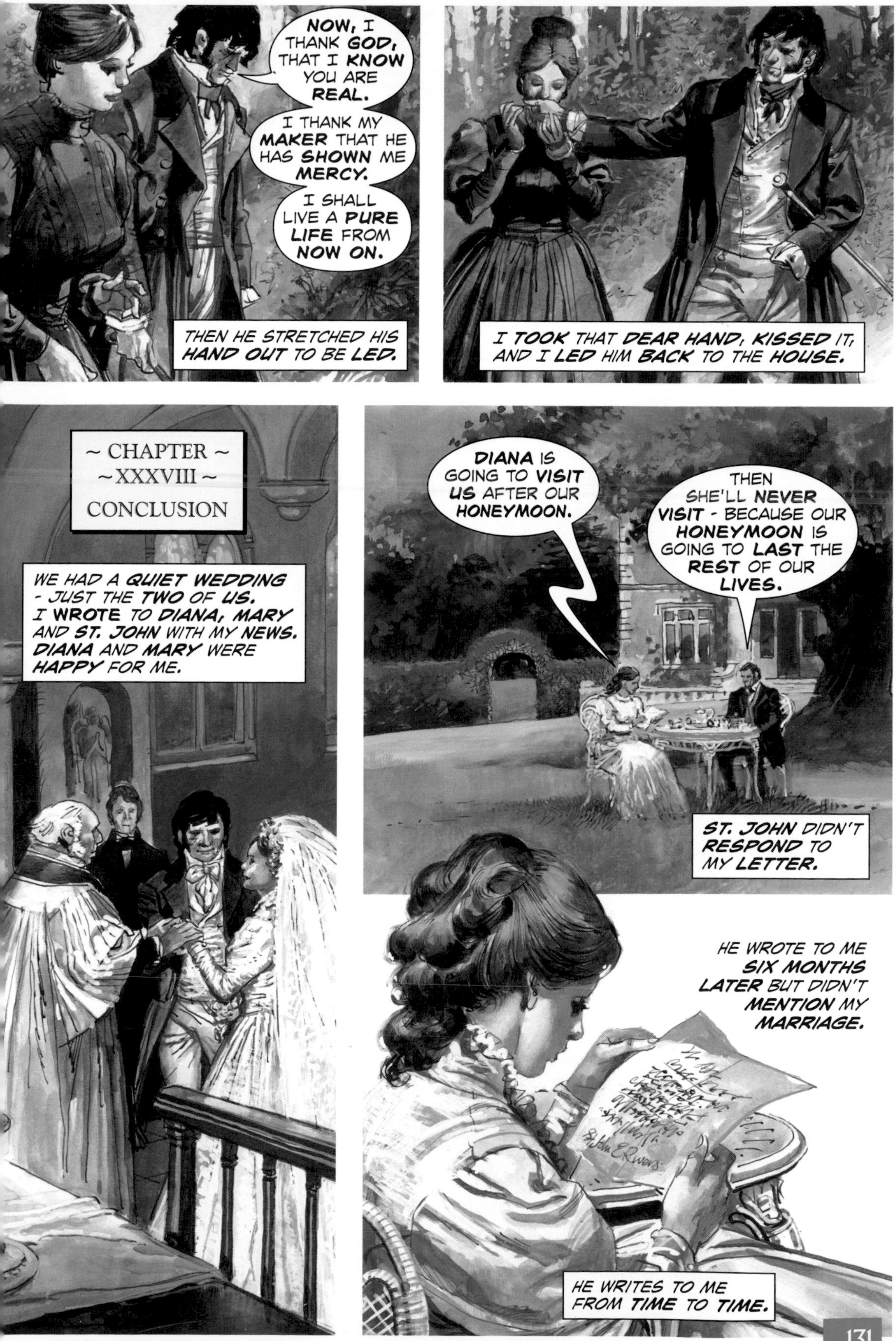
NOW, I THANK GOD, THAT I KNOW YOU ARE REAL.
I THANK MY MAKER THAT HE HAS SHOWN ME MERCY.
I SHALL LIVE A PURE LIFE FROM NOW ON.
THEN HE STRETCHED HIS HAND OUT TO BE LED.
I TOOK THAT DEAR HAND, KISSED IT, AND I LED HIM BACK TO THE HOUSE.
~ CHAPTER ~
~ XXXVIII ~
CONCLUSION
WE HAD A QUIET WEDDING - JUST THE TWO OF US. I WROTE TO DIANA, MARY AND ST. JOHN WITH MY NEWS. DIANA AND MARY WERE HAPPY FOR ME.
DIANA IS GOING TO VISIT US AFTER OUR HONEYMOON.
THEN SHE'LL NEVER VISIT - BECAUSE OUR HONEYMOON IS GOING TO LAST THE REST OF OUR LIVES.
ST. JOHN DIDN'T RESPOND TO MY LETTER.
HE WROTE TO ME SIX MONTHS LATER BUT DIDN'T MENTION MY MARRIAGE.
HE WRITES TO ME FROM TIME TO TIME.

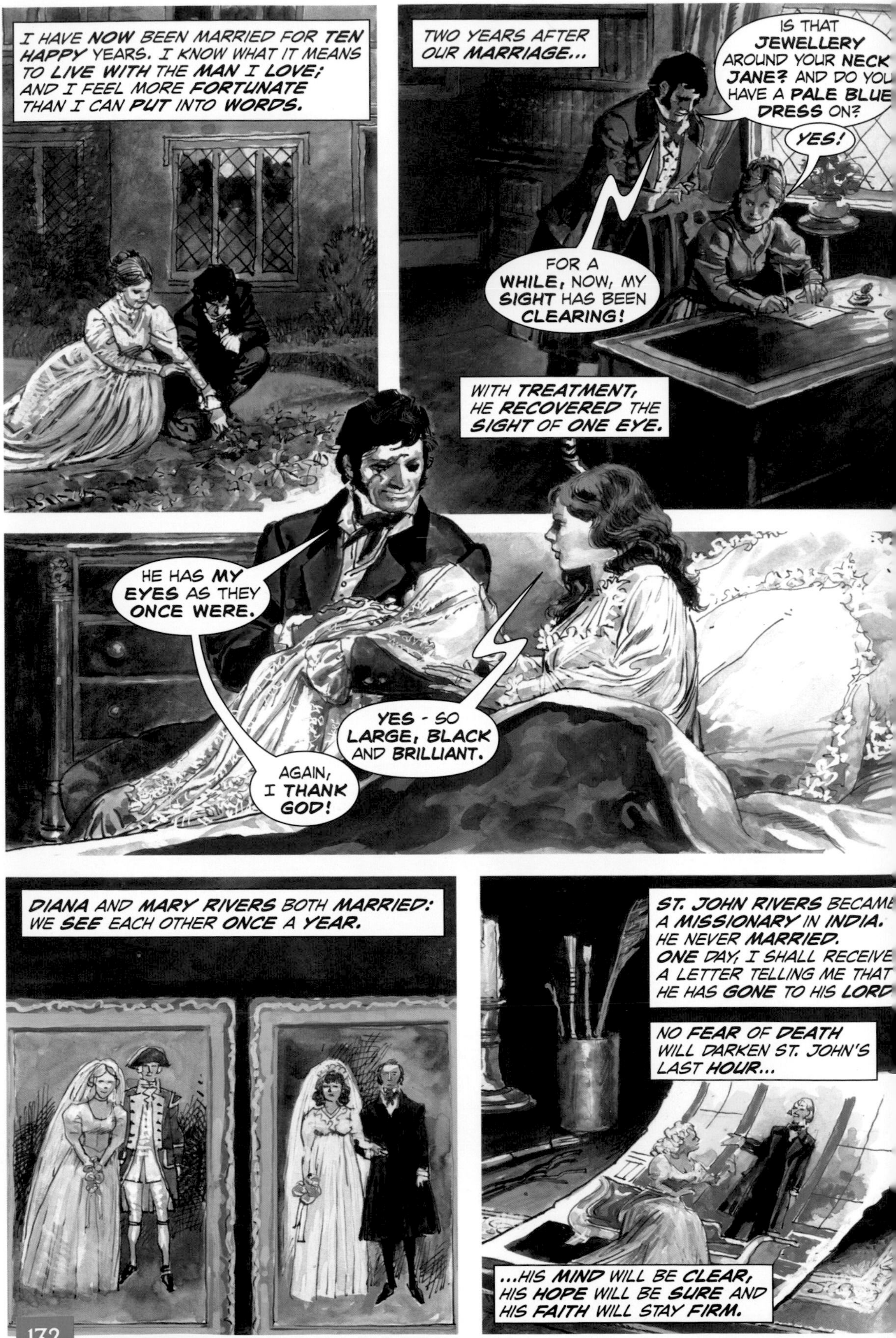

I HAVE NOW BEEN MARRIED FOR TEN HAPPY YEARS. I KNOW WHAT IT MEANS TO LIVE WITH THE MAN I LOVE; AND I FEEL MORE FORTUNATE THAN I CAN PUT INTO WORDS.
TWO YEARS AFTER OUR MARRIAGE...
IS THAT JEWELLERY AROUND YOUR NECK JANE? AND DO YOU HAVE A PALE BLUE DRESS ON?
YES!
FOR A WHILE, NOW, MY SIGHT HAS BEEN CLEARING!
WITH TREATMENT, HE RECOVERED THE SIGHT OF ONE EYE.
HE HAS MY EYES AS THEY ONCE WERE.
YES - SO LARGE, BLACK AND BRILLIANT.
AGAIN, I THANK GOD!
DIANA AND MARY RIVERS BOTH MARRIED: WE SEE EACH OTHER ONCE A YEAR.
ST. JOHN RIVERS BECAME A MISSIONARY IN INDIA. HE NEVER MARRIED. ONE DAY, I SHALL RECEIVE A LETTER TELLING ME THAT HE HAS GONE TO HIS LORD
NO FEAR OF DEATH WILL DARKEN ST. JOHN'S LAST HOUR...
...HIS MIND WILL BE CLEAR, HIS HOPE WILL BE SURE AND HIS FAITH WILL STAY FIRM.

Jane Eyre

The End

Charlotte Brontë

(1816 –1855)

"Literature cannot be the business of a woman's life..."

Poet Laureate Robert Southeys' letter to Charlotte Brontë in 1837

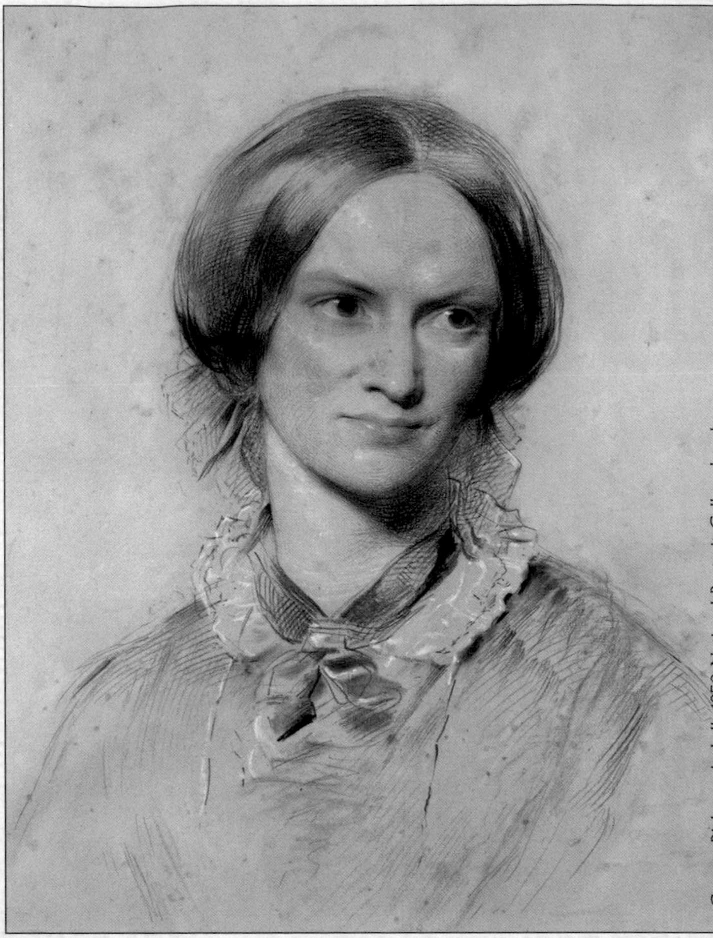

George Richmond, chalk, 1850 National Portrait Gallery, London

Charlotte Brontë was born on 21st April 1816, at 74 Market Street in the village of Thornton near Bradford, Yorkshire. She was one of six children born to Maria Branwell and Patrick Brontë: Maria (1814), Elizabeth (1815), Charlotte (1816), Patrick Branwell (who was known as Branwell, 1817), Emily (1818) and Anne (1820).

Her father, Patrick, was an Irish Anglican clergyman and writer, born in County Down, Ireland, in 1777. His surname was originally Brunty, but he decided to change his name, probably to give the impression of a more well-to-do background, giving the world the now familiar "Brontë." Charlotte's mother, Maria, was born in 1785, to a prosperous merchant family in Cornwall. Patrick and Maria met in Hartshead, Yorkshire, while she was helping her aunt with the domestic side of running a school.

In April 1820, when Charlotte was four years old, the family moved a short distance from Thornton to Haworth, where Patrick had been appointed perpetual curate of the church. Maria's sister, Elizabeth joined them a year later to help look after the children and to care for her sister, who was suffering from the final stages of cancer. She died in September 1821 - Charlotte was still only five years old.

The Parsonage at Haworth was a literary household. From early childhood, the Brontë children had written about the lives, wars and sufferings of people who lived in their own imaginary kingdoms. The story goes that Branwell had been given a set of toy soldiers in June 1826, and from these the children developed imaginary worlds of their own. Charlotte and Branwell wrote stories about their country — **"Angria"** — and Emily and Anne wrote articles and poems about theirs — **"Gondal"**. These sagas, plays, poems and stories were written down in handmade "little books" – books that they made from paper sheets stitched together. In a letter to author and biographer Elizabeth Gaskell, Patrick Brontë wrote:

> **"When mere children, as soon as they could read and write, Charlotte and her brother and sisters used to invent and act little plays of their own."**

In July 1824 Maria (ten) and Elizabeth (nine) were sent to the Clergy Daughter's School at Cowan Bridge, near Kirkby Lonsdale in Lancashire. Charlotte (eight) and Emily (six) joined them there in August. Life at boarding school must have been grim. Maria became ill and was sent home in February 1825; she died at Haworth in May. Elizabeth fell ill that same month and, like her sister, was sent home; she died just a few months later. Both sisters died of tuberculosis (also known as "consumption") and as a result of their deaths, Emily and Charlotte were withdrawn from the school. These events obviously had a great impact on Charlotte, who drew on the experience for *Jane Eyre* when she described Lowood School and the death of Helen Burns.

In fact much of the novel mirrors Charlotte's own life. Charlotte, like Jane, spent many years as a governess for a number of families - a career which she viewed with some distaste (a view which appears in Chapter 30 of this book, at the bottom of page 95). Having no personal fortune and few respectable ways of earning a living, this was the only socially acceptable option for many genteel young ladies. Emily and Anne also became governesses, although Emily's career as a teacher was short-lived; it is reported that she told her pupils at Miss Patchett's School in Halifax that she much preferred the school dog to any of them!

In 1842, Charlotte and Emily travelled to Brussels to study at the Pensionnat Heger – a boarding school run by Constantin Heger and his wife. Their Aunt Elizabeth Branwell paid for this trip, with the plan that they would set up their own school at the Parsonage when they returned. However, the girls were forced to return to England later that year when their Aunt Elizabeth died – just as in this book when Jane Eyre returns to Gateshead Hall when her Aunt Reed is on her death-bed.

Charlotte travelled alone to Brussels in January 1843 to take up a teaching post at Pensionnat Heger. This second stay was not a happy one: she was lonely without her sister, homesick, and had become deeply attached to Constantin Heger. She returned to Haworth a year later in January 1844. Her time at Pensionnat Heger became the inspiration for parts of two other books: *The Professor* and *Villette;* and her attraction to the married Constantin would seem to reflect Jane Eyre's love for Mr. Rochester.

Of the three sisters, Anne was the most successful teacher; but by 1845 the entire family, including Branwell, were all back at The Parsonage. Branwell returned home somewhat in disgrace for "proceedings bad beyond expression" - most likely a love affair with his employer's wife.

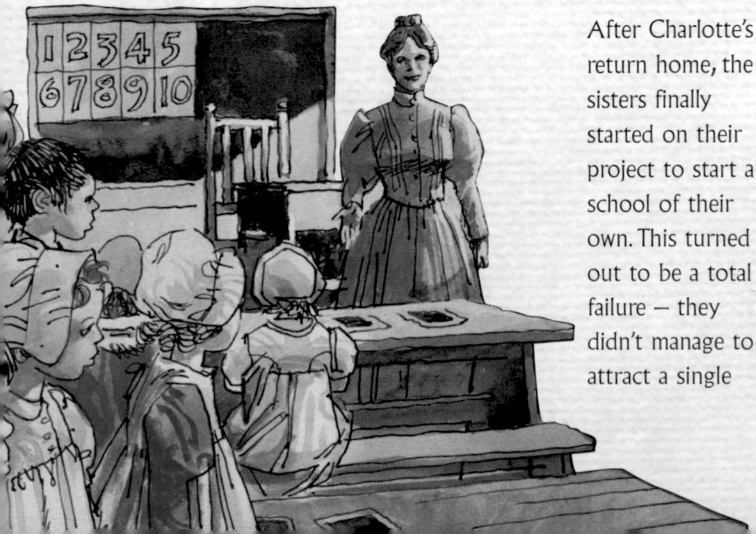

1 2 3 4 5
6 7 8 9 10

After Charlotte's return home, the sisters finally started on their project to start a school of their own. This turned out to be a total failure – they didn't manage to attract a single student! However that was probably to the world's advantage. Over the years, the sisters had continued their writing, and in 1846 – having abandoned the idea of starting a school - they decided to publish a selection of their poems. The title was simply *Poems* and it was published under different author names: Currer (Charlotte), Ellis (Emily) and Acton (Anne) Bell. One thousand copies of the book were printed, at a cost of around £50, which they funded themselves. The book received some favourable reviews, but sold only two copies in the first year.

Charlotte gave an explanation for these psuedonyms:

> "Averse to personal publicity, we veiled our own names under those of Currer, Ellis and Acton Bell; the ambiguous choice being dictated by a sort of conscientious scruple at assuming Christian names positively masculine, while we did not like to declare ourselves women, because - without at that time suspecting that our mode of writing and thinking was not what is called 'feminine' - we had a vague impression that authoresses are liable to be looked on with prejudice; we had noticed how critics sometimes use for their chastisement the weapon of personality, and for their reward, a flattery, which is not true praise."

In the same year that *Poems* was published, Charlotte also completed her first novel, *The Professor*. It was rejected by a number of publishers, but despite that, Charlotte remained undeterred. The following year saw the publication of Charlotte's *Jane Eyre*, Emily's *Wuthering Heights*, and Anne's *Agnes Grey;* all published under their assumed "Bell" names.

The sisters hid behind their assumed names until 1848, when Anne's second novel, *The Tenant of Wildfell Hall* was published; and the sisters were forced to reveal their true identities.

These first successes for the sisters were overshadowed by sadness. Their brother, Branwell, had been subjecting himself to alcohol and opium abuse for many years; and he died in 1848 – officially from tuberculosis, but thought to be brought on by his drug and drink habits. He was just thirty-one years old.

At the same time, Anne and Emily both became ill with tuberculosis. Emily died in December 1848, aged thirty.

Charlotte took Anne (who was now her only sibling) to Scarborough in May 1849, hoping that the sea air would help to cure her. Unfortunately, Anne died just four days after their arrival, aged only twenty-nine. She was buried in Scarborough so that their father didn't have to suffer the pain of yet another family funeral.

Shortly afterwards, Charlotte wrote:

> "A year ago – had a prophet warned me how I should stand in June 1849 – how stripped and bereaved....I should have thought – this can never be endured..."

Charlotte turned to her writing for comfort in these bleak times; and her next novel, *Shirley* was published in October 1849. She was now quite famous and attracted a great deal of attention. For instance, during one of her many visits to London she not only met her literary idol, W.M. Thackeray, but she also had her portrait painted by popular High Society artist George Richmond (reproduced at the top of page 134).

Her next novel, *Villette* published in 1853, was to be her last.

During this time, Charlotte had also attracted the personal attention of her father's curate, the Reverend Arthur Bell Nicholls. Charlotte initially rejected Reverend Nicholls' proposal for marriage, probably due to her father thinking that he was not worthy of his now-famous daughter. Eventually, however, he softened, and Charlotte married Reverend Nicholls in Haworth Church on 29th June 1854, and they spent their honeymoon in Ireland. Once again, this is mirrored in *Jane Eyre*, where Jane attracts the interest of a religious man, and also where Mr. Rochester suggests sending her away to Ireland. More interestingly, however, these actual events took place after *Jane Eyre* was written!

Charlotte became pregnant; and at the same time, her health began to decline. Elizabeth Gaskell, Charlotte's earliest biographer, writes that she was attacked by

> "sensations of perpetual nausea and ever-recurring faintness."

Charlotte and her unborn child died on 31st March 1855, three weeks before her thirty-ninth birthday. Her death certificate gives the cause of death as phthisis (tuberculosis).

Her husband, Reverend Nicholls, looked after Charlotte's father, Patrick, for six years until his death in June 1861 at the age of eighty-four.

Other than Patrick, none of the Brontës of Haworth enjoyed a long life, and none of them had any children to carry on the literary name.

"Gentle, soft dream, nestling in my arms now, you will fly, too, as your sisters have all fled before you:"

(from Jane Eyre, written while her younger sisters were alive).

The Brontë Family Tree

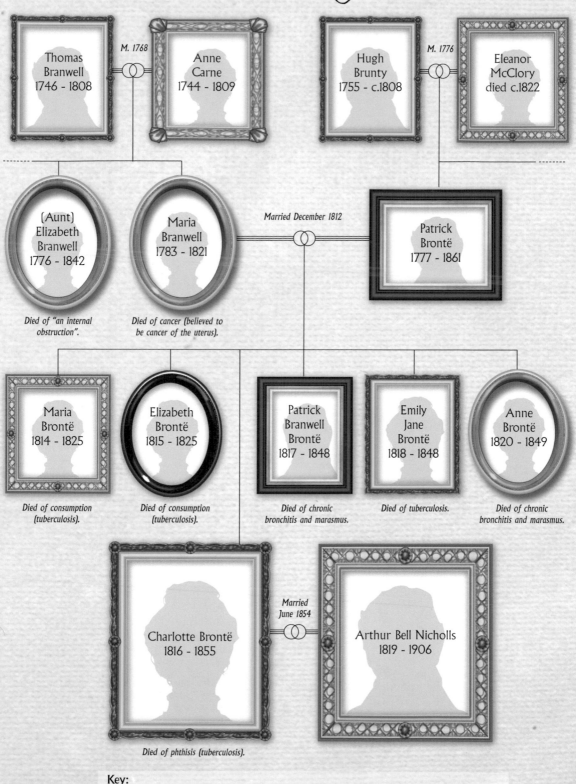

Thomas Branwell 1746 - 1808 — M. 1768 — Anne Carne 1744 - 1809

Hugh Brunty 1755 - c.1808 — M. 1776 — Eleanor McClory died c.1822

(Aunt) Elizabeth Branwell 1776 - 1842

Died of "an internal obstruction".

Maria Branwell 1783 - 1821 — Married December 1812 — Patrick Brontë 1777 - 1861

Died of cancer (believed to be cancer of the uterus).

Maria Brontë 1814 - 1825

Died of consumption (tuberculosis).

Elizabeth Brontë 1815 - 1825

Died of consumption (tuberculosis).

Patrick Branwell Brontë 1817 - 1848

Died of chronic bronchitis and marasmus.

Emily Jane Brontë 1818 - 1848

Died of tuberculosis.

Anne Brontë 1820 - 1849

Died of chronic bronchitis and marasmus.

Charlotte Brontë 1816 - 1855 — Married June 1854 — Arthur Bell Nicholls 1819 - 1906

Died of phthisis (tuberculosis).

Key:
Parent of ————
Married

Due to the lack of official records of births, deaths and marriages within this period, the above information is derived from extensive research and is as accurate as possible from the limited sources available.

A Chronology

1816   **21st April:** Charlotte is born at Thornton, Yorkshire, the third daughter of Patrick Brontë and Maria Branwell Brontë.

1817   **26th June:** Patrick Branwell Brontë is born.

1818   **30th July:** Emily Jane Brontë is born.

1820   **17th January:** Anne Brontë is born.

        February: Patrick Senior is appointed curate at Haworth.

        April: the Brontë family moves to Haworth.

1821   **September:** Maria Brontë dies of cancer. Her sister, Elizabeth Branwell, moves in with the family.

1824   **July:** Elizabeth and Maria are sent to the Clergy Daughters' School at Cowan Bridge, Lancashire.

        August: Charlotte and Emily are also sent to the Clergy Daughters' School (the school became a model for Lowood School in Jane Eyre).

1825   Elizabeth and Maria both return home from school in ill health. Maria dies in May, Elizabeth dies in June (both from tuberculosis, or "consumption"). Charlotte and Emily are removed from the school and sent home.

1826-1831   To entertain themselves, the children fill the pages of miniature homemade books with stories about imaginary kingdoms, inspired by some toy soldiers given to Branwell as a gift.

1831   **January:** Charlotte attends Miss Wooler's school at Roe Head, Mirfield. Here she meets lifelong friends Mary Taylor and Ellen Nussey.

1832   **June:** Charlotte leaves Roe Head to return home and teach her sisters.

1835   **July:** Charlotte returns to Roe Head as a teacher, taking Emily with her as a free pupil.

        October: Emily returns home, and Anne takes her place.

1838   **December:** Charlotte resigns her position and returns to Haworth.

1839   **March:** Charlotte rejects a marriage proposal from Reverend Henry Nussey, Ellen's brother.

        May to July: Charlotte works as a governess in Lothersdale.

        July: Charlotte rejects another marriage proposal, this time from Mr. Pryce – an Irish curate.

1841   Charlotte works as a governess at Rawdon from March to December.

1842   **February:** Charlotte and Emily go to Brussels to study languages at the Pensionnat Heger.

        October: Their Aunt Elizabeth dies.

        November: Charlotte and Emily return to Haworth.

1843   **January:** Charlotte returns to Brussels alone, but is lonely and becomes depressed. She forms an attachment to Constantin Heger, the head of the school, whose intellect appeals to her. Madame Heger's jealousy necessitates her departure.

1844   With all of the siblings now back at Haworth, the family try to start a school at the Haworth parsonage, but it is not a success.

1845   The Reverend Arthur Bell Nicholls becomes curate at Haworth.

1846   **April:** Charlotte, Emily, and Anne publish at their own expense a joint volume of *Poems* by Currer, Ellis, and Acton Bell. Only two copies are sold. Charlotte's novel *The Professor* is rejected by publishers.

        August: Charlotte begins *Jane Eyre* while caring for her father who was recovering from an eye operation.

1847   **October:** *Jane Eyre* is published, and is an immediate success. It starts off life as *Jane Eyre: An Autobiography Edited by Currer Bell* as if Jane Eyre was a real person and Charlotte Brontë, working under her assumed name of Currer Bell was merely the editor.

1848   **September:** Charlotte starts *Shirley*; Branwell dies of tuberculosis.

        December: Emily dies of tuberculosis. Anne also becomes ill.

1849   **May:** Charlotte tries to nurse Anne back to health and takes her to Scarborough. She dies four days after they arrive there.

        October: *Shirley – A Tale by Currer Bell* is published.

1849-1851   Charlotte travels frequently. She is invited to London as the guest of her publisher, where she meets Thackeray.

        She also visits the Lake District, Scotland, and Manchester, where she meets with Elizabeth Gaskell, her future biographer.

1851   **April:** She rejects a marriage proposal from James Taylor, a member of her publishing house.

1853   **January:** *Villette*, a novel set in Brussels is published, still by Currer Bell.

1854   **June:** Charlotte marries her fourth suitor, Arthur Bell Nichols, her father's curate. She begins but does not finish a novel, *Emma*.

1855   **March:** Charlotte dies during her pregnancy and is buried at The Parsonage at Haworth.

1857   **March:** Elizabeth Gaskell's *The Life of Charlotte Brontë* is published.

        June: Her previously rejected novel *The Professor* is published posthumously.

A letter from Charlotte

This is a letter written by Charlotte Brontë on 24th September 1847 to her publisher, Messrs. Smith, Elder and Co., thanking them for their punctuation of her manuscript for *Jane Eyre*. Interestingly, she signs it as C. Bell, which was the name under which she wrote *Jane Eyre* (see page 135). Seeing the finished book today, it is hard to imagine a time when the classic tale didn't exist; but like any other work, it had to be conceived and written. This letter, then, is like a time capsule - linking us back to when the book was still a work-in-progress:

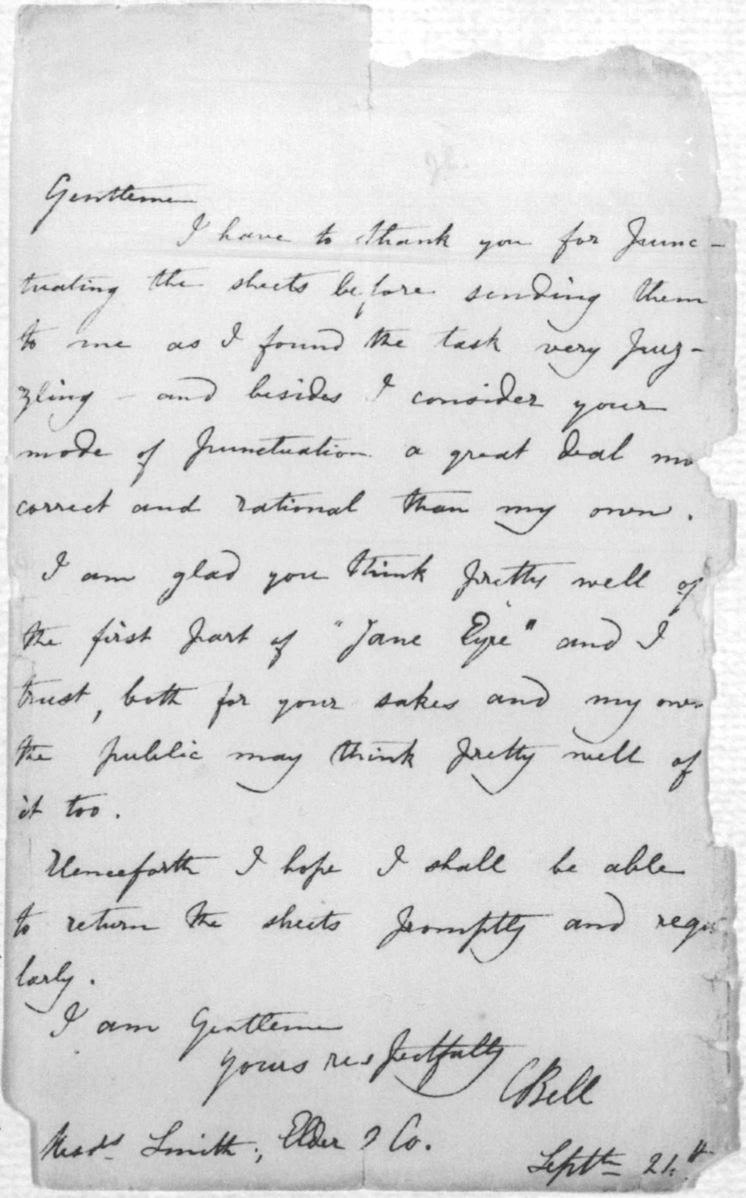

Gentlemen
I have to thank you for punctuating the sheets before sending them
to me as I found the task very puzzling - and besides I consider your
mode of punctuation a great deal mo
correct and rational than my own.
I am glad you think pretty well of
the first part of "Jane Eyre" and I
trust, both for your sakes and my own
the public may think pretty well of
it too.
Henceforth I hope I shall be able
to return the sheets promptly and regularly.
I am Gentlemen
Yours respectfully
C Bell
Messrs Smith, Elder & Co.
Septbr 24th

"Gentlemen,

I have to thank you for punctuating the sheets before sending them to me as I found the task very puzzling - and besides I consider your mode of punctuation a great deal mo[re] correct and rational than my own.

I am glad you think pretty well of the first part of "*Jane Eyre*" and I trust, for both your sakes and my own the public may think pretty well of it too.

Henceforth I hope that I shall be able to return the sheets promptly and regularly.

I am Gentlemen
Yours respectfully
C Bell"

To Messrs. Smith, Elder and Co.,
24th September (1847)

Page Creation

In order to create two versions of the same book, the story is first adapted into two scripts: Original Text and Quick Text. While the degree of complexity changes for each script, the artwork remains the same for both books.

432. Jane kisses his cheek tenderly, smoothing his hair with her hand.

	Original text	QUICK TEXT
JANE:	I am going, sir.	I am going, sir.
ROCHESTER:	You are leaving me?	
JANE:	Yes. God bless you, my dear master! And keep you from harm and wrong – direct you, solace you - reward you well for your past kindness to me. Farewell!	God bless you, my dear master! And keep you from harm and wrong. Farewell!
ROCHESTER:	Oh, Jane! My hope – my love – my life!	Oh, Jane! My hope – my love – my life!

433. Before sunrise, in the 'dim dawn', Jane leaves Thornfield House, dressed in her ordinary black stuff dress again, with her straw bonnet on, her shawl pinned and carrying a parcel.

JANE (CAP):	I rose at dawn to leave Thornfield Hall. In Mr Rochester's chamber, the inmate was walking restlessly from wall to wall. I knew what I had to do, and I did it mechanically.	I rose early to leave Thornfield Hall. Mr Rochester was awake in his room.
JANE (CAP):	I was out of Thornfield. There lay a road which stretched in the contrary direction to Millcote; thither I bent my steps.	

434. Birds are awake and fluttering in the thickets and undergrowth. Jane weeps as she rushes down the road, mad with grief. Her shawl is pinned in such a way as to make her look bird-like, as if her wings are flying in the morning wind. She is flying away.

JANE (CAP):	I thought of him now, in his room, hoping I should soon come to say I would be his. I longed to be his; it was not too late. I could go back and be his redeemer. Birds were faithful to their mates; birds were emblems of love. What was I? I had injured – wounded – left my master. I was hateful in my own eyes. Still I could not turn, nor retrace one step. I was weeping wildly as I walked: fast, fast I went like one delirious.	Away from Thornfield, I thought of him, in his room, hoping that I had changed my mind. It wasn't too late - I could go back. I had injured – wounded – left my master. But I couldn't return to him. Weeping wildly, I walked on.

435. A coach stops beside Jane Eyre. The coachman looks down from his perch, holding his whip upright.

JANE:	Where are you going?	Where are you going?
COACHMAN:	Whitcross – for thirty shillings, Miss.	Whitcross - thirty shillings, Miss.
JANE:	I only have twenty.	I only have twenty.

A page from the script of *Jane Eyre* showing the two versions of text.

CAP
A CAP
48*

The pencil drawing of page 91.

CAP
CAP

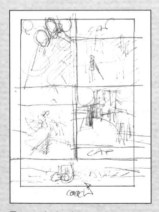

The rough sketch created from the above script.

Jane Eyre artist John M. Burns guides us through the creation process:

"First off, I make A5-ish thumbnails of the page layout. These are transferred to the art board which is then masked with tape while at the same time making any alterations to the page layout.

I then start the finished pencil drawings.

The next process is to ink these drawings. For Jane Eyre I mixed the ink I used (black, yellow ochre, and burnt umber). This gives the drawings a slight period look and is not such a contrast as black.

The ink drawing in this case is more a guide for the colour. However I will work up an inked drawing if I feel a flat colour will work.

After the ink stage the fun begins (the painting)."

The inked image, ready for colouring.

Jane Eyre character study

Adding colour brings the page and its characters to life.

Each character has a detailed Character Study drawn. This is useful for the artist to refer to and ensures continuity throughout the book.

The final stage is to add the captions, sound effects, and dialogue speech bubbles from the script. These are laid on top of the coloured pages. Two versions of each page are lettered, one for each of the two versions of the book (Original Text and Quick Text).

I AM GOING, SIR.
YOU ARE LEAVING ME?
GOD BLESS YOU, MY DEAR MASTER!
AND KEEP YOU FROM HARM AND WRONG.
FAREWELL!
OH, JANE! MY HOPE - MY LOVE - MY LIFE!
I ROSE EARLY TO LEAVE THORNFIELD HALL. MR. ROCHESTER WAS AWAKE IN HIS ROOM.
AWAY FROM THORNFIELD, I THOUGHT OF HIM, IN HIS ROOM, HOPING THAT I HAD CHANGED MY MIND. IT WASN'T TOO LATE - I COULD GO BACK. I HAD INJURED - WOUNDED - LEFT MY MASTER; BUT I COULDN'T RETURN TO HIM. WEEPING WILDLY, I WALKED ON.
WHERE ARE YOU GOING?
WHITCROSS - THIRTY SHILLINGS, MISS.
I ONLY HAVE TWENTY.
THAT WILL HAVE TO DO. GET INSIDE.
MAY NO-ONE EVER FEEL WHAT IT'S LIKE TO HURT THE ONE THEY LOVE.
91

These are then saved as final artwork pages and compiled into the finished book.

LOOK OUT FOR MORE TITLES IN THE CLASSICAL COMICS RANGE

Frankenstein: The Graphic Novel

Published: 29th September 2008 • 144 Pages • £9.99
• Script Adaptation: Jason Cobley • Linework: Declan Shalvey
• Colours: Jason Cardy & Kat Nicholson • Art Direction: Jon Haward • Letters: Terry Wiley

True to the original novel (rather than the square-headed Boris Karloff image from the films!) Declan's naturally gothic artistic style is a perfect match for this epic tale. Frankenstein is such a well known title; yet the films strayed so far beyond the original novel that many people today don't realise how this classic horror tale deals with such timeless subjects as alienation, empathy and understanding beyond appearance. Another great story, beautifully crafted into a superb graphic novel.

Original Text

I SANK TO THE GROUND AND MY INJURER ESCAPED INTO THE WOOD.
I HAD SAVED A HUMAN BEING FROM DESTRUCTION, AND AS A RECOMPENSE I NOW WRITHED UNDER THE MISERABLE PAIN OF A WOUND WHICH SHATTERED THE FLESH AND BONE.
THE FEELINGS OF KINDNESS GAVE PLACE TO HELLISH RAGE. INFLAMED BY PAIN, I VOWED ETERNAL HATRED AND VENGEANCE TO ALL MANKIND!
76

Frankenstein
THE GRAPHIC NOVEL

ISBN: 978-1-906332-15-0

Quick Text

I SANK TO THE GROUND AND THE MAN ESCAPED INTO THE WOOD.
I'D SAVED SOMEONE'S LIFE AND AS A REWARD, I HAD A SHATTERING WOUND.
IN GREAT PAIN, I VOWED ETERNAL HATRED AND VENGEANCE TO ALL MANKIND.
76

Frankenstein
THE GRAPHIC NOVEL

ISBN: 978-1-906332-16-7

A Christmas Carol: The Graphic Novel

Published: 13th October 2008 • 160 Pages • £9.99
• Script Adaptation: Sean Michael Wilson • Pencils: Mike Collins
• Inks: David Roach • Colours: James Offredi • Letters: Terry Wiley

A full-colour graphic novel adaptation of the much-loved Christmas story from the great Charles Dickens. Set in Victorian England and highlighting the social injustice of the time, we see one Ebenezer Scrooge go from oppressor to benefactor when he gets a rude awakening to how his life is, and how it should be. With sumptuous artwork and wonderful characters, this magical tale is a must-have for the festive season.

Original Text

HOW IT IS THAT I APPEAR BEFORE YOU IN A SHAPE THAT YOU CAN SEE, I MAY NOT TELL.
I HAVE SAT INVISIBLE BESIDE YOU MANY AND MANY A DAY. THAT IS NO LIGHT PART OF MY PENANCE.

A Christmas Carol
THE GRAPHIC NOVEL

ISBN: 978-1-906332-17-4

Quick Text

I HAVE SAT BESIDE YOU FOR MANY DAYS. YOU COULD NOT SEE ME.

A Christmas Carol
THE GRAPHIC NOVEL

ISBN: 978-1-906332-18-1

OTHER CLASSICAL COMICS TITLES:

Great Expectations
Published: January 2009
Original Text 978-1-906332-09-9
Quick Text 978-1-906332-11-2

Romeo & Juliet
Published: July 2009
Original Text 978-1-906332-19-8
Plain Text 978-1-906332-20-4
Quick Text 978-1-906332-21-1

Richard III
Published: March 2009
Original Text 978-1-906332-22-8
Plain Text 978-1-906332-23-5
Quick Text 978-1-906332-24-2

Dracula
Published: September 2009
Original Text 978-1-906332-25-9
Quick Text 978-1-906332-26-6

The Tempest
Published: May 2009
Original Text 978-1-906332-29-7
Plain Text 978-1-906332-30-3
Quick Text 978-1-906332-31-0

The Canterville Ghost
Published: October 2009
Original Text 978-1-906332-27-3
Quick Text 978-1-906332-28-0

For more information visit www.classicalcomics.com

TEACHERS' RESOURCES

To accompany each title in our series of graphic novels, we also publish a set of teachers' resources. These widely acclaimed photocopiable books are designed by teachers, for teachers, to help meet the requirements of the UK curriculum guidelines. Aimed at upper Key Stage 2 and above, each book provides exercises that cover structure, listening, understanding, motivation and comprehension as well as key words, themes and literary techniques. Although the majority of the tasks focus on the use of language in order to align with the revised framework for teaching English, you will also find many cross-curriculum topics, covering areas within history, ICT, drama, reading, speaking, writing and art; and with a range of skill levels, they provide many opportunities for differentiated teaching and the tailoring of lessons to meet individual needs.

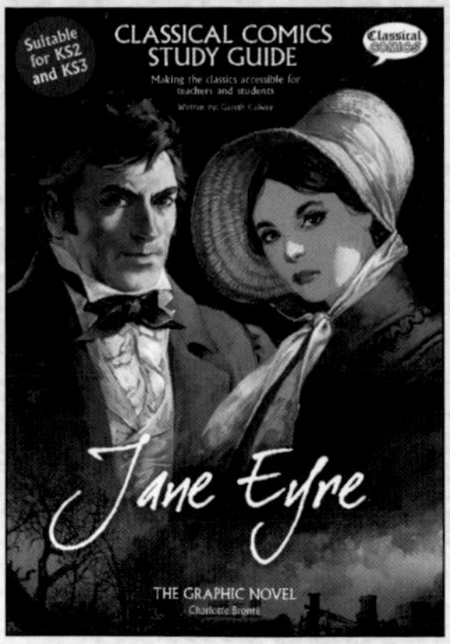

Suitable for KS2 and KS3
CLASSICAL COMICS STUDY GUIDE
Classical Comics
Jane Eyre
THE GRAPHIC NOVEL

Classical Comics Study Guide: Jane Eyre

Black and white, spiral bound A4 (making it easy to photocopy).

Price: £19.99
ISBN: 978-1-906332-12-9
Published: October 2008

DIFFERENTIATED TEACHING AT YOUR FINGERTIPS!

"Because the exercises feature illustrations from the graphic novel, they provide an immediate link for students between the book and the exercise – however they can also be used in conjunction with any traditional text; and many of the activities can be used completely stand-alone. I think the guide is fantastic and I look forward to using it. I know it will be a great help and lead to engaging lessons . It is easy to use, another major asset. Seriously: well done, well done, well done!"

Kornel Kossuth,
Head of English, Head of General Studies

"Thank you! These will be fantastic for all our students. It is a brilliant resource and to have the lesson ideas too are great. Thanks again to all your team who have created these."

B.P. KS3

"Thank you so much. I can't tell you what a help it will be."

A very grateful teacher, Kerryann SA

"...you've certainly got a corner of East Anglia convinced that this is a fantastic way to teach and progress English literature and language!!" *Chris Mehew*

"With many thanks again for your excellent resources and upbeat philosophy."

Dr. Marcella McCarthy
Leading Teacher for Gifted and Talented Education,
The Cherwell School, Oxford

"Dear Classical Comics,
Can I just say a quick "thank you" for the excellent teachers' resources that accompanied the *Henry V* Classical Comics. I needed to look no further for ideas to stimulate my class. The children responded with such enthusiasm to the different formats for worksheets, it kept their interest and I was able to find appropriate challenges for all abilities. The book itself was read avidly by even the most reluctant readers. Well done, I'm looking forward to seeing the new titles."

A. Dawes, Tockington Manor School

"I wanted to write to thank you - I had a bottom set Y9 class that would have really struggled with the text if it wasn't for your comics, THANK YOU."

Dan Woodhouse

"As to the resource, I can't wait to start using it! Well done on a fantastic service." *Will*

OUR RANGE OF OTHER CLASSICAL COMICS STUDY GUIDES

Henry V	*Macbeth*	*Frankenstein*	*A Christmas Carol*	*Great Expectations*
Published: November 2007	Published: March 2008	Published: October 2008	Published: October 2008	Published: January 2009
Price: £19.99	Price: £19.99	Price: £19.99	Price: £19.99	Price: £19.99
ISBN: 978-1-906332-07-5	ISBN: 978-1-906332-10-5	ISBN: 978-1-906332-37-2	ISBN: 978-1-906332-38-9	ISBN: 978-1-906332-13-6

BRINGING CLASSICS TO COMIC LIFE

Classical Comics has partnered with Comic Life to bring you a unique comic creation experience!

Comic Life is an award-winning software system that is used and loved by millions of children, adults and schools around the world. The software allows you to create astounding comics in a matter of minutes – and it is really easy and fun to use, too!

Through RM Distribution, you can now obtain all of our titles in every text version, electronically for use with any computer or whiteboard system. In addition, you can also obtain our titles as "No Text" versions that feature just the beautiful artwork without any speech bubbles or captions. These files can then be used in Comic Life (or any other software that can handle jpg files) enabling anyone to create their own version of one of our famous titles.

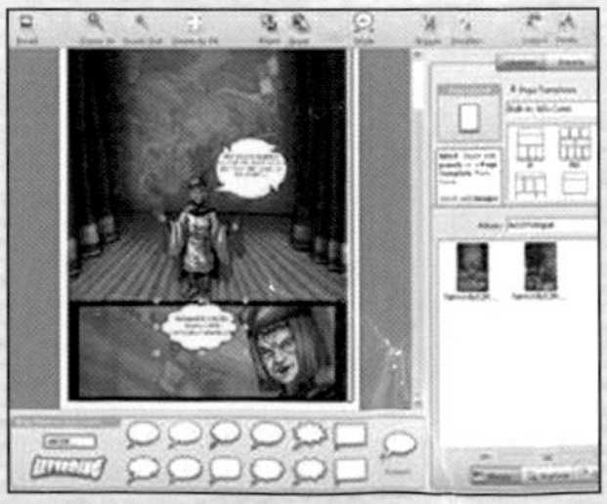

All of the digital versions of our titles are available from RM on a single user or site-license basis. For more details, visit www.rm.com and search for Classical Comics, or visit www.classicalcomics.com/education.

Classical Comics, RM and Comic Life - Bringing Classics to Comic Life!